MW00814125

Selected Letters of Bret Harte

Literature of the American West
William Kittredge, General Editor

Selected Letters of Bret Harte

Edited by Gary Scharnhorst

University of Oklahoma Press : Norman and London

Also Written or Edited by Gary Scharnhorst

The Lost Life of Horatio Alger (Bloomington, Ind., 1985)
(ed.) *Bret Harte's California: Letters to the Springfield Republican and Christian Register, 1866–67* (Albuquerque, N.Mex., 1990)
The Pursuit of William Rounseville Alger: An Experiment in Biography (Lewiston, N.Y., 1990)
Bret Harte (New York, 1992)
Henry David Thoreau: A Case Study in Canonization (Columbia, S.C., 1993)
(ed.) *American Literary Scholarship* (Durham, N.C., 1995)
Bret Harte: A Bibliography (Metuchen, N.J., and London, 1995)

This book is published with the generous assistance of the Wallace C. Thompson Endowment Fund, University of Oklahoma Foundation.

Harte, Bret, 1836–1902.
[Correspondence. Selections]
Selected letters of Bret Harte / edited by Gary Scharnhorst.
p. cm. — (Literature of the American West ; v. 1)
Includes index.
ISBN 0-8061-2897-6 (alk. paper)
1. Harte, Bret, 1836–1902—Correspondence. 2. Authors, American—19th century—Correspondence. 3. Authors, American—West (U.S.)—Correspondence. 4. Western stories—Authorship.
I. Scharnhorst, Gary. II. Title. III. Series.
PS1833.A4 1997
813' .4—dc20
[B] 96-18191
CIP

Text design by Debora Hackworth.

The paper in this book meets the guidelines for permanence and durability of the Committee on Production Guidelines for Book Longevity of the Council on Library Resources, Inc. ∞

1 2 3 4 5 6 7 8 9 10

Selected Letters of Bret Harte, edited by Gary Scharnhorst, is Volume 1 of Literature of the American West.

To Sandy,
the darling of Poverty Flat

Contents

Illustrations

Following page 216

A Note on the Photographs

Though he often sat for photographs, as early as 1870, in a note to Howells (letter 20), Harte disputed the accuracy of their "idealized" representation. Some sixteen years later, he reminded his wife, Anna, of "the cruel and disappointing flattery of photography."[1] For whatever reason—e.g., changes in facial hair, fluctuations in weight caused by illness, even the early technology of the art—Harte's appearance changed dramatically in the dozens of photographs taken of him over the years. Jeanette Gilder, editor of *The Critic*, once joked that "Whenever I see the portrait of a literary man and do not recognize the face, I am pretty sure of being right if I call it Bret Harte. No two pictures of Mr. Harte are the same."[2] Josephine McCrackin, a fellow journalist, similarly remarked that she had "never discovered a picture of Bret Harte that looked like him."[3]

1. BH to AH, 15 Mar. 1886 (UVa).
2. *Critic*, 8 Mar. 1890, 118.
3. *Overland Monthly*, n.s., 67 (Jan. 1916):13.

Acknowledgments

I owe special thanks to John Bret-Harte for granting me literary rights to his great-grandfather's letters; to the Right Honorable Lady Polwarth for permission to publish letter 199; to Houghton Mifflin for granting me permission to reprint texts published in *The Letters of Bret Harte*; to Duke University Press for permission to reprint letter 22; to Robert C. Ritchie and the staff of the Huntington Library for a Mayer Fund Fellowship which enabled me to work in residence there; and to the members of the Research Allocations Committee of the University of New Mexico for grants in support of this project. I also wish to acknowledge the following groups and institutions for permission to quote Harte manuscripts and/or to reproduce photographs in their collections: Special Collections Department, University of Virginia Library; University Research Library, University of California at Los Angeles; Boston Public Library; Rare Books and Manuscript Division, Berg Collection, and Research Center for the Performing Arts, New York Public Library; San Francisco Public Library; Fales Library, New York University; Dartmouth College Library; Seymour Library, Knox College; Hampden-Booth Theatre Library, New York; Leeds University Library; Rutherford B. Hayes Presidential Center, Fremont, Ohio; Morristown National Historical Park, Morristown, New Jersey;

Massachusetts Historical Society; Minnesota Historical Society; Special Collections and Archives, Wesleyan University Library; the Trustees of the National Library of Scotland; Brown University Library; Princeton University Libraries; Bancroft Library, University of California, Berkeley; University of Southern California Library; Ella Strong Denison Library of the Libraries of the Claremont Colleges; Haverford College Library; Wilson Library, University of North Carolina at Chapel Hill; Pierpont Morgan Library; Mark Twain House, Hartford, Connecticut; Rare Book and Manuscript Library, Columbia University; Department of Special Collections, Stanford University Libraries; Division of Rare and Manuscript Collections, Cornell University Library; Harry Ransom Humanities Research Center, University of Texas at Austin; Huntington Library; Beinecke Rare Book and Manuscript Library, Yale University; and Houghton Library, Harvard University. Charlotte Brown of UCLA Special Collections, Kathy Nicastro of the National Archives, and Frank Carroll of the Library of Congress assisted me beyond the call. Special thanks to Kim Wiar, Sarah Iselin, and the staff of the University of Oklahoma Press; to Glen Love, Patrick Morrow, and John Seelye for reading the manuscript and sharing their suggestions with me; and to Tom Quirk, Eric Atherton, Patricia Sprott, Lennie Cassuto, Hugh Witemeyer, Jim and Connie Thorson, Ross and Susie Humphreys, Walter Putnam, Dick Etulain, Harriet Elinor Smith, and all my friends at Scalo.

Abbreviations

AH	Anna Harte
Aldrich	Lilian Aldrich, *Crowding Memories* (Boston: Houghton Mifflin, 1920)
ALS	Autographed letter signed
Ballou	Ellen B. Ballou, *The Building of the House: Houghton Mifflin's Formative Years* (Boston: Houghton Mifflin, 1970)
Bancroft	Bancroft Library, University of California, Berkeley
Barnett	Linda Diz Barnett, *Bret Harte: A Reference Guide* (Boston: Hall, 1980)
Berg	Henry W. and Albert A. Berg Collection, New York Public Library, Astor, Lenox and Tilden Foundations
BH	Bret Harte
BH's California	*Bret Harte's California*, ed. Gary Scharnhorst (Albuquerque: University of New Mexico Press, 1990)
Claremont	Denison Library, Claremont Colleges, Claremont, Calif.
Cummins	Ella Sterling Cummins, *The Story of the Files* (San Francisco: Cooperative Printing Co., 1893)

Daly	Joseph F. Daly, *The Life of Augustin Daly* (New York: Macmillan, 1917)
Duckett	Margaret Duckett, *Mark Twain and Bret Harte* (Norman: University of Oklahoma Press, 1964)
FH	Frank Harte
Hampden-Booth	Hampden-Booth Theatre Library, New York
Harvard	Houghton Library, Harvard University
Hayes	Rutherford B. Hayes Presidential Center, Fremont, Ohio
Howe	M. A. DeWolfe Howe, *Memories of a Hostess* (Boston: Atlantic Monthly Press, 1922)
Huntington	Huntington Library, San Marino, Calif.
If Not Literature	*If Not Literature: Letters of Elinor Mead Howells*, ed. Ginette de B. Merrill and George Arms (Columbus: Ohio State University Press, 1988)
JBH	John Bret-Harte (private collection)
LC	Library of Congress, Washington, D.C.
Letters	*The Letters of Bret Harte*, ed. Geoffrey Harte (Boston: Houghton Mifflin, 1926)
Life in Letters	*Life in Letters of William Dean Howells*, ed. Mildred Howells (Garden City, N.Y.: Doubleday, 1928), 2 vols.
Literary Friends	W. D. Howells, *Literary Friends and Acquaintances* (New York: Harper & Bros., 1910)
LS	Letter signed
MT–H Letters	*Mark Twain–Howells Letters*, ed. Henry Nash Smith and William M. Gibson (Cambridge, Mass.: Belknap, 1960), 2 vols.
MT in Eruption	*Mark Twain in Eruption*, ed. Bernard De Voto (New York: Harper & Bros., 1940)
NA	National Archives, Washington, D.C.
Pemberton	T. Edgar Pemberton, *The Life of Bret Harte*(London: Pearson; New York: Dodd, Mead, 1903)
SFPL	San Francisco Public Library
Stewart	George Stewart, *Bret Harte: Argonaut and Exile* (Boston: Houghton Mifflin, 1931)
Texas	Harry Ransom Humanities Research Center, University of Texas at Austin

UCLA	Department of Special Collections, University Research Library, University of California at Los Angeles
UNC	A. P. Watt Records, General and Literary Manuscripts Collection, Wilson Library, University of North Carolina at Chapel Hill
UVa	Bret Harte Collection (#5310), Clifton Waller Barrett Library, Special Collections Department, University of Virginia Library
Wesleyan	Wesleyan University Library, Middletown, Conn.
Yale	Yale Collection of American Literature, Beinecke Rare Books and Manuscript Library, Yale University

Editor's Introduction

Editor's Introduction

However minor his art or modest his modern fame, Bret Harte deserves to be resurrected from the footnote. As the editor of a pair of popular California literary magazines, he was mentor to an entire generation of western American writers, among them Mark Twain, Ambrose Bierce, Joaquin Miller, Ina Coolbrith, and Charles Warren Stoddard. As Twain later allowed, Harte "trimmed and trained and schooled me patiently until he changed me from an awkward utterer of coarse grotesquenesses to a writer of paragraphs and chapters that have found a certain favor."[1] In such stories as "The Luck of Roaring Camp," "The Outcasts of Poker Flat," and "Tennessee's Partner," Harte staked his own claim to a rich vein of California local color. His poem "Plain Language from Truthful James," commonly known as "The Heathen Chinee," was one of the most popular poems ever published, cited by both foes and defenders of Chinese immigration. At his death in 1902, the London *Spectator* declared that Harte had "probably exerted a greater influence on English literature than any other American author,"[2] and no less a luminary than Henry Adams averred that he was one of "the most brilliant men of my time."[3] Henry Seidel Canby later claimed, with pardonable hyperbole, that "the literary West may be said to have founded itself upon the imagination of Bret Harte."[4] At his best, Harte was a preeminent satirist, an astute critic of sham sentiment, and an elegant stylist. His gradual disappearance from American literature anthologies may be attributed more to the shifting trade winds of literary fashion than to the intrinsic qualities of his best writing.

For better or worse, Harte was also a prototype of the man of letters as a man of business. As the most cursory reading of these letters reveals, he allowed the nexus of the market to dictate both his rate of production and the venue of publication. Lured east in 1871 by the promise of literary fame and fortune, he left California never to return. W. D. Howells later compared his trip across the continent with "the progress of a prince, in the universal attention and interest which met and followed it."[5] Removed from the West, however, Harte soon exhausted his welcome and began to trade on his name. The highest-paid writer for the most prestigious magazine in America in 1871–72, he was free-lancing hackwork to the Sunday feuilleton of such daily newspapers as the *New York Times* and *New York Tribune* only two years later. An indifferent public speaker, Harte nevertheless exploited his popularity by delivering his lecture "The Argonauts of '49" well over a hundred times between 1873 and 1875, traveling from New England to Nebraska, Canada to Georgia. He often disappointed audiences who expected a deadpan rustic like Petroleum V. Nasby; by comparison, he seemed a pompous dandy who dressed in neat suits, wore a pin in his tie, and spoke in a whispered monotone. Though his publisher Elisha Bliss sold serial rights to his novel *Gabriel Conroy* (1875) sight unseen to *Scribner's* for six thousand dollars, the novel was a critical and commercial flop. Horace Scudder complained in the *Atlantic Monthly*—the very magazine that had once featured Harte among its distinguished stable of contributors—that all its "dark passages" lead finally "not into the light, but into the vegetable cellar."[6] Though Harte sold dramatic rights to his script *Two Men of Sandy Bar* (1876) for a small fortune to the comic actor Stuart Robson, the play bombed on Broadway and in the provinces. To counter the negative publicity, Harte replied to his critics (letters 73, 76, and 78)—an impetuous maneuver that embroiled him in controversy for weeks and indelibly tarnished his reputation. His coauthorship with Mark Twain of the play *Ah Sin* (1877) was perhaps the most disastrous collaboration in the history of American letters and effectively ended their friendship. Harte's later tales were mostly written according to the same tired and tested formula. "I grind out the old tunes on the old organ and gather up the coppers," he lamented in 1879.[7] He tailored these stories to the standards of the magazine market, willingly accommodating the demands of editors such as Richard Watson Gilder (letter 251). "I must not try to *force* the market for my work, for the sake of momentary gains," he wrote his wife, Anna Harte, in September 1885, "and I must not let the publishers think I am getting anxious."[8] By the 1890s, Harte's agent was peddling his stories—like so many feet in a mine sold at shares—to such newspaper syndicates as the National Press Agency and Tillotson & Sons. In the end, he became the writer the market made him. Less a craftsman than a literary celebrity, he gauged the demand for his brand of California local color with a calculating eye and, as Howells put it, "wrote Bret Harte over and over again as long as he lived."[9]

The joke made the rounds that Harte had reversed the path of the sun, rising in glory in the West and setting in darkness in the East. Twain, his former friend, scorned Harte in 1907 as a johnny-one-note of western fiction. "When Bret Harte started east in his newborn glory," Twain claimed, "he had lived all of his life that was worth living. . . . He was entering upon a miserable career of poverty, debt, humiliation, shame, disgrace, bitterness, and a world-wide fame which must have been odious to him."[10] To be sure, as these letters suggest, Harte was haunted to the end of his life by the specter of the hardscrabble winter of 1877–78 when he literally lived from hand to mouth, relying on loans from such friends as the New York broker Thomas Musgrave, in debt to hostellers, publishers, tailors, and grocers. At the nadir of his career, he begged William Waldorf Astor for a job (letter 93) and scolded his friend James R. Osgood for failing to rush his short novel *The Story of a Mine* into hardcover so that he might receive an advance on it (letter 92). Yet he was by any fair measure a more complex figure than this litany of grievances may suggest.

Born in Albany, New York, to the teacher Henry Hart and Elizabeth (Ostrander) Hart in 1836, young Francis Brett Hart (whose parents later added an "e" to the surname) was educated in small academies and ordinary schools in the Hudson River valley. With his younger sister, Margaret, he sailed for San Francisco in 1854 to rejoin his mother and her second husband, Andrew Williams, the first mayor of Oakland. He soon left for the mining district in Tuolumne County, where he opened a school that failed for lack of students. He then spent several weeks in placer mining but "met with very indifferent success."[11] Over the next five years, he worked as an agent and messenger for Wells, Fargo & Co., a druggist's clerk in Oakland, a tutor for ranching families in Humboldt County, a soldier, and a printer's devil for the weekly *Northern Californian* newspaper. Early in 1860, in danger from an outraged citizenry, he fled to San Francisco after he editorially condemned a massacre of Indians near Eureka. He went to work as a compositor for the *Golden Era*, a weekly literary paper, to whose pages he contributed dozens of pieces over the next several years. His writings caught the eye of Jessie Benton Frémont, who helped him find employment in the offices of the U.S. Surveyor General, the U.S. Marshal, and the U.S. Branch Mint. "If I were to be cast away on a desert island," Harte later wrote Frémont, "I should expect a savage to come forward with a three-cornered note from you to tell me that, at your request, I had been appointed governor of the island at a salary of two thousand four hundred dollars."[12] By 1862, he enjoyed local renown as a poet and humorist, and in the spring of 1864 he cofounded an upscale literary weekly, the *Californian*. With so distinguished a literary apprenticeship, Harte was the logical first choice to fill the editorial chair of the *Overland Monthly*, founded in 1868 by the San Francisco publisher and bookseller Anton Roman, though he continued to harbor doubts "whether sufficient material of a proper character to interest magazine readers could be secured" from local writers.[13] Not surprisingly, Harte became his own most valued contributor. "The Luck of Roaring Camp," published without signature in the second number of the magazine, "reached across the continent and startled the Academists on the Atlantic Coast," as Kate Chopin later noted.[14] The *Springfield Republican* hailed it as "the best magazine story of the year,"[15] and within a twelvemonth the *Overland* sold as many copies in the East as in the states of California, Nevada, and Oregon.[16]

During the nearly forty years (1864–1902) covered by his extant letters, Harte played a variety of roles—poet, editor, critic, storyteller, lecturer, playwright, consul, and diplomat, as well as brother-husband-father. He knew, sometimes intimately, many of the most prominent

American and English writers of the day, including Howells, Twain, Emerson, Longfellow, Lowell, Holmes, Whittier, Whitman, Adams, Henry James, Thomas Bailey Aldrich, Bayard Taylor, Mary E. W. Sherwood, Thomas Hardy, George Eliot, Sir Wemyss Reid, Robert Browning, Havelock Ellis, Bram Stoker, William Black, J. A. Froude, Richard Monckton Milnes (Lord Houghton), Florence Henniker, and Hamlin Garland. During the course of his career he wrote for such leading editors and publishers as Gilder, J. T. Fields, J. R. Osgood, Samuel Bowles, Nicholas Trübner, Charles A. Dana, Donn Piatt, S. S. McClure, Bernhard Tauchnitz, Houghton Mifflin, and Chatto & Windus. He freely associated with theatrical figures (Augustin Daly, Lester Wallack, Dion Boucicault, Adah Isaacs Menken, John T. Ford, Edwin Booth, Lawrence Barrett, Bronson Howard, Genevieve Ward, John McCullough, Annie Russell, J. L. Toole, Joseph Hatton, Clara Morris, Charles and Daniel Frohman, Sir Charles Wyndham, Edward S. Willard, D'Oyley Carte, Sir Arthur Sullivan) as well as politicians (John Hay, Rutherford B. Hayes, Carl Schurz, William Evarts, Herbert Bismarck, the Earl of Crewe). Whatever his faults—and I make no attempt to whitewash them here—his career was, in fact, a long and honorable one, not the "short, happy life" sketched in the standard literary histories.

Nor were the events of his career all in a single minor key. The tone of his correspondence changes markedly over the years. In the early letters, for example, Harte was often ingratiating and occasionally arrogant, as when he curtly rejected Whitman's "Passage to India" for publication in the *Overland* (letter 11) or spurned an invitation to write for *The Galaxy* (letter 17). In these early letters, too, he vented his frustrations about California and his ambivalence to things western, prefiguring the flight back to "civilization" of his character Miss Mary at the close of "The Idyl of Red Gulch" and his own imminent departure for the East. As he wrote Howells in letter 28, even in the first years of his career he was not a prolific letter writer: "I generally rise from my task with dark thoughts and bitterness toward my correspondent. Writing doesn't come to me naturally." "I write so seldom to anyone and am so painfully conscious at the present moment of vast arrears of correspondence that you may really consider this a rarity," he explained to a young friend in 1874.[17] He was, he said, "the laziest and meanest of correspondents" (letter 65).

As his career spiraled downward in the 1870s, Harte often punctuated his notes home with expressions of concern for his family, and he became more prickly in the cards he sent editors, publishers, and lecture agents (e.g., letters 50, 57, and 60). He routinely quarreled with the middlemen of literary production who controlled his access to the public and set the prices paid for his writings (e.g., letters 26, 46, 90, and 134). As Robson remarked in 1876, amid the flap over *Two Men of Sandy Bar*, moreover, Harte had "never been popular with the press; he fails to possess that knack of getting along with its representatives which is so invaluable to an author or an artist."[18]

His letters to family and friends from Crefeld, Germany, where he represented the United States as consular agent between 1878 and 1880, and from Glasgow, where he was stationed as U.S. consul between 1880 and 1885, were perhaps the most literary of his entire correspondence. Harte routinely revised them in manuscript, though he insisted in a note to his sister Eliza (letter 123) that "*I hate to write letters* especially *family* letters." The task seemed to him contrived and artificial. "I must get an amanuensis for my business correspondence," he later reported. "I have answered *forty five* letters in two days—and I have not got through the pile awaiting me."[19] Harte was, in truth, never at home in Germany or Scotland. He disliked the climate, the customs, the clerical work. As a "residence for a nervous impressionable literary man," he complained in early 1880 (letter 129), "no place could be more outrageously absurd than Crefeld." Unfortunately, as he wrote ten months later, after his transfer, Glasgow "is a hundred times worse than Crefeld."[20] At each post, he was fortunate to hire an efficient vice-consul who handled the affairs of the office, freeing him to write and travel and, after 1882, to live in London with the Belgian diplomat Arthur Van de Velde, his wife, and their children.

Whereas many of his letters in the 1870s were unvarnished appeals for money, in personal letters of the 1880s and the 1890s he inveighed against old creditors and worried about family expenses. In 1884, foreseeing the loss of his consular salary, Harte hired an agent, A. P. Watt of London, who adroitly managed his business affairs by selling his "wares," arranging for favorable publicity, and occasionally advancing him money. To compensate for his lost consular income after 1885, Harte became more prolific, often writing stories at the rate of a thousand words per day, publishing at least one volume of new fiction every year until his death, by far the bulk of his collected works. On average, Harte wrote about a hundred thousand words and earned about ten thousand dollars annually after leaving the Glasgow consulate. Indeed, he found little time for letter writing amid the press of fiction writing. "I have a pile of unanswered letters on my table, and the few lines I have scrawled to you and Frank are the only ones I have been able to write," he complained to Anna Harte in 1885.[21] He often bemoaned the "terrible grind" of literary work,[22] "this perpetual grinding out of literary copy which is exhausting me, and no doubt the public" (letter 191). The only escape from the treadmill, he thought, would be to script "a good popular play" that might pay him upwards of "$3000 a year for a year or two" (letter 162). He repeatedly tried his hand at playwriting, ever mindful of the mistakes that had spoiled *Two Men of Sandy Bar* and *Ah Sin*. Between 1882 and 1897, he wrote eleven plays and two librettos, usually based on his own stories. With his hostess Mme Van de Velde, for example, he wrote a dramatic version of "The Luck of Roaring Camp," changing the title character into an ingenue who visits Paris in company with a gaggle of gold miners. He cowrote *Sue*, based on another of his stories, with his friend T. Edgar Pemberton, drama editor of the *Birmingham Post*. With the American actress Annie Russell in the title role, the play was staged in New York in 1896 and in London in 1898.

During the final seventeen years of his life in England, Harte moved in a small circle of friends and avoided the limelight. He was at once a voluminous and a circumspect correspondent, both a clubbable fellow who frequented London theatres and restaurants and an intensely private man who rarely expressed strong emotion in his letters except in his recurrent complaints to family about his health or straitened circumstances. He regularly visited his wife, Anna, and their daughter Ethel after they came to England in December 1898, though he repeatedly warned (most insistently in letter 254) that they should decrease their expenses. To the end of his life, Harte was a painstaking correspondent who refused, as he said, to "write letters 'on the wing'" (letter 221) and who, according to the testimony of a friend, "often made four or five copies of a note accepting an invitation to dinner!"[23]

Since the first blush of his fame, his letters have been treasured by those who received them. In July 1871, scarcely four months after Harte's arrival in the East, Louise Chandler Moulton praised their "monogramed paper, handsome chirography," and "dainty elegance of diction."[24] Even today, with his critical reputation in eclipse, Harte's letters are prized by collectors, often selling for several hundred dollars per leaf.[25] Of course, many letters Harte is known to have written do not survive. Josephine Clifford McCrackin, who joined the *Overland* staff during Harte's tenure as editor, reported that virtually all of her letters from him were destroyed in the forest fire that consumed her house in the Santa Cruz Mountains in 1899.[26] Similarly, Ina Coolbrith's cache of correspondence was destroyed in the earthquake that devastated the Bay Area in 1906;[27] many letters Harte sent the poet Mary E. W. Sherwood—"so full of fun, affection, and belief"—were burned in a hotel fire;[28] and most of the letters Harte sent his daughter-in-law Aline, carefully preserved between sheets of blotting paper, were inadvertently destroyed when they "were thrown into the fire as scraps, by the cook."[29] Other significant lacunae also mar the biographical record: The texts of only two of Harte's letters to Mme Van de Velde survive, both of them printed in Pemberton's authorized biography of the author. All the manuscript letters they exchanged have disappeared, presumably destroyed after Harte's death. That is, the precise nature of their relationship, long the subject of speculation, is forever lost in a biographical blind spot. Some of the letters Harte sent his sons and wife over the years have also been lost.

Even the letters that do survive sometimes hide or obscure more than they reveal. For example, Harte concealed his "Jewish birth," as Twain put it, "as carefully as if he considered it a disgrace," even failing to mention to Havelock Ellis in 1889 (letter 193) that his paternal grandfather, Bernard Hart, was an orthodox Jew. Nor did he acknowledge anywhere in his letters to Anna in 1878–79 that the young daughter of his cousin, Callie Cooper, was studying in Düsseldorf, presumably sharing his apartment, and traveling with him to England and Switzerland, though she figured often in the letters he addressed to his European friends. Harte was even more discreet about a six-week Swiss vacation he took in company with Mme Van de Velde in the summer of 1895. Though it is clear they rendezvoused near Geneva, Harte did not travel there with the friends who accompanied him to the continent, nor did he mention her name in any of the extant letters he wrote during the excursion. As George Stewart has noted, his letters to his wife after 1893 "were generally only brief notes enclosing the monthly remittance, never the long gossipy letters of earlier days."[30] Yet these letters also emphatically belie the charge—spread by Twain in his autobiographical dictation—that Harte abandoned his family when he left the United States in 1878. According to Twain, there was "no possibility of doubt" that Harte "never sent them a dollar" and "never intended to send them a dollar."[31] In fact, as these letters prove, over the last twenty-four years of his life Harte sent his wife and family some sixty thousand dollars (by his own estimate in letter 254). The Hartes' marriage was, to be sure, extremely unconventional, even in an age before divorce was commonplace. As his grandson Geoffrey Harte explained in an unpublished memoir, for over twenty years "they lived apart and maintained across three thousand miles of ocean a polite correspondence and the fiction of re-union in the near future. This fiction found expression in my grandfather's letters in an ever green plan to return to the United States."[32] Over the years, Harte offered a remarkable variety of excuses for his failure to return—the threatened loss of his consular post, his fear of lawsuits pressed by his creditors in the United States, his health, the expense of transatlantic travel, the complicated copyright situation, even the assassination of James Garfield.

The present edition of Harte's correspondence is only the second such volume to be published, the first since his grandson edited *The Letters of Bret Harte* (1926) for Houghton Mifflin. According to a note he sent the publisher, Geoffrey Harte chose the 355 letters in his collection from a pool of about nine hundred holographs.[33] Many of the letters he selected were quite ephemeral, mere social notes in which the elder Harte replied to dinner or theatre invitations or thanked his correspondent for a holiday gift; and the vast majority—over three hundred of them—were written after Harte left the United States in 1878. Some of the texts reproduced in the 1926 *Letters*, moreover, are corrupt transcriptions. In most cases, the errors were inadvertent, the consequence of Harte's crabbed handwriting, as when Geoffrey Harte has his grandfather thank "dear Colonel Laking" instead of "dear Carl Schurz," the secretary of the interior, for approving his diplomatic appointment in 1878.[34] Harte routinely apologized to his correspondents, as in letter 215, for his "illegible scrawl," and Gertrude Atherton fairly observed that his manuscript, especially late in life when he suffered from rheumatism, was "so fine and small that one finds it almost necessary to use a microscope" to read it.[35] In other cases, the changes were deliberate. The entire first paragraph of Harte's letter to his wife dated 20 November 1888 (letter 186) was omitted from the 1926 *Letters*,[36] for example, and Ferris Greenslet of Houghton Mifflin wrote Geoffrey Harte while *The Letters of Bret Harte* was in production to demand the deletion of a passage from Bret Harte's letter to Anna Harte of 17 April 1887 (letter 180) in which the author claims that Houghton Mifflin was "swindling" him.[37] Like Twain's jaundiced reminiscences in 1907, such omissions and corruptions had the effect of misrepresenting Harte and coloring the record of his career. Still, despite occasional reservations about its "erroneous and inadequate" editorial apparatus, the volume was mostly praised by reviewers. Fred Lewis Pattee asserted in the *New York Herald Tribune* that the letters vindicated Harte against charges of debt and dissipation, for example, and C. Hartley Grattan in the *New Republic* remarked on his long and gallant struggle to earn a living.[38]

Over the years, there have been piecemeal attempts to repair some of the gaps in Harte scholarship, to place some of the letters unknown or overlooked by Geoffrey Harte on the historical record. An additional hundred or so letters were published, most of them in three journal articles: Bradford Booth's "Unpublished Letters of Bret Harte," *American Literature* 16 (May 1944):131–42; Booth's "Bret Harte Goes East: Some Unpublished Letters," *American Literature* 19 (January 1948):318–35; and Brenda Murphy and George Monteiro's "The Unpublished Letters of Bret Harte to John Hay," *American Literary Realism* 12 (Spring 1979):77–110. These vagrant letters, like single pieces of a puzzle, add little more than bits of color to the record unless they are read in a larger context, however, and with the exception of the twenty-eight letters in Murphy and Monteiro's article none of Harte's published letters has been annotated.

This new edition of Harte's correspondence includes clear texts of 259 letters, 144 of them previously unpublished and/or new to scholarship, chosen from over two thousand letters from Harte's hand known to survive. That is, the texts in this edition have been selected from a pool over twice as large as the one Geoffrey Harte tapped in 1926. Many of the hundreds of additional letters are located in the collections of the University of California at Berkeley, the University of Texas at Austin, the Boston Public Library, the San Francisco Public Library, the New York Public Library, the Huntington Library, and the National Archives. By far the largest collection of Harte's letters, nearly seven hundred in all, is located in the Alderman Library, University of Virginia. The collection there includes original manuscripts of many letters first printed in Geoffrey Harte's 1926 edition as well as several dozen unpublished holographs sent to the novelist Florence Henniker, daughter of Harte's friend J. A. Froude; Rudolph Schneider, Harte's vice-consul in Crefeld, Germany; and his wife, Clara Schneider. To provide a rounded perspective on Harte's life and preserve narrative continuity, I have reprinted a number of private letters first published in Geoffrey Harte's edition or in other venues, though I have reedited them from original holographs in all but twelve cases. In several places I have restored omissions or corrected misreadings of Harte's handwriting, and in all cases in which I have worked from manuscripts I have retained the spelling and punctuation of the originals. Fortunately, though Geoffrey Harte sold virtually the entire collection of family letters in a series of public auctions between November 1925 and February 1926,[39] almost all of the holographs were eventually deposited in archives and thus are accessible. I also include complete texts of all eleven extant letters Harte sent Twain, the last in April 1877 during rehearsals of *Ah Sin*. In short, I have designed this edition of Harte's letters for use by both general readers interested in Harte's life and the literary and social milieu of the late-nineteenth century as well as specialists and other scholars who expect textual accuracy.

1. *Mark Twain's Letters*, ed. A. B. Paine (New York: Harper & Bros., 1917), I, 182–83.

2. London *Spectator*, 10 May 1902, 715.

3. *Henry Adams: Selected Letters*, ed. Ernest Samuels (Cambridge, Mass.: Belknap, 1992), 424. See also George Monteiro, *Henry James and John Hay* (Providence, R.I.: Brown University Press, 1965), 180.

4. Henry Canby, "The Luck of Bret Harte," *Saturday Review of Literature*, 17 Apr. 1926, 717.

5. *Literary Friends*, 290.

6. Horace Scudder, "Harte's Sketches and Stories," *Atlantic Monthly* 50 (Aug. 1882):266.

7. *Letters*, 154.

8. BH to AH, 15 Sept. 1885 (Bancroft).

9. *Literary Friends*, 299.

10. *MT in Eruption*, 267.

11. "Francis Bret Harte," *Chicago Tribune*, 20 Nov. 1870, p. 6, col. 6.

12. Jessie B. Frémont, *Souvenirs of My Time* (Boston: D. Lothrop & Co., 1887), 204–205.

13. Anton Roman, "The Genesis of the Overland Monthly," *Overland Monthly*, n.s., 40 (Sept. 1902):220.

14. Kate Chopin, *St. Louis Republic*, 9 Dec. 1900, Sunday magazine, 1.

15. *Springfield Republican*, 30 Sept. 1868, p. 2, col. 2.

16. Bayard Taylor, "Through to the Pacific," *New York Tribune*, 5 Aug. 1870, p. 2, col. 1.

17. BH to Bessie Ward, 19 Sept. 1874 (UVa).

18. *Baltimore Gazette*, 12 Oct. 1876, p. 1, col. 4.

19. BH to AH, 24 May 1880 (UVa).

20. *Letters*, 191.

21. BH to AH, 15 Jan. 1885 (UVa).

22. Bradford A. Booth, "Unpublished Letters of Bret Harte," *American Literature* 16 (May 1944):140.

23. S. R. Elliott, "Glimpses of Bret Harte," *Reader* 10 (July 1907):126.

24. "Boston," *New York Tribune*, 4 July 1871, p. 6, col. 2.

25. A two-page Harte letter in fine condition is priced at $750 in a 1990 sales catalogue (#193) issued by Kenneth W. Rendell, Inc., of Wellesley, Mass.

26. *Overland Monthly*, n.s., 66 (Dec. 1915):468.

27. Charles W. Stoddard, "In Old Bohemia," *Pacific Monthly* 19 (Mar. 1908):269.

28. *New York Times Saturday Review of Books*, 10 May 1902, 308.

29. Geoffrey Harte, unpublished memoir (JBH).

30. Stewart, 306.

31. *MT in Eruption*, 291.

32. Geoffrey Harte, unpublished memoir (JBH).

33. Geoffrey Bret Harte to Ferris Greenslet, 24 Dec. 1924 (Harvard).

34. *Letters*, 65.

35. San Francisco *Daily Evening Bulletin*, 6 May 1902, p. 1, cols. 6–7.

36. *Letters*, 333.

37. Ferris Greenslet to Geoffrey Bret Harte, 13 Aug. 1925 (Harvard).

38. Barnett, 256–59.

39. American Art Association sales catalogues for 24 November 1925, 11 December 1925, 11 and 12 January 1926, 17 and 18 February 1926.

Selected Letters of Bret Harte

1. TO ANTON ROMAN, 8 JANUARY 1866

San Franci^co^
Jan. 8th, 1866

My dear Sir,[1]

I have to thank you for yours of the 9th ult. and the eastern notices of "Outcroppings."[2]

You will learn from Mr. Allen that the book has created considerable excitement here, and that the compiler has been abused beyond his most sanguine expectations.[3] All of which ought to make the volume sell.

I understand that Miss Tingley disavows your right to use her selections. I trust you have written to her before this, and relieved me of responsibility in the matter.[4]

From your remarks concerning the cost of the volume &c., am I to infer that you propose to recompense me from the profits of the edition? I do not think we made any agreement whatever as to the amount or manner of remuneration but I certainly cannot consent to any that is to be *contingent* upon the success of the volume if that is your intention. I may misunderstand you; pray write to me more particularly upon this point. It is better we should understand each other at once. If you will recall our interviews you must remember that I was not sanguine of the success of this venture, and certainly did not base my ideas of payment on such a contingency.

I have some idea of publishing a little book of my California sketches and burlesques including the "Condensed Novels" which have been widely copied and seem to be popular in the East.[5] Let me know what you think of it, and if you would to undertake it. Of course I should depend entirely upon its sale in the East.

Yours very sincerely,
Fr Bret Harte

A Roman Esq
New York

Provenience: Fales Library, New York University (ALS).

1. Anton Roman immigrated to California in 1850 and started a bookstore and publishing company in San Francisco in 1860.

2. BH compiled *Outcroppings*, an anthology of forty-two poems by nineteen writers, for publication by Roman in November 1865. The book had been reviewed at least twice in the East—in the *Springfield Republican* (22 Nov. 1865, p. 1, col. 1) and the *Boston Courier* (24 Nov. 1865, p. 2, col. 2)—before Roman wrote BH on 9 December 1865.

3. Critical reviews of the book in the Virginia City *Territorial Enterprise*, *Oakland News*, *Pajaro Times*, *Golden Era*, and San Francisco *American Flag* had been excerpted on the front page of the San Francisco *Daily Evening Bulletin* on 6 January 1866. As BH reminisced in "My First Book" (*Idler* 4 [Jan 1894]: 553–61), "The big dailies collected the criticisms and published them in their own columns with the grim irony of exaggerated headlines. The book sold tremendously on account of this abuse."

4. In his preface, BH acknowledged that he had selected some of the poems in the volume "from material collected three years ago for a similar volume, by Miss M. V. Tingley" and submitted to Roman. Some sixty-four years later, Mary V. Tingley Lawrence still claimed she had been robbed: "Bret Harte deliberately broke into my 'Outcroppings of California Early Writers' and . . . dishonestly appropriated them" in a book whose very title he stole. "He was a deliberate thief" (24 Aug. 1929, UVa).

5. According to his obituary in the San Francisco *Daily Evening Bulletin* (7 May 1902, p. 1, cols. 5–7), BH's condensed novel *Fantine*, a parody of Victor Hugo first published in the *Golden Era* for 3 August 1862, was his first work widely copied in eastern newspapers.

2. TO HENRY W. BELLOWS, 15 SEPTEMBER 1866

San Franc[co]
Sept. 15th 1866.

My dear Sir,[1]

I differ from my young friend Stoddard,[2] and am satisfied that his eloquent note and beautiful poem needs no other help to your notice. But he insists that I shall add a few words of introduction to the enclosure.[3]

I can think of nothing to say except that he is yet young—about twenty one—and exhibits indications of poetic excellence in my opinion, beyond any other writer on the coast.

He is full of poetic sensibility—a good deal like Keats in disposition as well as fancy.[4] Perhaps as much out of place in this very material country as Pegasus in a quartz mill. How he can father "epithetic honey" on the scrubby sand hills of S.F. or keep the fine edge and delicate temper of his fancies in this community excites my wonder as well as my admiration.

He has a weakness for autographs rather than criticism.[5] I have not forgotten that *I* have yours in acknowledgement of certain verses, and although I have never shown it to him or any other of the tuneful tribe, for certain prudential reasons, which I know you will thank me for, I, without much hesitation commend him to your kindly notice.

With best regards to your wife & family

I am
Yours Sincerely
Francis Bret Harte

Rev. H. W. Bellows
N. Y.
P.S. I see that Stoddard speaks of the *Xn Examiner*—he means I think the *Inquirer.*[6]

Provenience: Bellows Papers, Massachusetts Historical Society (ALS).

1. Henry W. Bellows (1814–82), minister of All Souls Unitarian Church in New York, met BH when he filled the pulpit of the First Unitarian Church in San Francisco between April and September 1864.

2. BH was an early patron of the poet Charles Warren Stoddard (1843–1909). He included four of Stoddard's poems in *Outcroppings* (1865), his edition of California verse; and he edited Stoddard's *Poems* for publication the next year. See Jacob Blanck, *Bibliography of American Literature* (New Haven: Yale University Press, 1959), III, 413, item 7239; and Roger Austen, *Genteel Pagan: The Double Life of Charles Warren Stoddard* (Amherst: University of Massachusetts Press, 1991), 31, 178. See also Stoddard's memoir "Early Recollections of Bret Harte," *Atlantic Monthly* 78 (Nov. 1896):673–78.

3. Stoddard's poem "A Brief Evangel" appeared in the *Christian Inquirer*, which Bellows at least nominally edited and published, for 8 Nov. 1866, 8.

4. In its review of *Outcroppings*, the *Sacramento Union* had earlier remarked upon the "Keats-like quality" of Stoddard's verse (Austen, *Genteel Pagan*, 31).

5. In his "eloquent note" dated 15 September 1866 (Massachusetts Historical Society), Stoddard wrote Bellows: "If the enclosed verses meet

with your approbation and afterward appear in the 'Christian Examiner,' I should be very happy. But if they are refused, so long as *your own* pen announces their fate, I shall still have reason to be proud and happy."

6. Stoddard confused a Boston Unitarian bimonthly, the *Christian Examiner*, with the New York Unitarian weekly, the *Christian Inquirer*.

3. TO SAMUEL BOWLES, 9 AUGUST 1867

San Franc.[co] Aug 9th/67

My dear Mr. Bowles,[1]

I send by this mail two letters to make up for past shortcomings. One is rather long, and what is worse, owing to its sinuosity and devious wanderings it can't be cut or divided so as to make two, wherein it doth differ from the sprightly angle-worm, which in my boyish days I firmly believed could be separated into specimens of *annelidae* with a distinct vitality and separate head and tail. The other letter is political. I dont like to write politics—but I can't reflect the spirit of our civilization if I don't. Be thankful that you have the disinterested views of one, who though an office-holder, is no politician.[2]

I sent you by the last mail a copy of the Poem I delivered before the Assc.[td] *Alumni* of the Pacific Coast.[3] It was pleasantly inappropriate and considered by some of my most intimate friends as the very best thing of the kind ever attempted. They had been reading Webb's refreshing notice of me in his correspondence with the *Republican*.[4] Seriously, what possessed that clever, audicious wretch to roast me after that fashion, and why did you, Bowles,—whom I love, whose book I have praised and defended[5]—lend yourself to such an unpious fraud on the public and yours &c?

Fr. Bret Harte

Provenience: Bancroft (MSS C-H 57).

1. Samuel Bowles (1826–78), founding editor and publisher of the *Springfield Republican*, traveled to California in company with Vice President Schuyler Colfax and wrote a series of letters about the trip for his newspaper, later collected under the title *Across the Continent* (1865).

2. As its California correspondent, BH contributed a series of eighteen essays to the *Springfield Republican* between 5 April 1866 and 8 October

1867. These "San Francisco Letters" have been collected in *BH's California*. BH refers in particular to his letter to the *Republican* dated 29 July 1867, "Summer in San Francisco" (printed 11 Sept. 1867, p. 1, cols. 3–4), and his 9 August 1867 letter to the same paper on the gubernatorial campaign (printed 4 Sept. 1867, p. 1, cols. 1–2). As secretary to the superintendent of the U.S. Mint in San Francisco, BH was an "office-holder."

3. BH read his poem "The Lost Galleon" at the fourth annual meeting of the Associated Alumni of the Pacific Coast in Oakland on 5 June 1867 (San Francisco *Daily Evening Bulletin*, 6 June 1867, p. 1, cols. 4–5). It was not reprinted in the *Springfield Republican*.

4. Bowles had hailed BH as the "best of the California humorists after all" in the *Springfield Republican* for 22 May 1867, p. 1, col. 6. Charles H. Webb (1834–1905), the owner of the *Californian* with whom BH had quarreled since the winter of 1865–66, asked in his own column in the paper (signed with his nom de plume "John Paul") why the editor had paid BH so "equivocal" a compliment "in saying that, *after all*, he is 'the best,' etc." (*Springfield Republican*, 29 May 1867, p. 4, col. 4).

5. BH had commended Bowles's *Across the Continent* in the San Francisco *Daily Evening Bulletin* 7 Feb. 1866, p. 1, col. 1. He was more critical of Bowles in two later columns in the *Overland* 2 (Feb. 1869):194; and 6 (Feb. 1871):192.

4. TO INA COOLBRITH, 22 JULY 1868

Editorial Rooms of the "Overland Monthly."
San Francisco, July 22d, *1868*

My dear Miss Ina,[1]

On my return to-day from Sta Cruz, where I have been staying for the last two weeks, I found a vicious little note lying among my papers, like an asp. I do not know how long it had been there—not long I should say, for it was quite lively and venomous yet.

Why, bless your heart, my dear young lady, "the poem was settled," as you call it, 8 days ago by adopting one of your emendations. (I forget wh. just now.)

It was sent to me at Sta Cruz., with a pretty little note (quite unlike your last) wh. I did not think required an *answer* but which

I am free to say ought to have been acknowledged. But I was sick and worried. The *Overland* was following me persistently and relentlessly, and each night I made up a mail for the city that left me no leisure for vacation in which belongs the answering of your letters. This is my explanation and now accept my apology.

The poem is already in print in the 1st form of the *Overland* for Aug. It is the 1st poem.[2]

Yours ever truly
Fr. Bret Harte

Miss Ina Coolbrith

Provenience: Bancroft (Coolbrith Collection, MSS C-H 23).

1. Ina Coolbrith (1841–1928) was, with BH and C. W. Stoddard, one of the "Golden State Trinity" of California writers. Appointed the head of the Oakland Public Library in 1874, she became an early patron of Jack London. In her posthumously published introduction to an edition of *Plain Language from Truthful James* (San Francisco: Nash, 1934), she remarked that "It was my privilege, the novelty and happiness of which I did not then understand nor properly appreciate, to be closely associated with" BH during his *Overland* editorship.

2. "In Blossom-Times," *Overland* 1 (Aug. 1868):145.

5. TO JAMES T. FIELDS, 30 OCTOBER 1868

San Franc^co^
October 30th 1868

My dear Sir,[1]

As the author of "The Luck of Roaring Camp" I have to thank you for an invitation to contribute to the Atlantic Monthly,[2] but as the Editor of the *Overland* my duties claim most of my spare time outside of the Govt. office in wh. I am employed. My opportunities for doing anything more than the usual cast-iron work are few. I have written but seldom for the body of the magazine. But I'll try to find time to send you something.

The *Overland* is still an experiment. Should it fail—should the bear get the better of the locomotive,[3] why I dare say I may be able to do more.

But I am glad of this opportunity to thank some one connected with the *Atlantic* for its very generous good-will toward me and my writings—particularly the book which G. W. Carleton of New York, malformed in its birth. There was an extra kindness in your taking the deformed brat by the hand, and trying to recognize some traces of a parent so far away.[4] For all of wh. I assure I [am]

Very gratefully Yrs
Fr. Bret Harte

The Editor of the Atlantic Monthly

Provenience: Huntington (FI 5078).

1. James T. Fields (1817–81) was the most prominent American publisher of the nineteenth century and editor of the *Atlantic* between 1861 and 1871. See James C. Austin, *Fields of the Atlantic Monthly* (San Marino, Calif.: Huntington Library, 1953).

2. BH reminisced years later about the circumstances in which he wrote this letter. In the midst of local controversy surrounding the publication of the unsigned "Luck of Roaring Camp" in the *Overland*, "there came an important letter. It was from Fields & Osgood, the publishers, and was addressed to me as editor. It requested me to hand the enclosed note to the author of 'The Luck of Roaring Camp.' The note was their offer to publish anything he chose to write, upon his own terms. This became known, and it turned the tide of criticism. Since Boston indorsed the story, San Francisco was properly proud of it" (Henry J. W. Dam, "A Morning with Bret Harte," *McClure's* 4 [Dec. 1894]:46).

Ironically, after BH published an earlier story, "The Legend of Monte del Diablo," in the *Atlantic* for October 1863, Fields refused BH's subsequent submissions on the grounds he "fails to interest. He is not piquant enough for the readers of the *Atlantic*" (Jessie Frémont, "What Makes Literary Success?" *Ladies Home Journal*, n.s., 9 [Feb. 1892]:18).

3. BH alludes here to the logo of the *Overland*, which he helped to design: a bear angrily turning its face down a section of railroad track as if to meet an approaching locomotive.

4. In a letter to S. W. Bush dated 22 November 1867 (Washburn Autograph Collection, Massachusetts Historical Society), BH had repudiated "the coarseness and vulgarity of the illustrations" Carleton had commissioned for the first edition of the *Condensed Novels*, a series of burlesques in which BH parodied such writers as Dickens, Cooper, Hugo,

and Wilkie Collins. This edition with the offending illustrations has been microfilmed in Wright's American Fiction series II, no. 1115, reel H-9. On 30 May 1870 (Huntington), BH wrote to thank Fields for commending in the *Atlantic* (21 [Jan. 1868]:128) the "charming parodies, so well known in California."

6. TO FIELDS, OSGOOD & CO., 23 APRIL 1869

Rooms of The Overland Monthly
San Francisco, April 23d 1869

Gentlemen,

In regard to your proposal to examine a collection of my California sketches with a view to republication, I fear that you have overestimated the number of my contributions to the *Overland* which are (of stories) but two—"The Luck of Roaring Camp," and "The Outcasts of Poker Flat." The latter was in the Jany. no.[1]

I am writing a little sketch similar in style for the June no. and have in view three or four more,[2] when the pressure of my editorial duties shall be lifted either by the suspension of the magazine or a division of its editorial work—wh. since the inception of the O. M. has fallen entirely on me. One or the other will happen about the 1st June.

I have one or two California sketches published before (but not in the *Overland*) and not included in the "Condensed Novels," but even these would not, together with the "Luck" & the "Outcasts" make a volume of the size suggested.[3]

As my contract with Carleton of N.Y. expired with his first and only edition of the "Condensed Novels" (1500 copies) would it be possible to translate one or two sketches from that?[4]

Will you be good enough to tell me also what the *Atlantic* would pay for stories like these proposed.

Yours very truly
Fr. Bret Harte

Messrs Fields Osgood & Co.
Boston

Provenience: Huntington (HM 12491).

1. BH's first two stories for the *Overland Monthly* were "The Luck of Roaring Camp," 1 (Aug. 1868):183–89; and "The Outcasts of Poker Flat," 2 (Jan. 1869):41–47.

2. BH's story "Miggles" would appear in the *Overland* 2 (June 1869):570–76. Before the end of the year he also published "Tennessee's Partner" 3 (Oct. 1869):360–65, and "The Idyl of Red Gulch" 3 (Dec. 1869):569–74.

3. The first edition of *The Luck of Roaring Camp and Other Sketches*, issued by Fields, Osgood & Co. in April 1870, reprinted the first five stories BH had written for the *Overland*, a story entitled "The Right Eyes of the Commander" from the San Francisco *Daily Evening Bulletin* (4 Jan. 1867), plus nine tales and sketches first published in the *Golden Era*: "High Water Mark" (6 Jan. 1861), "A Lonely Ride" (22 Feb. 1863), "The Man of No Account" (7 Oct. 1860), "M'liss" (9 and 16 Dec. 1860), "Notes by Flood and Field" (7 and 14 Sept. 1862), "The Mission Dolores" (22 Mar. 1863), "John Chinaman" (5 Apr. 1863), "From a Back Window" (8 Mar. 1863), and "Boonder" (22 Feb. 1863). The second edition of the volume, issued later in 1870, also included an additional text, "Brown of Calaveras," first published in the *Overland* 4 (Mar. 1870):284–90.

4. In fact, Fields, Osgood & Co. would issue a new edition of BH's *Condensed Novels* in May 1871. See also letters 13 and 19.

7. TO JOHN H. CARMANY, 7 JUNE 1869

San Francisco June 7th 1869

John H. Carmany, Esq.[1]
Sir,

I will continue in the editorial charge of the Overland Monthly, upon the following terms:

1st. That I have the exclusive control, as formerly, of its literary and critical conduct.

2d. That I shall be privileged to select and occupy for that purpose, a private office, as formerly—where rent shall not exceed $30.00 per mo.—chargeable to the *Overland*.

3. That I shall receive as compensation $200 per mo. payable weekly, and receive the same amount paid other contributors, per page, for all contributions to the body of the magazine, exclusive of Etc. and Book Reviews.

4. That when the business, or income of the magazine shall justify the expenditure, I shall have acceptable editorial assistance.
5 That this contract shall continue in force for one year.

[signature removed]
Ed. *Overland*.[2]

Provenience: Bancroft (MSS C-H 57).

1. John Carmany (d. 1910) immigrated to California in 1858, founded the San Francisco *Commercial Herald* in 1867, and bought Anton Roman's interest in the *Overland* in mid-1869. See Cummins, 144–46.

2. In a letter to Carmany the next day, BH adamantly insisted he would neither "modify nor alter any of the prospositions in the terms I offered. They were made upon careful deliberation, and are, in my opinion, essential to the safety of the magazine and my operation. . . . If I do not hear from you by to-morrow 10 A.M. I shall consider myself at liberty to enter into other negotiations, elsewhere" (Bancroft, MSS C-H 57). On 9 June 1869, in apparent response to a reply from Carmany, BH reiterated that he would continue as editor of the *Overland* only on the terms "I offered two days ago, which I have never changed and do not intend to change" (*Letters*, 8). Carmany had capitulated to BH's terms by 11 June 1869. As he recalled later ("Supplement" to *Overland*, n.s., 1 [Feb 1883]:11), "At the time I purchased this periodical from Mr. Roman, some little difficulty was experienced about the retention of Mr. Harte as editor. Why he was disposed to hold off or be somewhat indifferent I could never learn."

8. TO W. D. HOWELLS, 5 AUGUST 1869

Rooms of The Overland Monthly
San Francisco. Aug. 5th *1869*

My Dear Sir[1]

My superior officer is Superintendent of the Mint and *not* Collector of the Port. But he is also Vice President of the Chamber of Commerce, Pres. of the Mer. Library, etc., etc. etc.,[2] and out of his omniscience in these several capacities he sends me the enclosed answer to yr. inquiry.

As for myself, my acquaintance with the Italian organ and scissors grinders of this city is limited by my ignorance of the Irish language.[3]

Dismissing your friend, for whom I confess I have not the slightest concern, I should like to tell you how much I admire your humor and your English, and shall do so, just as if you had not complimented me in your late note with such a pleasant blending of both. Indeed, when I first read your *Venetian Life* I came to the conclusion that I had perhaps overrated Hawthorne for a quality of composition which after all, was not so peculiar to himself as it was to good writing. Perhaps if I didn't like your prose so well, I should like your poetry better. I have, it is true, never read any of the latter but *No Love Lost*—wh. I admired for the rare restraining taste that kept it from being better or worse. I liked the *Italian Journeys* so well that as a lazy man and a fastidious one, I should have been willing to have seen Italy by proxy. I think you have such a rare faculty of not liking things in a likable manner. Any one can be charmingly enthusiastic, but so few can be even tolerably skeptical.[4]

But what I meant to say before I fell into this attitude of criticism was that I like your writings and you—in so far as you seem to me to be projected in them—and that perhaps I only voice the opinion editorial-wise—of clever folk, in saying so. This is particularly true of some bright young men in S.F.—of course contributors to the *Overland* who haven't in their exuberance of animal spirits forgotten how superior is cultivated repose.[5]

Should you ever come to San Francisco, I shall be glad to explain this letter. Perhaps I may see you in the East—whither I long to go for a visit & relief, for I am hardly overworked for a lazy man, and, having the sole editorial burden of the O. M. on my shoulders, sometimes think I am unfair to myself & readers. You, who are in the *Atlantic* I believe might come here and exchange pulpits.

I had some questions to ask of you—something as practical as yours, but I'll put it off, for I intend to write again, when I leave the Mint, and have more leisure and here I am at the end of my letter and yr. patience.

Truly yours
F. B. Harte

Provenience: Harvard (bMS Am 1784 [210]). By permission of the Houghton Library, Harvard University.

1. W. D. Howells (1837–1920) was the central figure and patron of a coterie of American writers, Henry James and Samuel Clemens foremost among them, who emerged after the Civil War. He joined the staff of the *Atlantic* in 1866 and became the editor in July 1871, a position he held for the next decade.

2. Superintendent of the San Francisco Mint between 1863 and 1869, Robert B. Swain (1822–72) was BH's "superior officer." Swain was also head of R. B. Swain & Co., commission merchants and insurance agents, and chair of the board of trustees of the First Unitarian Church in San Francisco, which BH attended.

3. BH refers sarcastically to the role of Irish organizations, especially the Fenians, in San Francisco at the time. See also his comments in his letters to the *Springfield Republican* dated 9 July 1866, 10 April 1867, and 15 June 1867 (*BH's California*, 51–52, 115, 128).

4. BH refers to Howells's *Venetian Life* (1866), a volume based on his Venice correspondence with the *Boston Daily Advertiser*; his long poem *No Love Lost* (1869); and his *Italian Journeys* (1867), based on his columns in the *Boston Daily Advertiser* and a series of articles for the *Atlantic Monthly*.

5. Some of the contributors to early numbers of the *Overland*, in addition to BH, were Stoddard, Coolbrith, Clemens, Prentice Mulford (1834–91), Ambrose Bierce (1842–1914?), Joaquin Miller (1837–1913), and Henry George (1839–97). All but Coolbrith and George subsequently contributed to the *Atlantic* during Howells's tenure as editor.

9. TO JOAQUIN MILLER, 19 AUGUST 1869

Rooms of The Overland Monthly
San Francisco. Aug 19 1869

My dear Sir,[1]

Although I shall not be able to use either of your poems, I think that I fairly appreciate the merit of their performance and promise. I cannot say that I as greatly admire your choice of subjects—which seems to me to be calculated to foster and develop a certain theatrical tendency and feverish exaltation, wh. would be better under restraint than development, just now. I see nothing in you worse than faults of excess, wh. you can easily check by selecting less sensational themes for your muse. You are, I think, on your way to become a poet, and will, by and by, learn how much strength as well as beauty lies in repose. The best thing in "*Peccavi*" is the quietest—the very felicitous and natural *lie* at its close. The rest is ecstasy—relieved by good phrasing—on a theme worn threadbare already by the best poets of your kind.

Yet I would not have you false to yr. dramatic tastes, but only suggest to you to develop your other faculties equally.

I have to thank you for yr. volume. Let this informal and well meaning attempt at criticism take the place of a notice in the O.M.[2]

I should be glad to receive something else from you. Try and condense something as long as "Sackcloth & Ashes"[3] into 30 or 40 lines.

Yours very sincerely
Fr. Bret Harte

C. H. Miller Esq

Provenience: Bancroft (MSS 79/47 C).

1. A resident of Oregon, Cincinnatus Hiner (later, "Joaquin") Miller moved to San Francisco in 1870 and joined the *Overland* circle. As he remarked in an interview (*Louisville Courier-Journal*, 2 Dec. 1875, p. 3, col. 4) he was "kindly received by Bret Harte."

2. BH subsequently reviewed Miller's *Joaquin et al.* in the *Overland* (4 [Jan. 1870]:104), praising "the true poetic instinct, with a natural felicity of diction and a dramatic rigor that are good in performance, and yet better in promise." Miller reminisced after BH's death that he "gave my first little book . . . a first-rate review in his Overland. I doubt if I should have tried to write more if he had cut me up as California is cutting him up now" (*New York Times Saturday Review of Books*, 31 May 1902, 360).

3. Neither "Peccavi" nor "Sackcloth and Ashes" appears in the standard edition of Miller's collected poems.

10. TO JOHN H. CARMANY, 11 (?) DECEMBER 1869[1]

Sat. Evening.

My dear Mr Carmany—

The proof of "San Francisco" was only completed by you at noon to-day.[2] It was only received by the author, whom I had been seeking all day, at 3 P.M. It required, as you know, great care in revision and correction, was already a page and a half beyond my limit, and could only be cut down by a careful consideration of the entire article as a whole. I had frequently explained this to you, as well as my anxiety to get the completed proof as soon as possible when I fully expected to have a day or night at least in wh. to remodel it with the author. And yet you think it "provoking" and something more that this proof wasn't returned to you in a couple of hours—less time than you usually give to an ordinary article.

It seems hardly fair that this particular article—wh. lay for two days in MS in your office, untouched—should be pushed through and slurred in that print wh. really requires the most care and attention. It was a special article, written for a specific purpose, and as you well know, I have—in the interests of the magazine as I fondly believe—bestowed upon it more personal care, actual time labor and anxiety—than I would upon a personal article or there is [*sic*: one that is] in the exact line of my duty. And I really do not think I should be reminded at such a moment of the *interests of the magazine*. Enough that I am quite as careful of them as you are—that our concern for the Overland should be identical—but that in questions of this kind I think that the contents of the magazine, on wh. its reputation is based, is paramount to all else. A day or two lost in time, hurts only a few subscribers; a poor magazine affects them all.[3] No one would be happier than myself, to be able to accept as Eastern editors do, only acceptable and properly prepared articles. But I must make the best of my material.

I return the proofs and copy. You will observe that there are two or three pages stricken out. It is part of my agreement with the author, that the cost of composition of these pages shall be deducted from his compensation, and was the only method I could hit upon to gain time and proper leisure.

Yours &c
Fr. Bret Harte

Provenience: Bancroft (Overland Monthly Records, MSS C-H 97).

1. This letter is dated by reference to the Watkins article in the *Overland* cited in note 2. BH is preparing to send copy to be typeset for the January 1870 issue of the *Overland*, which was issued on 1 January 1870.

2. This article by the local journalist James T. Watkins appeared in the *Overland* 4 (Jan. 1870):9–23.

3. Carmany later claimed that BH resigned the editorship of the *Overland* and went east in 1871 rather than sign a contract that would oblige him to have the magazine "ready for press on a certain date monthly, a point on which Harte was weak, for he was very dilatory" (Cummins, 145).

11. TO WALT WHITMAN, 13 APRIL 1870

Rooms of The Overland Monthly
San Francisco Apl 13th *1870*

My dear Sir,

I fear that the "Passage to India" is a poem too long and too abstract for the hasty and material minded readers of the O.M.[1]

With many thanks I am,

Your obt. svt.
Fr. Bret Harte Ed O.M.

Mr. Walt Whitman
Washington, D.C.

Provenience: Feinberg Collection, LC (ALS).

1. In a cover letter dated 4 April 1870, Whitman (1819–92) had offered his poem as the "leading article in either the June or July number" of the *Overland* for a price of two hundred dollars and twenty copies of the issue in which it appeared while reserving "the right to print it in future book" (*Walt Whitman: The Correspondence 1865–1875*, ed. Edwin Haviland Miller [New York: New York University Press, 1961], 94). Though impressed by BH's "The Outcasts of Poker Flat" and "What the Engines Said," in the *Overland* for January and June 1869, respectively (*With Walt Whitman in Camden*, ed. Horace Traubel [New York: Appleton, 1908], IV, 208), Whitman remarked in December 1871 that BH "is a sharp, bright fellow, but entirely cut off from what he writes about by having cultivated foppishness and superiority" (Clara Barrus, *Whitman and Burroughs, Comrades* [Boston: Houghton Mifflin, 1931], 64).

12. TO JOHN H. CARMANY, 5 OR 12 MAY 1870[1]

San Rafael
Thursday night

My dear Carmany—

I shant have any brevier copy before Saturday.[2]

I enclose "Dow's Flat." I intended it for a few verses like "Jim," but its grown to the length of "Her Letter."[3] I'm afraid of it—so send me a proof Friday night, that I may wrestle with it.

The *Republicans* notice of "The Luck" is sheer ambitious nonsense. I dont like it at all! The writer who classes *George Sand* with Shakespeare & Cervantes as a creator of character—that French slut never wrote anything but supersensuous sentiment—is an enormous ass.[4]

I cant think that Bowles did it. Then the allusion to Bacons proof-reader is in such bad taste[5]—I'm dreadfully disappointed.

Truly yours
H.

Provenience: Bancroft (Overland Monthly Records, MSS C-H 97).

1. This letter is dated by references to the review of *The Luck of Roaring Camp and Other Sketches* in the *Springfield Republican* for 25 April 1870 and BH's poem "Dow's Flat," published in the June 1870 issue of the *Overland*. It is unlikely BH could have seen the review by Thursday, April 28, and it is unlikely he would have been still writing material for the June issue of the magazine as late as Thursday, May 19. The most likely Thursday on which BH wrote this letter is thus either May 5 or 12.

2. BH refers to the copy for book reviews and the "Etc." section of the *Overland*, set in 8-point or "brevier" type.

3. BH alludes to three of his poems in the *Overland*—"Dow's Flat" 4 (June 1870):569–70; "Jim" 4 (Feb. 1870):186; and "Her Letter" 3 (Dec. 1869):567–68.

4. The particular target of BH's ire is this statement in the *Republican* (25 Apr. 1870, p. 2, col. 3): "He has produced . . . a few characters that are as real as any that ever trod the paths of fiction . . . such as Shakespeare and Cervantes and George Sand have depicted." Ironically, George Sand later translated BH's story "The Rose of Tuolumne" in *Contes d'une Grand'mère* (Paris: Paetz, 1877), 115–47.

5. To BH's dismay, the reviewer repeats the story about the proofreader, almost certainly Sarah B. Cooper, who objected to BH's depiction of the prostitute Cherokee Sal and to the elliptical curses of the miners in the title story. This proofreader nearly succeeded in killing the story in proof. BH himself sometimes repeated the anecdote in later years, as in the "General Introduction" to the collected edition of his *Writings* (London: Chatto & Windus, 1880), xiii, and in his essay "The Rise of the 'Short Story,'" *Cornhill*, n.s., 7 [July 1899]:7).

13. TO FIELDS, OSGOOD & CO., 30 MAY 1870

San Francisco
May 30th 1870

Gentlemen:

I cannot, of my own knowledge, say to whom the copyright of the "Condensed Novels" belongs; but here are some facts which your better judgement and experience may make available.

The material for the book was forwarded to A. Roman & Co's agent at N.Y. with directions to arrange with some publisher for its publication. The agent presently wrote that he had given the book to G. W. Carleton who was to publish it at his own expense and pay me 10¢ per copy on all copies "for copyright." I accepted these terms—the book being already in press—by letter—but there was no other or more formal contract.[1]

When the book appeared I was so incensed at its circus clowns dress and the painted grins that Mr Carleton had scattered through its pages,[2] that my correspondence with him was very brief, and I determined to get it out of his hands. This appeared simple enough, for he had written to me that it sold slowly, and I accordingly directed the *Overland's* agent in N.Y. to get from him a statement of a/c, and to bargain cautiously for the stereotype plates. Mr Carleton refused to recognize him as my agent—said that he did not know whether the plates were destroyed or not, and that he did not intend to print any more. A few months later I received a statement of a/c of 1800 volumes—(the edition)—showing a balance on hand of 100 copies with the remark that he *did not intend "to print any more."* Mr. Roman tells me that in answer to some orders which he has sent Carleton for the "Novels" the answer has been returned that the book is "out of print."

Now I know nothing of the *usual* contracts between Author and publisher, but from the terms of the written contract between Fields Osgood & Co. and myself, it seems to me that it is tacitly understood in an unwritten contract, as well as a condition of a written one, that the publisher shall supply the demand, and that when he ceases to do so, he virtually abandons the publication & the contract is void.

Pray give me the benefit of your advice and experience.[3] If I have the right to dispose of the "Novels," it is my wish to arrange with you for a revised edition—an edition which should exclude all but the "Novels"; the excluded sketches being also revised and possibly added in part to some future edition of "The Luck" (also revised) so as to make two books, each being much more distinctive and unique.

Truly Yrs
Fr. Bret Harte

Provenience: American Authors Collection (M122, box 2, folder 30), Department of Special Collections, Stanford University Libraries (ALS).

1. Samuel Clemens had predicted in a letter to Stoddard from New York on 23 April 1867 that "Bret is publishing with a Son of a Bitch who will swindle him, & he may print that opinion if he chooses, with my name signed to it" (*Mark Twain's Letters*, ed. Harriet Elinor Smith and Richard Bucci [Berkeley: University of California Press, 1990], II, 30).

2. See letter 5 and accompanying note 4.

3. James R. Osgood (1836–92), junior partner in the firm of Fields, Osgood & Co. and senior partner in the successor firm of J. R. Osgood & Co. from 1868 to 1878, soon opened negotiations for rights to BH's *Condensed Novels* but thought Carleton's price for the plates too steep. See Ballou, 185: see also letter 19.

14. TO PARKE GODWIN, 9 JULY 1870

Rooms of The Overland Monthly
San Francisco, July 9th *1870*

My dear Sir—[1]

Your letter was to some extent supplemented by one from Mr. Putnam,[2] wh. I handed to Mr. Carmany of the O. M. for his consideration. He has answered it I believe, but as his answer was unfavorable to Mr Putnam's later proposition, I return to that wh. you made more directly to myself. I should have replied before, but I have been absent from town and somewhat ill.

I should greatly like to take hold of Putnam's magazine if, with your valuable assistance, I could control it editorially, observing my own methods and after my own fashion as I do the O.M.—for I think there is room for an American magazine. But as I should give myself up to it entirely, I should expect a salary of at least $5000 per annum, *guaranteed for one year.* I do not know that Mr. Putnam could make this pay; I only know I could not afford less.[3]

Having said this I can the more disinterestedly thank you not only for the chivalrous kindness which you evidently feel for me and my future, but for the rare delicacy good taste, and critical faculty wh. which you have expressed it through the pages of a magazine which I fear must still remain the *Overlands* rival.[4]

Very truly Yrs
Fr. Bret Harte

Mr. Parke Godwin

Provenience: UVa (ALS).

1. Parke Godwin (1816–1904) was one of the members of the Brook Farm community, one of the editors of the original *Putnam's* (1853–57), and first editor of the revived *Putnam's* (1867–70).

2. George Palmer Putnam (1814–72), publisher of *Putnam's.*

3. The story soon circulated that Putnam was amenable. See the New York *World*, 1 Sept. 1870, p. 5, col. 1: "Brett Harte is said to have been offered the editorship of *Putnam's Magazine.*"

4. BH alludes particularly to a piece probably written by Godwin and printed the month before in the magazine, "A Star in the West," n.s., 5 (June 1870):721–22.

15. TO WHITELAW REID, 1 SEPTEMBER 1870

Rooms of The Overland Monthly
San Francisco Sept 1st *1870*

My dear Sir:[1]

I cannot, just now, forecast my work for the next year, but I think it possible that I may find the time, as I already have the inclination, to write for you.[2] The main difficulty, I apprehend, wd. be in getting something to write abt. Literary and Art items wd. not occupy a letter once in a year, while Society as it has gained in respectability, I fear has lost in picturesqueness, and differs now but little from that of most American second rate towns. The tourists have already exhausted superficial California and what is below is hard, dry and repulsive. Perhaps in more than one sense "placer" California is—to use an expressive localism—"played out." So that you wd. have to be content with different material from that wh. made Mrs Calhoun's letters[3] bright and sparkling. Epigrammatic California, is, I fear, only seen by tourists. I am a sixteen years' resident, and it eludes my analysis and defies my prophecy.

I am hoping that University business may give me an opportunity to visit the East this fall,[4] in wh. case I should be glad to talk further with you on this subject, but meanwhile you can consider whether the stuff I wd. be likely to offer you wd. be that most attractive to the readers of the *Tribune*.

Truly Yrs
Fr. Bret Harte

Provenience: LC (ALS).

1. Whitelaw Reid (1837–1912) was managing editor of the *New York Tribune* and, from 1872 to 1905, its editor-in-chief.

2. J. H. Carmany remembered later that BH had received an offer from the *New York Tribune* "of fifty dollars per letter, no matter as to length or subject" ("Supplement" to *Overland*, n.s., 1 [Feb. 1883]:12).

3. Lucia G. Calhoun, later Runkle (b. 1844), an editorialist for the *New York Tribune*, visited California in the summer of 1869 in a party with Vice President Schuyler Colfax and Samuel Bowles. Her travel letters appeared in Saturday editions of the *Tribune* in November and December 1869.

4. The San Francisco *Alta California* reported on 4 October 1870 (p. 1, col. 3) that BH had been offered the position of professor of recent literature and curator of the library and museum at the new University of California in nearby Berkeley but that he had declined on the grounds "it would interfere with his profession" and a visit he planned to "the Atlantic States."

16. TO FIELDS, OSGOOD & CO., 16 SEPTEMBER 1870

Rooms of The Overland Monthly
San Francisco. Sept. 16th *1870*

Gentlemen

My construction of your letter of the 21st June was that you would, at some future time, make me an offer to connect myself with your periodicals, upon a pecuniary basis of $5,000 per annum—the income named by me as essential to my removing East. But this proposition of a future proposition was, as I understood it, also contingent upon my satisfying you what I could do for the money.

This I did not then and do not now propose to do—believing that you ought to be aware by this time what are my abilities and usefulness, and not being willing, at any price and under any circumstances to agree to furnish any specified amount of "copy"—or to undertake any specific performance, except that which I now perform in the *Overland*. As Putnams and the Galaxy had both made me direct propositions for direct editorial work,[1] I did not deem it necessary to wait for yours.

I have not yet however entered into any contract or made any promise or pledge to any editor or publisher in N.Y. or elsewhere. I am still anxious to make my home in the East. To stay here I am offered a professorship in the University which will not interfere with my editorial work on the O.M. both of wh. offices will make my income amount to abt. $6,000 (gold) per annum.[2] Can you do as well for me, and how?

Touching the collection of my poems, I have enough already for a volume, and will receive a proposition from you.[3]

Truly yours,
Fr. Bret Harte

Messrs Fields Osgood & Co
Boston

Provenience: UVa (ALS).

1. See letters 14 and 17.

2. See note 4 to letter 15.

3. Fields, Osgood & Co. released a new edition of BH's *Poems* on 22 December 1870.

17. TO F. P. CHURCH, 18 OCTOBER 1870

Rooms of The Overland Monthly
San Francisco. Oct 18 *1870*

My dear sir:[1]

I have received your telegram of the 4th Octo. and yr. letters of Septem. 26th and Octo. 6th. The offer of Messrs Sheldon & Co, to wh. they refer I have, as you will probably learn, already declined.

That you may more fully comprehend my reasons for so doing, permit me to assure you that if I chose to furnish the amount of "copy" required by *The Galaxy*, I could by disposing of it elsewhere, realize twice the sum wh. *The Galaxy* offers. During the last 18 mos. I have propositions for more copy than I could possibly furnish. A publishing house in Boston have offered me $5,000 per year to retain me for their periodicals, without specifying the amount of "copy,"[2] and it is but due to your apparent frank concern for my well-being to assure you that *The Galaxy* has made me the lowest and least advantageous offer wh. I have yet had the honor to receive from any one.

Appreciating, my dear sir, the kindness of your notices,[3] I fear that I must conclude by saying that thus far our correspondence has developed nothing that would lead me to infer that a business connection with *The Galaxy* would be advantageous to either it or myself.

Very truly yours
Bret Harte

Mr F. P. Church
N.Y.

Provenience: Bancroft (MSS C-H 57).

1. Francis P. Church (1839–1906) edited *The Galaxy* in collaboration with his brother, William Conant Church.

2. See letter 16. Harper & Bros. also offered BH $100 to $150 "for every poem of yours accepted for their publications (S. L. Conant to BH, 15 Dec. 1870, LC).

3. *The Luck of Roaring Camp and Other Sketches* had been reviewed in the magazine, 9 (June 1870):850–51.

18. TO W. D. HOWELLS, 5 NOVEMBER 1870

Rooms of The Overland Monthly
San Francisco. Nov. 5th, *1870*

My Dear Mr. Howells:

The conviction being strong upon me that I should be somewhere near Boston at this date, I withheld myself, photo-and- autographically that I might burst upon you as an actual and joyous presence with somewhat of that "breezy freshness," wh. you Eastern Critics are fond of finding in the O. M. While thus impending I thought of many clever things to say to you extemporaneously—the wh. I have now forgotten.

My coming being postponed, I send you two sun-flattered pictures of myself.[1] I am told by disinterested friends that they are infinitely better looking than I am—one went so far as to declare the taking of them "sinful,"—but you shall give the nicest one to my fair but unknown admirer, whose acquaintance thereafter I shall prudently drop.

You are responsible for the spoiling of one photographic plate. At that supreme moment during the "sitting," while I was trying to look at the usual uninteresting speck on the wall with an interested expression, the operator turned his back upon me, and I thought of your fancy of his "hiding his tears" and laughed to the destruction of the plate. The general sadness of these pictures is the natural reaction.

I expect still to see you this winter. Until then I shall read you—for it might be that a closer and more intimate knowledge of your methods might spoil your work for me. Do you really go through "a day's pleasuring" grimly, with the intention of *ex post facto* reflections? These and many other impertinent questions I shall ask you, O, most excellent writer of excellent English! Until then, *adios*.[2]

Bret Harte

Mr. Howells, Cambridge.

Provenience: Harvard (bMS Am 1784 [210]). By permission of the Houghton Library, Harvard University.

1. See photograph 1, Harte in 1870. This photograph, by Bradley & Hulofson of San Francisco, was subsequently engraved by W. J. Linton for the cover of *Every Saturday*, 14 January 1871.

2. Elinor Mead Howells (1837–1910) soon reported to the Howells family that "Brett Harte has sent Will a nice photo of himself and a nicer letter with it" (*If Not Literature*, 132).

19. TO FIELDS, OSGOOD & CO., 1 JANUARY 1871

San Francisco, Jan 1st. '71.

Gentlemen,—Pray accept my thanks for the dozen presentation copies of the *Poems* as well as for their neat and tasteful appearance.[1] If you can obtain from Carleton *The Condensed Novels* by another attempt, I should be gratified to have my works together, in your hands. Carleton might be made to understand that there is neither money nor reputation for him in the reproduction of that monstrosity. However, he has not written to me, nor do I know anything of the no. of copies he has printed nor of its success.[2] To balance an a/c with the London & San Francisco Bank here, at the close of the year, I took the liberty to give a draft upon your house for Fifty-five 50/100 Dollars (gold) at sight, which I presume is due to me on a/c of the *Luck* and wh. I trust you will duly honor. It is my intention to visit the East, leaving here on or abt the 1st Feby—at wh time, if you are successful in obtaining the *Novels*, we can arrange for its republication.

Very truly yours,
Bret Harte

Provenience: Adrian Joline, *Meditations of an Autograph Collector* (New York: Harper, 1902), 125–26.

1. The Fields, Osgood edition of BH's *Poems* was issued in Boston on 22 December 1870. Within five days, the firm had sold out the first two printings of eleven hundred copies each and begun to sell a third printing of eighteen hundred copies (Ballou, 185).

2. Osgood had reopened negotiations with Carleton for rights to BH's *Condensed Novels* a few days before. Carleton had withdrawn his earlier offer to sell the stereotype plates of the book when, as he explained to Osgood on 28 December 1870, BH's popularity began to soar in the wake of the publication of his poem "Plain Language from Truthful James" in the *Overland* for September 1870, and

> I saw my property rapidly increasing in value. . . . If I sold you these plates now at the bagatelle price (which you evidently didn't consider them worth, or you would have jumped at them) I would be losing, and you gaining, enormously. The book is a real good book, & Bret Harte's popularity is so great just at this time, that either you or I could print from 3 to 5,000 at once, advertise it strongly as by the author of "Heathen Chinee" etc., and sell the whole edition in less than a month, at a profit of 1 to 2000 dollars—and with Harte's increasing reputation the plates would be a good paying property for a long time. There is an author's copyright of only 10 cents on each copy sold.
>
> I prefer keeping the plates, but if you want them for $1000. *cash*, you may have them! This offer I keep *only three days*.

Osgood acceded to Carleton's terms and bought the plates, woodcuts, and seventy-four copies of the book on 3 January 1871 (Ballou, 186–87).

20. TO W. D. HOWELLS, 24 JANUARY 1871

San Franc^co^
Jany. 24th/71

My dear Howells:

I've just accepted an invitation from Mr. Fields to meet you and other distinquished folk at the Saturday Club on the 25th prox. I would this had been put off until the tidal wave of my present cheap popularity had subsided, or until I had done something more worthy—say, my tragedy in 5 acts or that great epic poem as truly American literature for which the world is anxiously waiting—but my daemon wills otherwise and I go three thousand miles to be found out. My only comfort is that you have probably detected me long ago, and I—well I shall not say what I know of the Saturday Club.[1]

But your revenge, my dear fellow, was already complete in the *Every Saturday* picture wh. I must confess presents a different face from the one that will confront the Saturday Club. Not that it was not capitally engraved—in fact it was done not "wisely but too well"—but it idealized an already idealized photograph.[2] Illustrations have already ruined me—the d——d wood-cutters have every-where risen up against me as if I were a Cedar of Lebanon—and now you, with your infernal Venetian duplicity, have bribed your artist to estop my coming except as an imposter. The press of California cry out and reject the flattering picture; even my wife—poor wench—(I quote the excellent language of the admirable Mr. Pepys) did vex me mightily about it.[3]

You have my thanks for the prose sketch which accompanied it, and in wh. you handled with your usual delicacy a very commonplace history. I was both amused and gratified at your gentlemanly doubts of certain newspaper reporters' facts—or rather their statement of facts—and the kindly way that you gave me the benefit of these doubts. You are a good fellow and I doubt not I shall like you.[4]

I go East from here on Feby. 1st and will telegraph from Chicago or N.Y. when you can meet me at the Worcester depot.[5] There will then step from the cars a tired man, in the habit of the American pilgrim; thin-flanked, round-shouldered dark-haired, with an expression like Malvolio's of being "sad and civil."[6] Two "olive branches" (see the graceful notice in the *Xn Union*)[7] will twine around his thin legs and excite terror by endeavoring to mix themselves up with the car wheels. He will affect not to notice your evident disappointment but will introduce you to his wife "a little black woman" (Mr Pepys is also responsible for this) and in his western hand shake you shall recognize your friend

Bret Harte

Provenience: Harvard (bMS Am 1784 [210]). By permission of the Houghton Library, Harvard University.

1. On his first full day in Boston, 25 February 1871, BH "dined with the Saturday Club," where he met, among others, the Harvard naturalist Louis Agassiz (1807–73); the poets Henry Wadsworth Longfellow (1807–82), James Russell Lowell (1819–91), and Oliver Wendell Holmes (1809–94); Ralph Waldo Emerson (1803–82); and Richard Henry Dana, Jr. (1815–82). See "Local Matters," *Boston Daily Advertiser*, 28 Feb. 1871, p. 1, col. 7.

2. See note 1 to letter 18. BH quotes *Othello*, V. ii. 344.

3. The former Anna Griswold (1832–1920) had been a contralto in the First Unitarian Church in San Francisco when she met BH. They were married on 11 August 1862 in San Rafael, California.

4. The biographical sketch (*Every Saturday*, 14 Jan. 1871, 42–43) that

BH presumed Howells had written was probably by the editor Thomas Bailey Aldrich (1836–1907).

5. BH actually left San Francisco on February 2, stopped in both Chicago and New York en route, and arrived in Boston on February 24.

6. *Twelfth Night*, III. iv. 5.

7. BH alludes to a hostile notice of his *Poems* in *Christian Union* (31 Dec. 1870, 407).

21. TO JOSEPHINE CLIFFORD, 3 MARCH 1871[1]

My dear Miss Clifford:[2] I presume you have heard through the public press how nearly I became editor and part owner of the Lakeside, and how the childishness and provincial character of a few of the principal citizens of Chicago spoiled the project.[3] For many reasons—some of which we discussed in San Francisco—I wanted the Chicago Magazine, although I have since found that financially at least, I can do much better in New York, or Boston. I have not yet concluded any engagement, but shall do so shortly. But whatever I do I shall be able, through my connection with the best publishers here, to take care of any MSS. you may send me, and to look after your interests quite as well as when I was seated on the editorial tripod in the sanctum on Clay street. For the present my address will be James R. Osgood & Co., Boston, where you may send any MSS. you may have. I have not yet given up the idea that I shall yet have a magazine of my own.

Ever sincerely,
Bret Harte.

Provenience: *Overland Monthly*, n.s., 40 (Sept. 1902):223.

1. Dated by the headnote to the letter. BH has taken rooms in the Lenox House, a fashionable Fifth Avenue hotel. See *Hartford Courant*, 10 Mar. 1871, p. 1, col. 8.

2. Josephine Clifford McCrackin (1838–1920) joined the staff of the *Overland* in 1869 and later contributed to the *Lakeside Monthly*, *Harper's Monthly*, and other magazines. See also her memoir "Reminiscences of Bret Harte and Pioneer Days in the West," *Overland*, n.s., 66 (Dec. 1915):467–68; and n.s., 67 (Jan. 1916):13–15.

3. "Paul," the Chicago correspondent of the *Cincinnati Commercial*, had offered a jaundiced view of BH's visit to his city in early February 1871 that was widely circulated in the press. As the story goes, several prominent Chicagoans, among them the lawyer Wirt Dexter, had raised enough money by subscription to buy the *Lakeside* on the condition BH would agree to settle in Chicago and edit it. As part of the plan, Dexter hosted a "brilliant party" at his home which BH failed to attend. "Mr. Harte promptly apologized, of course, as became a well-bred gentleman, but the apology was voted unsatisfactory, and it was resolved to cut his acquaintance and destroy the subscription" ("Bret Harte in Chicago," *Cincinnati Commercial*, 23 Feb. 1871, p. 12, cols. 5–6). See also "Our Bret Harte Correspondence," *Chicago Republican*, 27 Feb. 1871, p. 2, cols. 2–3.

22. TO AMBROSE BIERCE, 5 MARCH 1871

New York
Mar. 5/71

My dear Bierce:

I got your note in Boston, but while there I was so wined and dined by the literary folk whom I used to scalp in the *Overland* that between remorse and good liquor I hardly knew where I stood.[1] I managed however to talk to Osgood abt you, and as I was an author whose book was then going off at 1000 per week—he listened to me.[2] He said he had written to you. As I had not seen your book, and you had not the decency to tell me about it before, I could only launch out on your general merits. Whatever may be the fate of this particular venture, you have that in you which he wd. be glad to publish. See that you get it out.

My most extravagant anticipations of the East are realized in climate, people, trade. Of the commercial value of my own stuff I really had no conception whatever. I have been offered $15,000 per annum and not less than $7,500. I have just accepted $10,000 per year from J. R. Osgood, tho merely for the exclusive right to such of my poems & sketches as I may turn out in that space—and this does not include the "half-profits" they offer me for republication. This, my dear boy, is of course confidential and is not to put into your papers.[3] Yesterday I was offered $10,000 down in advance, for four lectures.[4] Think of this and think of Carmany backing out of my modest offer of $5,000 per annum, and a quarter of the O.M. and a percentage of my lectures. Think that he hadn't confidence enough in me to risk the experiment for *three mos.* and the expenditure of $600. Why he might have made $15,000 the next year, or sold out his right to me for $20,000. Can I ever be sufficiently grateful to him for expressing so sublimely in himself the quintessence of California ignorance blindness and self conceit.

I have to thank you for making me acquainted with Major Eaton—a most refined and gentlemanly young fellow; indeed he and his partner Major Brown,[5] were the highest type I found in the West. Some time I'll tell you my Chicago experience wh. was very funny.[6] Yet spite of all I saw more enterprise and more energy in Chicago than I ever saw during my long residence in California. Indeed they are *really* all that Eastern people *believe* California to be.

Remember this is confidential. I do not care for the Californians generally to know of my good fortune from me.

Ever yours
Bret Harte

Provenience: *American Literature* 19 (Jan. 1948):324–25.

1. BH had reviewed Lowell's *Poems*, *The Cathedral*, and *Among My Books*; Emerson's *Prose* and *Society and Solitude*; and Thomas Wentworth Higginson's *Malbone* and *Army Life in a Black Regiment*, among other works, during his tenure as editor of the *Overland*.

2. BH's *Poems*, issued in Boston by Fields, Osgood & Co. on 22 December 1870, sold out six editions during its first five days in press (San Francisco *Alta California*, 8 Jan. 1871, p. 2, col. 2).

3. Bierce was editor of the *San Francisco News Letter and Commercial Advertiser*. He recalled these circumstances over twenty years later in his "Prattle" column in the *San Francisco Examiner*, 31 Jan. 1892, p. 6, col. 5: "After Harte had made a 'hit' with 'The Luck of Roaring Camp' and other stories in the same vein, Fields engaged him for *The Atlantic*—or thought he did. Harte received ten thousand dollars for whatever he should write for one year." See also Stanley T. Williams, "Ambrose Bierce and Bret Harte," *American Literature* 17 (May 1945):179–80.

4. The same day BH wrote this letter to Bierce, Howells wrote his father that BH "thinks of lecturing" next winter, "though none of his plans are

matured yet" (*Selected Letters of W. D. Howells*, ed. George Arms et al. [Boston: Twayne, 1979], I, 366). The *Independent* subsequently reported (11 May 1871, 4) that BH was offered five thousand dollars for twelve lectures "and has had the good sense to decline. The public is the goose that lays golden eggs for its favorites, but Mr. Harte is unwilling to slaughter the goose."

5. Francis F. Browne (1843–1913), who served in the 46th Massachusetts Regimental Volunteers during the Civil War, was editor of the *Lakeside Monthly*. Browne later reprinted BH's lyrics "The Society upon the Stanislaus" and "Dickens in Camp" in his collection *Golden Poems* (Chicago: Jansen, McClurg, 1881) and "Our Privilege" in his anthology of war verse, *Bugle-Echoes* (New York: White, Stokes & Allen, 1886). In addition, he was probably the author of the letter to the editor of the *Chicago Tribune* signed "B." (25 Nov. 1876, p. 6, col. 7) which praised BH's play *Two Men of Sandy Bar* when it was staged in Chicago.

6. See note 3 to letter 21.

23. TO JAMES R. OSGOOD, 6 MARCH 1871

New York
Mar. 6th/71

My dear Osgood:

I accept your offer of $10,000 for the exclusive publication of my poems and sketches (not to be less than 12 in no.) in your periodicals for the space of one year commencing Mar. 1st 1871.[1] It would be better that we should sign some contract to the above effect, wh. might if you choose be confidential. Of course I was sorely beset and tempted here on my return, and I have made some pecuniary sacrifice for the sake of keeping my books in the one house, and of giving a preference to my earliest publisher. But I am satisfied. I hope you are.

I had some talk with Eytinge this morning, and think I gave him several ideas about the "Heathen Chinee" and his Pagan brother—the California miner.[2] I have also promised to mark the passages in the "Luck &c" which I thought best fitted for illustration, with marginal notes and directions.[3]

Will you please get the amount of my carriage hire bill from

Mr. Howells and pay him—charging to my a/c. I had not time as we barely caught the train Sat. a.m.[4]

I go to Rye to-morrow—but any letter sent to 16 Fifth Avenue[5] will be forwarded to me.

Very truly yours
Bret Harte

Mr Osgood.

Provenience: Bancroft (MSS 79/47 C).

1. The agreement specifically does not cover plays or dramatic literature, even though in the summer of 1870, before leaving California, BH contracted to write a play entitled "In the Sierras" for the actor Lawrence Barrett (*New York Clipper*, 27 Aug. 1870; *Springfield Republican*, 30 Mar. 1871, p. 2, col. 4). The agreement also permits BH to earn additional money by lecturing.

2. Sol Eytinge, Jr. (b. 1833), illustrated works by Dickens, Holmes, Lowell, and others for Fields, Osgood & Co. Eytinge's illustrations for "Plain Language from Truthful James" first appeared in the 20 April 1871 issue of *Every Saturday* and were soon reissued in a chapbook edition of the poem by Fields, Osgood.

3. BH apparently means to refer not to *The Luck of Roaring Camp and Other Sketches* but to *Condensed Novels*. Eytinge illustrated its second edition, issued by Fields, Osgood in 1871. See also note 12 to letter 26.

4. Howells reminisced over thirty years later about this event in his "Editor's Easy Chair," *Harper's* 108 (Dec. 1903), reprinted under title "A Belated Guest" in *Literary Friends*, 303–304: Howells had rushed BH to the station to catch the train to New York and followed him on board "for those last words in which people try to linger out pleasures they have known together." Suddenly BH "started up in the discovery of having forgotten to get some cigars. They rushed out of the train together, and after a wild descent upon the cigar-counter of the restaurant, Harte rushed back to his car. But by this time the train was already moving with that deceitful slowness of the departing train, and Harte had to clamber up the steps of the rearmost platform." The train left the station with BH "blandly smiling" at Howells and "waving his hand with a cigar in it."

5. The New York address of BH's older sister, Eliza Knaufft.

24. TO JAMES RUSSELL LOWELL, 27 MARCH 1871

No. 72 Fifth Avenue
March 27th/71

My dear Sir,[1]

If I could hold out against the force exerted by the President of the Phi Beta Kappa Society whom I dont know, I should certainly fall before the infinite persuasion of the man I do know, so I hasten to accept and shall write to Professor Sanger this very night bidding him prepare the sacrifice. If I promise to make the usual mental exposure at the time and place specified, I have only to ask that, having lately excused myself to Dartmouth College on the plea of preoccupation,[2] you will considerately antedate this acceptance.

And now, if you were as well pleased with me as I have been with you, you would indicate something for me to say. You know my limitations—abt. 5 1/2 octaves I should say. I am ill at didactics; since one half the press has taken to cursing and swearing in rhyme and the other half holds *me* responsible for it, I am shy of "dialect." I am afraid too, that I am expected to be improper.[3] Briefly, what do the "more distinguished graduates of the university" want from

Your friend
Bret Harte

J. R. Lowell Esqr.
Cambridge

Provenience: Harvard (bMS Am 765 [378]). By permission of the Houghton Library, Harvard University.

1. Not only had BH reviewed Lowell's *The Cathedral*—not entirely favorably—in the *Overland* 4 (Apr. 1870):386–87, he had discussed "his dislike for something overliterary" in the poem with Lowell personally at the gatherings in Cambridge in late February (*Literary Friends*, 294). BH and Lowell had met on February 25 at the meeting of the Saturday Club in Boston. See note 1 to letter 20. Lowell also entertained BH at Elmwood, his home in Cambridge, on February 28 (*Letters of Henry Wadsworth Longfellow*, ed. Andrew Hilen [Cambridge, Mass.: Belknap, 1982], V, 405).

2. A week earlier, BH had spurned an invitation to speak at Dartmouth: "I fear I must reluctantly decline the proffered honor of acting as yr. Poet from sheer inability to determine whether I shall ever have more

time than I seem to have at present to prepare myself for such an occasion" (to Henry A. Folsom, 20 Mar. 1871, Dartmouth College Library).

3. In retrospect, BH's sense of foreboding seems perfectly justified. As Howells later recalled, he came "to that august Harvard occasion [on 29 June 1871] with a jingle so trivial, so out of keeping, so inadequate that his enemies . . . must have suffered from it almost as much as his friends" (*Literary Friends*, 300). According to the *Boston Daily Advertiser* (30 June 1871, p. 1, col. 6), BH "made so little effort to be heard that scarcely any one caught the meaning of all his lines, while people in the more distant parts of the church could not hear him at all." Lowell allowed that "he read it so low that it did not hit as it would had he pitched his voice higher" (*New Letters of James Russell Lowell*, ed. M. A. DeWolfe Howe, [New York: Harper, 1932], 154). Lilian Aldrich also remembered that BH "made his appearance in gaudy raiment and wearing green gloves" and that his "poem was as inappropriate as his dress" to the occasion (Aldrich, 142). Not only was his performance disappointing and his appearance surprising, BH merely recycled an old poem, "The Lost Beauty," first published in *Golden Era* for 28 December 1862, under a new title, "Aspiring Miss De Laine." Still, Alfred Munroe, the Massachusetts correspondent of the *New York Times*, rose to BH's defense by blaming Lowell for the fiasco, albeit not by name: BH was "notified of his election as poet, and strenuously urged to accept, the point being dwelt upon that he would have until Midsummer to write it . . . , the writer of the note forgetting, though a Cambridge man, that the Commencement time had been changed from July to June" (6 July 1871, p. 6, col. 1). Letter 25, in which BH mentions his promise to deliver the Phi Beta Kappa poem "this summer," lends credence to this explanation. Though BH and Lowell both served as U.S. diplomats in Great Britain in the early 1880s, this event effectively poisoned relations between them. As Howells tactfully noted, "Afterward in London they did not meet often or willingly" (*Literary Friends*, 294).

25. TO JAMES T. FIELDS, 1 APRIL 1871

Lenox House, 5th Avenue
April 1st/71

My dear Mr. Fields,

I send you the "Truthful James" autograph. Had it not been from a sense of duty, which made it—to speak after the nice fashion of men—a sort of ought-to-graph to you, I wd. have withheld it on account of all this "damnable iteration" and inordinate quotation wh. have divested it of all meaning to me, and make me loathe it so that I can not even copy it legibly. But such as it is it is yours. As the swan like Bard says: "Were I twice as tedious I could bestow it all upon your lordship."[1]

I look back tenderly to Boston from this noisy yet lonely city where they set such infinite values on finite and valueless things. Yet if we could avoid its vices it wd. be a pleasant place to live in just as Boston would be bearable if we could forego its virtues. So I think somewhat of going to Springfield eventually, where Truth in the person of Bowles resides between these extremes.[2]

And how are all those pleasant Cambridge folk? I trust they are well—for I have rashly promised to deliver the Phi Beta Kappa poem there this summer.[3] But before that time I shall drop in upon you at Boston—perhaps within the next fortnight.

My wife joins me in regards to Mrs Fields,[4]

Very Sincerely Yours
Bret Harte

Mr Jas. T. Fields,
Boston.

Provenience: Huntington (FI 1087).

1. BH consistently denigrated his popular poem "Plain Language from Truthful James," which he had originally published as filler in the *Overland* 5 (Sept. 1870): 287–88, probably because his satire of anti-Chinese prejudice was widely misread to reinforce that prejudice. BH slightly misquotes *Much Ado about Nothing*, III. v: "if I were as tedious as a king, I could find it in my heart to bestow it all of your worship."

2. Some two weeks before, BH had discussed with Samuel Bowles the possibility of settling in Springfield, Massachusetts, for the summer. See George S. Merriam, *The Life and Times of Samuel Bowles* (New York: Century, 1885), II, 170–71. On Bowles, see letter 3 and accompanying notes.

3. See letter 24.

4. Annie Adams Fields (1834–1915) was a poet, editor, and literary patron in her own right. See Howe; and Judith A. Roman, *Annie Adams Fields: The Spirit of Charles Street* (Bloomington: Indiana University Press, 1990).

26. TO JAMES R. OSGOOD, 1 APRIL 1871

72 Fifth Avenue
April 1st/71

My dear Osgood

I sent yesterday per express the *MS* of "Lothaw"[1] and send today by mail the autographs for the French Fair.[2]

I enclose, for what use you may put it to, Mr Brownes denial of the *News Letter* paragraph wh. I thank you for forwarding.[3] I should not have taken the trouble to call the *Lakeside's* editor's attention to it, but that the substance of this slander, magnified by personal malice, was sent as a telegraphic despatch to the *Associated press* here by their agent Col. A. S. Evans of S.F. an infinitely small rascal whose *MS* I once rejected and whose book I once reviewed in the O. M.[4] The Press suppressed the despatch in N.Y., but it had already been telegraphed all over the West and was finally copied in the *Sun* here.[5] The Associated Press have promised to telegraph the refutation, the *Sun* has already done so,[6] and you might if you choose ask Mr Aldrich if he could not print a moral from it in a paragraph in *Every Saturday*. The same fellow also sends a letter to a paper here called *The Globe* charging me with rejecting some fulsome female's *MS* and afterwards incorporating one of its "finest passages" as my own in an article I "published lately in an Eastern paper entitled "Journeyings in California."[7] I dont know whether it is worth while to answer this by stating the simple fact that I have never written or published any such article in any Eastern paper or any other paper; or reiterate the fact—which most publishers know—that I have never written any prose article for any Eastern publisher within the last 5 years. I fear that if I begin to notice these things publicly I shall have my hands full as well as foul. I observe, moreover, that the Western News Co. through the *Chicago Republican* are calling me "avaricious & ungrateful &c &c"—the result of yr. endeavors to stop their piracies.[8] I am surprised that, with such a tremendous broadside as you could bring to bear on the Chicago illustrations by giving Eytinge's designs voice in the columns of *Every Saturday* that you delay.[9] Nast will surely get ahead of you in Harpers.[10] I think that Eytinges designs would dispose of this tiresome "Chinee" business at once—by showing the inferiority of all of the other illustrations. Read what the *London Daily News* says of the Poem, and how they are giving praise to Hull's designs—simply because they have seen nothing else.[11]

I thank you for forwarding the specimen leaf of the "Condensed Novels."[12] Typography and paper are both excellent but—dont you think it would have made a neater book to have been in finer type and uniform in size and shape with the "Poems," rather than with the "Luck"? These are only suggestions; I shall invariably make them I fear; but I wish you always to believe that I defer to your better judgement.

I shall probably remain in N.Y. for six weeks or at least until May 1st, but I shall run up to Boston for a day's visit within the next two weeks. I shall want some money soon, and regularly, if I make my household life here. Shall I draw upon you, or how?

I hope you are getting the better of your dyspepsia, and sincerely sympathize with you. I have hardly recovered my own strength yet although I am gradually becoming acclimated.

Truly Yours
Bret Harte

Mr. Jas R. Osgood.

Provenience: Harvard (Harry Elkins Widener Collection). By permission of the Houghton Library, Harvard University.

1. "Lothaw," a parody of Benjamin Disraeli's *Lothair*, appeared in *Every Saturday* for 6 May 1871 and was BH's first contribution to the Fields, Osgood magazines under the terms of his contract. BH had previously reviewed *Lothair* in the *Overland* 5 (Aug. 1870):192–96.

2. According to a sales catalogue of the American Art Association, a copy of BH's *Poems* (1871) inscribed "to the French Fair with the compliments of Bret Harte. Boston, April 1871" was sold at auction in New York on 14-15 January 1926 (item #359). BH also autographed at least one printed slip raffled at the fair, a bazaar to raise money for the victims of the Franco-Prussian War. This slip is now in the Massachusetts Historical Society.

3. At BH's request, F. F. Browne (see note 5 to letter 22) had written to deny the allegations of his misconduct while in Chicago, the substance of the "slander" that had been widely copied.

4. Albert S. Evans (d. 1872) was the San Francisco agent of the Associated Press, which enjoyed a virtual monopoly on news telegraphed

to local papers across the country. BH had reviewed Evans's *Our Sister Republic* in the *Overland* 6 (Feb. 1871):197–99, criticizing in particular "the excessively opulent language of the gallant Colonel" whose "prejudices are, unfortunately, more dominant than his taste."

5. See note 3 to letter 21.

6. The "refutation" BH supplied the New York *Sun* was, simply enough, that he and his family stayed in Chicago with AH's sister, who "through some inadvertence or neglect had not been properly invited" to the Dexter dinner and on whose "account both Mr. and Mrs. Harte stayed away" (6 Mar. 1871, p. 2, col. 4).

7. This allegation also appeared in the *Chicago Republican* for 14 March 1871 (p. 2, col. 2): "Yesterday's telegrams told of his purloining manuscripts intrusted to him as editor of the *Overland*." Quotation marks appear here as they appear in the original manuscript.

8. The *Chicago Republican* also claimed that, during his late visit to Chicago, BH had skulked around the State Street offices of the Western News Company, which had published a popular edition of *The Heathen Chinee* with illustrations by Joseph Hull: "He sneaked around the counters, made inquiries of the cash-boys, and took notes of what he saw." In Boston, he urged Fields, Osgood & Co. "to interdict the further sale" of the Hull version "by virtue of a copyright on his collected poems. He did not succeed, however, though we understand the matter is still the subject of correspondence between the two establishments." The last copies of the Western News edition were destroyed in the Great Chicago Fire of October 1871, before the matter was settled legally.

9. As BH anticipated, Eytinge's illustrations of "Plain Language from Truthful James" proved so popular that the 20 April 1871 issue of *Every Saturday* "was immediately bought up" (New York *World*, 28 Apr. 1871, p. 2, col. 3).

10. Thomas Nast (1840–1902), the famous cartoonist for *Harper's Weekly*.

11. The London *Daily News* (21 Mar. 1871, p. 5, cols. 1-2) editorialized that in Hull BH found "an illustrator who is likely to become illustrious, not only for the exactness with which he has caught the spirit of the author, but by reason of a physiognomical accuracy in his caricature." This article was later excerpted in the *Boston Transcript* (4 Apr. 1871, p. 2, col. 2), and BH was "so amused" by it that he "always kept it" in his personal files (Pemberton, 11).

12. The second edition of the *Condensed Novels*, published by Fields, Osgood & Co., appeared in late May.

27. TO JAMES T. FIELDS, 13 MAY 1871

Lenox House
13th May.

My dear Mr Fields,

I was greatly relieved and most joyfully surprised in taking up last evening's paper to find that you had read my verses.[1] "Greater love hath no man than this"[2]—that he consent to face an audience with the untried unpublished MS of his friend. This by way of abstract truth. But in particular I at once felt that you were the man to make something out of that Yankee Cincinnatus, whom I had attempted to outlive in the few verses wh. I wrote only an hour or so before the mail closed on Thursday. The fact is I was alarmed at finding myself set down for that dreadful thing—a "Poem," when I had been assured by Mr Lyman that only a "few verses" would be required of me,[3] and for three or four days I labored over some exalted patriotic rhetoric and only recovered my good sense and original intention at noon Thursday. That is why the verses were so bad. Wherefore I pray you attaint that arch traitor Lyman of high crimes and misdemeanors. He hath beguiled a simple citizen of Dutch Flat; yea, he hath played it low down on the chosen minstrel of Calaveras.

The N.Y. papers of to-day give your felicitious introduction and praise your reading.[4] So do I. Did I not wisely to evade Boston?

I hope Mrs Fields has entirely recovered. Remember me to her kindly & believe me

Always yours
Bret Harte

Mr Jas T. Fields of Boston.

Provenience: Bancroft (MSS C-H 57).

1. Fields read BH's poem "The Old Major Explains" at the Globe Theatre in Boston on 12 May 1871 on the occasion of the reunion of the Grand Army of the Potomac.

2. John 15:13.

3. Col. Theodore Lyman (1833–97) had organized the reunion. In his letter to Lyman dated 11 May 1871 (UVa), BH confessed he was "much

disconcerted by being put down for 'A Poem,' when your letter to me asked only for a 'few verses' to close the exercises."

4. Both the New York *Evening Post* (p. 1, col. 7) and *World* (p. 1, col. 2) for 13 May 1871 printed BH's poem with praise for Fields's declamation of it. The poem also appeared two weeks later in *Every Saturday* (27 May 1871, 499) though BH would not count it among his contributions under the terms of his contract with Fields, Osgood & Co. See letter 51. Fields prefaced his reading of BH's poem with the following verses (subsequently published in *Society of the Army of the Potomac Report of Proceedings* [New York: Crocker & Co., 1872], 21):

If the poet whose absence to-day we deplore
Had struck but one note for his country's disgrace,
If his lyre had betrayed you, ye heroes of war,
I could not and would not stand here in his place.

But his soul was responsive to all that was grand,
And his loyal young spirit leaped up in a flame;
And he fought with his pen for his dear struggling land,
As you with your swords, sons of glory and fame.

And so, for my friend, I will take up his song,
And give it a voice, though, alas! not its own.
To him the quaint verse and his genius belong;
To me but the accents of friendship alone.

28. TO W. D. HOWELLS, 15 MAY 1871

Lenox House
May 15th/71

My dear Howells,

I enclose a few lines to Mr. Boott who I think means well. Many things are to be forgiven a musician.[1]

I was so glad to hear from you again even after this enforced fashion that I accepted your ingenious explanation of yr. previous silence. For myself I frankly admit I do not write letters without great artifice and dissimulation. I generally rise from my task with dark thoughts and bitterness toward my correspondent. Writing doesn't come to me naturally. I am inclined to think that Dogberry was quite right when he said that reading and writing "come by nature."[2]

We are still house hunting. It is hard unsympathetic work. I dont like to tell people that I dont like their houses; that their tastes are vile, and their sense of beauty limited. If you had not so fully occupied the field before me I should like to make my experience merchantable in a paper for the *Atlantic*. The amount of unreliable human evidence that I have accumulated regarding the insalubrity or healthfulness of the country seats around New York is frightful. And, dear me, what have become of all the farms I knew as a boy? Where are the farm yards—meadows, barns, orchards? There is nothing now between the shanty and villa. Think of being offered the fact that the milkman comes regularly, and that the trains will bring me fresh vegetables from N.Y. as an inducement to live 50 miles from the city!

And how is the sincere Booah? And the coquettish Winnie? My boys long for them to play with and abuse.[3] I have told them that when we get a country house you and your wife are to bring them to make us a visit. As a conscientious family man you will feel the importance of keeping faith with the boys.

I have not congratulated you, my dear fellow, on coming into your own in the *Atlantic*,[4] for with your conscientiousness the position will be irksome and I do not know that you are to be congratulated except in this public recognition of your past valuable service. I, who am just out of harness and who never was troubled with any grave sense of editorial duty

"Am weary thinking of your load[.]"

My wife sends her regards to Mrs H. I think she is gradually recovering strength to bear her usual ill health. Write to me often. Remember how easy it is for me not to answer your letters.

[signature removed]

Mr. Howells
of the Atlantic.

Provenience: Harvard (bMS Am 1784 [210]). By permission of the Houghton Library, Harvard University.

1. Francis Boott (1813–1904) set six of BH's lyrics to music in 1870–71, including "Jim," "Chiquita," and "Plain Language from Truthful James." Each of these songs was published by Oliver Ditson & Co. of Boston. BH's 15 May 1871 letter to Boott (Cincinnati Historical Society) was a short note of thanks for sending him copies of the sheet music.

2. Dogberry, the constable in *Much Ado about Nothing*, says that "To be a well-favored man is the gift of fortune, but to write and read comes by nature" (III. iii. 16).

3. "Booah" or John Mead Howells (1868–1959) and "Winnie" or Winifred Howells (1863–89) were the Howells children. BH's sons were Griswold Harte (1863–1901) and Francis King Harte (1865–1917). For the record, Elinor Mead Howells commended the manners of the boys during the week-long visit of the BH family to the Howells home in Cambridge (*If Not Literature*, 137).

4. Howells would formally succeed Fields as editor of the *Atlantic* on 1 July 1871.

29. TO W. D. HOWELLS, EARLY JUNE 1871

"Edgar Cottage"
Harrison Avenue[1]
Newport R. I.

My dear Howells,

I suppose it was from hearing in Boston that you had gone out West somewhere,[2] that I instantly felt like writing to you at Cambridge. Perhaps it was that I wished to carry to you my disapprobation of your not being at your post to read my proof which had nobly concluded to let you correct, revise and ornament.[3]

But my next idea is to invite you and your family to visit us at such time and season as may suit you at our new house in Newport, to which we are now rapidly adjusting ourselves. I think you and Mrs Howells might enjoy yourselves for a week or two, perhaps longer,[4] tho' at the end of that time, I dare say, we should begin to criticise each other to our respective wives. Our children with nobler directions would have quarrelled and made it up before then. There is a large and blank expanse of barn on our property on which Booah could retaliate the deep-seated and ineradicable injuries of your cellar door. (I may state here that both my boys deny that charge, and have successively attributed the outrage to grown-up people, whose names they do not know positively, but think are Longfellow or Lowell.) And then we have a good-sized library in wh. "The Night Drawers Play," enlarged and rendered more intelligible to a grown-up audience, could be performed. (Franky is inclined to refer the defects of that first representation to a want of proper scenery.) There is a strip of beach near the house much frequented by the simple but hardworking clam, who amuses himself at twilight by expectorating on the legs of the sentimental tourist. Hither we could walk at the sunset hour and together abuse the literary first-born of Egypt.

But to restrain this mad-[illegible]-ness, we have, as we think, a very charming, roomy, comfortable house, and we want you to run down here with your wife and boys and enjoy it with us. Choose your own time but let us know a few days before. Just now the weather *is* somewhat sloppy and they say that "dear June" is not the best month but suit your own tastes.

Ever Yours,
Bret Harte

Provenience: Harvard (bMS Am 1784 [210]). By permission of the Houghton Library, Harvard University.

1. BH settled with his family in a rented house in Newport no later than early June 1871. Marie J. Pitman ("Margery Deane") listed BH's name among the renters that season in her Newport correspondence with the New York *Evening Post* for 7 June 1871 (p. 1, col. 4); and Pitman subsequently reported that BH "has taken Newbold Edgar's place on Harrison avenue" (17 June 1871, p. 1, col. 3), "a pretty, picturesque place near the fort" (24 June 1871, p. 1, col. 4). Louise Chandler Moulton reported in her column in the *New York Tribune* (14 June 1871, p. 8, col. 1) that BH "has taken a house in Newport" with "a Blue Room" complete with a "ghost of high degree, for she rustles in heavy, old-fashioned brocade, and her jewels glitter through the darkness. . . . Bret Harte has been in strange company before now, and he may as well add a ghost to his visiting list." BH based his poem "A Newport Romance" in the *Atlantic* 28 (Oct 1871):481–82, yet another submission under the terms of his contract with Fields, Osgood & Co., on the local legend.

2. Between 1 June and about 15 June 1871, Howells was traveling in New York and Ohio with his father.

3. BH's story "The Poet of Sierra Flat," his second contribution to Fields, Osgood & Co. under the terms of his contract, appeared in the *Atlantic* 28 (July 1871):115–20.

4. When the Hartes had visited the Howellses in late February and early March, the couples had talked of vacationing together by the sea. See *Selected Letters of W. D. Howells*, ed. George Arms et al. [Boston: Twayne, 1979], I, 365. The younger Howells later wrote his father (15 Oct. 1871, Harvard) that there had been a misunderstanding about the dates and the vacation had been called off.

30. TO ANNA HARTE, 6 SEPTEMBER 1871

Boston
Sept. 6th/71

My dear Anna,

I received your telegram some 12 hours before your letter. I am glad that you happen to like Mt. Vernon in spite of its good report from other people.

I finished the poem—wh. is poor stuff—the night you left.[1] The next morning I met Mr. Fields who of course pressed me again to go with him that afternoon to Manchester and I did, returning this morning.

Mrs Fields met us at Beverly with the pony carriage and drove us to Manchester over a pleasant road past quaint old-fashioned farm houses. There was an autumnal suggestion in the air that was very pure and sweet. The New England Coast here is much finer than at Newport; the rocks are more picturesque and the trees—wh. are large and generous—almost overhang the ocean. We stopped on the way to call on a Mrs Cabot (I think), a friend of the Fields, whose house for really beautiful surroundings surpassed anything on our foggy little peninsula. There was very little wind—no fog—the sea even was sad and silent. There was a thoughtfulness over everything, as if the whole landscape had been surprised into reflection over some subtle premonition of the coming winter that we could not detect. I never believed that autumn could be so tenderly beautiful![2]

I have had a telegram from Watkins[3] saying that he would send me some copies of the News Letter, but as yet nothing has come from him or San Francisco and I must wait here until it does. I shall try to go up to Mt Vernon to-morrow afternoon, if not will come with Mr Clark[4] on Friday. I am not very well and sleep and eat but little.

Yrs affectionately
Frank

Provenience: UCLA (ALS).

1. "A Newport Romance." See note 1 to letter 29. The New York *Evening Post* agreed with BH's assessment of the poem: It "is pleasing but not level with his fame, and has the blemish of a grammatical error" (20 Sept. 1871, p. 1, col. 4).

2. See Annie Fields's account of this trip in Howe, 236–37.

3. James T. Watkins, an occasional contributor to the *Overland*, had become editor of the *Baltimore Bulletin*. BH wrote on 20 September 1871 (Pierpont Morgan Library, New York, MA 4064) to thank him "for your prompt attention to my request" and to invite him to visit his family in Newport. See also note 2 to letter 10 and Watkins's sketch of BH in the *Baltimore Bulletin*, reprinted in the *San Francisco Chronicle*, 2 Feb. 1871, p. 3, col. 2.

4. John Spencer Clark (b. 1835) was a junior partner in the firm of J. R. Osgood & Co.

31. TO JOHN HAY, 21 SEPTEMBER 1871

Newport, R. I.
Septem. 21st/71

My dear Mr. Hay,[1]

My wife's long continued ill health has somewhat thickened my affairs[2] or I should have thanked you before for the Tobacco Testimonial. I dimly remember now to have seen somewhere a ¶ stating that an English critic had spoken of me as a Mr. Benjamin with the soubriquet of Bret Harte and tho't it a newspaper joke, but I never before seriously contemplated its vast absurdity as a statement of fact. After all, I dont know but that the flings of one's own countrymen are better borne than foreign praise.

It is not strange that my real name should be tho't a *nom de plume* but it *is* queer that such an evident *nom de plume* as that of the historian of all Jewry with the prefix of "Mr." should be tho't genuine. A lady quite recently and very seriously asked my wife at a dinner what her real name was. "I mean, my dear, what did you used to call each other?" she added in explanation. My wife, who I think felt the integrity of her marriage certificate threatened replied with some feminine acidity.

I think that you or I could do better imitations than the Tribunes.[3] At heart *I* am conscious of an ability to burlesque myself better than that. By the way what kind of carving does Mr. Greenough[4] call that stuff which Mrs. Moulton sends to the Tribune?[5] Think of it being read aloud at a picnic which I attended the other day. Yet the people were well-bred, respectable, refined folk, as society goes, and I was their guest, and the reader was a clergyman!

Yours cordially
Bret Harte

Col. John Hay
P.S. Pray give my regards to Mr Brooks.[6]

Provenience: Brown University Library (ALS).

1. BH had met John Hay (1838–1905) in New York on 31 March 1871 (*American Literary Realism* 12 [Spring 1979]:78). Hay had worked in Washington as Abraham Lincoln's private secretary during the Civil War, had lately embarked on a journalistic and literary career, and would serve as U.S. secretary of state during the final seven years of his life.

2. BH "gave up his cottage" in Newport after a few weeks "and went inland, the sea air disagreeing with Mrs. Harte's health" (New York *Evening Post*, 31 July 1871, p. 1, col. 3).

3. "The Battle of Bards," a series of burlesques of Whitman, Harte, Hay, and Joaquin Miller, had appeared in the *New York Tribune*, 9 Sept. 1871, p. 4, col. 6. Though unsigned, they were written by Bayard Taylor and reprinted in *The Echo Club* (Boston: Osgood, 1872), 168–74.

4. The sculptor Richard Saltonstall Greenough (1819–1904).

5. Ellen Louise Chandler Moulton (1835–1908) was Boston correspondent for the *New York Tribune* between 1870 and 1876. Greenough's parody of the Harte and Hay style of dialect verse, entitled "Grit Moll,"

appeared in Moulton's column in the *Tribune* for 18 Sept. 1871 (p. 2, col. 1).

6. Noah Brooks (1830–1903), assistant editor of the *Overland* during BH's tenure, joined the staff of the *New York Tribune* in 1871. See also Brooks's several memoirs, "Harte's Early Days," *New York Times Saturday Review of Books*, 24 May 1902, 350; "Bret Harte: A Study and an Appreciation," *Book Buyer* 24 (June 1902):358–62; and "Bret Harte: A Biographical and a Critical Sketch," *Overland* n.s., 40 (Sept. 1902):201–207.

32. TO THE EDITOR OF THE *NEW-YORK STANDARD*, 28 MARCH 1872

To the Editor of the New-York Standard:

My Dear Sir: I fear that your correspondent, J.M.F., is misinformed in attributing to me the authorship of certain verses, entitled "Darling Kathleen," inclosed to the STANDARD of March 28.[1] I certainly have no recollection of ever writing such verses, or, indeed, any verses in praise of Miss Kathleen, and "several years ago" I was several thousand miles distant, and beyond the probable sphere of her active fascination. As the only time I could possibly have written "for a church fair in this city" was at the age of eleven, I cannot claim to have celebrated the incomparable charms of this young lady with that dexterity of epithet—to say nothing of the maturity of appreciation—so finely indicated in the unknown author's noble lines. May I beg you to restore the bays to their rightful owner, when he shall appear, and permit me to silently suffer the double deprivation of never having enjoyed the acquaintance of Miss Kathleen, or the privilege of having recorded her charms.

Bret Harte.

No. 217 East Forth-ninth street, March 28, 1872.

Provenience: *New-York Standard*, 3 Apr. 1872, p. 2, col. 2.

1. BH disclaims authorship of a poem printed in the *Standard* for 28 Mar. 1872 (p. 2, col. 7). The correspondent who submitted the lines claimed they "were printed a number of years ago in a little sheet issued at a church fair in this city" and asserted they were "too good to be lost." The following is the first of five stanzas:

I wonder if any wine ever was made
    As red as the lips of my love?
I wonder if any eyes ever so mocked
    The blue of the heavens above,
As the soul-lighted eyes of my darling Kathleen,
The bonniest maiden that ever was seen?

The subsequent stanzas refer to the lady's "tresses so brown," her "white brow," "ravishing form," "womanly breast," "snowy-white breast," "passion-dewed kiss," and "warm-loving kiss."

33. TO SAMUEL L. CLEMENS, 1 APRIL 1872

217 East 49th St.
April 1st '72

My dear Clemens,

Thank you for your remembrance, and accept the hearty congratulations of this household.[1] I was, I confess, slightly surprised; Mrs Harte by some occult feminine instinct was not. These women assume a superiority at such times which is simply disgusting.

I am glad its a girl. If she behaves herself she shall marry my Franky, provided her father does the right thing in the way of dowry and relinquishes humor as a profession. My Franky has early exhibited those talents calculated to render a woman happy, and as a circus rider, car conductor, negro minstrel or butcher's boy would attain professional eminence.

What I want to say, however, is that we send all kinds of good wishes to you and yours, and let loose a shower of blessings on the cradle of the little stranger. My wife I think accepts it as a good omen for herself, and in her present not very robust state she needs that comfort.[2] I hope before another six weeks passes you can return these congratulations four-fold—no! thats too many!—I mean in kind.

Mrs. Harte sends her sympathetic love to your wife and I am always

Yours
Bret Harte

Provenience: Bancroft (Mark Twain Papers).

1. BH writes to congratulate his friend on the birth of his daughter Olivia Susan (Susy) Clemens (1872–96), born the previous March 19.

2. AH is pregnant with daughter Jessamy Harte (1872–1962).

34. TO JAMES T. FIELDS, 2 MAY 1872

217 East 49th St
May 2d

My dear Fields,

That was a good, honest, impulsive note you wrote me three weeks ago, and I carry my gratitude still, even though you have had time since then to change your mind.[1] When I got the note I tried to bully—I think that's the proper word—Mrs Harte into sending to you her thanks and all the pleasant feminine things she had said to me about your "Yesterdays"[2] wh. she kept tucked under her pillow during the weary "to-days" and apprehensive "to-morrows" of her protracted invalidism, but in vain. She had the popular fallacy that all criticism to be valuable must be cold blooded, rhetorical and in the formal attitude, as if God rest! we could not enjoy a flower without specifying its class and genera. At all events I failed to use her after my *fainéant* fashion, to thank you for a favor done to myself. I fear that her idea was to get me to write an elaborate review of your book and enclose it to you as her own—a suggestion I promptly and scornfully rejected.

We missed you greatly at a little feed which Osgood gave Howells last evening. We, that is Howells and myself—tried to make up the deficit by telling your story of the blaspheming peach-can opener.[3] The folks received the *disjecta membrae* kindly and buried them but H & I thought we came off badly. The gentle Howells swore frightfully in the conscientious performance of his duty—as a *raconteur*—but I fear to no purpose.

My service and loyal regards to your wife to whom Mrs Harte sends love and greeting. She (Mrs H.) still expects. She has learned to wait at least if the other part of the injunction has offered itself.

Yours Ever
Bret Harte

Mr "T. Fields!"

Provenience: Huntington (FI 1085).

1. Probably a note about BH's poem "Concepcion de Arguellö," which Fields would have read before publication in the May 1872 *Atlantic*.

2. AH is reading *Yesterdays with Authors* (Boston: Osgood, 1872), Fields's reminiscences, originally published in the *Atlantic*, of his association with Dickens, Hawthorne, and other literary lights of the nineteenth century.

3. Fields had told this joke at a famous luncheon in BH's honor attended by Clemens, Howells, and Aldrich hosted by Ralph Keeler (1840–73) at Ober's restaurant in Boston on 2 November 1871.

35. TO SAMUEL L. CLEMENS, 17 JUNE 1872

217 E. 49th St
June 17th

My dear Clemens,

Many thanks for your kindly concern, my dear fellow, but notwithstanding all these delays in the process the result was all right.[1] Slote[2] bro't a note (wh. as Pegotty says "is rhyme though not intentional")[3] and his cheque, and I found Butterworth[4] the next day.

I liked Slote greatly. He is very sweet, simple and sincere. I think he is truly "white" as you say, or quite "candid" as Mr Lowell would say in his Latin-English.

I enclose your diamond stud, wh. I wore in the cars. My general style and tone wont admit of jewelry, and when a gentleman with a black moustache in the smoking car called me "Pard," and asked me to join him at draw poker and a remarkably over-dressed young lady offered me a seat in her carriage home I concluded to take the diamond off.

Let me hear from you about Bliss.[5] Tell Mrs Clemens I deputize you to kiss the baby for me, as I havent yet been able to perform the osculatory act for mine own.

You ought to be very happy with that sweet wife of yours and I suppose you are. It is not every man that can cap a hard, thorny, restless youth with so graceful a crown,[6] and you are so lucky that, like the Banuacide, I almost tremble for you.

Let me hear from you soon

Always Yours
Bret Harte

Mr. S. L. Clemens

Provenience: Bancroft (Mark Twain Papers).

1. BH accepts Clemens's congratulations on the birth of his daughter Jessamy on May 31.

2. Daniel Slote (1828?–82) was a stationery manufacturer in New York, had been a fellow passenger with Clemens on the *Quaker City* voyage in 1867, and figured prominently as one of the "boys" in *The Innocents Abroad*.

3. In chapter LXIII of *David Copperfield*, Mr. Peggotty says, "friends is dear, and I am here.—Which is verse . . . though I hadn't such intentions."

4. BH's landlord.

5. Elisha Bliss, Jr. (1822–80), president of the American Publishing Co. of Hartford, a subscription house. Clemens is acting as an intermediary between BH and Bliss, who are negotiating terms for a novel. See also letter 71. BH would sign a contract to write a novel for the Hartford company on 8 September 1872.

6. Clemens had named BH among a list of men who might give testimonials to his character in a letter dated 29 December 1868 to his prospective father-in-law, Jervis Langdon. BH's comment here suggested he was contacted by Langdon and favorably recommended his friend. Certainly Clemens later nursed a grudge against several of the men he had named who failed to aid his courtship of Olivia Langdon (1845–1904), whom he married on 2 February 1870. See also *Mark Twain's Letters*, ed. Harriet Elinor Smith and Richard Bucci (Berkeley: University of California Press, 1990), II, 359.

36. TO W. D. HOWELLS, 22 JUNE 1872

217 E 49th St,
June 22d

My dear Howells,

I enclose a poem for the *Atlantic*—one of half a dozen I hope to write, when the seed that is in me shall germinate.[1] I want to make some dramatic dialogues and monologues like my "Jim" & "Cicely"[2]—minus the dialect and the California flavor—for I find men and women pretty much the same on 5th Avenue as in Dutch Flat, and there is abundant material here. I dont think anybody is likely to follow me in this, and I know no one has preceded me. I purpose another to be called "Ten Minutes before Dinner" another "Over the Piano"[3]—all dramatic and I think not inconsistent.

My story still hangs fire, but I think you shall have it in a day or two.[4] In the last two months the baby has occupied my attention as an author to the exclusion of all else. Let me know if the poem will do, and what you think of my plan.

Ever yours
Bret Harte

W. D. Howells, Esq

Provenience: Harvard (bMS Am 1784 [210]). By permission of the Houghton Library, Harvard University.

1. Howells apparently declined this poem, probably "Dolly Varden," printed a week later in *Harper's Bazar* (29 June 1872, 434).

2. BH refers to two of his poems in the *Overland*: "Jim" 4 (Feb. 1870):186; and "Cicely" 5 (Oct. 1870):378–79.

3. BH subsequently published a poem entitled "Half an Hour before Supper" in the *Atlantic* 30 (Sept. 1872):272. He published no poem with the title "Over the Piano."

4. Probably "Mrs. Skaggs's Husbands," a two-part story that Howells apparently declined to publish in the *Atlantic*. As Howells later noted, "the long breath was not his" (*Literary Friends*, 300). BH's story first reached print in his collection *Mrs. Skaggs's Husbands and Other Sketches* (Boston: Osgood, 1873). See also letter 51.

37. TO SAMUEL L. CLEMENS, 25 JULY 1872[1]

Grand View House,
Morristown N.J.

My dear Clemens,

Thanks for your two letters.[2] That was a seductive picture you gave of Fenwick Hall—particularly to one who doesn't know how to play billiards and has spent most of his days trying to evade the companionship of people greatly older than himself. I fear, however, that the sea-side is not "indicated," as the Doctors say, in Mrs Harte's case. She has hardly got over her last summer at Newport and longs for mountain air.[3] I'm afraid that this will mean Mt. Washington or the Cattskills or some other remoteness, unless I can find something tonic nearer at hand. I think Holyoke or Mt. Tom would have fitted. Will there be any chance there about 1st August or later? Save Mrs Harte's persistent weakness and my own attempts to do work in an atmosphere and surroundings that inculcate laziness as a moral virtue we are doing pretty fairly here at Morristown. The wet-nurse—who is a well-disposed mammal—is bringing up the baby wonderfully, and we have lost at least all present anxiety, whatever you may see in the future.

This is a capital place for children. The air, without being at all bracing is pure and sweet; the scenery pretty and pastoral; the house—a very comfortable family hotel kept by my sisters husband—is 2 1/2 miles from Morristown and 1 1/2 hours from New York. It is near enough to the city to permit me, when I get quite desperate with the sleepy *dolce far niente* air, to rush to my empty house on 49th st for a days quiet work there—for work here is almost impossible. Could not you and I find some quite rural retreat this summer where we could establish ourselves (after your Elmira or Buffalo fashion) in some empty farm house a mile or two away from our families, and do our work, with judicious intervals of smoking, coming home to dinner at abt 3 P.M.?— Think of it.—

I've not yet directly heard from Bliss, but I fancy he will write to me after you have answered that note you enclosed. I'll get at the book as soon as this press of unfinished work is done.

When you write, address in "care of E. P. Dutton & Co 713 Broadway, Cor[ner] Washington Place"; its almost as direct and much more certain than this Morristown P.O. Regards to Mrs Clemens & love to baby

Ever Yours
Bret Harte

Provenience: Bancroft (Mark Twain Papers).

1. This letter is dated from the postmarked envelope.

2. With the exception of his 1 May 1867 letter to BH (Yale), all of Clemens's letters to BH are unrecovered and presumably lost.

3. See note 2 to letter 31.

38. TO THE EDITORS OF THE *BOSTON DAILY ADVERTISER*, 16 NOVEMBER 1872

To the Editors of the Boston Daily Advertiser:—

As you have already given the remarks of Mr. James Redpath before the Boston Lyceum course concerning my omission to lecture for him on the 13th instant,[1] will you allow me a few words of reply?

For the last two years Messrs. Redpath and Fall of the Lyceum Bureau have repeatedly solicited me to enter the lecture field under their auspices.[2] I finally acceded, and in August last in an interview with Mr. Redpath stated very clearly the conditions, and the only conditions, under which I would lecture. On the first of November I received from them a list of engagements whose conditions were totally at variance with those I had named. I at once informed them by letter that I would not accept them, and reiterated my former demand. To this I received no reply, but on the 9th of November, four days before the date of my Boston engagement, not wishing to disappoint a gathered audience pending these purely private and personal negotiations, I telegraphed to Messrs. Redpath and Fall that they must postpone that date. They replied by telegraph the same day that it was impossible, adding that Hartford (my first engagement) would accept my conditions. I at once wrote to them that until *all* my engagements were made equally satisfactory, they must postpone or cancel both, and that I would not permit Hartford to be forced, at the last moment, into accepting conditions of which they had not been previously aware. To this I added that the Boston fire, then burning,[3] was a sufficient excuse for postponement—an excuse that afterward in the case of two distinguished lecturers was considered valid and not particularly "insulting" to a Boston audience.

With a perfect understanding of these details, and with my letter in his pocket, Mr. James Redpath rose before an audience *which he had permitted to gather to hear a man who he knew would be absent*, charged me with insulting them, depreciated the wares he had asked permission to peddle exclusively—all in the most extraordinary performance, I trust, ever given before a New England lyceum.

I have only to add that it is still my intention to lecture before a Boston audience,[4] but not for Mr. Redpath, nor of him.

BRET HARTE.

New York, Nov. 16.

Provenience: *Boston Daily Advertiser*, 20 Nov. 1872, p. 2, col. 5.

1. "Local Matters," *Boston Daily Advertiser*, 14 Nov. 1872, p. 1, col. 7: "A good audience gathered in the Music Hall last evening in the expectation of hearing Mr. Bret Harte lecture upon 'The Argonauts of '49' as advertised. At 7:30 Mr Redpath stated, without attempting to conceal his annoyance, that after every effort on the part of the committee they had been unable to hold Mr Harte to his engagement. 'This,' said Mr Redpath, 'is the third time that "the Heathen Chinee" has insulted a Boston audience, and I think it is time this man was taught his place.'" No doubt this news item was a source of embarrassment for BH. Longfellow, for example, sent a clipping of the column to his friend George Washington Greene the very day it appeared in the *Advertiser* (*Letters of Henry Wadsworth Longfellow*, ed. Andrew Hilen [Cambridge, Mass.: Belknap, 1982], V, 616).

James Redpath (1833–91) founded the Boston Lyceum Bureau in 1868 and over the years counted among his clients such figures as Emerson, Clemens, and Horace Greeley. The two earlier "insults" to Boston to which Redpath alluded were BH's irreverent performance before the Phi Beta Kappa Society at Harvard commencement in 1871 (see note 3 to letter 24) and his failure to appear at the reunion of the Grand Army of the Potomac to read his poem (see letter 27). Redpath replied to BH's letter in the *Boston Daily Advertiser*, 22 November 1872, 4:1

2. Shortly after BH's arrival in the East, Redpath had published a poem, entitled "The New Evangel" and dedicated "to the Heathen Bretee," which hailed the new fashion in American literature; e.g., "St. Matthew's played out and St. Luke's no account./It takes our St. Bret holy deeds to recount" (*Independent*, 3 Aug. 1871, 12). See also note 1 to letter 23.

3. The Great Boston Fire of 9–10 November 1872 consumed about sixty-five acres of the business district west of the harbor.

4. In fact, BH delivered his address under the auspices of the American Lecture Bureau in Tremont Temple in Boston on Friday evening, 13 December 1872. See note 1 to letter 41.

39. TO JAMES R. OSGOOD, 18 NOVEMBER 1872

Novem 18th
6 P. M.

My dear Osgood,

Here, thank goodness, is the last ms. of Mrs Skaggs Husbands. Let me have a proof as soon as you can—but let it be complete.[1]

Did you get my card for the *Advertiser*.[2] What a delightful phase of New England character your Mr Redpath exhibits. He has, after his insult, *a la mort*, on the 13*th*, resumed (on his part) his business correspondence; quietly, as before, having found that my exhorbitant demands on the Lyceums have in all cases been quietly acceded to and that I am worth more than he thought. Can it be possible that my omission to have anything more to do with him, or even to inform him of that fact will be construed into an insult to Boston! My hair rises with the thought.

Yrs
Bret Harte

P.S. Ask Clark to let me know how my a/c stands & oblige
B. H.

Provenience: Texas (ALS).

1. See note 4 to letter 36.
2. Letter 38.

40. TO W. D. HOWELLS, 1 DECEMBER 1872

214 East 49th St.
Sunday P.M.
Decem. 1st

My dear Howells,

I received your pleasant note enclosing Freiligraths translations at a time when considerable nervous worry and business pre-occupation was added to my usual incapacity to answer letters. When I tell you however that Freiligraths one letter to me (a very sweet one, by the by, received some two months before) is still unanswered, and that I am holding the miserable excuse that the photograph he wanted me to send him is not yet taken, you will see, my dear fellow, that you are not elected to any special incivility (as Redpath believed a Boston audience was)[1] but are merely a victim of my general incompetency. Coming home from Baltimore, where I have been lecturing, last night,[2] I find more copies of *Die Gegenwart* redirected in your own chaste and beautiful hand. This makes three complete files of this journal that I have, and I am by this time fully convinced that the countrymen of the incomparable Göethe are fully awakened to the fact that he has a formidable rival in Harte.[3]

It was very good in Mr. Longfellow to ask you to send me the little slip, but why couldn't he have sent it himself with an autograph?[4] F[ields] referred me [to] Longfellow for his "character."

I hope to see you soon, when I come to Boston to lecture, wh. perhaps is not so indefinite and uncertain as my infelix reputation would indicate. But then, I am not consistent even in my vices, for I am always

Yours
Bret Harte

W. D. Howells, Esq.

Provenience: Harvard (bMS Am 1784 [210]). By permission of the Houghton Library, Harvard University.

1. See note 1 to letter 38.

2. After opening his lecture season in Springfield, Massachusetts, on 25 November 1872, BH gave his lecture, "The Argonauts of '49," in Baltimore on 29 November 1872 (*Baltimore American*, 30 Nov. 1872, p. 4, col. 3).

3. Perhaps the most gifted German poet of his generation, Ferdinand Freiligrath (1810–76) published six translations of BH poems in *Die Gegenwart* in 1872: "Dickens im Lager" ("Dickens in Camp"), 3 Feb. 1872, 25; "Im Tunnel" ("In the Tunnel"), 3 Feb. 1872, 25–26; "Die Sozietät am Stanislaus" ("The Society upon the Stanislaus"), 24 Feb. 1872, 72–74; "Die Heimkehr" ("The Return of Belisarius"), 2 Mar. 1872, 88–89; "Im Missionsgarten" ("In the Mission Garden"), 2 Mar. 1872, 89; and "Eine Friedensbotschaft" ("A Sanitary Message"), 18 May 1872, 265. Freiligrath published three additional translations in *Die Gegenwart* in 1874: "Habichtsnest" ("The Hawk's Nest"), 2 May 1874, 278–79; "Was die Lokomotiven fragten" ("What the Engines Said"), 9 May 1874, 294–95; and "An einen Seevogel" ("To a Sea-Bird"), 23 May 1874, 327. All nine

of these poems, plus translations of two others, "Lone Mountain" and "Das Idyll von Battle Hollow" ("The Idyl of Battle Hollow"), appear in Freiligrath's *Sämtliche Werke.* See also Hermann Kindf, "Freiligrath und Bret Harte," *Die Gegenwart*, 17 June 1876, 393–94.

4. Presumably a notice of BH's lecture in Springfield.

41. TO JAMES T. FIELDS, 18 DECEMBER 1872

Sturtevant House,
Decem. 18

My dear Fields,

Your charming note anent my Boston success[1] I think bore my sinews "stiffly up" before a New York audience on Monday night and helped me to make that "decided hit" which the papers were good enough, one and all, next day, to say that I achieved.[2] It was a dismal night, "with hoar frost on the fringe part and thaw upon the track," and doing under foot all that it threatened overhead, yet the house was completely filled, and with the best people.[3] Perhaps they were not as alert and quickly-responsive as that bright-eyed crowd that flashed at you and me on the Boston platform—but they seemed to be very agreeably surprised with me, and indeed I was myself. My voice was good—"I roared 'em as gently as any sucking dove."[4]

Many thanks to you my dear Fields, for your service on that eventful night in Boston.[5] It was your goodness that, I think, kept the fire from coursing Boston Common during the recent conflagration, and a few such men as you would have averted the calamity entirely. Verily you shall have your reward hereafter—besides being secured before the expiration of the next twenty days.

I trust there are "pieces of eight" and "pistoles" in the lecture, but it is rather late in the season now to rake them in. Nevertheless, my agent is quietly informing the country lyceums, with a circular and notices, what they are losing.

With the greatest of remembrances to Mrs Fields in which Mrs Harte joins, I am

Always yours
Bret Harte

J. T. Fields. Esq. of Boston.

Provenience: Huntington (FI 5184).

1. BH puts a favorable spin on the events in Boston of 13 December 1872. While his lecture at the Tremont Temple in Boston had been well attended and favorably reviewed, he was also arrested by a sheriff as he left the stage at the close of the lecture and the receipts for ticket sales were seized by his creditors. See *Life in Letters*, I, 251, and *Literary Friends*, 298.

Fields's 15 December 1872 letter to BH is published in Pemberton, 134–35. In it, Fields reports that many of his friends "fairly boiled over with delight" at the lecture and "swore so good a lecture, so delightful a lecture, had not been produced on that platform for many a year!"

2. According to the *New York Tribune*, BH's lecture was "a most gratifying and genuine success" (17 Dec. 1872, p. 8, cols. 1–2); and the New York *Evening Post* suggested that "his effort was level with the very high reputation for wit, humor, observation, and tenderness . . . which he had established by his writings" (17 Dec. 1872, p. 2, col. 2). Similarly, the *New York Times* reported that BH "kept the entire audience in a continuous roar of laughter" for ninety minutes "and in retiring was loudly applauded" (17 Dec. 1872, p. 5, col. 3); the New York *World* averred that BH "has proven himself to be an excellent speaker as well as a capital original writer" (17 Dec. 1872, p. 5, col. 1); and the *New York Herald* concluded that BH "combines the language of the poet with the form and color inborn in an artist" (17 Dec. 1872, p. 10, col. 3).

3. The *Evening Post* noted that the "large and brilliant audience" had "come through driving snow and rain to hear" the lecture (17 Dec. 1872, p. 2, col. 2).

4. Bottom in *A Midsummer Night's Dream*, I. ii: "I will aggravate my voice so that I will roar you as gently as any sucking dove."

5. Fields had introduced BH to the Boston audience on 13 December 1872. Lilian Aldrich also remembered many years later that BH's publisher, presumably Fields, had interceded on his behalf with the sheriff who waited to arrest him at the close of the lecture (Aldrich, 137).

42. TO SAMUEL L. CLEMENS, 26 DECEMBER 1872

Sturtevant House
Decem. 26/72

My dear Clemens:

I have been lately pretty well abused from unexpected sources but I think the enclosed caps the climax. Do you remember the man to whom you gave $50; for whom I raised $60 and procured by begging a first class passage to San Francisco and to whom I sent anonymously $25, when I was rather poor myself? Well—this is the reptile! And worse than all, this is the second or third time that he has thus requited me.[1]

Now, what in the name of all that is diabolically mean, am I to do. I don't mind his slander; that I can refute—but how am I to make this dog know that he is a dog and not a man?

You wrote me from London that you had heard that Osgood had taken £50 from Hotten and given him the copyright of my new book.[2] I believe Osgood did it for the best, but as I had no idea of condoning that pirate Hotten's offenses for £50, I repudiated it at once. I told Osgood not to send him advanced sheets of my new story and to say that Mr Harte annulled the contract. He did so—and I see by the Spectator that Hotten has quietly reproduced all the book except that story, without even paying the £50, and further has had the advantage of his previous announcement that he was "authorized by Mr. Harte &c." Further the book contains somebody else's story foisted upon me.[3] But that'll do to-day. I'll see you I hope on the 3rd.[4] I saw your brother-in-law at Elmira the other day.[5]

Yours
Harte

Provenience: Bancroft (Mark Twain Papers).

1. BH refers to W. A. Kendall and his article "Frank Bret Harte" in the *San Francisco Chronicle* for 15 December 1872 (p. 1, cols. 1–2), which alleged that BH "was a loose and not infrequent borrower of considerable sums, and then a cool ignorer of the gracious loaners." Kendall also intimated that, as editor of the *Overland*, BH had pocketed hundreds of dollars owed to contributors. Kendall, who had contributed to both the *Golden Era* and the *Overland*, was "utterly prostrated in health, and was poor and destitute, living on weekly contributions from newspaper men" in 1872. He attempted suicide in June 1875 and died by his own hand in January 1876. See "Poor Kendall," *San Francisco Chronicle*, 20 Jan. 1876, p. 1, col. 3; and "A Forgotten Poet," *San Francisco Chronicle*, 14 July 1889, p. 8, cols. 4–5.

Ironically, Clemens cited this article nearly six years later in a letter to Howells: "John Carmany, publisher of the Overland Monthly, charges [BH] with stealing money delivered to him to be paid to contributors," an allegation "W. A. Kendall . . . dared him" to deny (*MT–H Letters*, I, 235).

2. John Camden Hotten had written the *Spectator* (28 Sept. 1872) that "When 'Bret Harte's' agent called upon me a few days since with a new copyright story, we at once came to terms." The story was no doubt "Mrs. Skaggs's Husbands." See also note 4 to letter 36.

3. The *Spectator* reviewed Hotten's edition of BH's *Stories of the Sierras and Other Sketches* in its 7 December 1872 issue. The story "foisted" upon BH was by Joaquin Miller.

4. Clemens was present for BH's lecture in Hartford on 3 January 1873 (*Hartford Times*, 4 Jan. 1873, p. 1, col. 1). On 22 March 1873, he replied to an inquiry that BH "has an excellent lecture this season, & reads it execrably" (*Mark Twain's Letters 1872–73*, ed. Harriet Elinor Smith [Berkeley: University of California Press, forthcoming]).

5. BH had lectured on 23 December 1872 in Elmira, New York, where he had met Charles Langdon (1849–1916), brother of Olivia Langdon Clemens.

43. TO FRANK H. MASON, 25 FEBRUARY 1873

Detroit
Tuesday Evening,

My dear Mason,[1]

I had not time before I left New York to thank you for your kind offer, nor indeed do more than send my acceptance and the date by telegram the day I left for Toronto. At that place I managed to make myself so acceptable to Her Majesty's lieges as to arrange for a series of lectures to be delivered throughout the Dominion in the latter part of March. I asked my agent to send you the Toronto papers and from the *Mail* I think you may be able to extract something to publish in view of Friday's lecture.[2]

The audience at Toronto waited for me as Beechers audience waited for him at Pittsburgh, and although I telegraphed for a special train from Hamilton I did not reach Toronto until 9 oclock. I dressed myself in the cars at the rate of 60 miles an hour—the most rapid and extraordinary toilette I ever made.

I go to East Saginaw to-morrow, and shall telegraph you from there when you may look for me at Detroit [*sic*: Cleveland]. Until I can thank you more fully in person for your kindness pray accept these scant acknowledgements of

Yours ever
Bret Harte

Done with a vile hotel pen this 25th February 1873
B. H.

Provenience: Fales Library, New York University (ALS).

1. Frank Holcomb Mason (1840–1916) had been a military attaché on James A. Garfield's staff during the Civil War, was affiliated with the Cleveland *Leader* between 1865 and 1880, and was later a U.S. diplomat. BH contributed a brief preface to Mason's hagiographical *The Life and Public Services of James A. Garfield* (London: Trübner & Co., 1881).

2. According to the review in the Toronto *Mail* (24 Feb. 1873, p. 2, cols. 3–4), BH's lecture in the local YMCA hall on 22 February 1873 had been well received: "Wherever the English tongue is spoken, Bret Harte may address an audience, and though he knows no more of the meretricious tricks of the platform than an oyster knows of Donner Lake or the waters of Tahoe, he may calculate on being heard with pleasure." The review was extracted in the Cleveland *Leader* on the very day BH spoke in Cleveland (28 Feb. 1873, p. 4, col. 8).

44. TO JAMES R. OSGOOD, 2 APRIL 1873

45 Fifth Avenue
April 2nd 73

My dear Osgood,

Yours of the 27th March was forwarded from Toronto[1] and only received by me to-day. If you think a "complete" edition would pay you here, by all means get it up.

I have your answer to my dispatch of yesterday saying that Hotten had not responded in any way. In the face of the enclosed note wh. I received three weeks ago, his conduct seems to me utterly inexplicable. Is he not responsible to you directly?[2]

I am *not* going to England next month as you might have known from the papers saying that I *was*.[3] I have too much unfinished work to complete here. I think I will "keep" for another year with my English friends.

I am very much irritated by the discovery of another California swindle upon me. In 1860, I wrote the "Story of M'liss," as it appears in "The Luck &c" for the *Golden Era* a weekly San Francisco paper with which I was then connected. Three years after (1863), at the request of the proprietor, Col. Lawrence,[4] I attempted to create a longer story or novel out of it, but after writing 9 or 10 chapters I wound it up in disgust. As I always preferred my first conception, I adopted *that* when I put it in the "Luck." I find now that the *Golden Era* is reprinting the second story in their columns with an advertisement saying that it will be completed in "*sixty-two*" chapters. Of course this means a swindle on the public, or a *forgery.* I regret to say that they are quite capable of doing either in California, and as I have received no explanation or notice from them, I expect the worst. I have written a "card" to be published in the *Bulletin* of S.F. and have sent a private note to the Editor.[5] Can you not frighten them by copyright? The whole transaction is infamous!

I have copyrighted my lecture in Canada for England, having heard that an English order had been sent to N.Y. for a stenographic reprint. As I copyrighted a "proof" or printed slip of it, this will prevent Hotten or any other pirate from printing it.

Yours
Harte

Provenience: Texas (ALS).

1. While BH had lectured in Toronto on 22 February 1873, he was in Ottawa, Montreal, and Ogdensburg, New York, in late March 1873.

2. In a letter of 20 February 1873, John Camden Hotten assured BH that he was "anxious to give you a financial interest in the sale of your books here in England, & if you will re-edit them for me I am prepared to pay you whatever is equitable" (Rogers Collection, Harvard). By permission of the Houghton Library, Harvard University.

3. The rumor was given new life in the Boston *Literary World*, 1 May 1873, 192.

4. Joseph E. Lawrence, publisher of the *Golden Era.*

5. The *San Francisco Examiner* reported on 15 March 1873 (p. 3, col. 2) that the number of the *Golden Era* "issued tomorrow" would contain

the opening chapters of "M'liss," which in BH's version "never got beyond the sixteenth chapter." By arrangement of the publisher, however, the serial "will be continued to the end" and afterwards "printed in book form." Not only was BH's card not printed by the editors of the *Bulletin*, they defended the "swindle": BH had brought the original story "to an abrupt conclusion" in the *Golden Era* in 1863, and in his continuation G. S. Densmore adheres to "the obvious plan of the original fragment" (19 Apr. 1873, p. 1, col. 7). Whereas BH's "The Work on Red Mountain" (1860) ran to about 10,000 words and his revised "M'liss" (1863) to about 25,000 words, Densmore's "completion" was about 160,000 words long. To BH's dismay, it was later published as a volume (New York: DeWitt, 1873; microfilmed in Wright's American Fiction series II, no. 1120, reel H–10). BH successfully sued to enjoin its sale on the grounds the book infringed upon both his copyright and "his right to his name as a trademark" (*New York Times*, 27 Jan. 1874, p. 2, col. 5; 11 July 1874, p. 8, col. 2; 24 Mar. 1875, p. 5, col. 5). As he wrote R. R. Bowker on 24 December 1873 (LC), "I shall push the matter to an end, as I am somewhat oppressed by the monotony of the various outrages to which my literary good name and property have been subjected." Bowker editorialized in the New York *Evening Mail* (27 Dec. 1873, p. 2, cols. 1–2) that BH seemed a "favorite" target of "the piratical craft."

45. TO ANNA HARTE, 11 APRIL 1873

Galt House
Louisville, Ky. April 11 *1873*

My dear Nan,

I am at last at Louisville in time for my lecture[1] although up to this morning I did not really know whether I would not have to add this town to my other failures. But here I am, at the Galt House, some four hours before the lecture begins, nervous as usual but thank goodness! safe and well—and in time!

I suppose I ought to be very thankful that I lost nothing more than my Hudson engagement, for we were often in great danger, and at all times utterly incapable of finding out when or how we would get through. From Syracuse to Rochester we literally felt our way along—the track being hidden below two feet of water and floating ice and railroad ties, and the engine fires narrowly escaping being put out. Since the Sacramento flood I never saw anything like it. I was forty nine hours coming from New York to Cleveland and although I came through on the first train when many passengers deemed it unsafe to go, and although I telegraphed to Hudson promptly stating the cause of my detention, the usual insulting paragraph about my "breaking forth" and not "keeping engagements" appeared in the *Cleveland Plain Dealer.*[2] When I reached Cleveland I again telegraphed to Hudson offering them the 15th and 16th after Wheeling, but with no effect. My telegraphing cost me $10.00 and I did not get even civility in return. My luck, just now, is pretty hard.

Yet considering that I have been for three days continually in the cars and have had no sleep for three nights, I am surprised that I feeling even as well as I do, and am grateful. If I could be sure that *you* were better I would not feel so anxious. I have been thinking of your miserable health when I left—of your pale face—and thinking how much paler and more nervous you would be with my worry added to your own. I should not have telegraphed you at Albany, but for five hours I did not know whether I would not have to return. I was out of funds too—and had to borrow $25 to enable me to get here. I will telegraph some money to you to-morrow. "Cheer up Dot!"

Yours
Frank

Provenience: UVa (ALS).

1. After missing his engagement in Hudson, Ohio, BH lectured in Louisville on April 11 and in Wheeling, West Virginia, on April 14.

2. *Cleveland Plain Dealer*, 10 Apr. 1873, p. 2, col. 2: "Bret Harte telegraphed that he could not keep his appointment to lecture at Hudson Wednesday evening, and directing that the money received for tickets be refunded. Bret is famous as an engagement breaker."

46. TO ANNA HARTE, 19 OCTOBER 1873

St. Louis,
October 19th/73
Sunday P.M.

My dear Anna,

As my engagement is not until the 21st at Topeka Kansas,[1] I lie over here until to-morrow morning in preference to spending the extra day in Kansas.[2] I've accepted the invitation of Mr Hodges, one of the managers of the lecture course to stay at his house. He is a good fellow, with the usual American small family and experimental housekeeping, and the quiet and change from the hotel is very refreshing to me. They let me stay in my own room—wh. by the way, is hung with the chintz of our 49th St house—and don't bother me with company. So I was very good to-day and went to church. There was fine singing. The contralto sang your best sentences from the *Te Deum* "we believe that there shalt come &c &c" to the same minor chant that I used to admire.

The style of criticism which my lecture—or rather myself as a lecturer has received—of which I send you a specimen, culminated this morning in an editorial in the *Republican* which I shall send you, but have not with me at present.[3] I certainly never expected to be mainly criticised for being what *I am not*, a handsome fop—but this assertion is at the bottom of all the criticism. They may be right—I dare say they are—in asserting that I am no orator, have no special faculty for speaking—no fire, dramatic earnestness or expression, but when they intimate that I am running on my good looks, save the mark! I confess I get hopelessly furious. You will be amused to hear that my gold "studs" have again become "diamonds," my worn out shirts "faultless linen," my haggard face that of a "Spanish-looking exquisite," my habitual quiet and "used up" way, "gentle and elegant languor." But you will be a little astonished to know that the hall I spoke in was worse than Springfield and *notoriously* so[4]—that the people seemed generally pleased, that the lecture inaugurated the "Star" course very handsomely and that it was the first of the first series of lectures ever delivered in St Louis.

My dates in Kansas are changed thus, Topeka, 21st, Atchison, 22d Lawrence 23 Kansas City, 24th[5]—but they are not distant from each other and I shall probably get any letters without trouble.

I hope to hear that you have got a house or are settled in your next letter. I shall write again this week, probably from Kansas City.

Your affec.
Frank

Provenience: UVa (ALS).

1. BH lectured in Chicago on October 14 and in St. Louis on October 17.

2. From "Local Personals," St. Louis *Missouri Republican*, 19 Oct. 1873, p. 2, col. 5: "Bret Harte leaves Monday morning on the St. Louis, Kansas City and Northern railroad for Topeka, Kas."

3. In "Bret Harte and the Lecturers," the St. Louis *Missouri Republican* for 19 October 1873 (p. 4, cols. 3–4) editorialized as follows:

> BRET HARTE, in full dress costume with spotless linen and diamond studs, and altogether most faultlessly gotten up, lectured here Friday evening. In quantity and quality the audience was magnificent, the appearance of the Spanish looking exquisite was most charming, the lecture itself was interesting reading matter, but notwithstanding all this it was an exceedingly dull affair. In the immense hall the voice of the young man was cruelly engulfed, and as neither earnestness nor energy was permitted to ruffle his gentle and elegant languor, fully one-half of the people failed to catch the discourse.

4. According to the *Springfield Republican* (26 Nov. 1872, p. 8, col. 1) BH's debut lecture had been marred by the "destructive echoes of the city hall."

5. In addition, BH lectured in St. Joseph on October 25 and in Omaha on October 26.

47. TO ELIZA KNAUFFT, 23 OCTOBER 1873

Lawrence, Kansas,
Octo. 23d/73

My dear Sister,[1]

I have nothing from you or Anna since her letter from Morristown, and I do not even know whether she has yet come in town, or if you have found a house. I shall not write again until I hear from some of you. You will know of my whereabouts by my drafts & newspapers which I shall send to 45 Fifth Avenue. I sent to-day by Wells Fargo & Co $100 in greenbacks, with receipt herein enclosed.

I've had a pretty hard, wearisome trip thus far—although being in the country of "Bret Harte" collars, and "Bret Harte" hats, and with a settlement named after me in the next township, I am among friends and admirers.

It is a strange weird country and all the originality of the nation seems to be concentrated here, west of the Mississippi valley. I rode the other afternoon fifteen miles on horseback to keep a lecture engagement. It was over a bleak prairie with the thermometer at the freezing point. I was watching the red sun going down over this limitless land, beaten flat by the wind, when I passed a wolf first, and then an emigrant train such as you see in pictures, and the oddity of my errand struck me very forcibly. The wagon contained the usual Missouri family, the withered bombazing woman as flat, as uninteresting, as bleak and yet as prolific as the prairie we were crossing; the 14 or 15 children all colty and lank, and the grizzled "old man." But one of the young men, after riding beside me for a few moments, suddenly asked me if I were not "Bret Harte." I answered "yes" and asked him why he asked the question. He said I looked like my picture, and produced it with the greatest naivete from his pocket, greasy with handling. He said all my books were in the wagon, and to my great astonishment repeated nearly everything I had ever written. It was a very funny experience.[2]

Good night. I'm sorry you've thrown off me your brother, but I shall hunt up some other sister in Kansas.

Your affec brother
Frank

This was handed to me on the Atchison St. Joseph & Santa Fe train, by a sooty looking fireman, who instantly retired to the further end of the car in bashful confusion and the timid consciousness of authorship.[3] Of course they got their passes, and I left directions that they should have reserved seats.

B.H.

Provenience: Bancroft (MSS 88/181 C).

1. Eliza C. T. (Harte) Knaufft was BH's older sister and the mother of four children, including the musicologist Ernest Knaufft (1863–1942).

2. Joseph Bucklin Bishop relates a very different version of this story, told to him by BH, in *Notes and Anecdotes of Many Years* (New York: Scribner, 1925), 172–73: While at a hotel in "a little town in the Far West on a matter of business," BH was approached by a fellow "in full

cowboy costume" who asked him if he was the author of "The Outcasts of Poker Flat." When he replied yes, "he threw wide his arms, clasping me in them, and exclaimed: 'You d——d old s—— of a b——!'" BH also related a version of the story to Clemens sometime before their estrangement in 1877, to judge from an entry in his notebook (*Mark Twain's Notebooks and Journals*, ed. Frederick Anderson et al. [Berkeley: University of California Press, 1975], II, 344) and his autobiographical dictation (*MT in Eruption*, 270–72).

3. Written on the reverse of this enclosure is the following verse:

To hear your Lecture we are much inclined
But our pay car unfortunately is 3 months behind
You could mend this matter Mr. Harte if you choose
By passing in this unfortunate R.R. crew
We would like very much your Lecture to hear
This from Fireman Brakeman & Engineer

48. TO ELIZA KNAUFFT, 29 OCTOBER 1873

Davenport, Ia.
October 29th/73

My dear Sister,

I wrote and telegraphed you from Omaha on the 27th and sent you draft for 200. I add to-day $200 more by dft. I have received nothing further from you or Anna since I left Omaha, either by mail or telegraph.

I need not say that I am greatly worried and perplexed by this still unsettled condition of my family. Anna wrote me on the 17th that she expected presently to telegraph me concerning some house in the country. It is now nearly 1st Novem. and nothing seems to have been accomplished. I trust to hear otherwise at Bloomington, South Bend or at least at Ann Arbor on the 1st.[1]

For myself I have been very lucky thus far in being able to keep my engagements, even in a rough country and with long distances and scant trains. Had I missed a train at any time it would have involved the loss of half a dozen engagements. So I have risen at midnight—have driven directly from the lecture to the depot, have spent three nights without sleep consecutively, until I wonder at what unknown resources of vitality I am drawing upon. I am so fagged out when I do arrive, and am so weary while traveling—there are no Pullman cars on these shorter lines—that I find it difficult even to write a letter. Even committee men, who generally have a vague idea that lectures drop directly from the clouds without impediment of land travel—even these have complimented me on my promptness and endurance. I trust I shan't collapse before it is over. I live mainly on beef-tea and champagne. Before I close my eyes—when I ever do get the opportunity—at night, I breathe a silent blessing on Leibig and that dear old monk, Dom Perignon.

Do you get the papers I mail you? They at least indicate the kind of folk here, better than any description I could give. They are not picturesque I am sorry to say. I know of no more dreary spectacle than a car load of them, mainly women and children, who make up oddly enough the traveling class here. The women are prematurely old and withered; they wear the most outrageous costumes, but mainly affect a kind of snuffy, frowzy bombazine—black and lustreless. They give you an impression that their underclothes are dirty, and their stockings not properly gartered; the very children have their youth overlaid with encrusted dirt and incipient disease and snuffiness. They are given to lunch baskets and bread & butter in the cars, and the combined stench and heat is something to howl at. I have often gone into the filthy smoking car for relief—I knew at least what *that* smelt of. Mem: These people I never see at my lecture.

It is snowing again, but the weather makes no difference in the attendance here. And that reminds me that it is time for me to beef-tea myself into a little more vitality. I keep the champagne for the lecture.

Your affec brother,
Frank

Provenience: Bancroft (MSS 88/181 C).

1. BH lectured in Davenport on October 29, in Bloomington, Illinois, on October 30, in South Bend on October 31, and in Ann Arbor on November 1 before returning home.

49. TO GRISWOLD HARTE, 4 NOVEMBER 1873

Delaware, Ohio,
November 4th/73

My dear Wodie,[1]

Your letter made me very happy, and I hope that you will try to always make me so by being as good, as gentle, as industrious and manly as you say you will. Papa expects a great deal of you, and when he is away from home, Mamma ought to be able to depend on you, and trust to you, because you are Papa's oldest boy, and must take Papa's place.

I have been far away on a very long journey, but I have been very fortunate and have met with no delay or accident. But if anything had happened to me and I never came back any more to Mamma or my little boys, you, Wodie, would have had to take my place. When Papa dies, you Wodie and Frankie are the only ones that will bear his name, and Papa wants you to be so good and clever, and honorable and manly, that you will always make and keep that name sweet and fresh before men. That, and because Papa loves you is the reason why he wrote as he did.

I am glad you are doing so well in your studies. I have been lecturing before the college and university students here in the west, and I have always thought of you, Wodie, when I did so, and thought how pleasant it would be to see my dear boy Wodie's face look up some time to me among the others.

Your affectionate
Papa.

Provenience: Bancroft (MSS 88/181 C).

1. Griswold's nickname; the boy was ten years old at the time this letter was written.

50. TO GEORGE L. FALL, 29 NOVEMBER 1873

45 Fifth Avenue, N.Y.
Novem. 29th/73

My dear Sir,[1]

I have just received a statement of a/c of commissions due Redpath & Fall during the winter of '72 & '73.

As Mr. Redpath's late partner you must be aware of his conduct toward me at the beginning of my lecture season in Boston.[2] This conduct left me no course but to break at once all business relations with an agent who had publicly slandered his principal and had as publicly abandoned him. I did this by letter—adding that I would pay him all commissions on the engagements he had made for me.

I found, however, to my astonishment, that in each instance I was obliged to make new and distinct agreements and engagements with each of the Lyceums that Redpath & Fall had treated with previously as my agents—that this was invariably due to Mr. Redpaths letters; that he had written to them (copies of wh. letters I have in my possession) stating that I was not to be relied upon—and even in some cases offering to fill my engagements with a substitute at lower figures. I was obliged in every instance, but the Springfield lecture,[3] to enter into new agreements (over my own signature)—the lyceums all declining to recognize the engagements of Redpath & Fall as binding, and sometimes even quoting Mr Redpaths letters as confirmation.

I say nothing here of the absolute pecuniary damage done me, at the outset of my lecturing career, by Mr Redpaths extraordinary conduct. That is a matter for legal adjudication if he sees proper to push his claim.[4] But I am willing to believe, sir, that you are not fully aware of the illegality, presumption and assurance of this demand and in this belief, contrary to the opinion of the lawyer before whom I have laid Mr Redpath's claim and my several personal engagements with the lyceums, I have written this reply.

Your obt Svt.
Bret Harte

Mr. Geo. L. Fall,
Boston.

Provenience: Bancroft (MSS 88/181 C).

1. George L. Fall was James Redpath's former partner.
2. See letter 38.
3. See note 2 to letter 40.
4. See letter 68 for the disposition of Redpath's suit.

51. TO JAMES R. OSGOOD, 12 DECEMBER 1873

Morristown, N. J.
Decem. 12th/73

My dear Osgood,

I confess I was considerably surprised by your note, as you had given me no intimation when I asked for my a/c in Boston a few days ago, of the position you intended to assume. Neither did I know anything of your plans to dispose of the *Atlantic*—and so render it out of my power to furnish you with the single article we agreed upon as due you in the spirit of our contract—until after you had consummated the sale of the *Atlantic*.[1]

When I offered you "Mrs. Skaggs's Husbands["] for the *Atlantic*, according to our contract, you agreed to waive your right to it in the magazine in consideration of its freshness for the new volume—accepting it, however, as the substitute for two articles for the *Atlantic*. This left the matter furnished to you on my contract as follows:

Prose

1 Poet of Sierra Flat[2]
2 Romance of Madroño Hollow[3]
3 Princess Bob.[4]
4 How Sta. Claus came to Simpsons Bar[5]
5, 6 } Mrs Skaggs Husbands[6]
7 Lothaw (in *Every Saturday*)[7]

Poetry.

8 A Greyport Legend[8]
9 A Newport Romance[9]
10 Grandmother Tenterden[10]
11 Concepcion de Arguello[11]
12 Idyl of Battle Hollow.[12]
13 Half an Hour before Supper.[13]
14 Chicago (Every Saturday)[14]

In addition I offered you "Handsome is as Handsome does," written for *Every Saturday* but on account of your relations with Cha Reade you declined it.[15]

There seemed however to be some misunderstanding between us regarding the *Every Saturday* material being applied to the contract, and I offered to furnish you at some future time a sketch or poem in addition without charge. The last time I met you in the city I spoke of this—saying that I was writing a Spanish legend for your maga. and for a new volume of verse about which I wanted to consult you.[16] I had the poem nearly completed when I received the news of the *Atlantics* sale—of which you had not then or at any time given me any previous intimation.

Remembering these circumstances I think you can understand my surprise at your note. I should like also to know what is your proposition, and in any event, I think I am at least entitled to a statement of my a/c with you.

Very Sincerely Yours
Bret Harte

To Jas R. Osgood, Esq.
J. R. Osgood & Co. Boston.

Provenience: UCLA (ALS).

1. Technically, as BH insists, he fulfilled the letter of his contract with Fields, Osgood & Co. by supplying the firm with more than the twelve submissions the contract specified as a minimum number while it was in force. See letter 23. That is, there is no truth to the legend, summarily stated by Howells, that the "net result in a literary return to his publishers" of the contract "was one story and two or three poems" (*Literary Friends*, 301). Still, Osgood complained to C. W. Stoddard later with some justice that "never in his business career had he gotten so little out of a contributor, or with such pains" (*Pacific Monthly* 19 [Mar. 1908]:266). In a financial pinch, Osgood sold the *Atlantic* to Hurd & Houghton. Formal announcement of the sale first appeared in the *Riverside Bulletin* of 15 December 1873. See Ballou, 163, 202–203.

2. See note 3 to letter 29.

3. *Atlantic* 28 (Sept. 1871):371–77.

4. "The Princess Bob and Her Friends," *Atlantic* 28 (Dec. 1871):759–66.

5. *Atlantic* 29 (Mar. 1872):349–57.

6. See note 4 to letter 36.

7. See note 1 to letter 26.

8. *Atlantic* 28 (Sept. 1871):357–58.

9. *Atlantic* 28 (Oct. 1871):481–82.

10. *Atlantic* 29 (Jan. 1872):105–06.

11. See note 1 to letter 34.

12. *Atlantic* 29 (Apr, 1872):496–97.

13. See note 3 to letter 36.

14. *Every Saturday*, 28 Oct. 1871, 426.

15. "Handsome Is as Handsome Does," BH's parody of Charles Reade, first appeared in *Condensed Novels* (Boston: Fields, Osgood & Co., 1871).

16. Either "Don Diego of the South," first published in the *New York Times* for 10 May 1874 (p. 3, col. 1), or, more likely, "For the King," first published in the *Atlantic* 34 (July 1874):15–19.

52. TO MESSRS CARPENTER & SHELDON,[1] 12 JANUARY 1874

713 Broadway, N.Y.
Jany 12th/74

My dear Sir—

Your letter reached me two weeks ago but I have been absent from town and did not think that its contents called for an immediate response. I do not know now that I could add anything to what I have already said to you upon the subject.

I have always believed that the West offered an excellent field for an original, first-rate magazine that should be purely and distinctively American. I still think so, and believe that, owing to the changes in the *Atlantic*, and the general indecision and want of distinctive flavor in the other magazines to-day there is no time better than the present. I have always been ready and am now to take the literary charge of such a venture.

I see no reason why such a magazine as I have indicated should not be published and established in Chicago. But, frankly, I fear that the strong local, provincial feeling which exists there and which has been such a powerful auxillary in building up the city and fostering all local interests because they were local—will be against it. The magazine I speak of will not be local, and I do not see how you are to have a venture controlled by Chicago Capital and patronized by Chicago interests that will not express or advertise anything but Chicago. You would want at least $100,000 subscribed because you could not expect to get a circulation of over 5000 copies in Chicago for a magazine that was not purely local—and your population are not quite literary enough to give a larger patronage to a magazine on its merits purely. I think you make the mistake of calculating too much on the local pride in supporting a magazine that is not local—not like an Opera house, a hotel or a public Art gallery. The magazine is to live, if live it can, by its subscriptions outside of Chicago, by St. Louis, by Cincinnati, by Omaha, by San Francisco. Can you get Chicago Capitalists to pay the first expenses of an enterprise like this? I hope you *can*—but I *doubt*.

You overrate again the value of local feeling or pride in the mere advertising of such a venture. If, as you say, you could "manage the Press" of Chicago it would quite ruin the enterprise. Let the Chicago papers puff it steadily as a Chicago venture and it would ruin it in St Louis and every other western town that was at all a rival—and certainly render it "suspect" in the East. Briefly you must have men to take an interest in it, pecuniarily and practically because it is *not* Chicago—because it is unlike any of your previous ventures there—and for its prospective merits alone. Have you got them?

If you have I will be ready to take the helm at any moment. As I should have to give myself up to it completely, and remove to Chicago, I could not do this under $10,000 a year—irrespective of my contributions in the way of a serial novel or sketches for which I should expect my usual price, guaranteeing only that no article of mine should appear elsewhere. I would be willing to take a part of the $10,000 in an interest or share in the magazine. But I have no money to invest in it otherwise.

Yours very truly
Bret Harte

Provenience: Louis I. Jaffé Papers (#9924), Special Collections Department, University of Virginia Library (ALS).

1. Publishers of the short-lived *Stag Weekly* and *Chicago Pulpit*, a religious weekly.

53. TO ANNA HARTE, 6 APRIL 1874[1]

Monday PM.

Dear Nan,

There's nothing like boldness when one has the least reason

to be bold, and so I asked the *Times* this morning $600 for my story and—*got it*![2] I believe if I had asked $750 I would have got that. But my interview with Smith the other day[3] and my great needs I think frightened me. I have given Eliza $300 to deposit to pay the more pressing bills until I return. I sent mother $100 also. Do the best you can with the $100 and the $30 cheque wh. is as good as the money now.

And now Nan, I leave to-night for Boston to meet that $340 draft. I shall force Osgood into some kind of settlement with me, or at least know where I stand.[4] I cannot shilly-shally any longer. I heard to-day that at the Trade Sale my books sold as well as ever, and there must be some balance in my favor even deducting the sum they assumed last winter. At all events I cannot use my time to better advantage. I will leave Boston to-morrow night, and get into N.Y. Wednesday morning.

Your affec
Frank

Provenience: Berg (ALS).

1. This letter is dated by reference to letter 56, in which BH brags that he received six hundred dollars from the *New York Times* for "The Rose of Tuolumne," and by reference to letter 54 below.

2. "The Rose of Tuolumne," *New York Times*, 12 Apr. 1874, p. 2, cols. 1–5; and 19 Apr. 1874, p. 2, col. 1–p. 3, col. 1.

3. Roswell Smith (1829–92), one of the founders of *Scribner's* and business manager of Scribner and Co.

4. For the results of this conference, see letter 54.

54. TO JAMES R. OSGOOD, 15 APRIL 1874

Morristown N.J.
April 15th 74

My dear Osgood,

I enclose herewith the poem; I have so extended and altered it—wh. accounts for my delay—that it is really a new poem; a vast improvement on the one I intended to send you, and is worth to me about $400.[1] That at least is what I should ask for it, were I to offer it for sale. I do not think I have done anything as good for the length; I am quite certain I have never done anything as elaborate. Read it anyhow. I think you will like it apart from your business interest in it, and give it [to] Clark to read to Mrs Clark.

It is yours, my dear Osgood, if you will so accept it, as my voluntary acknowledgement of your conscientious fulfillment of your part of our late contract, and as an effort on my part to adjust the little differences which exist between us in regard to my performance, and a recognition of and atonement for my delay in execution. It will make according to the statement I furnished you, fifteen articles given to you between the date of our first contract and today, and covered and compensated by the $10,000 paid me during the twelvemonth of our contract.[2]

If you dont like it—or this, please enclose the poem at once to 713 Broadway. I want the poem in any event to go into print soon.

Yours always, my dear Osgood,
Bret Harte

Jas. R. Osgood, Esq

Provenience: Yale (ALS).

1. "For the King," *Atlantic* 34 (July 1874):15–19. In letter 53, BH indicates he owes Osgood $340; that is, he is settling his debt by giving Osgood the poem.

2. See also letter 51.

55. TO HIRAM CORSON, 25 APRIL 1874

Morristown, N.J.
25th of April '74

My dear Professor,[1]

The books came promptly, the letter duly—I am the only one derelict, dilatory and discourteous. Mea culpa, mea culpa, mea maxima culpa!

But then this is the first letter I have written for many weeks. I returned from the West with inflamed eyes to work that had to be done and at once. The result was that in a week I was nearly blind. I never could make use of an amanueusis; I never could borrow another's eyes without getting their other organs thrown in in a way utterly discomposing to my habits of composition. So I groped on in some solitary way to an end; the last intelligent and satisfactory work that I got out of them being the reading of your book.[2] But I didn't dare tax them further to respond, and I did not care to put a third person's hand between yours and mine.

But I am so much better now that I am quite sanguine of finishing my work before the summer fairly sets in, although my projected trip to Europe will have to be deferred. As soon as my doctor admits that I can "focus" perfectly I'll write you more at length.

Meanwhile I want you to believe that I thoroughly enjoyed my Ithaca visit—that it was a most grateful crown and capital to my writer's lecturing experience.[3] I am fearful that I never shall be able to criticise fairly the admirable and patient research shown in your Chaucer. I only know it is of a kind that a lazy, impatient, unmethodical worker like myself looks upon with respectful awe and shameless envy.

Make my grateful acknowledgements to Mr Beardsley for his photographs. They are like, very like—a little savage perhaps, as with a presentiment of weak eyes ahead—but very good. Yours, which, just now, looks I fancy, very forgivingly on me from the wall, is perfect.[4]

Always, dear Mr Corson,
Your friend,
Bret Harte

Professor Hiram Corson
Cornell University, Ithaca, N.Y.

Provenience: Hiram Corson Papers (Collection #14/12/449), Rare and Manuscript Collections, Cornell University Library.

1. Hiram Corson (1828–1911) was professor of English literature at Cornell between 1870 and 1903.

2. Corson was the author of *Chaucer's Legende of Goode Women* (Philadelphia: F. Leypoldt; New York: F. W. Christern, 1864).

3. BH lectured in Ithaca on 6 March 1874. As he wrote AH on 7 March 1874 (*Letters*, 33), his Ithaca auditors "were by far the most

appreciative I have had, not excepting Boston and N.Y. From the time I made my first appearance on the platform they had made up their minds to be pleased, and followed me through, rising at all the delicate points like a trout at a fly."

4. BH also noted in his 7 March 1874 letter (see note 3) that Corson "was a capital good fellow—as sweet and gentle as the old poets he lives among—and he gave me his picture. I had to sit for mine, for the students, before I left there this morning."

56. TO SAMUEL L. CLEMENS, 8 AUGUST 1874

Morristown, N.J.
August 8th/74

My dear Clemens,

The *Times* paid me $600 for the "Rose of Tuolumne" which occupied a page and a column of the Sunday edition[1] and $500 for "John Oakhurst."[2] These were my own figures,—I might have asked and got more I dare say—particularly for Oakhurst which I estimated as occupying less space but which really was longer than my first story. I only asked what I would have received from any first class magazine for the same material. My dealings—which only consisted in my naming my price and handing the MS (unread) in response to an invitation from Jennings—were with Jones, the Publisher.[3]

I think *you* ought to get more, as you are much more valuable to a newspaper than I am.[4] I certainly shall say so, if they condescend to consult me. Of one thing you may be certain, *I* shall keep up the market price—I can afford, less than you even, to lower it, for, as you know I write slowly and with exceeding labor. More than that I think that you and I owe it a duty to our profession to keep up its dignity at least in this way—and to the crowd of traders this way is the most telling. And still more—you and I have raised the compensation of other literary men about 50 per cent, by simply demanding and *getting* these prices.

Of course the other fellows dont see this. A day or two after it was reported in the papers that I received $400 for a poem in the *Atlantic*[5] a poet cut me dead in the street, and afterwards wrote a savage *critique* in wh. he endeavored to show how much a line I asked and that it wasn't worth the money. Yet I happen to know that he asked and received $50 more for his own stuff—in consequence of what he was pleased to term my "insolence"—for his publisher told me so with the added remark that I "was ruining his trade." Another publisher told me that you and I had "spoiled" the market—"men that were content with $2.50 a page now asked $5.00," because you and I asked $50.

You know as well as I that a man couldnt get $50 a page if he turned them out every day—and that even at these extravagant prices I make barely a decent living by my work in the magazines. Please God, with my novel—if I ever get it done—I'll be able to pay my debts and lay something by. And yet there are people who hearing that I got $500 for a story of 8 pp. imagine I'm rolling in wealth, and rush to me for a donation of $100 to "assist struggling genius &c. &c."

Of course all this is confidential. You will continue to inform people that I habitually turn out my $50 page per day and that it is my usual custom to eat from gold plate with a butler in a white cravat before me. That you have always deplored my extravagant prices, and that only personal friendship kept you from doing my work at one third the price in the interests of literature.

Raymond tells me you have dramatized your last book and that its good.[6] I never thought of you in that way. I dare say you will get before the footlights before I do—but the stage is large and there is audience for us both. Wherefore go on, my dear boy, and conquer. No one will applaud louder than myself—among the *claque*.

I'm sorry to hear of the exceeding insecurity in the supply of natural nourishment for your latest born.[7] I've been through all that—and have walked Bellevue Hospital at night through the female wards looking for the biped cow, with a telegram from my wife in my pocket that my poor little girls life hung upon that chance.[8] I never before analyzed the sensations I used to experience on beholding the female breast; I am satisfied now that what I thought was frivolity and weakness was simply the premonition of the father.

Heaven send your little one a good cow—who doesnt make too much of her importance to your well being. Give my best regards and Mrs Hartes quickest sympathies to your wife. My own house is, and has been all summer but little better than a hospital. Mrs Harte has been very sick, my mother and stepfather both old,[9] are very infirm, and the doctors horse stops of his own accord at our gate. For myself I'm very blue and dyspeptic, but for all that, dear Clemens,

Always yours
Bret Harte

Provenience: Bancroft (Mark Twain Papers).

1. See note 2 to letter 53.

2. "A Passage in the Life of Mr. John Oakhurst," *New York Times*, 28 June 1874, p. 2, col. 1–p. 3, col. 1.

3. Louis J. Jennings (1836–93) was senior editor of the *New York Times*. George Jones (1811–91) was the majority stockholder.

4. BH in effect explains how to negotiate terms with the *New York Times*, for which Clemens would soon write a pair of sketches, "On Accident Insurance" and "Sociable Jimmy."

5. See note 1 to letter 54.

6. The comic actor John T. Raymond (1836–87) was best known for his role as Colonel Sellers in Clemens's dramatization of *The Gilded Age*, first staged at the Park Theatre in New York on 16 September 1874. BH's comment tends to support the theory that Clemens did not merely put his name on G. S. Densmore's adaptation of the novel that Raymond had performed in San Francisco but substantially rewrote the script. See also Duckett, 120–21.

7. Clara Clemens (1874–1962) had been born the previous June 8.

8. BH wrote Minna Godwin on 7 July 1872 (Bryant-Godwin Collection, Rare Books and Manuscripts Division, New York Public Library, Astor, Lenox and Tilden Foundations) that his daughter Jessamy's "critical condition has kept Mrs Harte a close prisoner, and myself a walker of hospitals in quest of a wet-nurse—wh. the Doctor says is all that will ensure the baby's recovery."

9. BH's mother died at his home in Morristown on 4 April 1875. BH's stepfather, Col. Andrew Williams, died in Oakland, California, on 19 January 1876.

57. TO W. D. HOWELLS, 8 SEPTEMBER 1874

713 Broadway, N.Y.
Septem 8th/74

My dear Howells,

When I tell you that, since my arrival East, I have never received so small an offer for any story as that made to me by Mr Houghton;[1] that the lowest offer from any magazine or newspaper was $150 *more* than his, and that before sending it to you I had already refused $450 for the MS that I might make it the basis of terms with the *Atlantic*, you can readily imagine that I was considerably exasperated, and I think justly so, to have waited a week for such a reply.[2]

I do not question Mr Houghton's right to appraise my work by its value to his magazine, but before soliciting exclusive contributions from a popular author it seems to me that he ought to have informed himself of the prices they are in the habit of receiving. I thought I had guarded against such a contingency by first giving my price to you before offering to treat with the *Atlantic* on general terms. To oblige you I sent the MS for examination—which I have never been required to do before by any editor or publisher. My stories have always been *contracted for, accepted* and the *price fixed* before I had put pen to paper.

I thank you for returning the MS promptly. *The N. Y. Times* took it, without examination, for $400—which was all I asked for it from them, as they were full and preoccupied with other stories when I proposed to write this for them.[3] I had no time to spend nor inclination to hawk my wares further, so I contented myself with losing $50 and a weeks time for the pleasure of knowing Mr Houghton's valuation of my services in the *Atlantic*.

I dont blame you, my dear Howells, and I believe you acted conscientiously and for my best as you regarded it. I think too, *I* did wrong in accepting Mr Houghton's Yankee cheapening of my poem from $200 to $125,[4] but I do wish you lived out of a literary atmosphere which seems to exclude any vision of a broader literary world beyond,—its methods, profits and emoluments. But this is treason!—

Ever Yours
Bret Harte

P.S. A horrible thought strikes me that perhaps Mr Houghton believes that it was worth $300 to me to appear in the *Atlantic*! The *Times* paid me $600 for "the Rose of Tuolumne" $500 for "John Oakhurst."[5] Scribner paid me $1000 for "Fiddletown"—16 pp. long and $500 for the "Monte Flat Pastoral," 7 pp.[6]

Provenience: Harvard (bMS Am 1784 [210]). By permission of the Houghton Library, Harvard University.

1. Henry O. Houghton (1823–95), a principal owner of Hurd & Houghton, the new publishers of the *Atlantic Monthly*.

2. BH had written Howells on 28 August 1874 to offer "The Fool of Five Forks" to the *Atlantic* for five hundred dollars. Howells had replied on 1 September 1874 that BH should first submit the manuscript: "It is indispensible that I should see this story before asking the publishers to buy it at an extraordinary price." If BH "were writing exclusively for us, it would be another matter," he added. Howells had in fact tendered BH an exclusive contract with Hurd & Houghton to write for the *Atlantic* (at much less money than he had commanded under his 1871–72 contract with Fields, Osgood & Co.) but BH had declined the offer. Howells had begged BH to reply no later than 7 September 1874—"After that it will not be so important." See William J. Scheick, "William Dean Howells to Bret Harte: A Missing Letter," *American Literary Realism* 9 (Summer 1976):277. Howells subsequently wrote Houghton's partner, Melancthon M. Hurd (b. 1828), that his "Bret Harte negotiations" had fallen through and that instead he had engaged Clemens to write a series of sketches for the *Atlantic* (*Life in Letters*, I, 194). That is, Twain's "Old Times on the Mississippi" appeared in the magazine in lieu of regular contributions by BH.

3. "The Fool of Five Forks," *New York Times*, 20 Sept. 1874, p. 2, col. 1–p. 3, col. 1.

4. "Ramon" would be BH's last contribution to the *Atlantic* 34 (Oct 1874):465–67.

5. See note 2 to letter 53 and note 2 to letter 56.

6. BH alludes to "An Episode of Fiddletown," *Scribner's* 6 (Aug.–Oct. 1873):433–39, 576–82, 696–703; and "A Monte Flat Pastoral," *Scribner's* 7 (Jan. 1874):343–50.

58. TO ANNA HARTE, 7 NOVEMBER 1874

Macon, Ga.
Novem. 7th/74

My dear Nan,

I found yours of the 30th awaiting me here, and telegraphed this morning acknowledging it. I trust you have Bliss's draft by this time;

I think it would have been paid simply on your telegram signed by my name. At all events you must have received the other $100 long before I received yours.

I have no engagement until the 9th at Montgomery, Ala, and will probably rest here quietly to-day and to-morrow. I abandoned the idea of Savannah, as I was fearful of making a pecuniary failure there on account of the brief time necessarily given to the announcement of my lecture—only two days. It was provoking;—I wanted to see Savannah, and wanted the $150 it ought to have yielded me, but I did not dare to take the risk on my own account at so short notice. But I am full of the idea of making it the excuse for a little trip down here later in the season with *you*. I want *you* to see something that I have seen here.—I want *you* to share the strange experience I have had. I think you would be affected very much as I have been.

I have had several applications to lecture here at different places, but none of them could be arranged to suit the dates of my present trip. Perhaps I could arrange for two or three later—still I would be content to come down for about 10 days to Savannah for only that one lecture, if we could manage to come here together. Think of it well. I believe it would do you "a heap of good" and there is no roughness in the journey, that your condition would make dangerous.[1]

I seem to have been away from home a year.[2] Never before in any trip has my experience been crowded so full of strange observation and impressions. Since I left Louisville I appear to be traveling in a foreign land, and among a foreign people. I am too full of it to talk about it—I have done nothing—I can do nothing but absorb. I have tried to write, but my novel seems a far-off thing; even my lecture never before appeared so vapid. How could I expect to interest a people who were infinitely quainter more original, more pathetic, more ludicrous than the life I had to talk about. Perhaps I am only lazy—affected by the climate which seems to me the most perfect realization of an indolent luxurious lotus eating dream. It is Indian Summer here—an Indian summer, purged of all grossness and asperity; dependent upon no beauty of coloring or fascination of any particular sense, but affecting you in the subtlest and most intoxicating way through all the senses, and lapping your nerves into a most delicious and profound tranquility. No wonder the people are what they are!—no wonder they stare with great hollow eyes at the profound statesmen of the North who project theories for their well doing based upon the temperature of New England and the habits of labor. They dont know how to work here. Their attempts at what they conceive to be it are indescribably amusing. I have watched them and heard them talk about it, until I was divided between a laugh and a cry—as indeed I have been continually divided ever since I came here. I cannot keep the smile from my lips when I am with them—or the moisture from my eyes when I think of them, alone. They are so shiftless, so helpless—so like spoiled and petted children—who have been suddenly punished and brought face to face with duty that I cant think of them seriously as men and women. And more mysterious than all, their unrestrained and continual familiarity with the negro has wrought between them a strange weird sympathy and even affection which neither slavery *nor freedom* has changed, and which makes their fate almost identical. What that fate is to be, God knows!—I dare not think. The outlook is hopeless.

You wonder, dear Nan, to hear me talk so strongly of a political question—knowing how little interest I have in it usually.[3] But I never before had such a fateful problem brought before my eyes—I never before stood by the bedside of a ruined and slowly dying people. If I were a statesman I should devote my life to save them. I can think of no loftier ambition for any man—any Northern man I mean—for they are helpless. Any Northern man who was large enough to see that it is not only the ex slave to be saved but the ex master.

And the "nigger"—the innocent, miserable wretched degraded, fore-ordained by race and instinct and climate to be forever helpless and useless as part of the nation—this "curse" lolls in the sunlight, slouches in the shadow evades his responsibilities, is truant to his duty to his future, to the north, to the South,—and is miserably free and wretchedly happy. He works only when want drives him to it and even then will drop his work to go on a picnic, or on the excursion or political meeting that occurs every day. And when he goes to the political meeting he is as likely to vote against what are called the "radicals" as he is in favor of what are believed to be his own principles. He has but one virtue—he still loves his old master—it is his *only* fidelity. And it is a fact—this was told me by a Northern man—that the ex-master is apt to be more kind, humane and considerate and less impatient than the Northern man, in his treatment of this quaint, utterly original and utterly useless people.

All through the South, over the old battle grounds, and among the very people who have fought upon them, I have been pained with the spectacle of the utter devastation and ruin brought by the war—and struck *always* with the noble resignation of those that have suffered. I have heard no complaint nor bitterness. "You will hear no unforgiveness or hatred from the men who have fought," said a confederate general to me and our own general in command at Nashville, at whose table I heard the statement, endorsed the fact. The ill-feeling, the Ku Klux outrages, are kept up by the men who stayed at home during the war. I have never heard a word of insult or prejudice from these poor fellows—only an anxiety to show me that they had been maligned: I have listened in the cars, during this election excitement, to the conversation of old "rebels," who did not know a Northern man was listening to them, and heard only a desire for peace and the restoration of the dying South.

Personally I have been fortunate in only knowing intimately the *best*—and then only on rare occasions has there been any allusion to the past. They have been uniformly kind and courteous to me—without much effusion—and I think they like me. They are old fashioned in everything—in literature, in art, in dress,—but their manners are frank and easy. I have heard no better English spoken anywhere—nor as good—as among the wives and daughters of the state of Georgia. And in manner, natural grace and gentlewomanliness—they are far superior to the New Englander. They are not generally as pretty, but always are finer ladies. They dress outrageously—their slim purses and a certain kind of local pride keep them "ever in the rearward of the fashion," but they always act like ladies.

My audiences generally have not been large—but I get the best—and the people are few. To many, a lecture is a novelty, of which I am the sole introducer in the far South. I think the better class are always pleased—there is of course a class in the audience, who stare and—are disappointed. I am sorry to say that some of these are Northern men who have come in since the war.

But my dominant impression—above everything, is one of sadness! The wasted, ill-kept fields, the scattered negro cabins, the decaying and fallen plantation, the badly-dressed people, the helpless and hopeless negro, and the dumb ill-regulated, but earnest striving of the best people for a better state of things, and their child-like trust in the power of the great North to help them—all are pathetic and form a picture over which this tender sky and this delicous atmosphere hang with an irony that is hopeless and cruel.

But that'll do, Nan. I am so full of this that I couldn't help talking about it. Dont think I am not longing for you and the dear children, even while I am being absorbed by the life around me. Give my love to Mother and say to her I would write if I could find time. Remember me kindly to the Col. You do not say that Aunt Caddy is with you. Dont get low spirited or worry. In less than ten days I will be back again, better in health than when I left. I weigh more than I ever weighed before—152 lbs. I am a little languid from the climate, and tired from my journey, but I'm ever so much better than when I left. I enclose a draft for $150, and will send another from Montgomery.

Always, dear Nan,
Your affec.
Frank

Provenience: UVa (ALS).

1. AH is pregnant with their daughter Ethel (1875–circa 1958).

2. BH had lectured in Louisville on October 26, in Nashville on October 28, in Atlanta on November 2, in Augusta on November 3, and in Milledgeville on November 5. After leaving Macon, he would lecture in Montgomery on November 9, in Selma on November 10 and 11, and in Knoxville on November 13.

3. In a letter to AH from Macon the next day (*Letters*, 43) BH again apologized for this "long letter" with "a lot of political talk of which I was full."

59. TO FRANK H. MASON, 4 DECEMBER 1874

Saratoga Springs,
Decem. 4th/74

My dear Captain,

I received yours of the 29th ult., just as I was starting off on another raid on the Lyceums,[1] and had no time for playful dalliance. By the way there's another letter of yours that remains unanswered, but its so long ago—away back in some remote age when people used the stylus and wax tablets—that I didn't write. But I have seen Miss Hilliard[2] in N.Y. since then, and I have another letter from you, condoning my offence, and I am happy. And now I am *en route* to Buffalo and shall see Grey if he calls on me, and shall have that good luck which invariably visits on the skillful and habitual procrastinator. I only wish I could add you and your wife to my Buffalo experience. I ought to—the immortals never appear alone! If I cant have you there I'll try hard to stop over one night at Cleveland, *en route* to Chicago, which I am trying to evade, but fear I cant.[3] I want to talk to you about Southern outrages, and Watterson,[4] and Halsted,[5] and Lecture Committees, and Landlords and I have a large supply of new and unused adjectives on hand, and am filled to the brim with splenetic humors. I long for a quiet hour with you, the genial exchange of profanity and salutary description.

I have been working hard all summer and have my novel about two-thirds done. If it were not that I have the proof sheets I should not believe it. Thank you, my dear Captain, for your praise of some of my performances. Oakhursts love experiences *was* good.[6] I think yours was the first commendation I received, however.

Possibly because I am of late apt to get blue and homesick when traveling, that Fate has becalmed me for several hours here at a watering place, out of season! Think of it! Imagine the ghostly denizens of this long bleak expanse of piazza and colonnade, where the dead leaves emulate the old time rustle of the skirts of dead and gone girls. My footfall in the dining room sounded like the commandoes tread in Don Giovanni, and seemed to summon up all the ghosts again—myself among the number,—apparently much more unreal and shadowy than the others. I wonder if Lelands band[7] are not impelled to come here in their sleep and play once again in these vast hollow drawing rooms the "Thousand and One Nights" for the shadows to waltz by. It was on that chilly looking iron bench, half covered with snow that the peerless Constantina and myself sat apart from the giddy throng—or would if I hadn't been afraid that some one would tell Mrs H. of it.

Such, my dear Sir, is the effect of Congress Water,[8] four glasses, incautiously taken out of season into a dyspeptic stomach. I fear this is not entirely sentiment. I have a pain. I must close this and go to the Bar for Brandy.

In haste
Yours always
B. H.

Provenience: Fales Library, New York University (ALS).

1. BH lectured in both Buffalo and Gloversville, New York, en route to Chicago.

2. BH had met Laura Hilliard, a friend of both Mason and John Hay, during his visit to Cleveland in early 1873. See *American Literary Realism* 12 (Spring 1979):83.

3. BH lectured in Chicago on 10 December 1874. He hoped to "evade" Chicago because he feared continuing repercussions from his visit to the city in early February 1871.

4. Henry Watterson (1840–1921), editor of the *Louisville Courier-Journal*, introduced BH at his lecture in Louisville on 26 October 1874. As BH wrote his wife on 28 October 1874 (UVa), he arrived in Louisville without his trunk, but "Luckily my friend Watterson of the Louisville Journal gave me his dress suit."

5. Murat Halstead (1820–1908), editor of the *Cincinnati Commercial*, a leading Republican newspaper.

6. Mason had praised "A Passage in the Life of Mr. John Oakhurst," in the *New York Times* for 28 June 1874.

7. BH is writing from the new Union Hotel in Saratoga, owned by the seven Leland brothers. Its dining room was two hundred feet long by sixty feet wide, with ceilings twenty feet high (*Frank Leslie's Illustrated Newspaper*, 28 May 1870, 167). William W. Leland (1820–79) was the brother most closely identified with the management of the hotel. Less than three years later, the banker Joseph Seligman and his family were refused accommodations at the same hotel, a blatant act of anti-Semitism that inspired BH's satirical poem "That Ebrew Jew," Washington *Capital*, 24 June 1877, p. 4, col. 3.

8. A popular mineral water from the Congress Spring in Saratoga, New York.

60. TO THE EDITOR OF THE *BOSTON EVENING TRANSCRIPT*, 11 JANUARY 1875

Morristown, N. J., Jan. 11, 1875

My Dear Sir—I find this statement in a late number of your paper:

> Bret Harte is said to have obtained, though influential friends, a $3000 position in the New York Custom House, as a relief from pecuniary embarrassments.[1]

Although I am the subject of a good deal of easy and varied misinformation, I think you will do me the justice to admit that I am not in the habit of troubling the press with corrections. But this paragraph seems to be quite as hard upon these alleged influential friends of mine as upon myself, and I trust you will give me the space to state very earnestly and frankly that there is not one iota of truth in it. I have never been an applicant for any office whatsoever, nor has any suggestion, advice or promise of the kind intimated in that paragraph ever reached me, directly or indirectly. I have always found my profession sufficiently lucrative and, but for the gossip suggested as the origin of such a statement, quite as honorable and manly as any.

I do not know that any reader of the Transcript will sleep better tonight for this correction, but it really seems to me that justice to myself, my friends, my profession and finally, perhaps, the present Administration demands that I should correct this false and perfectly gratuitous report.

Very sincerely, dear sir,
Yours,
Bret Harte

To the Editor of the Transcript, Boston, Mass.

Provenience: *Boston Evening Transcript*, 13 Jan. 1875, p. 4, col. 2.

1. This brief news item, which has not been located in the extant files of the *Boston Evening Transcript*, apparently appeared as filler in an edition of the paper that has not been preserved. The *Springfield Republican* gave the rumor a different spin in its issue of 7 January 1875 (p. 4, col. 5): "Bret

Harte finds shelter in the New York custom house. His autograph on the monthly pay roll will be creditable to his penmanship and the government."

61. TO ANNA HARTE, CIRCA 16 MARCH 1875[1]

Tuesday noon.

My dear Nan,

I have no draft yet from Bliss—not even a letter since the telegram I sent you,—which I believe was only an excuse. He is evidently waiting until I send in the full installment of 100 pages complete and I am now writing the last 20 today, although I am so nervous I can hardly hold a pen.[2] I hear nothing from Boston.

It is hard for me—Nan—but it is worse for you, poor dear girl, alone and sick there![3] I would have returned each night, but for the expense and the certainty that my presence there without money would only provoke my creditors. God knows how you are getting on—I dare not think! I am almost beside myself with apprehension. I never will again come over here to put myself in this position. Better for me to wait there.

I shall finish the last pages today. If Bliss intends to keep his word at all—he will surely send to me by Thursday. He will have no excuse. I have spent all yesterday trying to borrow the sum—but without hope.

Keep up, Nan,—this cannot last long.

God bless you, dear,
Your own Frank

Provenience: Bancroft (MSS 77/166 C).

1. This letter is tentatively dated by reference to a letter BH wrote to Bliss on 7 March 1875 (Huntington, HM 7166), in which he indicated he had submitted forty-two pages of copy (about eleven thousand words) on 2 March 1875 and enclosed sixteen additional pages (about four thousand words). BH also reported that he would send another fifteen thousand words by March 14 to complete the installment.

2. In 1907, in his autobiographical dictation, Clemens reflected on BH's habit of working on his novel *Gabriel Conroy* only when he needed money and on Bliss's niggardliness in advancing him the money he needed: "About once a month Harte would get into desperate straits; then he would

dash off enough manuscript to set him temporarily free and carry it to Bliss and get a royalty advance. These assaults upon his prospective profits were never very large, except in the eyes of Bliss; to Bliss's telescopic vision a couple of hundred dollars that weren't due, or hadn't been earned, were a prodigious matter" (*MT in Eruption*, 280). However delinquent BH may have been in completing his novel, his misgivings about the publisher do not seem entirely misplaced. As Hamlin Hill notes, Bliss's "scruples and business ethics required constant scrutiny" (*Mark Twain's Letters to His Publishers* 1867–94 [Berkeley: University of California Press, 1967], 5).

3. BH had left his family in Morristown to work on the novel, probably in New York City.

62. TO JAMES R. OSGOOD, 18 APRIL 1875

Morristown N.J.
Apl. 18th/75

My dear Osgood,

I've forgotten whether I sent you the enclosed before. The final decision was reached last week "perpetually enjoining" the defendants, with costs &c &c. I suppose I might have recovered damages had I asked them.[1]

I am anxiously waiting the decision regarding the Lord & Taylor discussion.[2] This delay is exceedingly embarrassing to me regarding future publications in Boston. I want to bring out the book of Sketches at once. I shall see Bliss in a day or two and shall doubtless get his consent to the publication of the Sketches without reference to the priority of the novel. If *that*—ie. the novel—is a success it will help the later sale of the sketches. My intention is to publish the sketches *without any* new story prefacing the others; I am satisfied that in the case of "Mrs Skaggs' Husbands" the freshness of the titular story did not help the sale of the book one iota.[3] On the contrary, being new, it called the attention and objection of the critics to the other stories being old, and gave them a chance to say it was a publishers trick. I think it better the book should be *all* original or *all* reprint.

Yet this immediate publication depends on the Lord & Taylor decision. If it is decided that they can, without separate process, seize all profits that are to accrue on my copyrights present or to come, I shall not trouble myself to provide pabulum for these cormorants. Apart from their hoggishness—I dont think it is just to the few of my creditors who have been patient and obliging. I will give up all further publishing in the state of Massachusetts rather than submit to this Yankee gouging.

I think there is another statement due in May. Suppose you forward a/c with cheque to Walker,[4] under the same conditions as before, *a little before the 1st or the day specified in our contract*. That is, if it be convenient to you.

Always Yours
B. H.

Provenience: General Manuscript Collection, Rare Book and Manuscript Library, Columbia University (ALS).

1. BH sends Osgood a clipping from a New York paper (e.g., "Bret Harte's Mliss," *New York Times*, 27 Apr. 1875, p. 2, col. 3) detailing his successful suit to enjoin Robert M. DeWitt from selling the "completed" "M'liss." See note 5 to letter 44.

2. BH's tailors had sued him in New York City Superior Court in 1874 and been awarded $1153.76 in claims. BH had tried to avoid payment on jurisdictional grounds: by living in New Jersey and collecting royalties from Massachusetts. Lord & Taylor then sued Harte and Osgood in Massachusetts to recover the debt, and the dispute had dragged on for months. BH wrote Osgood on 8 January 1875 (UVa) that "the Lord & Taylor men hang back on the proposed compromise. If they wont take it, I shall guard myself in any arrangement I may make with you for a new book—as I can legally." In a letter to Osgood on 26 May 1875 (*Letters*, 52), he derisively referred again to "the Jarndyce & Jarndyce decision," the interminable lawsuit Dickens satirized in *Bleak House*. Finally, on 4 September 1875 the Massachusetts Supreme Court rendered summary judgment against Harte and ordered Osgood "to account with the plaintiffs for such sums of money as may now be due or hereafter fall due to Harte under the contracts, until his debt to the plaintiffs, with the interest thereon and the costs of this proceeding, shall be fully paid" (*Massachusetts Reports* 118 [June–Oct. 1875]:271–74).

3. See note 4 to letter 36.

4. BH's lawyer, Stephen A. Walker.

63. TO ELISHA BLISS, JR., 8 MAY 1875

N.Y.
May 8th 75

My dear Bliss,

I enclose remainder of chap. Mr Smith of Scribners Monthly writes to me that he shall renew with you the negotiations of last summer regarding the publication of the story in his magazine.

I do *not* think it a good place, but I defer to your better judgement and larger experience. If you think favorably of it you and I will talk over terms.[1]

In haste
B.H.

Provenience: Huntington (Box 4, Charles M. Kozlay Collection).

1. According to Clemens, Bliss "became alarmed" when he "realized that *Gabriel Conroy* was a white elephant. The book was nearing a finish, but, as a subscription book, its value had almost disappeared" so "he sold the serial rights" in it "to one of the magazines . . . and a good trade it was, for the serial rights were not really worth the money" (*MT in Eruption*, 280–81). Incredibly, Roswell Smith of Scribner & Co. agreed to pay six thousand dollars, to be divided equally between Bliss and BH, for rights to the novel, and it was serialized in *Scribner's* between November 1875 and August 1876. In the end, the arrangement proved a mixed blessing: Bliss delayed publication of *Gabriel Conroy* in book form until 2 September 1876, almost exactly four years to the day after BH had contracted to write it. The contract specified that Bliss would pay a royalty of 7 1/2 percent on U.S. sales and 10 percent on sales in England (*MT-H Letters*, I, 92). However, Bliss never afterwards supplied BH with a sales statement or paid him royalties because, it seems, the book did not earn sufficient royalties to cover Bliss's advances to the author prior to publication. According to extant records, *Gabriel Conroy* sold only 3,354 copies in its first year in print (Hamlin Hill, *Mark Twain and Elisha Bliss* [Columbia: University of Missouri Press, 1964], 92); and when BH left for Europe in 1878 he still owed about twenty-five hundred dollars to the American Publishing Co., a debt he never fully repaid (Ballou, 252). See also letter 71 and accompanying notes. BH was predictably outraged in 1884 when he learned that Bliss had sold dramatic rights to the story without either consulting him or sharing the proceeds. See letters 130 and 158.

64. TO JOHN H. CARMANY, 13 SEPTEMBER 1875

Cohasset, Mass.
Septem. 13th/75

My dear Mr Carmany,—

It is some two weeks since I received your note. At that time I was exceedingly busy with the last act of my new Play,[1] and as your wish for an answer by telegraph was only based on the answer being affirmative, I thought it better to wait than send you a curt "no," without explanation or reason, which was about all my preoccupation would then allow.

The Play is done now and I have time to thank you for your pleasant offer, and give you my reasons for saying "No."[2]

1st. Although you have mentioned no terms, knowing as I do, the prices that are considered fair literary compensation in California—knowing that however liberal you may wish to be—you must as a business man be limited to the conditions, ideas and patronage of the people among whom you live and do business, I am satisfied that as a business proposition I could not accept your terms. In other words I can make here, by my pen, with less drudgery, with more security, honor and respect thrice as much as I could make in California at the head of the Overland.—taking the past as an estimate. So far as I can see the tastes, habits and ideas of your people have not changed since you and I were forced to part company, because I could better myself here.

Second, If we could come to terms—I do not see how I could make the Overland's "sanctum" the literary Mecca of the West, after the Prophet had been so decidedly renounced by his disciples. I think that even a California community would see the ridiculousness of my returning to a magazine that had, under the thin disguise of literary criticism, abused me at the *expense of its own literary record.*[3] And even if this stultification should not be inconsistent with Californian ideas—I should lose, as I would deserve, the honorable respect of many thousand readers East who were more shocked than even myself at that spectacle of shameless ingratitude, and blundering malice!

Permit me to thank you again for your offer. I believe you are very honest and manly in it. Nothing but a very positive preference for myself, and a kind disposition to confess a mistake—which however I think you yourself will see is *irretrievable*—would have prompted your pleasant offer.

Truly, dear Mr Carmany,
Yours
Bret Harte

Provenience: Bancroft (Overland Monthly Records, MSS C-H 97).

1. BH moved to Cohasset, Massachusetts, in July 1875, near Marie Villa, the home of the actor Lawrence Barrett (1838–91), to work on the script of his play *Two Men of Sandy Bar* for the comic actor Stuart Robson (1836–1903). BH had known Barrett in San Francisco as early as 19 January 1869, when the actor read BH's dedicatory poem at the opening of the California Theatre, and Barrett had witnessed the signing of the contract for the play between BH and Robson on 13 October 1875. According to the *Chicago Tribune* (4 July 1876, p. 7, cols. 1–2), Robson and Barrett then "beguiled Mr. Harte to the sea-side" to write the play.

2. Carmany readily conceded in later years that "the glory of the *Overland* went with Bret Harte" (Cummins, 145). After failing to entice BH back to San Francisco to assume editorial control of the magazine, Carmany suspended its publication at the end of 1875. He was often quoted later to the effect that he was "the man who spent $30,000 to make Bret Harte famous."

3. After BH's departure from California in 1871, the *Overland* reviewed his books quite critically. See the notices in the magazine of *East and West Poems*, 8 (Jan. 1872):97–98; of *Mrs. Skaggs's Husbands and Other Sketches*, 10 (Apr. 1873):390–91; and especially of *Echoes of the Foothills*, 14 (Mar. 1875):292–93. The latter review, which particularly galled BH, compared him with "the sputtering falling stick that went up so lately [in] one blazing pyrotechnic glory. . . . Bret Harte, *the* Bret Harte, is gone 'where the woodbine twineth,' where the plesiosaurus hunts the dodo."

65. TO LAWRENCE BARRETT, 22 SEPTEMBER 1875

Cohasset, Mass.
Septem. 22/75

My dear Barrett,

Your good wife has kept us thoughtfully advised of your

California movements, but I was quite taken aback by the unexpected alternative of a letter from you in the midst of your business. It has knocked a few lines of reply out of me—the laziest and meanest of correspondents.

Your success in S.F. did not astonish me.[1] When your wife showed me your telegram about poor Ralston's death,[2] I told her that it would not affect your engagement. A living man is always vastly the superior of a dead one in California, and I have no doubt, my dear fellow, that you, the player, thought more frequently of Ralston that first night than did any of the audience.

Of course, I know nothing more of Ralston's death, or what preceded it, than what the California newspapers delivered to us here, but familiar as I am with California lying—the exceeding awkwardness of and bungling of the despatches astonished even me. I frankly came to the conclusion, that having been for many years, the great and accepted exponent and illustrator of California energy and materialism and success, he was at last in a moment of trial, deserted and forsaken by the very men who had praised him and called themselves his disciples. You know I never admired Ralston for that which so many thought admirable—and always doubted his good influence on the character of the people—but he was the best that they had—and he lived and died a bold, self-sustained, proud man, as incapable of any moral meanness as he was of any lofty enthusiasm; as direct and prompt and ready as people are apt to be with short aims—in fact about as nearly a hero as California can make one. And now it appears that the *Bulletin* is to bear all the blame of everything! What perfect children they are out there!

To return, California-fashion, to our matter. *The play is done.* Ten days ago I read the last act to Robson, and day before yesterday he took the altered, revised and alas!—deeply *excised*—copy in print to N.Y. As I first handed it to him in type, it would play about 4¼ hours. I have boldly—*heroically*! cut it to the extent of 17 pages. It is more than assault and battery—it is mayhem! And I am afraid it too long now. Nothing more can be worked upon its defenseless body but *dramacide*! Still if you were here—I should boldly hand you over the scissors. I fear it will be *too* late to send you a copy for revision.[3]

There has been a slight improvement in our hospital on Skunkmill Heights.[4] The patients are convalescing—and only one new case, my stepfather, who rashly visited us is reported![5] We are looking anxiously forward to the 1st of October, and relief in some *inland* mountain village, where we trust to gain sufficient strength to get to New York. The southwest wind, which always blew in the dry days has left us in the first chilly Autumn days. The wind is East now, and the house as unbearable from cold as it once was from heat! We are out of water! Another skunk has fallen in the well! "Bring me no more reports!"[6]

Your wife has been very noble and neighborly—and has always been ready to drop in with a plaster or linger with a box of pills. I dont know what we would have done without her. Anna has been very patient and long-suffering, but even she has expressed her opinion that she did not like Cohasset.

I am glad you met Sam Williams.[7] He is one of the best of fellows and the most loyal of friends. I wish he were as near to me in person as he is in spirit—but I'll hold up here and write to him at once.

Yours ever
B. H.

Provenience: Special Collections and Archives, Knox College Library, Galesburg, Ill. (ALS).

1. Barrett opened a four-week engagement at the California Theatre in San Francisco on 6 September 1875.

2. William C. Ralston (b. 1826), the manager of the Bank of California in San Francisco, died on 27 August 1875, an apparent suicide, the day after the bank failed.

3. Robson later claimed that "in its first form" BH's play "would have occupied six hours. I suggested changes, but Harte fought against the alteration of a line. . . . As fast as the play was written it was sent to Osgood & Co. and put in type, and the proof-sheets furnished us. I sent the play in this form to Lawrence Barrett, then in California, who made the changes he thought necessary to get it into working order" (*San Francisco Chronicle*, 14 Oct. 1877, p. 1, col. 9).

4. BH had written Barrett on 11 July 1875 (Hampden-Booth) to ask him and his wife, Mollie, to furnish the house he had rented for the season: "[W]e must leave the furnishing entirely to you. Mrs. H. places an abiding confidence in your wife's judgment. Tell her to go on in her noble work. The eyes of posterity are upon her. Her mission divinely appointed, is to furnish houses for B.H." When BH left at the end of the summer, he was

in arrears to both the landlord and the furniture dealer. "[T]o avoid appearing in an unpleasant controversy over bills," Barrett "paid the house rent and the furniture bills" ("Bret Harte's Old Friends," *San Francisco Examiner*, 1 May 1892, p. 10, cols. 1–2).

5. See note 9 to letter 56.

6. *Macbeth*, V. iii. 1.

7. Samuel Williams (1824?–81) was a reporter and book editor for the San Francisco *Daily Evening Bulletin* and, not incidentally, one of BH's creditors when he left California. See William C. Barrett, "Samuel Williams, Journalist," *Californian* 4 (Oct 1881):323–30; Charles Howard Shinn, "A Journalist of the Old School," *Springfield Republican*, 1 June 1890, p. 2, cols. 4–5; and "Bret Harte's Old Friends," *San Francisco Examiner*, 1 May 1892, p. 10, col. 1.

66. TO ANNIE ADAMS FIELDS, 27 SEPTEMBER 1875

Cohasset, Mass.
Septem. 27/75

My dear Mrs Fields,

I know all! I know now why Fields has become a popular lecturer on authors, living and dead.[1] He is only basely utilizing—for a puerile, personal, pecuniary purpose the faculty of elegant compliment which belongs to *you*! *He*—this wild Manchester Pirate and Rover of the Gloucester Shores!—is demanding from a timorous and credulous public seventy-five cents, (Reserved Seats, one dollar) for the graceful compliment and kindly and truthful appreciation which drops spontaneously from your tongue and pen. He lies in wait, apparently engaged in the preoccupation of hitching his trousers, while you and I are talking, and appropriates to his own aggrandizement the good things that your good heart and good taste dictate. He, with a wicked, salty eye—apparently scanning the horizon for wrecks or a change in the weather—overlooks your kind pages, and—is—a Pirate still![2]

Dear Mrs Fields, I have not forgotten, if you have, that when I published my *first* book, I received as kind, as considerate, as charming and as graceful a compliment in the same handwriting and over the same signature as your last—and I know you will believe that I am doubly grateful.

But then—**He**—*He* had not tasted the intoxication of salty seas; his trousers were securely sustained as was his moral character—He was of the Earth—Earthy,[3] and not of the sea—salty. No wild dream of Lafitte or Kid or Blackbeard had entered his brain. He passed for a peaceful man—with a tendency to "jibe" but not in a nautical sense.

I have excited the pallid envy of countless householders—among them the mistress of my own house—by extravagant descriptions of Gambrel Cottage and its interior. They have accepted everything but the India matting on the wainscotting of the halls. There they pause, breathless and incredulous! Then I sling in an account of the procession of heathen deities in outline on the entablature. Then they succumb! And I stand over them, with a continuous and florid narrative of the hall window and its red cushions, and retire, with the field to myself![4]

I spent two—to me—delightful hours with Mr Longfellow on Saturday last. He was looking so much better than I had reason to expect that I do hope he saw some of the joy in my eyes. He was as sweet, as fine, as ever—I could find no better simile than his own fancy of the Schoolmaster's compliment to the "fair Almira"—"as pure as water and as good as bread."[5] I should not have intruded upon him, but that, breakfasting with Lord Houghton and his son on Friday in N.Y.,[6] I had partly promised to go with them to luncheon at his house Saturday, but they failed to come. So I had him all to myself—the luncheon meanwhile getting cold in the other room and Longfellow patient and polite in the library—for I could not prolong my visit until the hour of the feast.

We expect to leave here on the 1st prox. and go to Berkshire for a couple of weeks—in quarantine—before we go to N.Y. But keep your weather eye—pardon the nautical phrase which slips naturally from my pen!—well open, from your salon window in Charles street, and some day you may see straggling into it—*First*: Mrs H. proudly bearing her last, at the heart,[7] followed by Eliza, the nurse, with infantive accompaniments, *Second* Lilla, a maid, leading Jessamy my second daughter, Third, Franky and Wodie, firing crackers, and attended by Policemen, R[ight] & L[eft], and after a decent interval—calm, irresponsible for the foregoing, an dwearing a jaunty, unmarried, rakish air,—

Your friend,
Bret Harte

P.S. Give my love to your husband. You may add, generally "Belay Avast! Ahoy!"—or any other nautical expression which an extended reading of the works of Captain Marryatt,[8] Fenimore Cooper,[9] & Professor Ingraham[10] may suggest.

Provenience: Huntington (FI 1086).

1. After his retirement from publishing, Fields became a popular speaker on literary topics.

2. Annie Fields noted in her diary on 18 September 1875 that BH "was bubbling over with fun, full of the most natural and unexpected sallies" during a recent visit. BH "said he was surprised to find J. T. F[ields] without a sailor's jacket and collar" (Howe, 242).

3. I Corinthians 15:47. See also note 3 to letter 100.

4. James and Annie Fields had moved into their new summer home near Manchester, Massachusetts, in July 1875. Originally named Gambrel Cottage after the shape of its roof, the house was better known as Thunderbolt Hill after the site on which it was built.

5. Longfellow suffered from neuralgia for most of 1875. BH quotes his poem "The Birds of Killingworth." See also letter 70, which quotes the same phrase, and accompanying notes 4 and 5.

6. Richard Monckton Milnes (1809–85), Lord Houghton, visited New York in October-November 1875. He reciprocated BH's hospitality in London in April 1879. See T. Wemyss Reid, *The Life, Letters, and Friendships of Richard Monckton Milnes, First Lord Houghton* (New York: Cassell, 1891), II, 385. See also note 4 to letter 101 and letter 226.

7. Ethel Harte.

8. Frederick Marryat (1792–1848), popular author of *Newton Forster* (1832), *Mr. Midshipman Easy* (1836), and other sea tales. BH had parodied Marryat in "Midshipman Breezy" in his *Condensed Novels*.

9. James Fenimore Cooper (1789–1851) was not only the author of the Leatherstocking series, but of such sea narratives as *The Pilot* (1823) and *The Red Rover* (1827).

10. Joseph Holt Ingraham (1809–66), author of such sea tales as *Lafitte* (1836), *Captain Kyd* (1839), and *The Chameleon, or The Mysterious Cruiser* (1848).

67. TO FRANK H. MASON, 30 SEPTEMBER 1875

Cohasset, Mass.
Septem 30th/75

My dear Captain,

If the voice of an unfettered Press has reached you with the intimation that "the Play" was done, I write this to corroborate it;—if, as is more likely, it has stated that somebody else has written a play for Stuart Robson, or that Stuart Robson has concluded to write one for me, I beg to here unequivocally deny it.

The play was done—more! *it was in type two weeks ago*, and is now in the managers hands.[1]

I have done a heap of work in the last year. Think of it!—a novel—(no slouch, but a 600 page—printed page—story, and d——d good if I say it!)—and a play of 100 pages. As to the latter's merit, I cant say—the actors like it and the man who bespoke it is satisfied. But I beg you again, my dear Captain, to think of the *quantity of matter* hammered out by me. 600 pages!—No!—you will not believe it![2]

All this is only preliminary to the statement that I intend to have a holiday, and come to Cleveland—soon. When shall it be?

My love to your wife & Miss Hilliard

Always, dear Captain,
Yours
B. H.

P.S. If you write, address me, as usual, at 713 Broadway (Dutton's). I leave here for a few days stay in Western Massachusetts, and then go to N.Y.

Provenience: Fales Library, New York University (ALS).

1. Annie Fields noted in her diary for 18 September 1875 that BH had brought manuscript copies of both his novel *Gabriel Conroy* and *Two Men of Sandy Bar*, "which are just now finished," to their home outside Manchester, Massachusetts, "for us to read. He has evidently enjoyed the play, and he enjoys the fame and the money they both bring him" (Howe, 243). The manager to whom BH refers is probably A. H. Palmer (1838–1905), who ran the Union Square Theatre in New York, where BH's play opened on 28 August 1876 after a brief trial in Chicago the previous July. As a letter from Leonard Glover, manager of the Adelphi Theatre in Chicago,

to Palmer makes clear (7 Aug. 1876, Hampden-Booth), Palmer tried to recruit a "play doctor" to revise BH's script before it was staged.

2. BH fails to add the one hundred manuscript pages of the play to the six hundred manuscript pages of the novel.

68. TO JAMES R. OSGOOD, 6 October 1875

Lenox, Mass.
Oct 6th/75

My dear Osgood—

Please settle the Redpath suit for $205 as proposed.[1] Pay it out of the $250 held by you as security for the Redpath bond. You will see by your a/c that the transfer of that amount antedates by a long time any proceeding of Lord & Taylors and cannot be accounted for to them. Send me the balance $45—and, by the way, you did not send me the balance of the advance on Tales of the Argonauts.[2] Is there a balance? I am short of funds.

I really do not see wherein Lord & Taylor's proposition differs at all from the remedy they expect to obtain by law—viz. all that is due me now, and all that is coming to me until the debt be paid.[3] I believe the judgment is about $1100. There is not more than half that sum due now on copyright, and I cannot see that it makes any difference if they take that by process of law, or by compromise—except that by law they might be kept longer about it. The notes at 6 and 12 months represent about the sums that will become due by copyright at those times. Indeed altogether the proposition reads to me that I am to save them the trouble of collecting half the principal by giving it to them, and then provide them with a *better* security for the balance than the more undetermined amount of copyright—*your* endorsement.

I think I am not yet quite driven to this extremity. I have done all a poor man, with a large family, can do toward settling a debt that he cannot pay outright—but which he is able to secure to his creditor. But this proposition is a little like imposition.

I shall do no more than I find proposed. I will pay L & T. $400 cash, and $400 a year in half yearly payments of $200 ea. out of my copyright, perfectly secured, with legal interest on all over the first 400.

If they dont take that, I have legal advice that will save me paying more than the amount due at the time of the service of proceedings and amply protect me from any further trouble from them.

Will you please send me a statement of the amount due now on copyright, and the sum for which suit was brought.

Yours always
B. H.

Provenience: UVa (ALS).

1. See letter 50.

2. Osgood would publish BH's *Tales of the Argonauts and Other Sketches* in late October 1875.

3. See note 2 to letter 62.

69. TO MARY E. W. SHERWOOD, 31 OCTOBER 1875

45 Fifth Avenue,
October 31st/75

My dear Mrs Sherwood,[1]

I have dispatched your translation—and a capital one it was too—to Mr Longfellow.[2]

Of course I have intimated to him that it was my own—a little thing I tossed off in the cars—this M.E.W.S. is my "name of the pen," and was the way we used to spell "muse" in Poker Flat, where a singular proficiency with the revolver estopped any criticism of inaccuracy.

I dont fancy the horse piece as well—I mean the original not the translation. I never had a horse act in that way. But then in California I used to ride a mule. That probably prevented me from marrying an heiress. It was a mule that eventually delivered me into the hands of Mrs Harte.

That person desires me to thank you for your flowers, from wh. you will imagine she has returned from Lenox and has overlooked your systematic and continual depreciation of her husband. The baby—who, by reason of your heartless abandonment at her birth has since developed all the infantile diseases, and who gets up her teeth in a way as awful and terrifying to the beholder as Cadmus got his,—that baby is here, and I am teaching her to revile you in her lisping accents. In fact whenever she wakes up in the night screaming—and she does it pretty regularly—and neither pain nor colic seem to offer a sufficient explanation, my simple suggestion that she is objecting to Mrs Sherwood—is accepted even by the physician as a sufficient cause.

Nevertheless Mrs Harte thinks that "Lizzie" is a pretty name, and says she dont believe that you intended that (alleged) Chinese vase as a mug, knowing as you do that our family preferences have always been for silver.

The object of all this impertinence being that you will probably come to 45 Fifth Avenue during the next few days to find out what it means. When I shall prudently be out—but

Always, dear Mrs Sherwood,
Yours
Bret Harte

Mrs Sherwood.

Provenience: Bancroft (MSS C-H 57).

1. The poet Mary Elizabeth Wilson Sherwood (1830–1903). See also Sherwood's memoir "Bret Harte," *New York Times Saturday Review of Books*, 10 May 1902, 308.

2. BH sent a copy of Sherwood's translation of Gustave Nadaud's "Carcassonne" to Longfellow with a cover letter also dated 31 October 1875 (Bancroft, MSS 77/166 C).

70. TO HENRY WADSWORTH LONGFELLOW, 9 NOVEMBER 1875

45 Fifth Avenue
Novem. 9th/75

My dear Mr. Longfellow,

I enclose Mrs Sherwood's delighted permission to you to use her poem and her name in your collection.[1]

The mysterious gloves were mine. You may safely lift them from your mind and table, and put them aside—leaving me the privilege of boring you some day under the hollow pretext of recovering them.

The "Pandora" came duly to hand yesterday.[2] My boys were sensibly touched with your kindness, and freighted me with their overflowing thanks. And when I told them you were preparing a book that would not only make Geography easy,—but charming!—I think they advanced you above George Washington.[3]

Let me thank you in a somewhat larger way for Pandora. I have often wondered if you cared to know how your work affected a writer like myself, whose methods, habits, experiences and education have been so widely different from your own. If you *do* care wont you let me say very frankly—without attitude of criticism, analysis, or even explanation—that you reach and touch me always with the simple directness of a summer landscape, an evening sky, or a sky larks song. You rest me as Nature rests me always—on a higher plane than my ordinary level, but always without the feverish processes of exaltation or preliminary delirium, something better than repose, a rest that has the slight beating of the spirits wings below it. I dont know that I make myself clear, but when I add that I always feel in your poetry a quality that my critical faculty and even my sympathy with your Art cannot analyze,—that you make me sometimes suspect I have a moral nature, and occasionally that I am a poet, perhaps I am more intelligible, and weak and human.[4]

You remember that the Schoolmaster in the "Birds of Killingworth" said of the fair Almira that she was "as pure as water and as good as bread."[5] Perhaps that is what I am trying to say of your poetry. And after having told you how that poetry affects me, I add that bread and water, however pure and good, has not been my regular mental diet, and that it has been my literary habit—like that Prince in the Arabian Nights—to put "pepper in the cream tarts" of my own composition,[6] you will appreciate the praise of this paradox.

I had no idea of saying all this when I began to thank you for your simple courtesies. But I do not know why I should be ashamed to say to a man who has given me so much honest pleasure how I love and respect him. You have done me much good, dear Mr Longfellow. God grant you may live long enough to get an equal acknowledgment from all you have benefitted.

Always
Your friend,
Bret Harte

Provenience: Harvard (bMS Am 1340.2 [2569]). By permission of the Houghton Library, Harvard University.

1. Sherwood's translation of Nadaud's "Carcassonne" subsequently appeared in Longfellow's edition of *Poems of Places: France* (Boston: Osgood, 1877), I, 96–98. Longfellow also reprinted twenty of BH's lyrics in the thirty-one volumes of *Poems of Places.*

2. Longfellow, *The Masque of Pandora and Other Poems* (Boston: Osgood, 1875).

3. In a letter to Longfellow dated 31 October 1875 (Bancroft, MSS 77/166 C), BH remarked that his sons "still remember the gentleman who spoke so pleasantly to them at Cambridge, and whom I think they dimly connect with George Washington."

4. As Howells recalled (*Literary Friends*, 295), "Longfellow alone escaped the corrosive touch of [BH's] subtle irreverence, or, more strictly speaking, had only the effect of his reverence. That gentle and exquisitely modest dignity of Longfellow's he honored with as much veneration as it was in him to bestow." In his memoir "Longfellow" (*Good Words* 23 [June 1882]:385–87), BH declared that the poet was "the man I most revered."

5. BH was fond of quoting this phrase, especially to Longfellow. See letter 66 and accompanying note 5. BH also quoted the phrase in his memoir "Longfellow" cited in note 4 above.

6. In his 17 September 1867 letter to the *Springfield Republican*, BH had written that "Californians, like the Arabian Prince, prefer their cream tarts with pepper" (*BH's California*, 140).

71. TO SAMUEL L. CLEMENS, 24 DECEMBER 1875

45 Fifth Avenue,
Decem. 24th 75

My dear Clemens,

Do you remember that some years ago when Bliss wanted a book from me for his House, you told him you would use your influence provided he did the decent and honorable thing to you in some contested point of business? Well, you remember I wrote a letter to him saying "that on the representations of my friend Mr. Clemens &c., I would accept &c." I remind you of this only that I want to ask a similar favor at your hands—I want you to use your influence with him for *me.*

I have asked Bliss to advance me a further $1000 on my copyright of "Gabriel Conroy." He has already advanced between $3 & $4000,[1] but by reason of his contract with Scribner & Co, has received $3000 of it back, so that his actual risk is only about $1500—if as much. Indeed, if his representations to me of the sale of his books are correct, he runs no risk whatever.

Bliss thinks he can't do it. I think he *can*. I want you to think he can. I need the money 1st, because my play at the Union Square Theatre may not see the footlights this season on account of Rose Michel,[2] 2nd because I dont want to sacrifice my dramatization of "Gabriel Conroy" for the "money down" that I need this minute. Raymond, who has written to me for it, will I believe make me as fair an offer as he did you if I can wait.[3]

So I ask you, in the common interests of our trade to help me—and to do the best you can to persuade our common enemy—the publisher to make this advance. You know Bliss better than I do—you are, I think one of his stockholders. You will of course satisfy yourself that the company runs no risk in an advance—but you, as a brother author, will appreciate my anxiety to get the best I can for my work—and why I may perhaps have to wait for it. At all events I know you will do your best for me, and I am, very confidently,

Always yours
Bret Harte

Saml. L. Clemens

Provenience: Bancroft (Mark Twain Papers).

1. This estimate corresponds to Clemens's recollection in 1907: Bliss "had advanced to Harte . . .—I think my figures are correct—thirty-six hundred dollars" (*MT in Eruption*, 281). There is no indication either that Bliss complied with BH's request for an additional advance or that Clemens interceded with Bliss on BH's behalf. Certainly BH's conflict with the publisher compounded his problems with Clemens and led in part to their eventual estrangement. According to BH, Clemens, as one of the directors of Bliss's company, profited from its failure to pay him royalties on *Gabriel Conroy*.

2. *Rose Michel*, a melodrama adapted by James Steele Mackaye from an original French play by Ernst Blum, opened at the Union Square Theatre

on 23 November 1875 with Robson in the cast and marked its hundredth performance on 28 February 1876.

3. On Raymond, see note 6 to letter 56. On the results of BH's negotiations with Raymond, see letter 72 below.

72. TO SAMUEL L. CLEMENS, 2 JANUARY 1876

45 Fifth Avenue,
Jan. 2d/76

My dear Clemens,

Raymond would not agree to my terms—so that our negotiations were at an end before I got your letter, and the question of his ability to play "Gabriel Conroy" was not mooted. I think you are right in the main in what you say,—certainly I should not have been shrewd enough to deliberate whether the running of two plays on alternate nights by the same actor would reduce our income.

So that I still am open to an offer and wait for the coming actor who can personate Gabriel Conroy. I thought I had found him in John McCullough,[1] who seemed to me to look the part,—who had a simple, natural strength and suggestion of pathos in his physical aspect, but he, although never doubtful of his ability to do Hamlet or King Lear, does not think he can play Gabriel Conroy.

I have been such a tremendous fool in disposing of my first play as I did—that I feel wary.[2] To think that Stuart Robson has it in his pocket while he is quietly drawing a good salary from his manager for not playing it, and that its appearance at all depends entirely upon a manager and an actor who can afford to do without it—is exasperating.

Try and make Bliss do something for me. You can if you choose make him think it the proper and in the end the profitable thing—certainly it is no risk to him.

Yours always,
B. H.

Provenience: Bancroft (Mark Twain Papers).

1. John McCullough (1832–85), a popular actor BH knew in San Francisco. Both Raymond and McCullough declined to sponsor the writing

of a script by BH based on the novel. Over a decade later, BH again considered dramatizing *Gabriel Conroy* (see letter 185 and accompanying note 1).

2. The terms of BH's contract with Robson, a copy of which survives in the Hampden-Booth Theatre Library, specified that the actor would pay the playwright a one thousand dollar advance on 1 April 1875, an additional one thousand dollars upon delivery of the manuscript, a third thousand on 1 August 1875, and a royalty of fifty dollars per evening performance and twenty-five dollars per matinee to a maximum of three thousand dollars—for a total of six thousand dollars. So long as the play was "in [Robson's] pocket" rather than on the boards, BH figured he was losing money.

73. TO THE EDITOR OF THE *NEW YORK HERALD*, 2 SEPTEMBER 1876

To the Editor of the Herald:—

If I did not at once apologize in the public journals for the perpetration and production of a play entitled "Two Men of Sandy Bar," at the Union Square Theatre last Monday night,[1] it was because I received a letter from Mr. Stuart Robson, which ran as follows:—

Union Square Theatre.

Mr. Bret Harte:—

My Dear Friend—Your play has passed what is called the ordeal; its success with the public is unmistakable and I trust you will not be discouraged by the tone of the New York press.[2] The "Two Men of Sandy Bar," as a work, answers my fullest expectations as an actor, and the public—the only true and infallible arbiter in such a matter—nightly testify their approbation. The abuse of the critics was not unexpected by me, as I am fully aware of the cause. The day when the dignified critical expression of the press could influence the multitude regarding the merits of a play or artists has passed. It has, I am sorry to say, become merely a vehicle of advertisement, the largest purse commanding the longest and strongest editorials.[3] This is a notorious fact, of which the play-going community are fully aware; and it is only necessary to remind you that the best abused plays of recent production have been the best received by the public and the most lasting successes. Congratulating you upon the presentation of this your first dramatic labor, I am yours, with respect,

STUART ROBSON.[4]

As the gentleman had already made me the unsolicited offer and payment of $6,000 for the play,[5] I did not think it honorable to dissent from the more experienced and practical judgment expressed in this letter. Herein I possibly erred. Knowing as I do with what alacrity and firmness all my critics would have rejected that sum, or even half of it, for an untried play; knowing as I do the singularly unselfish devotion they have for their art, and the superb indifference they have always shown to mercenary approaches or the suggestion of emolument, I should, perhaps, have publicly apologized, withdrawn the play and refunded the $6,000. But I regret to say that Mr. Robson would not permit it. Following, doubtless, the evil example of Colonel Sellers and Bardwell Slote,[6] he preferred to continue on in the face of criticism, in his ill-advised and incautious progress toward the characterization of American life in American comedy.

Against the infatuation of such a man it seems to me at present, Mr. Editor, that little can be done. Possibly one thing. I have not yet seen the play, having been absent from town, but I shall take an early opportunity to do so. If I find it half as bad as my most friendly critics have alleged I shall probably abandon it to this most unfortunate and infatuated man, and in my functions as a critic, I doubt not, shall now and then castigate it as his property. But if, on the other hand, I shall find that my critics are prejudiced, envious, ignorant or mistaken, why, I may demand through your friendly columns to be tried by a jury of my peers. At least I may oblige the critic who tells me that a pitiable drunkard on the stage is a vulgar and "disgusting object," to disprove the existence of "Rip Van Winkle" as a successful play;[7] that the question of the morality of my characters, settled by public sentiment here and abroad several years ago, shall not be obtruded now without impertinence;[8] that he who criticises the good taste, judgment or cleanliness of my style shall do it in English, free from those objections,[9] and that one critic who assumes to know me thoroughly shall know that I have written something else than a "comic song."[10]

As to the play, it must stand or fall "in the light of the public square." Only a fool could hope that its real defects could be atoned for by explanation or apology—only an ass would believe that adverse criticism could detract from its real merits.

BRET HARTE.

Provenience: *New York Herald*, 3 Sept. 1876, p. 5, col. 4.

1. BH's play starring Robson opened on 28 August 1876 for a scheduled engagement of five weeks.

2. As will become clear, the play was unceremoniously panned by reviewers. The consensus was, as one of them put it, that *Two Men of Sandy Bar* resembled "a dime novel struck by lightning" (New York *Commercial Advertiser*, 5 Sept. 1876, p. 1, col. 2). BH remarked later that the criticism the morning after the play opened in New York "evinced such personal malignity that it suffocated itself by its multitudinous abuse" (Washington *Capital*, 1 Oct. 1876, p. 1, col. 3).

3. That is, Robson—and BH in printing this letter—has alleged that the poor reviews of the play were the result of their refusal to pay off the New York theatrical critics.

4. In his interview with the Washington *Capital*, BH remarked that he had been concerned for Robson, who had invested "his entire wealth in the pecuniary success of the play," and that he had been surprised when they met the next day to find Robson

> cheerful to hilarity over what he regarded as the success of the piece. Finding me so despondent over the prospect of his pecuniary success, he wrote me a letter, I think only with the intention of satisfying me that I was not a swindler and that he was not a dupe. . . . I asked him, as he had made grave charges, if he was willing to let me use the letter as it was; if he could substantiate it. He assented at once. I asked if he had any proof. He said the proof was as plenty as blackberries. (1 Oct. 1876, p. 1, cols. 3–4)

On his part, Robson vigorously disputed BH's version of events the day after the première: "When I waked up that morning and read what the papers had to say of me and my play I felt very bitter, and I wrote a note to Mr. Harte that was not intended for publication. Harte *did* publish it, and when it was published I certainly stood by it. I merely asserted that the play would not be well received because I had not paid *certain* critics, and I was very much surprised by the row it caused" (*San Francisco Chronicle*, 14 Oct. 1877, p. 1, col. 9).

5. See note 2 to letter 72. In all, Robson lost about ten thousand dollars on the production (*Saturday Evening Post*, 11 Feb. 1899, 521).

6. BH refers to the roles popularized by John T. Raymond in Mark Twain's *The Gilded Age* and W. J. Florence in E. B. Woolf's *The Mighty Dollar.*

7. The New York *Evening Post* (30 Aug. 1876, p. 2, col. 4) had complained that a "visible and tangible drunkard" like Sandy Morton "excites disgust rather than pity or sympathy." BH responds that the stage version of *Rip Van Winkle* starring Joseph Jefferson, a perennial favorite, also featured a drunk.

8. William Winter (1836–1917), drama critic of the *New York Tribune* and one of the first eastern critics to champion BH's work, lamented the "blackguards" who composed the cast of characters and their "vociferous profanity. . . . They are probable, natural, and so is a garbage barrel" (29 Aug. 1876, p. 5, col. 1). Similarly, the New York *World* suggested that the characters almost without exception were "fit subjects either for missionary enterprises or the police" (29 Aug. 1876, p. 5, col. 2).

9. The New York *Commercial Advertiser* (29 Aug. 1876, p. 1, col. 3) criticized the "very wearisome" dialogue of the play, which was "filled with platitudes. There are not two striking things in it. There is none of that epigrammatic, pregnant composition found in nearly every one of Harte's writings." Similarly, the *New York Herald* (29 Aug. 1876, p. 5, col. 4) suggested that BH "has lived upon his reputation" since leaving California and that "we have never known so celebrated a writer to produce such a worthless work."

10. The *New York Times* (29 Aug. 1876, p. 5, cols. 4–5) condemned the play as "the most dismal mass of trash that was ever put into dramatic shape before a New-York audience" and added that it proved that "the ability to write a comic song ["Plain Language from Truthful James"] does not qualify one to write a play." Again in his interview with the Washington *Capital* a few weeks later BH complained that he had awakened on 29 August 1876 "to find my entire reputation resting on what one critic called a comic song" (1 Oct. 1876, p. 1, col. 3).

74. TO A. C. WHEELER, 3 SEPTEMBER 1876

Demarest, N.J.
Septem 3d/76

My dear Sir,[1]

As I have not the pleasure of knowing you personally, will you let me thank you, in this somewhat formal way, for the honorable intent and manly sincerity of your criticism in last Sunday's *World*.[2] It is the only one that the "Two Men of Sandy Bar" has received, wherein the writer shows that he is able to exercise his judgement as a critic without losing his respect for himself, his Art, or the subject he criticises. I thank you for showing these journalists that the functions of a critic are not incompatible with the instincts of a gentleman.

Will you further let me express my honest admiration of the manner in which you speak of your own failure as a dramatist.[3] As I have never seen your play I know not how far your modesty influences your judgement. But I cannot help seeing that while it is undoubtedly a fine thing to write a successful play, it is incomparably finer to be able to speak of one's own failure to do so, as gallantly and clearly as you do.

With great respects, dear Sir, believe me,

Yours
Bret Harte

To Mr. Wheeler.

Provenience: UVa (ALS).

1. Andrew C. Wheeler (1835–1903), drama critic for the New York *World*.

2. Under his pen name "Nym Crinkle," Wheeler had reviewed BH's play in the New York *World* for 3 September 1876 (p. 6, cols. 1–3): "I see nothing in 'The Two Men of Sandy Bar' to disturb my faith in its author. On the whole I see much in it that is bright, clever, dexterous and fresh." Ironically, that is, BH was delighted by a review of the play in the *World*, the very paper he subsequently implicated in his 21 September 1876 letter to the editor of the New York *Graphic*. Wheeler was later caught up in the scandal, presumably for defending BH, to judge from a report by the

New York correspondent of the St. Louis *Daily Globe-Democrat* (21 Jan. 1877, p. 3, col. 4): "A. C. Wheeler (Nym Crinkle) has either left, or is about to leave, the *World*, I understand, in consequence of some disagreement between himself and the publishers, growing out of the charges made by Bret Harte, in connection with the 'Two Men of Sandy Bar.'" Wheeler moved to the *Sun* where, in an otherwise critical review of *Ah Sin* (5 Aug. 1877, p. 5, cols. 3–4), he again asserted that *Two Men of Sandy Bar* may have "owed its failure to [BH's] artistic integrity."

3. Wheeler's play *The Twins* (1862).

75. TO SAMUEL L. CLEMENS, 5 SEPTEMBER 1876

713 B'way, N.Y.
Septem. 5th[1]/76

My dear Clemens,

I have received the enclosed note to-day.[2]

The Baron is a good fellow. Considering the fact that we have no copyright on the Continent, and that he *could* steal but *wont*, and that his editions are the perfection of letter press, and that to be on his list is a kind of guarantee to the English reading people there I'd advise you to accept his offer. He will send you from £50 to £100 according to the size of the book—as a gratuity. Of course as his books are contraband in England, it doesn't interfere with your rights *there*.[3]

You have, of course, read all the critics have said about my play. And yet, it is drawing well, and, honestly, I dont think [it] is a bad play.[4] It seems to me a little like the three parts of a charade with the answer left out, but it's pretty and picturesque and Robson is satisfied. If you come in town, let me send you tickets.[5]

I cannot understand why Bliss delays my book.[6] He promised to bring it out on the 1st Sept. but I have heard nothing of it, and it seems to be dead. You are a stockholder in the Concern. Shore him up.

Yours ever
Bret Harte

Mr Sam. Clemens

Provenience: Bancroft (Mark Twain Papers).

1. The date seems to be a "3" overwritten by a "5."

2. BH forwards a letter from the Leipzig publisher Bernhard Tauchnitz dated 21 August 1876 inquiring about the possibility of reprinting *The Adventures of Tom Sawyer* on the continent. This letter is published in Duckett, 99.

3. Clemens later wrote Howells that Tauchnitz was "a mighty nice old gentleman" who paid him "about 6 or 700 fr. for Tom Sawyer (it being new)" (*MT-H Letters*, I, 262).

4. The *Hartford Courant* reported on 5 September 1876 (p. 1, col. 8) that either the "play, or the criticisms on it, fill the Union square theatre nightly." Robson and BH apparently stirred the controversy over the play to counter the adverse reviews and to publicize it, a possibility underscored by Robson's comment to an interviewer: "The row we had with the critics helped us a little" (Washington *Capital*, 6 May 1877, p. 4, col. 5–p. 5, col. 1; see also *Baltimore Gazette*, 12 Oct. 1876, p. 1, col. 4). The *New York Tribune* implied the controversy was largely manufactured in its editorial reply to Robson and BH's allegations: "to get up a discussion about a play, through the medium of 'your friendly columns,' is thought to be wholesome for the business of the theatre" (4 Sept. 1876, p. 4, col. 5). The *New York Clipper*, a theatrical paper, also noted that the controversy "secured a good deal of cheap advertising" for the play (23 Sept. 1876, 202). Certainly the play completed its entire five-week engagement in New York as originally scheduled.

5. Clemens attended a performance of *Two Men of Sandy Bar* in New York before September 14. Robson subsequently quoted a letter from Clemens to BH which he claimed to have read: "I saw your piece last night, my dear Bret, for the first time, and did not laugh once, for the simple reason that you have sold that piece for a sum you should have received for three months' performance of it" (*Baltimore Gazette*, 12 Oct. 1876, p. 1, col. 4). See also *MT-H Letters*, I, 152. In his autobiographical dictation, he again remarked that BH once "wrote a play with a perfectly delightful Chinaman in it—a play which would have succeeded if anyone else had written it" (*MT in Eruption*, 275).

6. See note 1 to letter 63. Nearly two months later, Clemens's neighbor Charles Dudley Warner (1829–1900) wrote C. H. Webb (27 Oct. 1876, Bancroft, MSS C-H 57) to complain: "In a flush time Bliss is more difficult to open than an Egyptian tomb." Both *Tom Sawyer* and Warner's own

Moslems and Mummies were in press with Bliss's company but not yet released, and "Bret Harte is in the same condition with Gabriel Conroy—only his book has not sold at all yet."

76. TO THE EDITOR OF THE NEW YORK *SUN*, 13 SEPTEMBER 1876

TO THE EDITOR OF THE SUN—*Sir*: I have been called upon by the various journals of the city to give the names of certain critics connected with the New York press, whom Mr. Robson, in a letter to me about "Two Men of Sandy Bar," charges with bribery and corruption.[1] Generally, I believe, it is the utterer and not the receiver of an alleged counterfeit who is called upon to make his tender good. But as the opinion has been expressed that in publishing Mr. Robson's letter, I tacitly endorsed his charges, why let me say that I certainly endorse them here, and have become thoroughly convinced of their truth. It is understood, therefore, that Mr. Robson's charge is reiterated; earnestly, I know; good temperedly, I trust, by Mr. Bret Harte. The issue here, at least, is squarely joined. But lest we should drift away from the intent and spirit of my late letter, I wish to state here that Mr. Robson's letter was published solely to show that the allegation of the critics that he was disappointed in his bargain, or, as it was insinuated by one critic, had been deceived and swindled out of $6,000 by me,[2] was maliciously impertinent and unqualifiedly false. If, however, the critics prefer to evade this charge made by me, and take issue on another charge made by another man, why I am willing to meet that also.

As to the names asked for, one has already been given to an influential journal of this city. It is the name of one of its employees who approached Mr. Theo. Hamilton[3] with the direct tender of the favorable critical expression of his paper for coin. Mr. Hamilton, I am informed, yielded the name at the request of the editor—a man, we will say, quite incapable of permitting or even suspecting the integrity of his subordinates.[4] It is possible that Mr. Hamilton remembered that this same journal had appealed to me, as a brother journalist, in the interests of a journalism worthy of Mr. Carlyle's epithet, to revoke these charges; and that, knowing this, he felt an honorable delicacy in giving to the public the meaner secrets of my profession, through the names of those who hang muddily upon its tattered fringes, and was satisfied that the wrong would be fairly redeemed by the journal in question.

If, however, further names and proofs are demanded, they can be evoked from me simply and readily. It is difficult to get a manager or actor to admit that they have paid for favorable critical services, but they may be obliged to testify under due process of law. An action for libel would call out the proof; but as I cannot bring such an action, not being able to conscientiously swear that the expression of these critics has damaged me or my play, I would propose that those gentlemen who are aggrieved by my charges should bring an action against me. It will enable us both to get at the truth, which, I trust, is all that is asked for. It will, at least, be a novelty.

If, owing to the habitual extravagance and prodigality of the literary man, it is doubtful if any damages could be collected from me, there is the play to fall back upon. Indeed, I know of no more beautiful instance of retributive justice than the sublime spectacle of these gentlemen nightly pocketing the proceeds of the play they have condemned and vindicating the art of the critic over the folly of the public. Standing beside the box office of the Union Square Theatre, sternly but sadly, with faces that shall indicate to the passing throng of giddy and unwise pleasure seekers an outraged æsthetic sense, mitigated and tenderly softened by the near prospect of pecuniary emolument, with one hand warningly raised against the public, and the other gently inserted in the box office, it seems to me that a spectacle like this would compensate somewhat for a preliminary disbursement to legal counsel.

Mr. Robson, I fear, must hereafter answer for himself. I'll have none of him. A man who, as the *Tribune* beautifully says, "mingles a noble grief with an imperfect syntax,"[5] and doesn't even now seem to know how much finer is an ignoble rage mingled with a perfect syntax, shall not insult the great profession of journalism without hearing from BRET HARTE.

Provenience: New York *Sun*, 14 Sept. 1876, p. 2, col. 6.

1. The New York *Evening Post* (4 Sept. 1876, p. 2, col. 3) had immediately urged BH and Robson to "give the facts" if either of them

"knows any critic belonging to any respectable journal of this city who has been bribed." The *Sun* (7 Sept. 1876, p. 2, col. 4), *Commercial Advertiser* (9 Sept. 1876, p. 2, col. 3), and the *World* (10 Sept. 1876, p. 4, col. 6) soon followed suit.

2. The *New York Times* asserted that Robson "paid an enormous sum for a piece of writing that has not a scintilla of wit, nor the slightest degree of literary merit" (29 Aug. 1876, p. 5, col. 4).

3. Theodore Hamilton was Robson's manager and played the part of John Oakhurst in the Union Square Theatre production of *Two Men of Sandy Bar*.

4. The *Sun* reported in its columns the day after this letter appeared that Theodore Hamilton had identified a stringer for the New York *World*, Paul Hamilton, as the corrupt critic. Paul Hamilton subsequently denied soliciting a bribe in exchange for a favorable notice (New York *Sun*, 15 Sept. 1876, p. 2, col. 4). Nevertheless, according to BH, he was "promptly dismissed" from the paper (Washington *Capital*, 1 Oct. 1876, p. 1, col. 4).

5. This phrase appeared in an editorial on the controversy in the *New York Tribune* (4 Sept. 1876, p. 4, col. 5). BH's final paragraph notwithstanding, Robson wrote BH from Washington on 6 October 1876 (Bancroft, MSS 79/47 C) that "I am well satisfied that I will soon get back the six thousand dollars the dignified 'Times' says you swindled me out of. . . . The 'literary lazzarone' of New York, who have treated us as if we were criminals instead of gentlemen, have accomplished nothing to our injury."

77. TO ROBERT B. ROOSEVELT, 21 SEPTEMBER 1876

713 B'way.
September 21st, 1876

My dear Mr. Roosevelt,[1]

Pray pardon me for having left your honest and thoughtful note so long unanswered. But I have been quite busy lately, and in my moments of leisure, have, I dare say, bestowed more attention on my adversary than on my friend.

Your criticism of the condonement of a mortal offense by one of the "Two Men of Sandy Bar" is a point well taken.[2] But it is a fault of *execution*, I think, rather than of *conception*. I erred,—as most men who are not born dramatists will err—in endeavoring to show by simple *narrative*, instead of *action*, the domination of a strong man over a weaker one—a case we have all had delivered to us in Brooklyn, *in re* Beecher, Tilton, *et al.*[3] And this explanation by dialogue is really one of the cardinal defects of the play.

As to the Chinaman, don't you think he would become tiresome and monotonous as the central figure in a three act play? And I can't help giving you the remark of that clever actor, Parsloe, when I suggested to him that I might, if he wished it, inject him in the first act. "Don't, Mr. Harte, give me a line more—to please *me*. I am content. I should only repeat myself, and may be disappoint the audience." This from the actor who has made the one decided "hit" of the piece, strikes me as worthy of consideration.[4]

Nevertheless, as actors are apt to look at "parts" rather than "wholes," are not generally good judges of *ensemble*, I'll look into the matter. Meantime, dear Sir, let me thank you for your kindly interest, and believe me,

Yours very sincerely,
Bret Harte

Provenience: *American Literary Realism* 21 (Fall 1988):60–61.

1. Robert B. Roosevelt !1829–1906), a banker, congressman, and popular magazinist, is best known today if at all as the uncle of Theodore Roosevelt. BH had known Roosevelt at least since 13 October 1872 (*New York Tribune*, 14 October 1872, p. 5, col. 3).

2. Roosevelt had apparently criticized John Oakhurst's willingness to permit the Duchess to leave Sandy Bar without acknowledging her crimes, including bigamy.

3. Henry Ward Beecher was charged with "criminal conversation," or adultery, by Theodore Tilton, husband of Elizabeth Tilton, in August 1874. The suit went to trial in Brooklyn City Court in January 1875 and ended, 112 trial days later, with Beecher's acquital by a sharply divided jury.

4. The comic actor Charles T. Parsloe (1836–98) played Hop Sing, a guileless Chinese laundryman, in *Two Men of Sandy Bar.* Though he delivered only nine lines and was on stage for less than five minutes, Parsloe was praised by the critics and applauded by the audience. Like Roosevelt, Clemens was also delighted by the character of Hop Sing. See note 5 to letter 75. Despite the misgivings he expressed in this letter, when BH proposed to Clemens that they write a play together "& divide the swag"

they chose to feature the "wonderfully funny creature, as Bret presents him—for 5 minutes—in his Sandy Bar play" (*MT-H Letters*, I, 157).

78. TO THE EDITOR OF THE NEW YORK *GRAPHIC*, 21 SEPTEMBER 1876

[*To the Editor of The Graphic.*]

The *World* of Sunday last contained the following editorial:

> The Sun gives Mr. Bret Harte and Mr. Robson pretty plainly to understand that it means to hold them to book as to their joint and several charges of venality and corruption against the dramatic critics of the New York press.[1] The *Sun* is in the right path and should be cordially backed by all its colleagues. So far as we have learned neither Mr. Harte nor Mr. Robson has yet made public the name of any person by whom either of them was approached, directly or indirectly, with any offer to sell the critical opinion of any newspaper in New York. It surely cannot be possible that either Mr. Harte or Mr. Robson can have deliberately made a sweeping charge of this sort without at least believing himself to possess some grounds for making it, such as he need not hesitate to avow when pressed so to do by the responsible conductors of the press. As the case now stands it is not the repute of the dramatic critics of New York which is in question, but the good faith of the authors of this tempest in a teapot.[2]

I am sorry to be obliged to state that both this statement and implication are utterly false. The *World* was in possession of one of these names for a week previous.

A day or two after that paper first asked for names, the name of one of its own employes—the name of the man who criticised my play "Two Men of Sandy Bar" in the *World*, and approached Mr. Hamilton for money—was given to that paper.[3] No public notice having been taken of the fact by the *World*, on Saturday last the same name was given to the *Sun* in answer to their public request for names, through an affidavit by Mr. Hamilton. An editorial allusion was made by the *Sun* to this fact, but the name of the critic and, what was more important to the public, the name of the paper, were studiously concealed.

If, after all this clamor, the first name that I offer to the press is thus withheld, I might well hesitate to intrust further names and proofs to such a tribunal.

The name of this critic is of little importance to the public, but the name of the journal is. I have been told that my charges were too general to admit of that legal redress I proposed to the critics. Let me make them more specific by charging the New York *World* with allowing a critic who demanded money from an actor to afterwards write the criticism for their columns. Let me further charge the *World* with knowing these facts, and yet publicly denying them. It seems to me that this charge, if false, is actionable, and that the *World* could readily bring such action against me. One such suit would be as good as a dozen to disclose the facts. At least it would enable the public to know something more of the truth of my general charges than the publication by the press of alleged interviews of reporters with actors and managers. It would enable me to be tried by a court whereof the judge, jury, and witnesses were not composed entirely of the parties accused.[4] BRET HARTE.

New York, September 21.

Provenience: New York *Graphic*, 21 Sept. 1876, 568.

1. The *Sun* was aggressively investigating Robson and BH's allegations. See note 4 to letter 76.

2. This editorial appeared in the New York *World* for 17 Sept. 1876, p. 4, col. 1.

3. BH omits a crucial detail here: Paul Hamilton reviewed *Two Men of Sandy Bar* for the newspaper *the previous July* during its Chicago debut. To be sure, the notice was highly critical of BH; e. g., "Abandoned to his fate, bound by the fetters of a golden contract to furnish a play at all hazards, the faint Harte spunked up and devised" the melodrama (New York *World*, 18 July 1876, p. 1, cols. 4–5). The tone of this review no doubt rankled BH, who groused in an interview that it had been "evidently written before the play ever saw the footlights" (Washington *Capital*, 1 Oct. 1876, p. 1, cols. 3–4). Since the publication of letter 73 in the *New York Herald*, his

ground of complaint had subtly shifted from wholesale condemnation of all New York theatrical critics to indictment of an out-of-town stringer. For the record, too, Paul Hamilton's name was the only one that ever publicly surfaced in the investigation of Robson and BH's allegations.

4. Most New York papers simply ignored this latest diatribe, although the *World* printed a rebuttal in its next issue. Early in September 1876, it seems, A. C. Wheeler wrote Theodore Hamilton "requesting the name of the person so inculpated," and the actor replied that he had been "instructed by Mr. Robson not to state any more facts in regard to this unpleasant business." The *World* had then publicly demanded that either BH or Robson name the culprit (see note 1 to letter 76). Because "no communication whatever has been received" by the editors of the *World* from either BH or the actor, "it is plain that Mr. Harte has himself alone to blame for appearing in the painful light in which he has put himself by his extraordinary outburst." When BH "recovers his mental equilibrium," the *World* concluded, "he will bitterly regret the injustice which he has done, not only to persons who have never wished him any harm, but to himself and his own good name" (New York *World*, 23 Sept. 1876, p. 4, col. 5).

79. TO JAMES R. OSGOOD, 3 OCTOBER 1876

713 B'way, Oct 3d 76

My dear Osgood,

Robson is willing and satisfied to have the "Two Men of Sandy Bar" printed as a book.[1] The lawyer's say that as *he* holds the prior dramatic copyright—*no one else has a right to interfere* and that the publication by printing through me, and the publication through representation by him are each distinct copyright that do not invalidate each other. So you may drive on!

Now can't you send me an advance of $150—enough to cover what I paid for printing the play? Send me your cheque—that's a good fellow. I am in want of the money. Then go on and sell 2 or 3000 copies at $1.00 each.

Yours
Bret Harte

Provenience: Yale (ALS).

1. *Literary World* 7 (Jan. 1877):130: "Having written a play called 'Two Men of Sandy Bar,'" BH sold it, "it is said, to Stuart Robson, for $6,000. He then came on to Boston, and arranged with Messrs. Osgood & Co. to publish it in book form, concealing this fact from Robson." See also note 3 to letter 65.

80. TO JAMES R. OSGOOD, 5 DECEMBER 1876

Hartford,
Decem. 5/76

My dear Osgood,—

Won't you send me proofs of "Thankful" as fast as your printer turns them out, and let me know the latest day I may return them?[1]

Also, regarding illustration, have you settled upon the artist? I can send you a photo. of a portrait of one of her descendants,—a mighty taking picture.[2]

And, finally, can't you send me a cheque for something by way of advance on the book, that I can use the Xmas times.

Please dont let these several interrogatories lie over for answer a week or two, but let me know as soon as you can. I shall be here in Hartford until Saturday noon.

Yours ever,
B.H.

J. R. Osgood. Esq.

Provenience: Huntington (HM 7168).

1. BH is visiting Clemens in Hartford and completing "Thankful Blossom," a story of the American Revolution, published serially in the Sunday editions of the New York *Sun* between 3 and 24 December 1876. This short novel was issued in book form by Osgood in late January 1877. In his autobiographical dictation, Clemens reminisced about BH's visit on this occasion: "He came to us once just upon the verge of Christmas, to stay a day and finish a story for the New York *Sun* called 'Faithful Blossom'—if my memory serves me." Charles A. Dana (1819–97), the owner and editor of the *Sun*, had promised him $250 "if he finished it in time for Christmas use. Harte had reached the middle of his story, but his time limit was now

so brief that he could afford no interruptions, wherefore he had come to us to get away from the persistent visits of his creditors." As Clemens recounts the incident, BH drank two quarts of whiskey and worked all night in his room to finish the manuscript. "The last half of that story was written under the unpromising conditions which I have described; it is a story which I have never seen mentioned in print and I think it is quite unknown, but it is my conviction that it belongs at the very top of Harte's literature" (*MT in Eruption*, 275–77). As this brief note to Osgood indicates, however, Clemens's memory is not to be trusted on all details. BH visited the Clemenses not "just upon the verge of Christmas" but early in December, and he remained in Hartford at least four days, from Tuesday the 5th to Saturday the 9th. He was proofreading the installments already printed in the *Sun* as well as writing the final chapters of the story. The original manuscript of "Thankful Blossom" in the Huntington Library, moreover, is heavily revised in BH's hand, suggesting that even if he drafted the second half of the story in one sitting he later revised what he had written before sending it to the *Sun*.

2. A private joke: BH offers to send his own photograph. He wrote in 1890 that, while the heroine of his story was "purely imaginary," her name "was an actual one, and was borne by a (chronologically) remote maternal relation of mine" (Julia Keese Colles, *Authors and Writers Associated with Morristown* [Morristown, N.J.: Vogt Bros., 1893], 123–24).

81. TO SAMUEL L. CLEMENS, 16 DECEMBER 1876

45 Fifth Avenue,
Decem. 16th/76

My dear Mark,

I got a short note from Parsloe yesterday, making an appointment to meet me at Dutton's at 10:30 to-day.[1] I was there, waited an hour, but *he* didn't come. At about 3 P.M. he called on me here, where after some desultory talk I read him those portions of the 1st & 2d act that indicated his *role*, and he expressed himself satisfied with it, and competent to take it in hand. As nearly as I could judge he was pleased.[2]

Of the contract, its nature, what would be his share of the profits, and generally what *we* should expect from him *I said nothing*. In fact I was only too glad to leave all that business with you. He talked,—a little prematurely I thought and with a certain egotism that I had noticed before—about his having made the fortunes already of certain people to whom he had been subordinate, and of his intention now of trying to make his own. He intimated that he was hereafter "going to look out for himself." To all of which I said nothing, and shall deliver him into your hands without committing you to even a single suggestion. He is to go with me to Hartford on such day as I may name early next week, and I shall give you notice by telegraph of our coming twelve hours before. You can, if you like, meet us at the station, and we can go to your lawyer's at once.

You will be surprised, I dare say, that with all my anxiety to push our play into print I am still halting and fussing over the manuscript. I've been revising the 1st and 2d Act—writing myself *up* and you down, that is trying to make myself more easily intelligible, and you not quite so *prononcé*. I find that Mrs H's opinion of the real Plunketts jumps with your wife's, and I think we'll have to modify *Miss P.* at least. I think that Mrs H. and Mrs C. represent fairly our feminine auditors, and as we are not constructing women "after our own image" or as we have seen them, I suppose we will have to defer to their ideas of what a woman ought to be.

I hope, dear old boy, that you are better in health, and that Nature has let up generally on your bowels. For myself, I was quite knocked up by one last day's work, and when I got back to N,Y. was for a day or two unable to do anything, and "the Ba"[3] might have put her finger on me as an illustration of "shop head" and "ledder heard."

Remember me kindly to your wife, Mrs Langdon and Miss Hess.[4] Tell Mrs Clemens that she must forgive me for my heterodoxy—that until she does I shall wear sackcloth (fashionably cut,) and that I would put ashes on my head but that Nature has anticipated me, and that I feel her gentle protests to my awful opinions all the more remorsefully that I am away; say to Miss Hess she isn't from Boston, and that I always agreed with her about the natural infamy of Man; tell Mrs Langdon I forgive her for liking you so much, and her general disposition to weakly defer to your horrible egotism and stubbornness; and then kiss Susie for me, and implore "the Ba" on your bended knees, to add me to the Holy Family.

Always, dear old fellow,

Yours B. H.

Provenience: Bancroft (Mark Twain Papers).

1. E. P. Dutton & Co. at 713 Broadway.

2. BH and Clemens want Parsloe to reprise his role as a Chinese laundryman as lead in their play *Ah Sin*. To do so, they would offer him a one-third interest in the play.

3. The baby, Clara Clemens.

4. Oliva Lewis Langdon (1810–90), Clemens's mother-in-law, and Fanny C. Hesse, his secretary.

82. TO SAMUEL L. CLEMENS, 1 MARCH 1877

713 Broadway, N.Y.
Mar. 1st 77

My dear Clemens,

As I've been writing for my bread-and-butter for the last few days, and as your letter called for no answer except I should receive one from Ford,[1] which I should have forwarded promptly, and as nothing has come from Ford, I have taken my own time to talk with you. Had I written the day after receiving your letter, I hardly think we would have had any further correspondence or business together. As it is I'm not anxious to write this. But there are a few things I must say to you.

First. As to the American Publishing Co.

If Mr. Bliss was a business man he would have sent *me* a statement of my a/c *when it was due*, and given me an opportunity of examining it—of knowing what he was doing and what he had done about my property, and what profit I was to expect from it. He would have exhibited his charge for "*interest on advances*"—a charge so preposterous and outrageous that if he will look at his contract he will see that it is so, and if he comes in contact with my lawyer he will know it is so.

Second—As to his sales of my book and the amount of copyright: *No publisher of any of my works, at any day, or time has done as badly as he has.* It is no answer to this to repeat your formula "that the book was delayed by me, that my reputation had suffered by it, that I had lost my popularity &c. &c. &c." The only test is what other publishers are doing now, and since then, and at the time of Bliss' publication, with my *other* books. Mr. Osgood offered Robson $250 *advance* (without *interest*, of course,) on the sale of the much abused play of "Sandy Bar"—which he would offer to the trade at 65¢. Inside of a month, Osgood had credited me on account of "Thankful Blossom"—a book published originally in a daily newspaper and sold by Osgood for 60¢—with one half the amount of copyright that Bliss shows for his sales in 5 mos of a book that a magazine paid $6000 for, and which he sells for $3.50. In brief, Osgood has sold more copies of "Thankful Blossom" in a month, than Bliss has sold of "Gabriel Conroy" in five months,—and on looking over my copyright accounts, I find I have never in my literary experience sold less than four or five thousand copies in the first three months of publication. Either Bliss must confess that he runs his concern solely in *your* interest, *and* that he uses the names of other authors to keep that fact from the public, or else he is a fool. No sane business man would advance $6000 dollars on a book,[2] of which in 5 mos he sold only 2000 copies, unless he had some other reason for it. I dont think his friendship for me goes as far as that. Possibly he may have carelessly made up his accounts. Ticknor of J. R. Osgood & Co,[3] to whom I stated the case, tells me that from his experience of the dealings of the regular trade with subscription houses, that Bliss has probably already disposed of at least 2000 copies to the trade *alone*. Even Bliss' advances of $6,000 cannot cover the loss I shall have from respectable publishers by publishing with *him*. Now, this is somewhere wrong, Mark, and as my friend you should have looked into Bliss's books and Bliss's methods, quite as much with a desire of seeing justice done your friend, as with the desire of seeing what chance you had of recovering any possible advance of $500 on our mutual work, if it failed.

I have written this on a separate page that you might show the preceding ones to Bliss. I only add one other fact (*to yourself solely*) which *you* may have forgotten. I had forgotten it, until looking for my contract with Bliss I found a letter from you of the same date. You requested me to tell Bliss that his contract with me was of *your* making and out of your influence with me as a friend, and you afterwards admitted to me that a disputed question of one or two thousand dollars was settled in your favor by *virtue of that contract so made.*[4] I am willing to admit that your loan of $750 wipes out that obligation,[5] nor should I have referred to it, but for the tenor of your letter the other day, which struck me as being inconsistent with the facts.

Now, as to "Ah Sin"! First:

Parsloe called here and showed me your letter. I dont object to San Francisco as the place of *début*, except that from my own knowledge they prefer something with an Eastern endorsement, and I really can't see how our main idea of bringing out the play in a small town so that we might be able to superintend rehearsals, is furthered by this.[6]

Secondly.

If there is any one thing that we are *sure* about, regarding our play—anything that we do *know*, by actual experience, by general report, by universal criticism, by the consent and acknowledgement of the public—it is that Parsloe is a perfect Chinaman![7] Now to spend five or six hundred dollars to send him to San Francisco *to study Chinese character* is simply *preposterous*—so preposterous, that even the honest fellow himself saw it. Without waiting for my opinion, he told me he wouldn't do it. And in saying this to you I think I have overlooked your implied insult—an insult I admit I felt keenly when he showed me your letter—of your offering this actor, in a mere whim and idiotic impulse—the very sum you refused to advance your *collaborateur* who called that actor into life,[8] who had given already four or five weeks of his time to you and whom you refused on the plea of *poverty*!

No, Mark, I do not think it advisable for us to write another play together. Your offer of "$25 per week and board"—is flattering I admit—but I think that if I accepted it, even *you* would despise me for it. I can make about $100 per week for a few weeks here at my desk—my only idea of asking you for an advance was to save me from the importunity of my creditors, and give me that quiet, which as a nervous man yourself, you ought to know is essential to composition. I had not the slightest idea of your speculating out of my poverty, but as a shrewd man, a careful man, a provident man, I think you will admit that in my circumstances the writing of plays with you is not profitable.

Allowing even that I came to you on a salary of $25 per week, as I could not, after your letter, break bread or eat salt with you—dont you see as an economic man, as a shrewd man, that my board at the cheapest hotel would cost me at least $7.50 per week and that I should have only $17.50 to support my wife and 4 children. I know it can be done cheaper than that, but I think I'll struggle on here on $100 per week—and not write any more plays with you.

As to the play, already written,—except a protest against your marring it any more by alterations until it is rehearsed, and a special, and I think not improper request that you will try to allow me some understanding of the characters I have created, you can do with it, according to your business shrewdness and sagacity, as you may deem best for both of us—subject to my endorsement.[9]

I think I object to San Francisco.

I have no answer from Ford. I shall telegraph him again tomorrow.

Yours, very respectfully,
Bret Harte

Mr. Saml L. Clemens
Hartford.
P.S. I have kept a copy of this letter.[10]

Provenience: Bancroft (Mark Twain Papers).

1. John T. Ford (1829–94), owner of the infamous Ford's Theatre in Washington, site of Lincoln's assassination, operated four theatres in Washington and Baltimore.

2. BH apparently confuses the six thousand dollars paid by Scribner & Co. for serial rights to *Gabriel Conroy* and the thirty-six hundred or so that Bliss had paid him in advances on the novel.

3. Benjamin H. Ticknor (b. 1843), the second son of Fields's old partner William D. Ticknor and a junior partner in the firm of Osgood & Co.

4. See letter 71.

5. In 1907, in his autobiographical dictation, Clemens claimed that "Harte owed me fifteen hundred dollars" when they worked together on *Ah Sin*; "later he owed me three thousand," the increase presumably BH's share of the losses on the play (*MT in Eruption*, 279). BH not only places his debt to Clemens at a much lower figure here but suggests that Clemens has forgiven the debt in acknowledgment of the earlier favor.

6. After its debut at the National Theatre in Washington and Ford's Opera House in Baltimore in May 1877, *Ah Sin* opened at Daly's Fifth Avenue Theatre on 31 July 1877 for a one-month engagement. The play

then went on the road to St. Louis, and then to a series of New York towns—Rochester, Elmira, Utica, Watertown, Oswego, and Syracuse.

7. The Washington correspondent of the San Francisco *Argonaut* (19 May 1877, 5) quoted Clemens on Parsloe's portrayal: "'Look at him,' said Mark; 'ain't he a lost and wandering Chinee by nature? See those two front teeth of Parsloe, just separated far enough to give him the true Mongol look.'" See also note 4 to letter 159.

8. BH had asked Clemens for a loan just before writing this letter during a visit to Hartford to plot out another play.

9. Clemens continued to tinker with the script without consulting BH. The extant fragments of dialogue in BH's hand do not appear in the sole prompt copy of the play that survives (*Ah Sin: A Dramatic Work*, ed. Frederick Anderson [San Francisco: Book Club of California, 1961], xvii–xviii). Clemens also wrote Howells on 3 August 1877 that he had "been putting in a deal of hard work on that play in New York, & have left hardly a foot-print of Harte in it anywhere" (*MT-H Letters*, I, 192). In 1907, however, Clemens allowed that BH's "part was the best part of it" (*MT in Eruption*, 278).

10. Clemens jotted on the back of this letter: "I have read two pages of this ineffable idiotcy—it is all I can stand of it."

83. TO SAMUEL L. CLEMENS, 2 APRIL 1877

Washington, D.C.
Apr. 2d/77

My dear Mr. Clemens,

Mr. J. T. Ford, who has theatres in Washington, Baltimore and Philadelphia came up from Balt. day before yesterday, by appointment, to speak to me about our play.

I learn from him, *first*,: That he has made an offer to Parsloe for the first week in Washington and the second in Baltimore, (the engagement to commence in the early part of May), on the following terms: Ten per cent. of the weekly expenses of the Theatre—i.e. Two thousand dollars, and 50 per *centum* on all gross receipts over the $2000. This gives a surety of $200 for each of these two weeks, and if he plays to a good business—(i.e. $6000 per week,) of course we come in for $2000, per week.

2d. By this arrangement we have an opportunity of attending rehearsals a week before, and the promise that, if on rehearsal, we desire to let the engagement go by—(to write up parts—) it shall not be at *our* expense.

My reasons are for favoring this:

1st. We shall know by May 1st *whether we have or have not* a play;

2d. We shall learn at the same time, whether *we have or have not an actor in the titular part.*

3d The $200 will at least pay our expenses here to find out that important fact.

4th If we fail—it is a local failure and will not hurt our other work as much as a metropolitan *fiasco.*

5th. That I dont see we can do anything else.

6th That I dont see that Parsloe is offering anything better.

When I dont see that Parsloe has either declined or accepted Fords offer it seems to me that we ought to do something about it. I want to realize on my work as soon as possible, and I dont think that either you or I can afford to have an actor walking around the streets of N.Y. with an unaccepted play of *ours*, in his pocket.

Please let me know by telegraph to 713 B'way if you accept Ford's offer. Then I can hunt up Parsloe, and make him give me a reason why he doesn't say yes or no, and make him say yes—if you agree with me.

Yours &c.
Bret Harte

Mr S. L. Clemens

Provenience: Bancroft (Mark Twain Papers).

84. TO JOHN T. FORD, 7 MAY 1877

My Dear Mr. Ford:—Won't you do for me what I hope some day to do personally, namely: thank your people for their honest endeavor and clever interpretation of the varied characters in "Ah Sin." So much of the author is usually left to the actor to deliver to the public that I was most agreeably surprised to find that the best of my *collaborateurs* and myself so honestly and fairly represented, and our failures are cleverly concealed.[1]

BRET HARTE.

Washington, May 7, 11 p.m.

Provenience: Washington *National Republican*, 8 May 1877, p. 1, col. 7.

1. After the première of *Ah Sin* at the National Theatre in Washington, Parsloe read a congratulatory telegram from Clemens. Though he was present at the theatre, BH was not publicly recognized; later that evening he sent this note to the theatrical producer and his company. On 16 May 1877, he sent the following telegram to Clemens: "Send my draft if any to Mrs Knaufft forty five fifth ave" (from the collection of the Mark Twain House, Hartford, Conn.).

85. TO ANNA HARTE, 24 JUNE 1877[1]

Georgetown, Sunday Evening.

My dear Nan,

I thought you understood from my last letter what the "good news" meant and why I stayed. I'm trying to *secure* an arrangement to write a story for the *Capital*, whose editor is an agent of Thompson for $2000 which shall be payable as I write it and put in bank for me.[2] I am to hear "yes" or "no" to-morrow. Mr Donn Piatt has been absent a week. I could not know until to-day, as to the details. I've had the offer in my hands.

It is a chance to get money quickly—which I must have or I shall go mad. I wrote some verses for the *Capital* last week, and sent you the money $30; I wrote some more this week and sent you $50, yesterday.[3]

I've not seen Evarts[4] since I wrote you last. Then it seemed to me from his very cautious and diplomatic speech, that I ought to have *political* influence. *I can get it if I choose.*

Shall I choose? Jones, the great millionaire and Senator from Nevada,[5] told me that he *demanded* of the President as part of his patronage an office for me. The member from New Mexico[6] not only offered his own personal influence but to pledge all the Territorial delegates for me. I can easily secure the whole California delegation. But what effect this may have upon the "Facing-both-ways" administration I dont know—nor do I care!

In five minutes I could make you understand why I am so sparing in my speech, why I am so sparing in my letters. I have "some new hope for each new day"—I can not return until I have *achieved something.*

Limick[7]

Provenience: UVa (ALS).

1. Dated by reference to the poems in note 3 below.

2. The editor of the weekly Washington *Capital* was the popular journalist Donn Piatt (1819–91). William Neely Thompson "was one of Piatt's most intimate friends" and a Washington insider (Charles Grant Miller, *Donn Piatt: His Work and His Ways* [Cincinnati: Clarke, 1893], 276). BH again wrote AH on 7 July 1877 that "Thompson has offered me (through a friend) $2,000 for a story like or shorter than 'Thankful Blossom.' Part of this sum, I think, I can get in advance. I shall know tomorrow (Sunday). I have given up all hope of getting anything from the Administration" (*Books and Autographs/. . ./Bret Harte Autograph Letters* [New York: American Art Assn., 1926], III, item 366).

3. "The Wandering of Ulysses/As Reported by Mary Jones, Maid to Mrs. Grant," *Capital*, 17 June 1877, p. 4, col. 2; and "That Ebrew Jew," *Capital*, 24 June 1877, p. 4, col. 3.

4. William Evarts (1818–1901) was a former U.S. attorney general, secretary of state from 1877 until 1881, and later a Republican U.S. senator from New York.

5. John Percival Jones (1829–1912) made a fortune in mining in California and Nevada before his election as a Republican to the U.S. Senate in 1873.

6. Trinidad Romero (1835–1918), a Republican.

7. BH's nickname.

86. TO ANNA HARTE, 8 JULY 1877

Georgetown,
July 8th/77

My dear Nan,

I sign a contract with Donn Piatt of the *Capital* to-morrow,[1] which will put $1000 in the Bank for me to check upon as I require it and furnish copy. I shall get an advance of about $150 at first the bulk of which I will send you.

For the first time in many years I have for the last few days been confined to my bed. The Doctor says it is Gastric Catarrh—which is the polite name for dysentery. I should not tell you or worry you about it, but that I am better and the Doctor says that with care I will pull through without a return of the active complaint. He sat by me from 3 A.M. until 9—but it was not until I was better that I felt at all frightened. You may be certain, Nan, that if I find any return of the symptoms I shall take train to Balt.—(only to stop there if I am not well enough to go on to N.Y.) and stay with Brantz Mayer who has been like a brother to me in all my worries.[2] And if I get frightened, I'll telegraph for you. But *I am determined not to get down sick yet.*

My work here will be worth about $2500 to me, of this I am *sure* of $1000.

As regards Appointments, I know nothing. Whatever is done now, must come to me without solicitation.

I shall see you in a few days. Did you get the $10 for the boys? It was all I had.

Kiss the chicks for me. God bless you, patient Nan, says

Limick

Provenience: UCLA (ALS).

1. BH contracts to write *The Story of a Mine*, published serially in the *Capital* between 29 July and 7 October 1877.

2. Brantz Mayer (1809–79) was AH's brother-in-law. See BH's 9 January 1873 letter to AH (*Letters*, 17–18). Mayer was also the author of *Mexico as It Was and It Is* (1844) and *Mexico, Axtec, Spanish and Republican* (1851).

87. TO CHARLES A. DANA, 16 JULY 1877

Washington, D.C.
July 16th/77

My dear Dana,

I enclose the sketch of the "Office Seeker"—the dead horse I have been carrying so long, and for which I am indebted to you.

I think quite honestly that the story has not suffered by delay.[1] At all events it is much longer than I intended to make it originally, and if it runs much over the usual length of my sketches for $100, I expect you to send me a modest little cheque for the balance.

"Thank God," as Mr Micawber remarked when he gave his I.O.U. to Copperfield, "Thank God I am out of debt now."[2]

Seriously, I worked on this all day Saturday and Sunday that I might be free to begin a story for the *Capital* next week.[3] I shall get that presently off my hands, and then I shall be ready to ply you with copy as long as you can stand it.

Did you publish the Critique on the Centennial Poems?[4] Did you get my letter anent it? Should I stay here a week longer would you like a rather free and easy Washington letter over my own signature?[5]

I have to collect some items for my story, but if within a few days a gaunt, haggard man walks into your office and demands alms, take him down tenderly to Dison's and tell him ghost stories on the beach to the sound of water lapping on the crags, and he will in time tell you wondrous tales of political enchantment, of the great and stupid Giant Civil Service Reform and of the good Queen Hayes who was always in the kitchen eating bread and honey &c &c.

Write me a line when you get this and if you use the sketch for next Sunday, let me have a proof promptly.

Yours always
B.H.

C. A. Dana Esq.

Provenience: UVa (ALS).

1. "The Office Seeker," New York *Sun*, 22 July 1877, p. 2, cols. 1–4.

2. In chapter XXXVI of *David Copperfield*, Wilkins Micawber hands Thomas Traddles an I.O.U., then declares he is "happy to recover my moral dignity." John Hay remembered that once, when he was complaining of his own straitened circumstances, BH told him it was his own fault: "Why did you fool away your money paying your debts?" (*The Life and Letters of John Hay*, ed. William Roscoe Thayer [Boston: Houghton Mifflin, 1915], II, 402).

3. Only the day before, BH had written AH (UVa) that he had "been writing hard day and night to get far enough along in my story so as to

draw $400 or 500 at once from Bank," though he was sending Dana a manuscript "early next week" so that "he shall not think I deserted him for the Capital."

4. BH's "The Poetry of the Centennial," a review of *Our National Jubilee*, ed. E. B. Treat (1838–1928), appeared without signature in the *Sun*, 15 July 1877, p. 2, cols. 2–4. In it, BH excoriates Holmes for a "wretched" poem, Bayard Taylor for his "ridiculous, cumbrous, and old-fashioned machinery," Bryant for "indifferent" verse, and Whittier for his heavy-handed moralizing.

5. BH was almost certainly the author of "The Wanderings of Ulysses," an unsigned whimsical sketch about President Grant's travels, in the New York *Sun* (1 Aug. 1877, p. 2, cols. 5–6).

88. TO ANNA HARTE, 22 JULY 1877[1]

Washington, D.C.
Sunday P.M.

Dear Nan,

I had no opportunity to write you yesterday, and nothing to write. I have nearly finished my story,[2] besides writing another article for the *Capital*.[3] Dana has sent me a telegram saying the story read so well he wouldn't bother me with proof, and would not publish until next Sunday.[4] He may give me something extra for the story as it is longer than my usual $100 sketches;[5] whatever he may send I'll send to you.

Donn Piatt, the ed. & prop. of the *Capital*, to-day made me an offer of $5000 per year (put in bank to my credit and payable monthly) if I will share with him the editorial labors—or he will give me a smaller salary (secured) and a 1/2 interest in the paper. Both offers are good; perhaps the $5000 in hand is worth the 1/2 interest in the bush—but I'm going to look into it to-morrow. It is a weekly paper—it will only require abt. 2 columns of writing per week or about as much as a single article for the *Sun* and will leave me, as Piatt says, ample time for my literary work elsewhere.

Washington is the place for a literary man to make money.

Think of it.—Remember the money will be secured me by deposit in bank as the $1000 is for my story. Let me know your advice. You must, also, remember that the payment of $5000 is not dependant upon my furnishing so much copy—it is a *salary*; if I should be sick or unable to do anything I could still draw it. And if I can write as well and as rapidly as I am writing now, I can easily double it in the *Sun*, by the articles Dana still wants.

Now I am utterly bewildered as to what *you* are to do—*just now.* I sent you $50 and will send you more to-morrow, at least enough to enable you to go anywhere you like, with a month board in advance in your pocket. But just now dont go to the Cattskills—its too far for me, and if you can possibly *wait* a few days longer for my return—do it. I want to get in another instalment of my story,[6] and get Piatts offer into a definite shape and contract to submit to you.

Every moment here is pecuniarily valuable to me. I will try and come early next week and if the roads are blocked by Strikers,[7] shall come by sea.

God bless you all. I think the tide is turning. At least I begin to feel my way ahead, slowly.

Your own
Limick!

P.S. I am writing with an old quill and can hardly read this, and my eyes are giving out. When you write or when you receive letters remember that Morristown is as far by mail from Washington as Boston is, and that by telegraph it is farther and twice as expensive as Chicago.

Provenience: UVa (ALS).

1. This letter is dated by the postmarked envelope.

2. BH is completing the first installment of "The Story of a Mine," published in the *Capital* the following week.

3. "An American Haroun al-Raschid," Washington *Capital*, 22 July 1877, p. 1, cols. 1–5.

4. Whatever BH understood Dana to mean, "The Office Seeker" was published this day in the *Sun*.

5. "The Office Seeker" filled over three columns of the *Sun* rather than the two columns BH's sketches usually filled.

6. *The Story of a Mine*. BH wrote Osgood on 18 July 1877 that he had already written "about 1/3" of the story (Box 4, Charles M. Kozlay

Collection, Huntington). However, the serial ran longer than he expected. See letter 89.

7. The "Great Upheaval of 1877" was sparked by pay cuts on the Pennsylvania, Baltimore and Ohio, and other railroads in July 1877.

89. TO DONN PIATT, 20 AUGUST 1877

713 Broadway, N. Y.
Aug. 20th/77

My dear Piatt,

My lawyers are drawing up the agreement between us based upon your proposition. There will, I think, be little alteration; at least the *spirit* of it will be the same. I only want to protect myself from any indebtedness of the Company over and above my share in it, should we fail.

I think you and I can make a team of it. If we *can*, there is money, and reputation, and self-respect in our venture. I am willing to risk it. There is much ahead for us both to do, if we will do it. I want to do it.

Tell me how the story goes on. It will be longer than I expected, but I dare say you dont care for that.[1]

My play is a sort of success. At least it's valuable enough for Parsloe to try and buy my third, which I dont intend to sell him.[2]

I've spoken to some newspaper men about my project; some (among them our friend Dana) do not think *any Washington paper* can succeed—*but I am satisfied to try.*

Did you ever think that in your innocent remark about my application for a foreign appointment the story of Evarts refusing me the China Mission (published I think in your Cincinnati correspondence,) would do me an awful mischief? It has. Every gutter snipe of the press, who hates me, rolls it as a sweet morsel over his tongue, and praises Evarts for his wisdom.[3] And to think its all a lie—and "it was not an enemy who did me this but a friend."

I'll forgive you, if you write me at once. I can be in Washington by the 31st, if you think it necessary.

Yours Ever,
Bret Harte

Provenience: Hayes (ALS).

1. *The Story of a Mine.*

2. The initial reviews of *Ah Sin* in Washington and New York were encouraging. The *New York Herald*, for example, thought it would make "two or three fortunes" and predicted "a long run" for it (1 Aug. 1877, p. 6, col. 5). Clemens reported to Howells on 3 August 1877 that the play "went a-booming at the Fifth Avenue. The reception of Col. Sellers [in the dramatization of *The Gilded Age*] was calm compared to it" (*MT-H Letters*, I, 191). Meanwhile, Clemens and Parsloe had forged an alliance in opposition to BH. Parsloe wrote Clemens on 9 March 1877 that he had seen BH, who had inquired about rehearsals of the play. Parsloe replied that he would keep BH informed if there was anything he ought to know, at which point BH's face turned red with anger and he stormed away (Duckett, 141). After the play opened in New York, BH contacted the theatrical impresario Augustin Daly (1838–99) for information: "I don't want any accounts from you or Parsloe, only a simple expression of your opinion as to whether the play was or was not successful, and as one of its authors, this does not seem to me to be an inconsistent request or calculated to wound anybody's—say Parsloe's—sensitive nature" (Daly, 236–37). As usual, BH made the wrong decision in refusing to sell Parsloe his interest in the play. Clemens finally admitted to Howells on 15 October 1877 that *Ah Sin* was "a most abject and incurable failure" (*MT-H Letters*, I, 206).

3. In his letter from Washington dated 6 August 1877 (*Cincinnati Enquirer*, 9 Aug. 1877, p. 5, col. 1), Piatt had written as follows:

> Harte was put forward by the Pacific slope as its candidate for the mission to China, and he found favor with the President, but not with Mr. Evarts. The Secretary of State read Bret's qualifications in his face by the light of the author's life in New York. . . . Now, Bret Harte has been carrying a heavy load in a wife and four children, to say nothing of some rather luxurious tastes and habits, upon the wit of his pen. In consequence he has had hungry creditors and financial complications. To add to his trouble he writes slowly and with no little labor, and when held by affairs he could not manage or control he found it impossible to write at all. From this came sundry allegations and stories not creditable to Bret in the ears of a commercial community. It can never forgive a man for being in debt.

> It would have been a graceful thing in Mr. Evarts to have ignored the commercial and looked only at the literary side, and provided for a man whose genius has given more respect to our name abroad than all the diplomats we ever possessed. A diplomat of our creating has nothing to do, and I know of no one more capable of doing it gracefully than my friend Bret Harte.

As BH complains in his letter to Piatt, these paragraphs were widely copied, as in "Why Bret Harte Doesn't Get an Offer" in the *Springfield Republican*, 13 Aug. 1877, p. 4, col. 5.

90. TO ANNA HARTE, 21 SEPTEMBER 1877

Washington D.C.
Septem 21st/77

My dear good, patient Nan, if you did not already know how foolish I am about not writing bad news you would guess, as I see by your kind letter you have, that I have had great trouble and perplexity here. The non-appearance of my story made annoyance—even to the meanness of its having been alleged by the *World* that I was bought off or frightened by a decision of the Attorney Generals's, in the New Idria Case,[1]—when as you and I know only the necessity of writing other things to pay my daily expenses caused the omission. It was still, a dreadful mistake. It lost me I fear many friends. It put me again in the shameful attitude of breaking my engagements. All of which there was no answer to,—dear Nan—It was my own fault, and I cannot blame people for not knowing everything.

When I handed Piatt the contract he said he was very sorry but that some old debts against the paper had lately come up unexpectedly and that he could not fulfill his promise regarding the 1/2 share.[2] Of course, I believed this only an excuse and that he had thought better of his bargain. But since then he assures me that he is most anxious to complete it—that he hopes to arrange matters so that we can go as he intended—and honestly (and this is one reason I have not told you this before) *I do not even now know whether he is sincere or not*, or whether he will, if sincere, be able to do what he offered. I have been kept for a week in the most wretched, lamentable state of anxiety.

But I shall to-night finish the story. It is longer than Thankful Blossom,—longer than I first intended, but I could not bear nor dare to put in poor work or hurry it. Please God I may yet get a couple of hundred dollars out of it from Osgood, and mayhap, something from England. It isn't a bad story—even if it has been written in the sorest trouble I have ever had.[3]

Dear Nan I have had no money since I have been here—I shall have none until the story is finished. I do not blame them. But it is hard. But it is not so terrible to me as the reflection that you are left alone, penniless, at that strange hotel, with me away.[4] If I could do anything by being *there* more than I am doing here I would come. *But I must come with money.*

God bless you, Nan, be patient a day or two longer.

Limick

Provenience: UVa (ALS).

1. No installment of *The Story of a Mine* appeared in issues of the *Capital* for 2 and 9 September 1877. BH alludes to an editorial in the pages of his old nemesis, the New York *World*, for 10 September 1877 (p. 4, cols. 5–6):

> Apropos of Attorney-General Devens's decision against the New Idria Mining Company in the famous [Billy] McGarrahan claim case, a Washington correspondent tells a story not overly favorable to Mr. Bret Harte, who has been, he says, printing in Donn Piatt's paper, the *Capital*, a serial called 'A Story of a Mine.' Piatt, according to the chronicler, is an attorney or friend of the New Idria Company and has always abused McGarrahan, and Bret Harte's story was a part of this abuse, as it makes out McGarrahan a robber and murderer and everything that is not pleasant. Last week the *Capital* contained "a card explaining the absence of the usual two or three chapters of the story by stating that 'for some unaccountable reason the manuscript did not come to hand.' The story is that Mr. Harte had been told early in the week that Mr. Devens intended to decide in favor of the New Idria Company, and had written up the chapters of his story to suit, and not until Friday night did he learn that the decision was the other way. He then knew that he would have to rewrite the concluding chapter

of the story, and he sent for the manuscript. After looking it over he thought it was too big a job, and he concluded not to work it up until next week. The card, he thought, would satisfy the readers of the story.

2. George Hill, Jr., a Georgetown paper manufacturer, had petitioned a judge to declare the Capital Publishing Co. bankrupt in July. In his response to the petition, Piatt denied the company was insolvent but acknowledged he had failed to pay a promissory note when it had come due the previous April (Washington *National Republican*, 18 July 1877, p. 4, col. 2).

3. Osgood published *The Story of a Mine* in early February 1878. The novel was published before the end of 1877 in England by Routledge and in Germany by Tauchnitz; it was issued in a German translation in 1878 and in a French translation in 1879.

4. AH and the children were living at the Sea Cliff Hotel on Long Island.

91. TO ANNA HARTE, 18 OCTOBER 1877

Thursday Night[1]

Thank you, dear Nan, for your kind, hopeful letter. I *have* been very sick, very much disappointed, but I'm better now, and am only awaiting some money to return. I ought to have, for the work that I have done, more than would help us out of our difficulties. But it doesn't come, and even the money I've expected from the *Capital* for my story is seized by its creditors. That hope and the expectations that I had from the paper and Piatt in the future amount to nothing. I have found that it is bankrupt.[2]

Can you wonder, Nan, that I have kept this from you. You have so hard a time of it there that I cannot bear to have you worried if there is the least hope of a change in my affairs as they look, day by day. Piatt has been gone nearly a month, was expected to return every day, and only yesterday, did I know positively of his inability to fulfill his promises. Neely Thompson came here, three days ago, and in a very few moments, I learned from him that I need expect nothing for the particular service I had done him. I've been vilified and abused in the papers for having received compensation for my services, when really and truly I have only received *less* than I should have got from any magazine or newspaper for my story.

I sent you the fifty dollars by Mr Dana, because I knew you must be in *immediate* need and there is no telegraphic transfer office on Long Island. It was the only fifty I have made since I've been here.

I am waiting to hear from Osgood regarding an advance on that wretched story; he writes me he does not quite like it.[3] I shall probably hear from him to-night. When the money comes I shall come with it.

God bless you and keep you and the children safe for the sake of

Limick

Provenience: UVa (ALS).

1. This letter is dated by reference to BH's note to Osgood cited in note 3 below and by his 19 October 1877 letter to AH (*Letters*, 61–62).

2. See note 2 to letter 90. Whatever the financial condition of the Capital Publishing Co., the paper did not suspend publication until 1890.

3. BH had sent Osgood the printed slips containing "The Story of a Mine" on 27 September 1877. In his cover letter, he plaintively asked: "How much can you advance me on the book?" (Charles Roberts Autograph Letters Collection, Haverford College Library, Haverford, Penn.).

92. TO JAMES R. OSGOOD, 6 DECEMBER 1877

713 B'way
Decem. 6th/77

My dear Osgood,

I sent the last proofs of the "Story of a Mine" in a separate cover to-day, excepting the concluding slip, which I enclose.[1]

As I told Mr Ticknor, I can find no better title for the story than the one I have already given it. I think the day of sensational titles is past, and in regard to this little romance, I think, if it proves successful, it will be rather from the contested title of the Mine it celebrates, than its own.

I wish you would add the dedication page I enclose.[2]

Of course I was disappointed to find my a/c balancing the wrong way. But why didn't you tell me this before, and why dont you send me the statement for November now? I dont doubt your figures, but

I'd like to know *how* my books sell, and whether I had not better learn some honest trade. An all ruling Providence prevented me from becoming a publisher in Washington.[3]

I may be wrong, but I honestly believe that neither you nor I would lose money, and that *we might make some*, by publishing at once a "Little Classics" copy of my later sketches. I sent you a copy of the English edition.[4] Since then, I have enough to make a good sized book without the poems. I have read the "Condensed Young American Pirate" novel to many, and I think it, alone, would sell the book.[5]

Now pray write me about it, or say in a few words that you haven't time to write, or you won't publish. Dont make me waste my substance in telegraphing to you for what a word or two by post might save.

Yours, possibly,
Bret Harte

P.S. I notice several grammatical errors in the revise. Wont you let your proof reader go over my English again carefully.

B.H.

P.P.S. I'll write you to-morrow as to the best terms of publication.

Provenience: Texas (ALS).

1. BH is returning the revised proof sheets of the story electrotyped from the newspapers slips he had sent earlier. See note 3 to letter 91.

2. BH dedicated the book to Udo Brachvogel (1835–1913), the editor of the New York *Belletristisches Journal* and New York correspondent of *Die Gegenwart*, "Whose clever translations of my writings have helped to introduce me to the favor of his countrymen." In a letter to Brachvogel (15 Apr. 1876, SFPL) BH had asked how he might "solely vest in you the right to hereafter translate my works in the German language." Brachvogel had translated *Gabriel Conroy* into German in *Deutsche Roman-Bibliotek* (Stuttgart: Hallberger, 1876), Band 1, and BH wrote again on 10 December 1876 (UVa) to thank him for a copy of the translation "in which you have incorporated so much of your own good work with mine." Brachvogel also translated BH's "Who Was My Quiet Friend?" under the title "Wer mein angenehmer Begleiter war" in *Die Gegenwart*, 6 Oct. 1877, 212–14, and "Two Saints of the Foothills" under the title "Die beiden heiligen der Vorberge" in *Deutsche Rundschau* 15 (Apr 1878):133–44. See also "Bret Harte in Germany," *Critic*, 21 Feb. 1885, 85, and Brachvogel's article "Bret Harte" in *Nord und Sud* (Nov. 1880).

3. The *Philadelphia Evening Bulletin* reported (1 Dec. 1877, p. 1, col. 4) that BH "has left Washington, severing his reported literary engagement there, and is now living at Sea Cliff."

4. The books in Osgood's Little Classics series were forerunners to paperbacks, cheap reprinted editions of popular texts. BH had sent Osgood a copy of his collection *My Friend the Tramp* (London: Routledge, 1877), which contained seven recent sketches and six recent poems.

5. "The Hoodlum Band, or the Boy Chief/The Infant Politician and the Pirate Prodigy," first published in *Godey's Lady's Book* 96 (Jan. 1878):33–40, and *Temple Bar* 52 (Jan. 1878):87–100. Osgood's edition of Harte's *Drift from Two Shores*, published in mid-July 1878, included several of the prose pieces in *My Friend the Tramp* as well as this condensed dime novel.

93. TO WILLIAM WALDORF ASTOR, 5 JANUARY 1878

713 B'way
Jan. 5th/78

My dear Astor,—[1]

You'll think me importunate, but even at that risk, I feel I must recall to you our conversation in your office, and ask you if you have any news for me yet. Is there anything I, myself, can do towards forwarding the matter? Have you heard of any position that you think I could fill, and is get-at-able? And if so, how?

I hate to bother you, knowing how much your time must be preoccupied with larger and just now more pleasurable things, but the fact is that I [am] becoming really very much distressed, and since my illness have been quite unable to do much with my pen.

I know you will keep this in your mind and in confidence. Send me a line—be the news good or ill, and believe me

Your friend
Bret Harte

W. W. Astor Esq.

Provenience: Autograph Collection (#9030), Special Collections Department, University of Virginia Library (ALS).

1. William Waldorf Astor (1848–1919), great-grandson of the founder of the Astor fortune, was employed in the management of the family estate.

94. TO JAMES R. OSGOOD, 10 FEBRUARY 1878

713 Broadway, N.Y.
Feb. 10th/78

My dear Osgood,

Your communication marked "Confidential" concerning the change in your firm, reached me 24 hours after I had read the news in the N.Y. papers.[1] You had probably been writing or talking *confidentially* to some one else, previously, so *I* had no show.

As I dont suppose my opinion will have the slightest might with you I withhold it for the present until I see how many additional thousand of my works the new firm dispose of, and observe the size of the cheque, which of course I suppose it is the intention of Houghton Osgood & Co to present to their authors by way of introduction. That is, if any of my works are to be published by the firm. In all of the published notices of the authors carried over into the new firm I observe my name is omitted.[2]

Thus much to the firm. To yourself, my dear Osgood, believe that I heartily welcome any change in your business affairs that will give you rest, and some surcease of trouble and anxiety. If this change will clear some of the worry from your brow, let up a little on your rheumatism and dyspepsia, and bring back the old, young Osgood to us again, I am sure that I and every one else who loves you for the pluck and honesty and manliness that has carried you through all that worry, will be heartily glad.

And even I will pay that debt of a dinner which you won of me through your superior knowledge of the general faithlessness of publishers.

When are you coming to New York? And what has become of Ben Ticknor?[3]

Always my dear Osgood, with or without a Houghton or a Co.,

Yours,
Bret Harte

Jas. R. Osgood. Esq.

Provenience: Harvard (Harry Elkins Widener Collection). By permission of the Houghton Library, Harvard University.

1. The partnership papers merging Hurd & Houghton with Osgood & Co. to form Houghton, Osgood & Co. were signed on 4 February 1878 (Ballou, 247). The *New York Tribune* carried news of the merger on 9 February 1878 (p. 4, col. 6).

2. While the *Tribune* report of the merger noted twenty names on the "brilliant list of authors" published by the new firm (e.g., Hawthorne, Longfellow, Emerson, and Dickens) BH's name was not among them.

3. Ticknor "was bought out for $40,000 in short-term notes and given a salesman's job with S. D. Warren & Co." (Ballou, 247).

95. TO JAMES R. OSGOOD, 9 MARCH 1878

713 Broadway,
Mar. 9th/78

My dear Osgood,—

Do you think you are treating me exactly right? It is now some three weeks since I wrote you from Baltimore regarding my new book of sketches and sent you some copy. I have no acknowledgement from you, nor any response to a later telegram.

If you are greatly preoccupied with other business, say so, and state when you can attend to mine. Your tardiness greatly embarrasses me in my bringing out an edition in England—copy having been already sent there.[1]

As this is my first dealing with your new firm, and as one of its members, Mr Houghton, was not particularly civil to me after he took the *Atlantic*,[2] I am anxious to know if this lengthy consideration of my proposition is to be taken as a form of declining, and if I am to have the privilege of trying my luck with another publisher. As I intend to publish the sketches, anyway, I think it only fair that I should know in ample time to make other arrangements.

I should also like to know something about "The Story of a Mine"—how it has been received and if it is selling.[3] I got a few copies from Mr. Dillingham as you had forgotten to send me the usual author's copies.

I hope to hear something from you by return mail.

Yours, always sincerely,
Bret Harte

Jas. R. Osgood Esq
Houghton, Osgood & Co Boston

Provenience: Bancroft (MSS C-H 57).

1. BH has sent Osgood copy for *Drift from Two Shores*. He has sent the same pieces to England for publication under the title *The Hoodlum Band and Other Stories* (London: Ward, Lock, and Co., 1878). That is, BH published some of his recent sketches twice in separate English editions. Both *My Friend the Tramp*, in press with Routledge, and *The Hoodlum Band and Other Stories*, in press with Ward, Lock, and Co., contained "My Friend, the Tramp," "The Man from Solano," "The Office Seeker," "Morning on the Avenues" or "Five o'clock in the Morning," "The Man Whose Yoke Was Not Easy," and "A Sleeping Car Experience."

2. See letter 57.

3. See note 3 to letter 90.

96. TO ANNA HARTE, 12 APRIL 1878[1]

Riggs'
Friday Night.

My dear Anna,

I'm considerably worried at not hearing from you. I have finished my poem; it makes over 400 lines, and I have written Lee to send you a cheque for $100.[2] I suppose he will; I see no reason why he should not be prompt, but people always take their own time, and only to-day have I got an answer from the *Independent* to whom I sent a poem last Thursday, with a request for them to send cheque at once. And the answer is—"that *the Editor has written* to me." Doesn't it beat everything?[3]

I have seen Stanley Matthews and he has promised me all his assistance,[4] and has, I hear from others, expressed great indignation at my having had to ask for a consulate. He told a friend that he would *make* the Administration *offer* it to me. I cannot help smiling at all this—but it may mean something.

I wrote to Watrous five days ago to see Dix for me.[5] No answer.

Here at least is something tangible. The Proprietor of the New Brazilian line of steamers will personally invite me to go on the first trip of the new steamer to Rio Janeiro. If all else fails, here is a trip and a rest for two months, sure.

God bless you. I wish I could send something more definite.

Limick

P.S. Dont forget to write—even if you have nothing new.

Provenience: UVa (ALS).

1. This letter is dated by reference to BH's letter to Homer Lee cited in note 2.

2. BH has completed his long poem "Cadet Grey" for *West Point Tic-Tacs* (1878), published by the artist and engraver Homer Lee (1856–1923). In a letter dated 12 April 1878 (UVa), BH instructed Lee to send a draft for one hundred dollars to AH at the Sea Cliff Hotel on Long Island, with this admonition: "I have given up my other work for this and am behind in my income."

3. The explanation is simple: The poem, "Miss Edith Makes It Pleasant for Brother Jack," had been refused. It first appeared in *Scribner's* 16 (Sept. 1878):721.

4. Stanley Matthews (1824–89), a Republican, was a U.S. senator from Ohio and later an associate justice of the U.S. Supreme Court (1881–89).

5. Charles Watrous was one of BH's friends from California who had relocated to the East. James Adams Dix (1798–1879), former U.S. senator (1845–49), secretary of the treasury (1861), minister to France (1866–69), and governor of New York (1873–75), was a member of the so-called Albany Regency and a Democratic power broker. That BH solicited the support of so established a Democrat as Dix tends to support Mark Twain's later charge that BH took neither side in the 1876 campaign because he had been promised "that he was going to be taken care of no matter how the contest might go" (*MT in Eruption*, 287–88).

97. TO ANNA HARTE, 19 APRIL 1878

Riggs House,
Friday night.[1]

My dear Nan,

I had an interview with Mr Seward yesterday,[2] which resulted in his confirming all and more than Stanley Matthews had said, and satisfied me, as far as evidence could go, that it was *the plan* of Mr Evarts to do something for me. Mr. Seward said "kindly" (like Frankie's schoolmistress) 'Mr Harte wouldn't you like to take the map and look at some of the places talked of for you. You know, however, that you are not supposed to know anything about it—until you are offered some place. But here is "Crefeld"—near Düsseldorf in Germany, on the Rhine; not much to do and its worth about $2500 now, and may be raised to $3 or 4000.[3] What do *you* think of it?—Mr Matthews was looking at it for you, and we've stopped the application of others for it at present. It is vacant now and has the advantage that you could take it at once.'

Of course I was wise enough not to commit myself—although you can imagine that, with all my disappointments, this seemed like a glimpse of Paradise. That it was well to wait, my interview with Matthews again this morning satisfied me, for he told me I could have the position of *First Secretary of Legation to St Petersburg*, salary $2600, if I wanted it! Of course this is away *up*, as honors go, but St. Petersburg is costly and very "swell," and I could barely keep up appearances on the salary. It would be pleasant, of course, to be with Stoughton[4] who is the Envoy, but I frankly told him why I thought I had better not take it, and he understood me. In looking over the "blue book," I noticed his hand and eye always rested on "The Hague," and always came the remark, "thats what you ought to have—the *Mission* there! But its filled, *and I dont know, yet, how we can get that man out!*" I only tell you this to show you that the estimation of my needs is increasing,—the places spoken of are *successively better*,—not that I expect or have a right to expect any thing better. But being in the saddle, I shall try to go as far as I can before I dismount.

And I have something else to tell you, which, happily, is a *fact accomplished*, and which, whatever is done hereafter cannot be undone. A paper or petition to the administration in my behalf has been circulated in Congress, and has received I dare not say *how* many great names and expressions of good will, recommending me to a Diplomatic or Consular appointment. It was an almost spontaneous movement in which they all have joined, irrespective of politics or party,—Democrats & Republicans, Northern & Southern men. One of the Senators told me that in the History of the American Congress, no such honor or compliment was ever before given to an American citizen. He said I should be proud of it—"if it brought me nothing"—but added, with a laugh, that no Administration was strong enough to dare to put themselves on the record as ignoring it.

There!—that'll do for today, Nan. I am to see Evarts to-morrow and I'll write—

No, I must tell you something else—in one respect *best of all*! I heard that—as indeed I had all-along feared—enemies were trying to poison Mr. Evarts ears with reports of my debts, extravagances, &c.[5] My friends took hold of the matter on the ground that Mr Evarts would be influenced by it, as this statement, if true, might show my unfitness for any financial trust.[6] In this extremity I remembered that I had held a pretty responsible position in the Mint, honorably, for 7 years. They were overjoyed at the news. I remembered also that John Jay Knox (now the Comptroller of the Currency)—a very high official—came out [to] California to investigate the Mint while I was there.[7] I went to see him:—he wrote a letter to Matthews (which Matthews sent to Evarts)—saying that I had held a most responsible position, and that in Swain's absence I was, virtually, Superintendent of the Mint and had been in the confidence of one of the best business men in California. So that, in one blow, all the stories of my extravagance, debts, &c. &c.—so far as they affected my having a responsible position under Government—were demolished! More than that, Knox's praise of me—absolutely clothed me with virtues of integrity, fitness, &. I didn't know I possessed.

So its all right, Nan—there!

I'll stop now and give you a rest. But I wanted you to get this before Sunday and have it to read over and think over then.

All that worries me now—is money. I'm at work writing again, although night and day, I keep at the other business. Matthews tells me to stay as long as I can. So be patient, and God bless you & the chicks!

Limick

Provenience: UVa (ALS).

1. This letter is dated by the postmarked envelope.

2. Frederick William Seward (1830–1915) was assistant secretary of state.

3. BH would in fact be posted in Crefeld, Germany, a town well known in the nineteenth century for the manufacture and sale of silks and velvets, from July 1878 until June 1880.

4. Edwin W. Stoughton (1818–82) had been a Republican member of the committee that reported on the Hayes-Tilden election of 1876 and served as U.S. ambassador to Russia (1877–79).

5. Among the "enemies" who opposed BH's diplomatic appointment was Clemens, who urged Howells on 21 June 1877 to inform Elinor Mead Howells's cousin Rutherford B. Hayes of the "disgrace of literature & the country which would be the infallible result of the appointment of Bret Harte to any responsible post" (*New England Quarterly* 58 [Mar. 1985]:89). Clemens also wrote Hayes to try to block the appointment (*MT-H Letters*, I, 235), though this letter has apparently been lost.

6. Ironically, Hayes had contacted Howells, prior to BH's nomination, to solicit his opinion. In his confidential reply of 9 April 1878, Howells vouched for BH and recommended him for the post: "From what I hear he is really making an effort to reform. It would be a godsend to him, if he could get such a place; for he is poor, and he writes with difficulty and very little. He has had the worst reputation as regards punctuality, solvency and sobriety; but he has had a terrible lesson in falling from the highest prosperity to the lowest adversity in literature. . . . *Personally*, I should be glad of his appointment, and I should have great hopes of him—and fears. It would be easy to recall him, if he misbehaved" (*Life in Letters*, I, 251–52).

7. John Jay Knox (1828–92) had been a Treasury Department official from 1862 to 1872 and served as U.S. comptroller of currency from 1872 to 1884.

98. TO ANNA HARTE, 23 APRIL 1878

Washington,

Tuesday Evening,[1]

Nan! Nan! Nan!

I have not written you because there was really nothing to say, and because I was so faint-hearted that I really could not feel that I could say anything. When I telegraphed to you that "I had succeeded" I meant that the President, the Secy. of State, and Carl Schurz, the Secy. of the Interior,[2] had all recognized my claims and had assured me *personally* of their intention of sending me to the Netherlands, Switzerland, or perhaps *a little higher up in the diplomatic scale.* I have been so fainthearted and ridiculously modest that until the day I telegraphed you I did not dare to believe in my success. But, when, after an interview with the President, the other day, in the Cabinet (where never before another civilian had been admitted) the President said that "he would unite with the Secy. of State in giving me an appointment["] and told me that "he did not mind saying that Mr Evarts["] (from whom I could not extract a word of positive encouragement before) "had sent in a list of preferred names and among them my own"—why, I could not help sending you that joyful telegram and feeling, as dear Carl Schurz said to me, that I was "all right." No one could have been kinder to me than this noble Teuton; no one has ever, I think, received such uniform courtesy and intelligent appreciation as I have. Whatever I receive from the Department of State I have *won by my own individual efforts*; I have not had to wet the sole of my shoe in the political mire— Even the Mason's with their "cousinry" really have not done anything for me,—and in the beginning I saw at once that I must stand alone.

I am so full of my experience that I cannot write, and wait until I can see you. Then I will talk for half-a-day. In my whole life I have never had such an experience, or one so fateful of good or ill.

You imagine I think, Nan, why I have delayed here. But when you remember that I came here with $20 in my pocket, and that until I sent to N.Y. to-day I had nothing more, you will know, why I lingered. And yet you will *be glad to know that every moment's delay has helped me—as I will explain to you.*

God bless you; Know that I will come when I can, and that I am perhaps making the turning point of my life.[3] Limick

Provenience: UVa (ALS).

1. This letter is dated by the postmarked envelope.

2. BH has conferred with Hayes, Evarts, and Carl Schurz (1829–1906), a liberal Republican, former U.S. senator from Missouri (1869–75).

3. BH posted his bond with the State Department on 11 May 1878 and formally accepted the appointment as U.S. commercial agent at Crefeld, Germany.

99. TO ANNA HARTE, 27 JUNE 1878

Off Staten Island,
Thursday 4 P.M.[1]

My dear Nan,

The morning baggage hasn't turned up yet, but I'm in hopes that it will before long. It would be a joke if—no it wouldn't be a joke at all. But I send this line back by the pilot to get you not to worry about it. The boys will tell you how they left me.[2] God bless you Nan, keep up a brave heart, and be patient and pray for

Limick

Provenience: UVa (ALS).

1. BH sailed for England aboard the *Suevia* on 27 June 1878 (*New York Times*, 27 June 1878, p. 3, col. 5).

2. His sons at his departure were fifteen and thirteen respectively; his daughters were six and three.

100. TO ANNA HARTE, 9 JULY 1878

Tavistock Hotel
London, July 9, 1878

My dear Nan,

As soon as I landed at Plymouth, yesterday morning, I telegraphed you, but, on arriving last evening, I found myself so fagged out that I did not write as I promised.

I know you are most anxious to hear about my health. I wish I could write more encouragingly, but I fear the voyage did me not even a temporary good. I was not seasick; I was simply heavy, dyspeptic, and sleepless. I do not think I have had one good night's rest since I left New York, except last night. In short, the voyage was a great disappointment to me—although from my recollection of my previous experiences at sea, I ought not to have built up much hope on that. Nevertheless, the trip was interesting—the weather, with the exception of one or two foggy days, delightful, and the sea, but for one or two days of rolling and roughness, quite calm and beautiful. I was not taken off my sea-legs, but spent most of my time day and night on deck; was thought to be a very good sailor, and secretly envied the passengers who were down in their berths, dreadfully seasick, and soon over it. Osgood was very jolly; Mrs. Waring very kind; the Colonel bright and self-complacent; and the few other passengers whose acquaintance I made were very pleasant. Hilgard, of the United State Coast Survey, was on board and gave me a chart on which I marked each day our reckoning, and which I sent to Wodie by mail.[1] It was a pleasant occupation and somewhat broke the monotony of the voyage. I made one or two notes of certain little experiences, of the exquisite colours of the ocean, which were new to me, and which I shall use hereafter.[2]

The run up, by rail, from Plymouth through southern and woodland England was so beautiful that it half atoned for the voyage. I never saw anything like it. There is nothing like it elsewhere. It is all I expected—and more! The island is one strong reality of vivid colour and verdure, but by no means a vision. Everything is comfortable and wholesome, even in its beauty. Nowhere is the earth so beautiful, but nowhere so thoroughly "of the earth—earthy."[3] There was to me something so new, and, as it seemed at the time, so comprehensive, in the revelation of England and the English character—a revelation I do not think has been made to any other writer, that I think I shall be able to make something of it. If I can get my health again—which I sometimes doubt—I think I can say some new things of England.

I am stopping at a quiet little hotel (Osgood's choice and selection) and have been already to see Routledge and Company, and sent my card to Charles Reade with Boucicault's letter last night.[4] I have not heard from him yet. Nobody has been to see me yet—it takes a long time, I suppose, for people to find you are in London, there being no publication, as with us, of hotel arrivals. It seems probable that I may be obliged to leave to-morrow, without seeing anybody—and that Joaquin Miller's ridiculous advice may be right, after all.[5] But I would rather go away unnoticed than follow it. And the programme Osgood and I propose may obviate it, which is this: I shall, unless I hear from Reade to-day, leave to-morrow for Paris, stay there a day, and go to Crefeld, take my place, present my credentials. Then a week later, when I have everything in order, a Vice-Consul appointed to act for me, I shall return to Paris, to meet Osgood there, stay a day or two with him, and then return with him to England, when anybody, if they come to see me, can find me. It seems to be the best thing to do at present. I may find some other place. At all events, I will write you from Paris or Crefeld, as again from here should I stay over to-morrow. Mr. Trübner,[6] of Trübner and Company, Osgood's friend, wants me to go down with him to see George Eliot and stay a day, but I dare not accept yet.

I have ridden four or five hours through London, and (from a hansom cab) have seen Saint Paul's, Westminster, and few other noted points.[7] But I reserve even a thought about them for the present.

I have only one very strong dominant feeling in this great, solid, earthly, powerful, and practical London. I am *awfully* lonely!

Frank

P.S. It was foolish of me not to ask you to write to London, for I shall not hear from you until I reach Crefeld.

Provenience: *Letters*, 75–78.

1. BH was accompanied on the transatlantic voyage by Osgood; the engineer Col. George E. Waring (1833–98), Waring's wife, Virginia; and Julius E. Hilgard (1825–91) of the U.S. Coast and Geodetic Survey.

2. BH used this material in the story "A Tourist from Injinny," published in the New York *Sun* on 29 September 1878.

3. I Corinthians 15:47. See also note 3 to letter 66.

4. The playwright and impresario Dion Boucicault (1820–90) has written a letter introducing BH to the novelist Charles Reade (1814–84), whom BH had parodied in "Handsome Is as Handsome Does" (see note 15 to letter 51).

5. As Miller reminisced later, BH "came to me in London on his way" to Crefeld with "a French dictionary in one pocket and a German dictionary in the other" (*San Francisco Examiner*, 7 July 1895, p. 25, cols. 1–2).

6. Nicholas Trübner (1817–84) was a prominent London publisher, the intimate of G. H. Lewes and George Eliot, among others.

7. Joaquin Miller remembered that he "had the pleasure of driving [BH] all day about London as he went through there, winding up [in Westminster Abbey] at the flat black stone with its brass letters above the dust of Dickens. He did not see the name under his feet, but was looking intently up at the bust of Thackeray. Then I touched his arm and pointed down, for it was almost dusk." In "the dim light that came in over the tomb of Chaucer . . . tears filled his eyes and fell on the big flat stone of Charles Dickens and I led him away" (*San Francisco Examiner*, 7 July 1895, p. 25, col. 2). Miller added a detail to this anecdote later: BH urged Miller to "read Dickens. He is the greatest of them all" (*San Francisco Examiner*, 7 May 1902, p. 3, col. 6). However, BH denied Miller's version of these events: "[T]here is no foundation in the story except that I was at Newstead Abbey when Mr Miller was there, and that I once met him in Westminster Abbey" (*Letters*, 289).

101. TO ANNA HARTE, 17 JULY 1878

Crefeld,
July 17th/78

My dear Nan,

At last! I arrived here at 8 oclock this morning, after a long sleepless ride of 12 hours from Paris and found your letter of June 28th awaiting me. It was only a days later news but it was the first one I had from home since I left three weeks ago.

I left London Friday morning and reached Paris the same night, intending to come here the next day, but I found myself so worn out that I lingered at Paris until last night—3 days. I saw Dora & Gertie[1]—they were both glad to see me, were very kind and found a nice little hotel for me, and helped me in many ways in my lingual helplessness, although I was dreadfully disappointed that they could not come to Crefeld with me, where so much depended upon my having some friend with me who understood the language. But I have audaciously travelled alone nearly 400 miles through an utterly foreign country on one or two little French and German phrases, and a very small stock of assurance, and have delivered my letters to my predecessor and shall take possession of the Consulate to-morrow. Mr Wausleben the present incumbent appears to me—I do not know how far I shall modify my impression hereafter—as a very narrow, mean, ill-bred, and not over-bright puritanical German. It was my intention to appoint him my Vice Consul—an act of courtesy suggested both by my own sense of right and Mr Seward's advice, but he does not seem to deserve it, and has even received my suggestion of it with the suspicion of a mean nature. But at present I fear I may have to do it, for I know no one else here,—I am to all appearances utterly friendless; I have not received the first act of kindness or courtesy from any one, and I suppose this fellow sees it. I shall go to Barmen to-morrow to see the Consul there,[2] who held this place as one of his dependencies and under whose direction Wausleben was—and try to make matters straight.

Its been uphill work ever since I left N.Y. but I shall try to see it through, Please God! I don't allow myself to think over it at all, or I should go crazy. I shut my eyes to it and in doing so perhaps I shut out what is often so pleasant to a travellers first impressions, but thus far London has only seemed to me a sluggish nightmare through which I have waded, and Paris a confused sort of hysterical experience. I had hoped for a little kindness and rest here. Perhaps it may come. But you must know that the only courtesy extended to me in London was through one of Osgood's friends, Mr. Trübner, of Trübner & Co who invited me to his house. While Reade whom I saw finally by going to him, was barely civil, made a lame excuse of intending to write to me, and said Boucicault had *not* written to him and that he, (Reade) never had anything to do with the new paper.[3] Houghton never answered or noticed my card.[4] But to day I found here (forwarded from London) a kind letter response to my card from Froude who invites me to come to his country place—an old seaport village in Devonshire.[5] If everything had gone well here—if I can make it *go* well here,—I shall go back to London & Paris for a vacation of a few weeks—and see Froude at least.

At least Nan, be sure Ive written now the *worst*; I think things must be better soon. I shall, please God, make some friends I trust in good time—and will try and be patient. But I shall not think of sending for you until I see clearly that I can stay *myself*. If the worst comes to the worst, I shall try to stand it for a year, and save enough to come home and begin anew *there*. But I could not stand it to see you break your heart here through disappointment as I mayhap may do.

Gertie told me that the French and English papers copied all the ugly things that were said about me. That may account for some of the incivility. I shall write again in a day or two when I have taken my place.

Your affec
Frank

P.S. My health is pretty fair. It would be unfair to judge of it now until I get over my worries.

Provenience: UVa (ALS).

1. Dora Griswold, the wife of AH's brother Charles. Her daughter Gertrude Griswold (1861–1912) was studying voice at the Conservatoire in Paris.

2. The U.S. consul in Barmen, near Cologne, was Edgar Stanton.

3. Ironically, according to Stuart Robson, a year before Reade "spoke of Harte in terms of the warmest admiration, declaring that his humor was so refined that it was delightful" (*San Francisco Chronicle*, 14 Oct. 1877, p. 1, col. 9).

4. Richard Monckton Milnes, Lord Houghton. See note 6 to letter 66.

5. The historian James Anthony Froude (1818–94) is best known for his multivolume *History of England* and a biography of Thomas Carlyle. BH had met Froude in New York in 1872 (*New York Times*, 16 Oct. 1872, p. 8, col. 1). On 23 July 1878 (JBH), Froude wrote BH that "It will be delightful to see you here and I really think the place will interest you or if not the place, at least the people. Come when you will or can and stay as long as you can."

102. TO JAMES R. OSGOOD, 19 JULY 1878

Crefeld,
July 19th/78

My dear Osgood,—

I've just answered your telegram—how satisfactorily I dont know. I should like to go with you to Switzerland, but if going means a giving up of Paris entirely let me rather perish![1] I saw so little of that highly glazed metropolis while was there that I couldnt identify it under oath. Most of my time was spent, *en famille*, with my sister-in-law and her daughter,[2] in style too decorous for you to understand much less imitate. The last two evenings I wrote letters.

I expect to be in Paris Tuesday night and at the *Hotel du Nouvel Opera, 48 rue de la Chaussée-d'Antin*, where I'd advise you to go at once unless you prefer to pay for gilded carelessness in the 7th *etagr* at the Grand Hotel. Its only a few squares away and is near the New Opera house—very central and convenient. Mdms Donvillé—proprietress—speaks English enough to keep you from forgetting it in your voluble French, and will give you a nice room for 15 francs a day with table d'hote or 8 francs a day without board.

I've just got the Consulate in running order, but it was a tough job in a town where no English is spoken, and the Consul himself is frightened as to almost forget it. I made the former incumbent, who was only Consular Agent, my Vice and as this is a kind of promotion, it softened his savage and outraged sense.[3] But you can readily imagine that there was very little desire here to assist the American stranger whose "hand had crept across the trade" of a native. So I had to play it alone on a few substantives and verbs and a great deal of assurance.

What does this Switzerland trip mean? I know you dont care to see mountains or glaciers. What kind of a looking girl is she, anyway?

Dis ess not orpsides Mr Osgoods, eh? This reminds me of a story. I went into a bookstore here where English is alleged to be spoken. After I had made my purchase—(another map!—) I noticed a German translation of one of my books lying on the counter. Thinking to ingratiate myself with my new fellow citizens I picked up the book and with a modest smile, pointed to my name in large letters on the cover and said "That is mine." *Der Buchhandler* without a smile, took the book quietly but firmly from my hand, said "das is fuer my brudder in Stuttgart," and turned scornfully away.[4]

Dont overdo things in Paris but wait for me.

Always Yours,
B. H.

I enclose your telegram. This attempt of yours to show you have forgotten your English is simply absurd.

Provenience: Harvard (Harry Elkins Widener Collection). By permission of the Houghton Library, Harvard University.

1. Osgood had invited BH to join him in Paris on July 22 to travel to Switzerland. Their "little excursion" fell through when BH was preoccupied in Crefeld in hiring a vice-consul. See Carl J. Weber, *The Rise and Fall of James Ripley Osgood* (Waterville, Me.: Colby College Press, 1959), 169–70. BH arrived in Paris on July 29 and, as he wrote Henry J. Winser, the U.S. consul in Sonneberg, Germany, on 1 August 1878 (Bancroft, MSS C-H 57), he expected "to stay a few days" there "without leave from the [State] Department. I shall at once apologize (when I return to my post) averring my ignorance as a novice." He returned to Crefeld six weeks later.

2. A private joke. See Aldrich, 137: "Mr. Harte came to dinner *en famille*, or, as he said a friend said to him in California, '*En famille*, with my family.'"

3. On 22 July 1878 (*Letters*, 82) BH wrote AH that Wausleben "backed out again." Instead, he hired Rudolf Schneider to be his vice-consul and to "take all of the work of the Consulate off my hands, for all the fees above $2500."

4. BH later wrote Lewis Rosenthal with a different version of this anecdote: "I think I was never more keenly and humanly touched with a sense of gratitude than on the first day of my arrival in Germany. I was wandering down the Königsallee of Düsseldorf, in the utter loneliness and friendliness of a foreigner to its language and people, when I caught sight of my own name, in German text, on certain little quaint-looking books, with queer titles, in a bookseller's window. It was like the hail of a friendly voice, and as I passed on, it seemed to me that I was no longer a stranger" (*Critic*, 21 Feb. 1885, 85).

103. TO GERTRUDE GRISWOLD, 18 AUGUST 1878

The Moult.
Salcombe, Kingsbridge, Devonshire,
Sunday, Aug 18/78

My dear Gertie,

I did not leave London until Thursday afternoon, and, had I known the trip here was as long as from London to Paris I should have given it up, or crossed the channel instead. But I dont regret it now, only I am a little punked to have spent so much time in London and travelling.

I left the train at Kingsbridge Road and took an old fashioned Stage Coach to where Mr Froude's carriage met me 12 miles beyond. The way lay through high green hedge rows, with glimpses here and there of the distant sea, and long reaches of undulating fields and commons, and part quaint old lodge gates, and queer little tumble-down villages of thatch and stone. It was quite late when Froude's carriage took me up but I kept on 6 miles further in the long English twilight over moors and commons, until we passed a gamekeepers lodge, and then a Paters lodge all roses and ivy, and began to descend a terraced slope and at last pulled up at a gray ivy covered entrance porch and I heard Froude's voice and knew I had arrived. But it was like a leaf out of some English novel. So thoroughly does it seem like something I have read that I fear I only half-enjoy it, and at times I am anxious to wake up and come back to reality again. I look out of my window upon these lovely lawns and terraces down to the deep blue sea, and the ruined castle on the promontory at one side, or I walk out in the hillside garden where the rotted walls hang with peaches and apricots, and where the sea wall holds a few cannon and a flag staff, and I seem to be as unreal and as much of a ghost myself as the scene. The crowning absurdity of it all is that when I go back to my room I read on the door the inscription "Lord Devon"—(for this is the Earl of Devons house and I occupy his room) and I seem to have died, and to be resting under a tombstone, with an inscription over me that lies even more than tombstones usually do. When I awake at night I expect to see that ingenious nobleman at my side, endeavoring to persuade me that he is B.H. and I'm mistaken.

Froude is a connexion of the Earl, and has hired the property for a summer house. It is not ostent[at]ious or grand, but perfectly lovely and tasteful. Think of all you have ever read of English Country houses, and imagine this as something between Locksley Hall, and the "High Hall Garden" where "Maud" used to walk.[1]

Now, as to the people: Of course Froude is *splendid*, awfully bound and elegant, tall, dark, deep-voiced and foreign looking, as all great Englishmen are, but simple and gentle as a child, and more loveable even than when I knew him in America.[2] The ladies of his family are four—but here comes in my oddest experience. The eldest daughter, but for her pronunciation, would be in style and intellect a perfect copy of an educated Boston girl. She knows all kinds of dreadful things,—Rationalism, Herbert Spencer, Politics &c&c. and more than all talks about them as freely as a man. Her sister is only 10 years old, yet, overhearing something I said to her father one day this child told her sister that "she feared Mr Bret Harte was inclined to be skeptical." Doesn't this beat any English story of Yankee children's precocity? Imagine how I regard this terrible infant![3] Then there is the usual, low-voiced uncomfortably civil governess, and the dowager sister-in-law of Froudes, who is the widow of a Bishop[4] and who looks like Queen Elizabeth, and asks me civil questions about America in a voice like Mrs Siddons.[5] I dont dare to ask about Mrs Froude, or if there *is* one—I ought to know but I've forgotten. She isn't here and I think she's dead, as they all were mourning.[6]

I walk and talk with Froude, whose conversation is delicious—but the rest of the time get rather low-spirited, although the others are very nice, and theres much to do and see here.

Yet I am not happy. I'm fearful I dont fit in here any better than I did in Paris. I wonder where I really belong.

I'm afraid this is not an earnest letter. Is it flippant? You dont know what you want.

I'm going back to London in a day or two, and then to Paris on my way back to Crefeld.

Please do not show this letter to any one out of your family. I hate to write anything about people I like, as I have written here. I write to you, confidentally. B.H.

Provenience: Huntington (HM 25909).

1. BH alludes to Tennyson's "Locksley Hall" and *Maud: A Melodrama.*

2. See note 5 to letter 101.

3. Froude's elder daughter was Margaret, the younger May.

4. Fanny Kingsley, Froude's sister-in-law, was the widow of Charles Kingsley (1819–75), formerly professor of modern history at Cambridge and canon of Westminster.

5. Probably one of the nursemaids BH had employed after moving east in 1871.

6. Froude's first wife, Charlotte, had died in 1860. His second wife, Henrietta, had died in 1874.

104. TO ANNA HARTE, 6 AND 10 SEPTEMBER 1878

Newstead Abbey
Nottingham
Sept 6th/78

My dear Nan,—

I came up from Froude's to London quite ill, and yet I had to wait here a few days for Osgood who was going back to America, and who I trust has sent you my note and a few trifles I gave him for the boys.[1] While waiting here, however, I got an invitation from Mrs. Webb, the hostess of Newstead Abbey to visit her there.[2] I think I am indebted somewhat to Mr. Miller for this first introduction to some of the best people in England—for he was visiting the Abbey at the time,[3] but after I arrived here, and since I have been here, all the kindness and excessive cordiality shown to me I think I won for myself. For I have heard much of English hospitality, but never was so pleasantly convinced of it. I have been told that this beautiful house must be considered my "English Home"—to come here whenever I want, do as I like—and always feel that my English "first cousins" would be glad to see me. And even the few days I have spent here quite draw me to believe in this pleasant illusion.

You have of course read all about this old home of Lord Byron's. Washington Irving was here when it belonged to Byron's old schoolfellow Col Wildman and has written about it.[4] There are many pictures of this old Norman abbey—(and some I shall send you—) and perhaps you already know *how* it looks; but neither photograph nor written description can give you an idea of its beauty, of its wonderful mixture of the romantic, the historical, the legendary, and the modern opulence of a *perfect* English country seat.[5] I thought Froude's place was beautiful, but here is so much beauty, with history, with a certain grandeur, and, above all, with all the melancholy of Byron's genius instinct in every line of the ruined chapel. It is grand and lovely as Byron, and as—sad. For the man has become a very real person to me since I have been here, and what I have always looked upon as his fancies and his affectations I now see were doubtless very genuine and sincere. To be *here*, where *he* played as a boy and know how dreadful it must have been for him to part with it; to see the great house of "Annesley" and even the "antique oratory" where he stood with Mary Chaworth, and feel in some queer way *why* he was unappreciated here—a feeling which the ludicrous self-conceit of these people here perpetuated by a hideous picture of an agonized Byron in a dark corsair's cloak looking in a window on the perfect happiness of Musters and Chaworth—to come back to the abbey and at night hear the wind sighing through the ruined central window of the chapel, and the wall left standing like a great screen, or to come up from the billiard room at night, through the old cloisters, when the light of your bedroom candle is but a foot from you, and from every arch the figure of the "black friar" seems to steal forth—then you begin to understand something about this proud, handsome, sensitive, lame boy. I never thought I should ever feel like crying over Byron. But I walk here alone in a dream, with only this beautiful, wicked, foolish, but awfully pathetic figure appealing to me out of the past until I forget everything but that.[6]

10th Septem. London

I take this up after leaving Newstead on my way back to Crefeld. I'm afraid you cant read it but I leave it for you to puzzle over. Leaving Newstead was like leaving home, in the week that I was there I felt more at ease than I have felt anywhere since I left America. These people have very truly made it "my English home."

Among the little photographs I have put away to send you is one of *my room*—"the Duke of Sussex Room" as it was called. It was next to the great ruined screen-like wall of the Abbey, and overlooked the lake. I tried to write you here and began two letters to the boys, but I was so full of everything I saw that I could not write a line. I slept one night in the Byron room—the haunted chamber—of course without anything coming of it—but that night I wrote a funny ballad called the "good Lord Byron"—being a sort of relief to the awfully gloomy stories of the dreadfully wicked Byron, and gave it to Geraldine Webb—whose picture I send you—for her album.[7] It was a great success and the whole countryside were anxious to have it to copy. I'll get a copy from the lady and send it to you. I remember only that it was very ridiculous and audacious, and that all the Byron ghosts headed by George Gordon himself, would have been justified in haunting me the next night.

I met many pleasant people. Among them was the Duchess of St Alban's—a sweet, bright, sympathetic, graceful lady to whom I took a great fancy.[8] I lunched at her house and she came over the next day with all her party from "Bestwood Lodge" to luncheon at the Abbey. She had, she confessed to me, set her heart upon taking me away from the Webbs and installing me at "Bestwood," and she at last got the Webbs to consent. But I knew they felt a little sore about it and they had been very kind to me, and so I declined as graciously as I could, and got out of it by promising to make the Duchess a visit in October if I could come to England. She sent me her photograph which I will send you and a book which she wanted me to read. I met her once or twice in my wanderings with the Webbs out toward "Annesley" and Hucknall, and have a very picturesque recollection of her coming through the graveyard at Hucknall Church where Byron is buried, with a train of some of the prettiest women in England behind her—but herself the nicest of them all. It was pretty to see the graceful suggestion of deference paid her by these other women—who were mostly her old schoolfellows and friends and who called her by her christian name—and the sweet little graceful way she accepted it—the whole thing more a sentiment than a formality. It was the only indication I ever saw of her rank—of her being the wife of the second oldest Duke in the Kingdom.[9] I always felt more at ease in her presence than I ever felt among American women. She was perfectly *natural*, and so indeed were they all. We had, a day or two afterward, a picnic in Sherwood Forest—and a visit to Lord Manner's great house, and Mrs Scott-Murray and her sister, and a Mrs Percy-Gore and her daughter (two beautiful women of apparently the same age)—helped me to poke fun at the paintings, and pretend to appraise the value of the furniture as if they had been two mischevious American girls—say the Godwins. This reminds me that I met Annie Godwin in Paris at the Hôtel Splendide. Her father and mother were in London, she was in company with a very "fast" American woman and her daughter, and of course there was no end of wickedness that she informed me she had not been up to. She had been to *Mabille Closerie Bougain* &c.&c.[10] I could not help laughing but I could not help remembering what these filthy Frenchmen think about our American girls. And I must say that the extravagances of some of our "fast" girls justify them somewhat. Gertie told me that she had to fight against this prejudice of the best people to the American girls when she first entered the Conservatory, and that she did not dare to be even civil to a gentleman.

The Webbs told me to tell you that you are to come to them as soon as you come to England, and the boys are to have the lake to row on and fish in. They have been very kind—but for all that I cannot say that I like England or should like to live there—or that I am very anxious to go there again. I am always heart-sick for my own country. I do not feel as if I could stop long in any place—and the thought of two years longer here sometimes makes me feel utterly hopeless.

My eyes are troubling me so that I must stop writing. They have been very weak lately. Hence this scrawl.

I hope Osgood sent you a cheque for some copy I gave him,[11] for I cannot send you anything until I get back to Crefeld. God bless you. I'll write from there. Limick

Provenience: Texas (ALS).

1. Osgood sailed for New York on 29 August 1878. On August 27, BH had written AH (Pemberton, 185) that he "dare not go with Osgood to Liverpool for fear I shall get on the steamer with him and return. So I try to forget that I have no house to go to, but must stay here, day by day."

2. BH's hosts at Newstead Abbey were Col. William Frederick Webb and Geraldine Webb.

3. As Joaquin Miller claimed later, "We last met at Newstead Abbey. . . . [T]he great good people there wanted to see him, and I had been se[n]t to decoy him to Newstead from his humble post of French-German Credfeldt" (*San Francisco Examiner*, 7 July 1895, p. 25, col. 2). Miller and Harte never saw each other again. "We parted at St. Albans, one morning after a shower. As we said 'good-bye' we stood beneath a rainbow" (*San Francisco Examiner*, 7 May 1902, p. 3, col. 6). But see also note 7 to letter 100.

4. Washington Irving visited Col. Thomas Wildman, who had known Byron at Harrow, at Newstead Abbey in January 1832. See Irving's "Abbotsford and Newstead Abbey" in volume 2 of *The Crayon Miscellany* (1835).

5. Ironically, BH had remarked in a review of *Notes in England and Italy* (*Overland* 4 [Mar. 1870]:295) that Sophia Hawthorne's "picture of Newstead Abbey, as restored and preserved by Colonel Wildman, is

excellent for its details" and she "indulges in none of the cheap poetry with which most sentimental pilgrims overflow at Newstead."

6. BH was intimately familiar with the story of Byron's schoolboy passion for Mary Chaworth, who lived in nearby Annesley Hall, married the squire John Musters in 1805, and was the subject of Byron's later poem "The Dream."

7. BH's original holograph of the unpublished "Moral and Instructive Ballad of the Good Lord Byron," in twenty-four quatrains inscribed to "Miss Geraldine/Her Book/from B.H./Newstead Abbey, Septem 1878," survives in the Bret Harte Collection (UVa).

8. Grace, Duchess of St. Albans (d. 1926).

9. The tenth Duke of St. Albans was William Amelius Aubrey de Vere (Beauclerk) (1840–98).

10. Annie Godwin, the fourth of Parke Godwin's seven children, had apparently visited a Parisian "pleasure garden."

11. "The Great Deadwood Mystery," subsequently published in *Scribner's* 17 (Dec. 1878):177–88.

105. TO GRISWOLD HARTE, 14 SEPTEMBER 1878

Crefeld,
Septem. 14th/78

My dear Wodie,—

I'm glad you wrote me about the boat, although I must leave it to mamma to say whether you should keep it or not. I read your description of it to the Webb family at Newstead Abbey, and they all thought that boats must run remarkably cheap in America.

I've mislaid or torn up a letter I began to write you, telling you something about Paris and the Exposition, and how I went *up* in a balloon, and *down* in the sewers of Paris.[1] But it seems so long ago now, that I can't remember it entirely. So I'll only say that when I went up in the balloon,—or rather when Paris and the whole earth seemed to drop away and sink from us I was *disappointed*. It did not seem grand nor terrible at all. It was a "captive" balloon—that is, was fastened by a long and strong cable of wire to the earth, so that it could not ascend above a certain distance. I was told afterwards that if the cable were to break, it would—relieved of all that weight—

shoot upward with the velocity of a cannon ball, and that every one would be killed as surely by its rapid flight *up*, as they would if they had fallen *downward* the same distance. I remember noticing that when we were half a mile up, every sound of the earth ceased. When we descended again the noise of Paris suddenly came back—like a shout!—as if a window had been suddenly opened.

The sewers of Paris are like underground rivers, running through streets brilliantly lighted with gas. There is scarcely any odor, and they say that the other day a romantic American lady, leaned back in the boat, quite forgot herself, and let her fingers trail in the water.

I had written you a good deal about *Notre Dame*, but all I remember now is that the *Sacristan* showed us the blood-stained clothes of the murdered Archbishop of Paris—who was assassinated by the Communist mob,[2]—and that while he was talking indignantly about it, the people who stood near us, who were all Parisians were staring and listening to him, but I remembered thinking that they were, after all the brothers and cousins of the men who did it, and would be just as likely to do it again. For they are the queerest people in the world. They get raving crazy quicker, and get sooner over it, than any other people in the world. I was in a shop one day and hearing a noise outside I went out and found my *cocher*, or driver, engaged in a furious quarrel with some man, and the whole neighborhood "assisting" with clenched fist and gesticulations, and the most awful threats and the highest of voices. I thought certainly that some one would be killed, and began to look around for another *cocher*, but before I could find any—suddenly my man reappeared as gentle as a lamb, smiling and wanting to know if he should still "*Attendez*"! or whether "M'sieu" would go on.

I saw the tomb of Napoleon at the *Invalides*—it is kept very much like a Saint's tomb, with lights, &c. &c.—and was very funny. All the 'big' things that the French attempt to do are funny. Their whole idea of grandeur is glitter—whether of *gas*, or *mirrors* or *gold*. But it must be always something shiny.

The Exposition was not as good as the Philadelphia one. There were some splendid works of art—but I dont remember seeing anything in the way of inventions or machinery that was more remarkable than a "swimming doll." It struck out in the water just like a human being.

At Newstead Abbey—I've written something about it to Frankie[3]—there was a large lake and on it ten little forts with cannons. One of the old Lords Byron built it for play and had a toy full rigged ship—the model size—brought through the forest (Sherwood Forest) from the nearest sea-port. One of the old servants hearing of it instantly fainted! Then she condescended to explain that there was an old story that mischance would come to the house of Byron—whenever a full-rigged ship came through Sherwood forest to Newstead Abbey. The mischance, it afterward appeared was the killing of somebody else by the old lord.

That will do for to-day, Wodie. I've something else to tell you another time.

Be papa's *good big* boy, and remember I'm

Your affec.
Papa

Provenience: Bancroft (MSS 88/181 C).

1. The Morse Collection at UCLA contains a copy of Ermete Pierotti's guidebook to Paris (1878) *ex libris* BH.

2. During "Bloody Week" (21–28 May 1871), when the Paris Commune was forcibly suppressed, the communards executed a number of hostages, including the archbishop of Paris.

3. BH's 11 September 1878 letter to FH (*Letters*, 97–100).

106. TO ANNA HARTE, 5 OCTOBER 1878

. . . *Crefeld*, Oct 5th/78

My dear Nan,

I was conscience-stricken and horrified when your letter came, to look back and find it was nearly three weeks since I had last written. But they were *very busy* weeks to me, all the business that had collected in my office during my absence to England, and all my first Quarterly Reports to the Department had to be got rid of. It is so late now that I must only send you a few lines with a draft for $100—and a promise, which I shall *surely* keep to write again within the next week and send you another draft. I wish I had more money *to send now.* For I want you to be able to make your arrangements to leave Sea Cliff, before the 1st November. You must not on any account stay there during the winter. I've so much to say to you for and against coming here this winter that I must not open the subject now. All I can say now is—that from *my own experience* (and it has been pretty general,) that I know of no happiness, comfort, pleasure—mental or bodily, that can be had by a residence in Germany—that cannot be had in America with less trouble and expense. You probably think I exaggerate—wait until I write again and I'll give you a few details—and personal experiences. I am not speaking of a visit, or the novelty of travel and sight seeing. I speak particularly of a home.

I think my health is better although I came back from England with a cold very much like my cold of last winter.[1] I think I have broken it up however by a very simple German remedy—so simple that I want you to try it. I take a goblet full of equal parts of hot *milk* and cold Selters water, every morning before rising. You know how I dislike milk; but the Selters water takes away the buttery taste, and makes a palatable drink—very much as I imagine cream sodawater tastes. There is enough salt in the Selters to give it a flavor. Try it. 1/2 glass of *hot* milk 1/2 glass of Selters, mixed before rising. It is a sovereign cure for a cold in the beginning.

You asked me to try the German wines. I did, but they did not agree with me, and the Doctor ordered me to drink red wine, (Bordeaux). Its too bad for the wines here are good and cheap. But almost every form of wine or alcohol disagrees with me. My dyspepsia has taken a new form of terrible distress and distension after each meal. I go often without my meals fearing to eat. But I'm better I think in other ways. I'm stronger. I can walk—without dizziness or trouble, and I walk nearly four times as much as I did in America. When I can afford it, I shall get me a horse. They are to be had cheap here—I mean on livery.

I was at first frightened as to my *work*. But I think I've got back my old strength and pleasure in my pen again. Its a great relief not to have to work against *time*, and to work for my own pleasure at my own leisure. And I shall have no difficulty in disposing of my work here, at good prices. I think I can make from my pen nearly twice as much as before. I hope to get something from the German publishers, and am in treaty with them now. The London journals write to me for copy. I've already accepted an invitation to lecture in Hull, England, for $250 this winter, and Froude thinks I will have no difficulty in making 10 or a dozen lectures in England.

My English friends have been very anxious to have me return to them for a visit. I enclose to you a letter from the Duchess of St Albans with an invitation I had to decline on account of my work here. I want you to observe from the letter that your own large handwriting is eminently aristocratic. She's a very nice woman. When I write again I'll send you her photograph, though it breaks my heart to part with it, of course!

Kiss the little girls and say that Papa has their pictures on his desk. Tell the boys I'll write to them presently, but not until after I write you again. Remember me kindly to Mr Devine. Ask Mr Dana if he got my sketch "a Tourist from Injinny" in time to publish it. I might have sent it elsewhere and got you a $100 for it, but I thought it better to send it to Dana to begin to pay up the money he so kindly advanced.[2] It will be all the better in the end if you can hold your own for a month yet. You will not then be troubled at all for want of money. My first settlement of accounts here make me nervous about drawing money, and I have kept one rule rigidly here. *I will not make a single debt.*

God bless you.

Limick.

P.S. I cant find St Albans letter, but I send a note of hers as a specimen of her handwriting.

Provenience: UVa (ALS).

1. On 10 September 1878 BH had written Gertrude Griswold from Crefeld (Huntington, HM 25910) that "Physically I'm a little better I think, morally I know I'm not."

2. See note 2 to letter 100. BH repays with "copy" the money borrowed from Dana to cover expenses until he could begin to draw his consular salary.

107. TO ANNA HARTE, 16 OCTOBER 1878

Crefeld. Oct 16th/78

My dear Nan,

I'm becoming very anxious to hear from you, as your last letter—

enclosing the pictures of Totty[1] and Ethel—came over six weeks ago. If you were waiting to hear from me I could understand it, but you have have long since received mine of September 15th and the package with the photographs from Newstead.

Ive not been so well since I wrote you a week ago. Perhaps I'm under the weather, or more probably as the Doctors think under the *climate*. It worries me sometimes to think that I may not be able to stay here, and I try to reassure myself by thinking how often I have said the same thing about the various places where I have lived. The climate is not exhilarating—perhaps it may be better for me if it is not—but I do not seem to be wholly myself, in energy or capacity to work.[2] Heaven forbid that I do not become like these lethargic, fat-witted Germans about me, who live altogether below their waists and whose hips and stomachs are the largest part of them. I have got their lethargy and dullness I fear without their health. Perhaps that may come later on. I think too that my dyspepsia is not so continuous, but more active when it does trouble me. I suffer *ridiculously* and yet most *painfully* from distension caused by flatulency, until I absolutely ache from the tension of the sinews of the abdomen. The doctor pounds me and thumps me for dropsy, but says its only acid, gives me some trifling medicine, and leaves me to feel stuffed and aching for hours after. I diet regularly and conscientiously, do not drink as much as the Doctor orders,—for I find that here the slightest stimulant instantly affects me—you would think me altogether a model—and yet I get up from a moderate repast with a feeling as if I were an helpless overfed boa constrictor. I say a *moderate* repast—temperance in eating here is a matter of necessity to me for the German cooking is poison to a dyspeptic. Grease, fried butter, half fermented preserves and some vegetables are the delights of the German table. Think of potatoes and *milk* and apples and *vinegar*, all in one dish. Think of them bringing you after your soup,—in which the grease stands quarter of an inch deep—compote or sweets, and the *roast* meat just before your cheese and coffee. Vegetables are always served *separately* as a course. Fish comes in at *any time*. You can readily imagine that I am obliged to have my meals separately cooked—and restrict myself to mutton and beef. The wines, which I thought I would like,—and capital Rhine wine they have here too—distresses me. I came at last to dread my meals—

and got very little comfort out of mere living. As to sleeping—there is not a decent bed in Germany. The single beds are bunks or berths—a little wider and deeper than a coffin, with a feather bed for a mattress and at the head and foot, under the mattress, two wedge shaped cushions, like this

so that the shape of the bed is thus

This is made to accommodate the ludicrous disgusting German *bottom* and hips, and this entire nation sleeps after this fashion

In this district of Germany it is absolutely *impossible* to get other beds—they dont understand you when you object to them—*they* could not sleep on an honest level spring bed any more than a club-footed man could wear an ordinary shoe. I have slept on sofas on chairs and on tables, and lately I took a room with two single beds and putting them side by side slept crosswise. The bedclothes to any nervous susceptible person are intolerable, the blankets are heavy, soggy, pancakey and scant in size, the sheets are narrow, and over all is the abominable "*bettdecke*" or "feather bed" placed on top of you, and reaching just above the waist.

It is utterly impossible for an American family to live here without bringing from America their own furniture and comforts, for they can never get them here. Although it is as cold here now—the middle of October—as it is in America in the latter half of November, and a dreary, chilling, foggy, misty atmosphere—there are no carpets to fit the floors, only square wig-like coverings, which leave a chilly margin of bare painted floor two or three feet wide around the walls. The only heating apparatus is an immense oven like iron stove placed in the corner against the wall, which does not give out as much heat as a foot warmer. There is consequently no hearth—no center in a room for a cozy disposition of chairs. You never are asked to draw your chair up to the fire—for you could not. You never see the fire—for it is hidden in two or three thicknesses of iron, you sit and shiver with your overcoat on—like the rest of them. The women always wear shawls in the house. When you ask them why they dont make fire places or have better stoves, they look at you helplessly. An American friend of mine at Barmen wanted to put a fire place in his house at his own expense, but the landlord objected, saying, that it would spoil the house for others—and he was right. My friend was the only American in Barmen, as I am the only American in Crefeld. It would be absurd to expect them to indulge what they think our expensive whims. Another American, the Consul at Elberfeld told me that it was lucky that my Barmen friend had not fitted up his grate & fire place as he could never have got coal to use in it. He then showed me the fuel he burned in his stove—the only kind that could be bought there. It was *absolutely* "*screenings*"—or coal *dust* mixed with water and clay—making a fire like dull coke. It is the fuel of the Rheinish provinces.

I might go on interminably, telling you of the discomforts of life here, how scantily water is furnished; how in even the modern houses, *baths* are unknown, how inexpressibly filthy all the water closet arrangements are, how impossible it is to get decent ventilation, how the sour and greasy smell of cooking permeates everything and everybody. How you can not get clothes to fit you ready made—nor even made for you,—how one or two English people that I know who have not particularly nice feet to trust of—are obliged to send to Paris for their shoes. I should like to see your narrow foot in one of these hideous "hoof pads" made for women. It is more like a chinese shoe in its short thick depravity than anything else.

Why do I tell you all this, Nan? It seems but trifling, but *you could not stand it* for a year—even for six months, or if you *could* you would sink to the level of these barbarians—for barbarians they are—with all their kindness and good humor. I think I suffer as much from the *idea* that I get of the *meaning* of such living as I do from its discomforts. When it no longer shocks me, I shall go away—for I shall feel that I have lost my sense of fineness and delicacy. I am not giving you only my *own* four months experience, but the general experience of the very few Americans that are between this place and Cologne.

One could stand the discomfort if one was sure that he got any thing in return. Everything that is peculiar to the country or for which it is especially noted can be got in America. Even the pictures and picture galleries are finer and more extensive in New York than in Düsseldorf. The best wines are sent to America; the best silks and velvets go there too. Perhaps it may be something to acquire the language. But it is a difficult language, and when acquired what then. It is at best, a barbarous tongue, overcrusted with gothic rudenesses. It will pass away, even as the uncouth German letters are now being abandoned by the younger German scholars to make way for the English or Roman script. Think of being obliged to spend a month over a printed and written alphabet which they themselves confess is a relic of barbarism, when you know it will be of no service ten or twelve years hence. Think how ridiculous it would be to bring up an American child on Old English letters—which have the same origin as the German, to enable it to read.[3] I am studying German with this dreadful feeling that it is time thrown away, except for my present convenience.[4]

I've forgotten one advantage here. Pianos—good ones—"Steinways" can be rented for $45 a year.

Summing it all up, I do not think you would be comfortable here this winter, and taking in the expense of coming, it would be a great deal dearer for you to come for six months or even a year than to stay where you are. I want you to be comfortable, Nan, and have no worry about money, and live where you think it best, and I shall try and send you enough to keep you from any fear of the future. My ideas of Germany may change before spring—I mean I may find means to make a comfortable home here—but at present I dont see it, and shall make no calculation upon it. I shall lecture in England this winter certainly *once*—perhaps a dozen times;[5] by moving around actively I shall keep off homelessness—but I shall feel very anxious until I know you are settled. The boys must go to school too. I had forgotten to say that they could not enter the schools here until they had a very thorough knowledge of German, so that really they would lose a year here at first.

I have been thinking to send you a silk dress by some returning tourist, but they are not plentiful—(I mean the tourists)—and I hesitate about asking a man to "smuggle" goods for me for it amounts about to that. When I return I intend to bring some things with me, but I shall first write to the Treasury Department for a permit. At present it seems to me best that I should,—instead of risking the confiscation of the silk or putting you to the trouble of going to the Custom House and paying the duties—get an order on a New

York correpondent of a Crefeld Exporter to give you a silk dress, of the quality I shall pick out *here*, and *pay for here*, and all you will have to do is to go [to] the importer, present your letter and select the silk yourself. It will be *Crefeld silk*, the same Limick invoices here, and just as good as if Limick himself put it up and sent it to you. But I dont want any "shenanigan" or "nonsense" about it—I dont want you to go to the importers and pick out instead stockings for the children, or curants for the boys—I want you to *choose a silk dress for yourself.*

I shall try to hit Christmas time, by sending some things from Crefeld to the children. If it isn't possible I'll send you the money to buy them there. The trouble about picking out anything here, is that everything that is rare or peculiar is immediately sent to America.

The Duchess of St Albans is very anxious for me to make her *that* visit. I am anxious too, for I know I would enjoy myself—and it would be quite a matter of *policy* in my coming lectures, to have friends among the best people. I enclose you one of her letters—but since then she has written to me to come on the 28th inst. I also send one of Froudes. He is a most delicious fellow. I will write again to-morrow, and send a draft. Kiss the chickens for me,

Limick

Provenience: UVa (ALS).

1. Jessamy's nickname.

2. Since leaving the United States, BH had published only one story: "A Tourist from Injinny."

3. In "Views from a German Spion" (see note 3 to letter 114) BH indicted Fraktur script, the "elsewhere-discarded, uncouth, slow-decaying text" that "plucks out the bright eyes of youth" and "bristles the gateways of your language" with "splintered rubbish."

4. BH complained to John Hay on 12 December 1878 (Brown University Library) that he was "doing very little here, except to wrestle with the language and wait for a verb to come round the corner and help me." He also wrote FH on 18 January 1879 (*Letters*, 124) that he had "begun to study German like a child . . . in the third and fourth reader" and "broken his heart and worn his eyes out."

5. See letter 112 and accompanying notes.

108. TO GEORGE W. SMALLEY, 9 NOVEMBER 1878

29 Upper Hamilton Terrace,[1]
London,
Novem. 9th/78

My dear Mr Smalley,[2]

I regret very much to have missed you to-day—the more so that my present stay in London is now limited to a few hours, and I leave for Crefeld to-night.

I need not tell you how, as a good American, it would have been my duty as well as my pleasure to have met you. But I must hope for another opportunity later on, when I again visit London. Perhaps next month—if not then, when I shall make arrangements to lecture in England this winter.

Very truly yours
Bret Harte

Mr George W. Smalley

Provenience: Bancroft (MSS C-H 57).

1. The Trübners' address in St. John's Wood, London.

2. George W. Smalley (1833–1916) was the longtime London correspondent of the *New York Tribune*. The two men likely met when BH returned to England to lecture in late January and February 1879. See *The Letters of Anthony Trollope*, ed. N. John Hall (Stanford, Calif.: Stanford University Press, 1983), II, 814, 832. Certainly Smalley praised BH's lectures in his *Tribune* correspondence (24 Feb. 1879, p. 6, col. 1; and 3 Mar. 1879, p. 1, col. 5). BH noted in his diary on 9 November 1883 (Berg) that he had "written Smalley" on behalf of his niece Gertrude Griswold; and he attended the dinner in London given Smalley upon his retirement (*New York Times*, 7 May 1895, p. 5, col. 3). Shortly before BH's death, Smalley complained that BH's most recent stories "lack freshness" and "have left no mark on current literature or thought" (*Munsey's* 26 [Mar. 1902]:774).

109. TO JOHN H. CARMANY, 10 DECEMBER 1878

Crefeld,
Decem. 10th/78

My dear Mr Carmany,—

I should not have left yours of the 14th Oct so long unanswered but I have been trying, through correspondence with America, to find out something more about Miss Coolbrith's missing poems. *First*, let me say that they are not in my possession, and have not been during the many years that have elapsed since I first offered them to the publishers here, or since I was first applied to to return them to her. They are not with my papers in America.[1]

Mr Osgood, of Houghton, Osgood & Co tells me that he returned them to me—either by mail or personally—but I have no recollection of anything more than what seemed to be the important fact that he declined their publication. I remember very distinctly of endeavoring to procure their publication by other publishers, but whether I sent them the poems I am unable to say. I always referred the publishers to the pages of the *Overland Monthly* for the quality of Miss Co[o]lbrith's verse. These publishers do not now remember whether they ever received or returned them. Mr Osgood alone remembers returning them to me.

I suppose I must refer my carelessness of the copy to the fact that the poems were all *newspaper slips* or *reprints*, and did not seem to have the value of MS in my eyes. I had read them all before in print and knew that the best of them were still extant in the pages of the *Overland*. I should never have thought of returning them, after having failed to procure a publisher, if I had not been written to about them, very shortly afterwards. I then answered, substantially what I say now.

I have done all I can to find and restore them. If they are lost I cannot see that their loss entails anything more serious than the labor of copying or clipping them from the pages of still-available magazines and periodicals,[2] and for that labor I am willing to pay. They were not many—If I remember rightly, were some 30 or 40 newspaper slips in an ordinary note envelope. I believe a few were MS copies of already printed verses.

I need not say that the personal regard I have for Miss Coolbrith and the high value I set upon her talents would compel me to do anything I could to assist her, even if I were not responsible for this missing copy. But I do not see how I can, in another quarter of the globe, do anything more than to trust to an uncertain memory of something that has elapsed eight years ago, and send her that in default of her "copy."

Yours very truly
Bret Harte

Provenience: Bancroft (MSS C-H 57).

1. The disappearance of Coolbrith's sheaf of poems was later added to the list of grievances against BH. The *San Francisco Examiner* (1 May 1892, p. 10, cols. 1–2) charged that "Miss Coolbrith gladly trusted her writings to the man who promised so much. Harte and the manuscript went East. To New Jersey went Harte; to the unknown went the verses. . . . Miss Coolbrith's book was never published in the East, nor did Harte ever give the publication attention." This version of events no doubt originated with Carmany, for Coolbrith bore no grudge. In a letter to Laurie Haynes Martin dated 9 February 1912 (Huntington, IC 209), Coolbrith defended BH: "What he was or did after leaving California I can say nothing for he passed out of my life; but while here I bear witness that he was one of the most genial, unselfish, kind, unaffected and *non*-conceited of all the writers I have known. . . . [T]hese repeated thrusts . . . come with a bad grace from California for which he did more in a literary sense, than all its other writers together."

2. In fact, Coolbrith subsequently assembled her first volume of poetry, *A Perfect Day*, in precisely this way. As her biographers Josephine D. Rhodehamel and Raymund F. Wood remark, "The compilation was not difficult. Of the sixty-three final selections, forty-six came from the *Overland*" (*Ina Coolbrith: Librarian and Laureate of California* [Provo, Utah: Brigham Young University Press, 1973], 156).

110. TO ANNA HARTE, 27 DECEMBER 1878

Crefeld,
Decem 27th/78

My dear Anna,

I've just received yours of the 11th. I wrote you a few days ago, and on the 23d telegraphed you $100, making $850. I hoped it would enable you to have a little money to spend on Xmas, even if you did not get something from Dana or Smith.

I was greatly mortified and angry at the letter Mr Smith sent you which you enclosed. I distinctly wrote Mr Smith that when he sent the article to Dana he was to fix *a price*. When I sent the "Tourist" to Dana I fixed no price and did not ask him to send the money to you. I am mortified that this pompous, *gossipping*[1] should know that I owed Dana money and *think* that I was trying to evade payment of it; I am *shocked* to think that Dana would imagine the same thing. It is enough to keep alive all the stories and lies about me that I am trying to live down, and which have partly exiled me from my own country.

A few days before Christmas I received a note from an Advocate in Crefeld, which like all my German letters I handed over to my Vice Consul to read and answer. He came to me in a few moments, and with a look of astonishment read it to me. It was about a bill of Leland's of the Sturtevant House dated 1874 for the balance of $300 that I owed him sent out here for collection and *suit*. I was so shocked and mortified and so angry at this kind of persecution by a rich man, for the Lelands are rich, and above all, the possibility of what I had always thought was impossible here, that I was completely *stunned*. It is of course quite improbable that any such bill can be legally collected here, the lawyers say, and at all events I have nothing they can take from me, but it will be known and I shall be ashamed and mortified—*and that is the object of this persecution*. Every creditor that I have can knock at my consulate door and worry my life out of me if they choose. I did not think it possible that I had any creditors so contemptible.

That was my preparation for Christmas, Nan. It was mighty hard. I had felt so secure—so free from that nervousness that daily bent me in N.Y. I have asked for a leave of absence to lecture in England and the Consul General at Berlin has approved it so I shall probably get some relief from that worry here.[2] I shall endeavor to tie up what money I make in England so that it cannot be touched. It can be very easily done.

I had two invitations out on Christmas or rather for the *two* days they celebrate as Christmas here; the 25th and 26th—one to an old fashioned German Christmas party with the *tree*. I'll write you more about them hereafter.

You have heard of course of Bayard Taylors death.[3] The Berliner Tageblatt, the great German paper telegraphed to me for an article on him and I wrote it and sent it. I wrote it Xmas day.—*that* was my Christmas. I had sat up all night to finish a long poem—a "Legend of Cologne" which I finished too.[4] So that I at least put that much work behind me. Ill send you them both—the poem I think is good.

God bless you all, and hoping that when this reaches you, you will have had a Happy New Year.

Limick

Provenience: Bancroft (MSS C-H 57).

1. At the top of the second page of his letter, in his haste, BH omits the noun that the adjectives modify.

2. On 17 December 1878 BH had requested a leave "for a period of seven weeks" to "lecture before various societies in Great Britain, on purely literary topics." His request was approved by Consul General Kreismann in Berlin on 23 December 1878 (NA).

3. Bayard Taylor (1825–78) was U.S. minister to Germany from April to December 1878. BH's essay "In Memoriam Bayard Taylor" appeared in German translation under the title "Zum Undenfen Bayard Taylors" in the *Berliner Tageblatt* for 29 December 1878. A manuscript of this piece survives at UVa; it has also been retranslated into English by Luther S. Luedtke and Patrick D. Morrow in *Markham Review* 3 (May 1973):101–105. As a boy in New York, BH heard Taylor lecture and, in the *Overland*, he reviewed Taylor's *By-Ways of Europe* (3 [Aug 1869]:195–96). BH likely met Taylor in California in July 1870 (see *New York Tribune*, 5 Aug. 1879, p. 2, col. 1), and he accepted Taylor's invitation to visit him in New York in March 1871 (UVa). Later, Taylor parodied BH's "Plain Language from Truthful James" (*The Echo Club* [Boston: Osgood, 1872], 158–60); and he criticized BH's *Two Men of Sandy Bar* (*Boston Globe*, 14 Nov. 1876, p. 3, col. 1). On his part, BH anonymously disparaged Taylor's Centennial ode (see note 4 to letter 87). On 20 July 1878, BH wrote Taylor from Crefeld to solicit his help: "Do you remember you once offered, if we chanced to be in Germany together, to make me known to some ducal friend of yours? Now, my dear fellow, I should be content to know even a Burgomaster or Police Inspector, if he lived in this District. For here I find myself quite

unknown" (*The Charles Meeker Kozlay Collection of Bret Harte* [New York: American Art Association, 1926], item 130). Taylor failed to respond in kind, to judge from BH's 22 January 1879 letter to AH (*Letters*, 128): "You remember that I did not feel very kindly toward him, nor had he troubled himself much about me when I came here alone and friendless, but his death choked back my resentment, and what I wrote . . . afterwards in the *Tageblatt* I felt very honestly."

4. Published in *Belgravia* 38 (Mar. 1879):44–51; and *Harper's Bazar*, 1 Mar. 1879, 134.

111. TO RUDOLF MORE, 2 JANUARY 1879

Crefeld,
Jan 2d/79

My dear Sir:

I have to thank you for your letter of Decem. 31st enclosing 200 marks. The copies of the *Tageblatt* have not yet arrived.[1]

In regard to the several proposals you were good enough to honor me with, I wish to say that I will give them speedy consideration. But I can say *at once* that your suggestion of my writing a series of frank, honest observations on my impressions of German Life and Character, not only fully agrees with my wishes but was my preconceived *intention*, and if you can give me an idea of the space you could afford in the columns of your journal, and how frequently, with the compensation you would be willing to make, I dare say we could come to an arrangement at once. It would be understood, of course, that I should retain the right to use the articles, in English, elsewhere than in Germany. I should also like to try the experiment of having the articles translated into German *under my own personal supervision and with my own ideas of equivalent expression &c &c.* And in making me an offer you might say—1st What you would give for the sketches in English. 2d What you would give for them in *German*. I only want to make the difference pay the cost of translation and copying. Consider this, and give me your answer as speedily as possible.

In regard to your publishing a novel of mine, there is time for consideration, as I have not at present any long story on hand. I fear that sketches like those I have given the *Rundschau* are not a good size for your *feuilleton*, and are perhaps too expensive for you.[2]

I have lately written a "legend of Cologne Cathedral."[3] But it is in *verse*, and would perhaps be too difficult for translation. If you would, however, like to see the English proof I'll send it to you.

Very respectfully yours
Bret Harte

Rudolf More, Esq
Editor Berliner Tageblatt

Provenience: General Manuscripts (Misc.), Princeton University Libraries (ALS). Published with permission of the Princeton University Libraries.

1. In payment for BH's memorial to Bayard Taylor. See note 3 to letter 110.

2. The *Deutsche Rundschau* had to date published two BH stories in German translation: "Die beiden heiligen der Vorberge" ("Two Saints of the Foothills") 15 (Apr. 1878):134–44; and "Vier-und-Siebenzig, Fünf-und-Siebenzig/Die Geschichte des grossen Deadwood-Geheimnisses" ("The Great Deadwood Mystery") 17 (Dec. 1878):449–68.

3. See note 4 to letter 110.

112. TO RUDOLF SCHNEIDER, 8 FEBRUARY 1879

Athenaeum Club
Pall Mall, S.W.
Feb 8th/79

My dear Mr Schneider,

Thanks for your prompt attention to the telegram, and the two letters I received to-day.

I am still very uncertain about my movements. The nearest decision I can come to is that I shall have the whole lecture tour postponed after my lecture at Nottingham on the 14th, and that I shall return to Crefeld immediately after. A month later I will come back to London again and have a big public dinner given to me and *then lecture* at St James Hall. This is the opinion of the best people here, who all say the tour has been frightfully mismanaged, and that I never should have lectured at the Crystal Palace at all. My instinct in regard to Carte's management was right *after all.*[1] I lectured at Hull on the 4th, but if it were possible to give up the Nottingham lecture and one at Southport I should do it and return at once.[2]

Its been a wretched blunder all through. Nothing has gone right, except the *Press*, and the *people.*[3]

Give my best regards to Mrs Schneider.

In great haste
Yours
Bret Harte

R Schneider, Esq.

Provenience: UVa (ALS).

1. The theatrical manager Richard D'Oyly Carte (1844–1901) produced many of the Gilbert and Sullivan operettas. BH had complained in a letter to AH the day before (UVa) that "Carte opened with me at the Crystal Palace at Sydenham, which would have been about equal to an *entree* in New York at Yonkers."

2. In addition to his dates in Sydenham (January 28), Hull, and Nottingham, BH lectured in Southport on February 11 and in Hastings on February 13. He cleared only about $200 over expenses. "I was bound in honor to perform them," he wrote AH on 21 February 1879 (*Letters*, 132), "or I should have returned when I found how I was *swindled.* Only a fear of repeating the 'Redpath' experience kept me from doing it."

3. BH's Crystal Palace lecture was favorably reviewed in the London *Daily News*, 29 Jan. 1879, p. 5, col. 6; *Athenaeum*, 1 Feb. 1879, 152–53; and *Punch*, 15 Feb. 1879, 60.

113. TO RUDOLF SCHNEIDER, 29 MARCH 1879

London,
Mar 29th/79

My dear Mr Schneider,

Many thanks for your note and enclosure.

We had, as you greatly suspected, a very tedious journey here—so boisterous and tempestuous in the channel that Callie,[1] in spite of her being a good sailor was nevertheless inclined to be a little sea-sick. It snowed and rained and did everything horrid. Yet in spite of want of sleep and neuralgia I arrived in tolerably good condition.

The Manchester lecture was a most decided *hit*—if I could judge from the expression and conduct of the audience. They received me with the greatest enthusiasm, applauded everything, *even to cheering me when I stopped to drink a glass of water*! Their anxiety to make me think they were satisfied with me was something very pleasant. The lecture was in *Free Trade Hall*—a large building but a dreadful barn of a place for speaking and there were about 1000 people present. I sent you the local papers.[2]

This is the *one* side of my experience. Unfortunately Mr Carte has with his usual infelicity subjected me to another kind of experience not so pleasant. The man who managed the lecture *paid me only 45 guineas*, or a little more than half the fee, alleging that he had not collected the rest but would pay it when he did. Of course *I* shall look to Carte for the whole amount—for nobody here seems to know if the manager of the lecture is a responsible man—and he may promise to pay and keep promising.

I was too tired to go out to Mr Shaws (the American Consul's) house at Sal[ford]—in the Manchester suburbs. But he and Mr Shepherd, our consul at Bradford, spent the evening with us.[3]

I shall probably return directly after the Birmingham lecture on the 7th—not taking any further engagements.[4]

Give my regards to Mrs Schneider and say that Callie is well and in good spirits. She has seen a few of the shows and we dine at the Trübners on Sunday where she will stay, probably, when I go to Halifax on the 1st.

Yours ever,
Bret Harte

Provenience: UVa (ALS).

1. Callie T. Cooper, daughter of BH's cousin Georgianna and David M. Cooper of Georgetown, studied painting in Düsseldorf in 1878–79. BH had stayed with the Coopers when he was in D.C. during the summer of 1877. He wrote Georgianna Cooper on 16 March 1879 (Bancroft, MSS C-H 57) that he was "trying to persuade [Callie] to go with me

to London when I go there to lecture, as I am satisfied she needs some change from the monotony of her life here. . . . Mrs Trübner, at whose house I stayed while I was in London would be very glad to have her pay her a visit."

2. According to a report in the *Manchester Guardian* (28 Mar. 1879, p. 6, cols. 3–4), BH's lecture was punctuated with frequent laughter and applause.

3. Albert D. Shaw (1841–1901) was U.S. consul at Toronto from 1868 to 1878 and at Manchester from 1878 to 1886. Shaw and BH remained on friendly terms after BH moved to Glasgow in 1880. They corresponded as late as 23 February 1883 (Bancroft, MSS C-H 57). Charles O. Shepard was U.S. consul at Bradford.

4. After his lecture in Manchester on March 27, BH spoke in Halifax on April 1, Brighton on April 3, and Birmingham on April 7.

114. TO ANNA HARTE, 25 APRIL 1879

Crefeld,
April 25/79

My dear Nan,

I've been trying for a long time to so arrange matters that you would hereafter be *secure* in regularly receiving money from me. The principal trouble thus far has been that I did not know from month to month how *much I could send you*, and how much I could depend upon your receiving from *the sale of my writings in New York*. I have at last arranged with Schroeder & Co to pay you regularly $150 per month—in such sum or sums as you may like on the 1st or 15th of each month. This is to be a surety—and you can depend upon it. Of course, Nan, you understand that I will send more *if I can*—and that in all probability the sale of my writings will amount to $50 or perhaps $100 more and that you are pretty sure of calculating upon $200 each month—but I want you to feel that you can depend regularly upon *something*, until my year in the consular service is over, which will be on the 18th July, and I will know how and where I stand.

I am not very hopeful of the future *here*.

I am hesitating about returning to England to go to the "Royal Academy Dinner" and the "Literary Fund Dinner" and the "Dinner of St John's College" at Cambridge—to all of which I am invited, and where I should be expected to make a speech. I am trying to leave out my personal feelings and look at it purely as *business*. It will be a good *advertisement*, and make some people I know of in New York and Boston ashamed—but it will cost me *some money*—at least $75—and in all my other trips I have made my lecturing pay my expenses. There is no lecture to come in as an excuse—and a recompense pecuniarily. And I am afraid that in America something may be said about my absence from my Consulate and my being continually in England. I have a leave of absence of 7 weeks from the Department,[1] and have not used it all—I have still a week at my disposal,—but that they dont know, and they might make a fuss in the papers, which of course the Department would not condescend to *answer*, but might wish had never occurred. Again, I find that this absence, if only for a week, retards my learning German greatly, and interrupts my study and besides that, I am getting backward in my story-writing. If I wrote one or two things—particularly good—it would do quite as much to keep up my reputation as a dinner—if not more. I wish you could advise me *what* to do!

I shall not continue my German sketches at present. Writing them for a German paper and living in a German community and above all holding a half-diplomatic position here, cramps my pen. Did I ever tell you that the people of Crefeld were very much annoyed by the Legend of Sammstadt—taking the extravagant speeches I put in Clinch's mouth as my own utterance?[2] Well, when I found them so thin-skinned, with the fear of truth before my eyes, when I sent my MS to the *Tageblatt* I asked them to be frank, and point out any passages that might be open to misunderstanding. They did—very frankly and kindly—condemning the ridiculous sensitiveness of their countrymen, offering to print as I wished—but pointing out three or four of my best passages as being "likely to be misunderstood." I have consequently written but the one article—and shall bide my time for the others.[3]

While I am writing this and just after I had satisfied myself that I *ought not* to go to London, comes a letter from Sir Fred. Leighton, Presd. of the Royal Academy, asking me if I will respond to the *toast of "Literature,"* as they wish to deviate from their regular custom of asking a British author *in honor to myself*![4] What shall I do?

Kiss the babies for Limick!—while I make up my mind.
P.S. Can you read this scrawl?

Provenience: UVa (ALS).

1. See note 2 to letter 110.

2. First printed in the New York *Sun*, 22 Dec. 1878, p. 2, cols. 1–5; and translated into German by Alfred Murenberg in *Eine Sage aus Sammtstadt und andere Erzahlungen* (Stuttgart: Abenheim'scher Verlag, 1879), 1–37.

3. BH refers to "Der Spion," published in German translation in *Berliner Tageblatt* in mid-Apr 1879. Under the English title "Views from a German Spion" this essay first appeared in the New York *Sun* for 25 May 1879, p. 2, col. 6–p. 3, col. 1.

4. Frederic Leighton, Baron Leighton of Stretton (1830–96), a painter and president of the Royal Academy of Arts. BH declined the invitation when his vice-consul fell ill—"too late I fear to avoid the trouble that would arise from a change in your programme," as he wrote Leighton (30 Apr. 1879, UVa).

115. TO T. WEMYSS REID, 24 MAY 1879

Crefeld,
May 24th/79

My dear Mr. Reid,[1]

That same lofty and self-sacrificing devotion to the interests of my Government, which kept me here at the Consulate certifying to invoices, when I might have been dining with Princes of the Blood at Royal Academy and Literary Fund banquets, three weeks ago, will, I fear, keep me from Royal propinquity at the Edinburgh University Dinner. Perhaps the authorities in Washington may reward me hereafter with promotion and translation to England, but for the present I must forego my social opportunities there.

Wont you, however, convey to your good friend Dr. Brown,[2] my thorough appreciation of his intended compliment, in such felicity of phrase as will naturally occur to you. I have quite exhausted my vocabulary of apology.

Rest assured I have not forgotten a single incident of our pleasant trip to Haworth.[3] As a shrine-breaking American citizen I suppose

I ought to go in for *change*, under the name of *improvement* and *rebuilding*, but if any word of mine could keep the old church intact; could fix forever to posterity its grim, hard unloveliness, could perpetuate the old churchyard sacred to unhallowed mediocrity, could preserve the religious discipline of those uncomfortable stiff backed pews, could secure a mortgage on that bleak lonely outlying moor beyond, the weary clambering prospectless hilly street, and the unsympathetic inn that made poor Branwell's dissipation[4] a necessity, could retain the grim, confining, limited atmosphere in which those sad sisters lived, and in which Charlotte's genius was developed—I'd say it, and try to make myself a little clearer than I do now. The church is not picturesque nor characteristic I suppose, but I am inclined to believe that the cradle of genius seldom is the one or the other.

I gathered from a letter of Consul Shepard's[5] that the demolition of the church was a *fait accompli* already.[6] How is this?

I believe I have to thank you for a copy of the *Mercury* received some time ago. I am delighted with your book on Charlotte.[7] Have I already said so?

Yours most sincerely,
Bret Harte

T. Wemyss Reid.

Provenience: Bancroft (MSS 77/166 C).

1. T. Wemyss Reid (1842–1905), journalist and biographer.

2. Probably John Brown, M.D. (1810–82), author of *Rab and His Friends* (1859).

3. An excursion to Brontë country during his visit to England in March 1879. The Morse Collection at UCLA contains a 1901 article clipped from the *Westminster Gazette* entitled "How Bret Harte Got into Haworth Parsonage" (Barnett, 147).

4. The brother, Branwell Brontë (1817–48).

5. Charles O. Shepard, U.S. consul at Bradford, England.

6. The Haworth church the tourist sees today was built around the old tower of the former structure.

7. Reid was editor of the *Leeds Mercury* between 1870 and 1887 and the author of *Charlotte Brontë: A Monograph* (1877). He probably sent a copy of the *Mercury* for 5 May 1879 that quoted Froude's accolade for

BH at the Royal Academy dinner (p. 3, col. 2). Certainly BH had seen a report of the dinner as early as 10 May 1879, the day he wrote Osgood (UVa) that Froude "said nicer things about me than I would have dared to say myself!"

116. TO ANNA HARTE, 29 MAY 1879

United States Consulate,
Crefeld.
May 29th/79

My dear Nan,—

On the 18th of July I shall have served the Government one year at this post, and I am thinking very seriously of applying to the Department for a transfer or *exchange*—(I dare not yet hope for any *promotion*)—to some other locality.[1] My strongest reason is my *health*, and I can get any number of certificates from the best German physicians here that this part of the country is injurious to my temperament and condition. You will perhaps smile and remember how you used to accuse me of making the like charges against every place where I ever lived. I only know that certain symptoms disappear when I leave Germany, if only for a week or two, and invariably return when I am here. Although I was by no means well in Paris and London, I am much worse here, and lately *neuralgia*, in all its disagreeable forms, has fixed upon me. I used to have little pity for people with the toothache, but since I've suffered with my jaws bound up in a towel, night after night, I can imagine nothing worse. I've had dentists examine my teeth, doctors stick things into my ears, and indulge in all sorts of speculation until they finally concluded that it was really *neuralgia*. I should have asked for an exchange before, but when I write to the Department, I must have *outside friends* to urge and speak for me. I shall write a private letter to Mr Seward, but *that* is not sufficient, and at present I cannot think of any one with influence enough in Washington to assist me. If I could hold on until a change in the Administration, I might be reasonably sure of success, but I cannot ask for an extended leave of absence, by reason of taking already so much in my lecture trip, to England, and the Doctor says I must go to Switzerland or the sea shore this summer positively.

You may have wondered why I did not ask before. I was quite ashamed so soon—but this belief that I cannot live here and be a strong, and healthy man with the power to work, has been slowly forcing itself upon me, and has been at the bottom of all my indecision in the plans for the future. I am only too glad that I have made none, and that the change—if I have to make one, will involve the movements of nobody but myself. It would have been no light matter to have moved a family.

I'll write to you again and more decidedly as to my intentions—*when I know them.* I hope you are in the country by this time, although it is but a shade or two warmer than an American March at this season here, and I sincerely hope you are all better. Dont worry about me either! The Doctors here who have examined me and probed me all over, say it is nothing but the climate acting upon a nervous sensitive American constitution. God bless you all.

Limick

Provenience: UVa (ALS).

1. BH would wait some three months after his anniversary date, until 7 October 1879, before writing the State Department to request an exchange. See note 2 to letter 125.

117. TO RUDOLF SCHNEIDER, 30 JULY 1879[1]

United States Consulate
Zürich

Bocken, Hargen,
Wednesday P.M.

My dear Mr Schneider,

We arrived here this morning.

After we left Mainz, some of the finest scenery and vegetation I have yet seen in Europe, were visible from the railway all the way to Strassburg. We reached there at 2 oclock, lunched at the hotel, went to the Cathedral, saw the clock strike a "five," drove round the city and went back to dinner. The next morning we left Strassburg at six, came in sight of some snow peaks at about 12 and at 2 got to Zurich. We staid there all night, and saw the lake by moonlight in all its glory.

We like Bocken very much so far—i.e. eight hours. It lies above the lake, looking over it, and towards the snow-peaks in the distance.

The weather is superb. It grew steadily warmer as we came here, and now it is really summer. I shall go and look at Obstalden in a day or two, but I think we shall stay here all the time.

Expecting to hear from you soon, I send you and Mrs Schneider my best wishes and hopes that your journey back was as pleasant as ours—in which Callie joins,—she having quite recovered her health and spirits—

Always Yours,
B.H.

Provenience: UVa (ALS).

1. Dated by reference to BH's 31 July 1879 letter to FH (*Letters*, 147–49).

118. TO ANNA HARTE, 11 AUGUST 1879

United States Consulate
Zürich Aug. 11th/79

My dear Nan,

I wrote a few lines to Frankie last week,[1] but I have had no time to write you the long letter I expected to send from Switzerland. I have been moving around from place to place,[2] hoping to fine some healthful spot to spend my vacation in—but in vain. Unfortunately I cannot afford to go to the most frequented places for the prices and the altitude are equally *high*, and if I stay in Switzerland I must find some spot that is cheap. Thus far my health has been no better; I did not expect to be delighted with the scenery so I am not disappointed then, but I did hope to be strong enough to take long walks and climb a little. The weather here has been intensely hot, and although it has cooled off a little within the last few days, I am still weak. I shall go to the Righi—about 4000 feet up—in a day or two, if I did not feel some exaltation or improvement from it I shall leave Switzerland and go to the sea side in Holland.

I have tried, when my head or my stomach was not aching, to appreciate Swiss scenery. I am living in the hills overlooking Lake Zurich—(whence the poem "by the margin of fair Zurichs waters") and I regret to say that the Zurichs waters are *not* "fair," and that the California mountains and coast range are really superior to these famous Alps—in every respect. As the Rhein is inferior to the Hudson so is Switzerland to California, and even to the Cattskills in New York. The snow peaks visible from my window are fine but I have seen finer views from a wayside hotel in Calaveras county.

Last night some infamous wastels extemporized a "jodel" call or cry which you probably remember to have read of or heard sung in the opera. It was like the caterwauling of 50 cats, with an obligato from a donkey.

I will write you after I have returned from the Righi. I have not received anything from you since the 25th of July—but I have not had my letters sent here from Crefeld and your letters may be awaiting me there.

God bless you all.

Limick

Provenience: UVa (ALS).

1. BH's 31 July 1879 letter to FH (*Letters*, 147–49).

2. BH's letters from Switzerland to his wife and son contain no hint he is traveling with Callie Cooper.

119. TO RUDOLF SCHNEIDER, 12 AUGUST 1879

Bocken,
Tuesday, Aug 12th '79

My dear Schneider,

Yours with enclosures and the affecting poem from the Appraisers Chief Clerk received. With such lofty inspiration in the Custom House I dont wonder the invoices are "raised."[1]

I was up on the "Uetliberg" yesterday. I have however come to the conclusion that I must try a higher air, and must go to the Righi, if I cannot get it elsewhere. I have thus far been deterred by the high prices charged there, but as I came to Switzerland for my health, it would be foolish for me to lose this chance through economy. I shall at all events *try it*. Byers[2] and I expect to go there to-morrow; Callie, who gets along very well here, and has a portfolio full of sketches already, does not care to change and will probably stay and sketch here or go to Wesen.

In view of my forcibly increased expenses perhaps you had better send me $100—(400 marks) against any contingency. Send it to me care of Consul Byers, Zurich.

Tauchnitz writes me that Chatto & Windus offered to sell him "The Twins" but that he refused saying that he always dealt with me directly.[3] Isn't this about the smallest bit of meanness you ever heard of! Think of C. & W. trying to get hold of what Tauchnitz gives to me virtually as a personal gift to an author!

I forgot to say that I was so weak and uncertain about myself the other day that I had to go to a Doctor in Zurich.[4] He said I must go to the Engadine—on the Righi—or Ragatz. The Engadine is two days journey away—and I should be bankrupt from travelling expenses. I almost wish I had not gone to Switzerland at all, but since I am here I suppose I must see it through.

I will write to you in a day or two where to send my American letters. As *anybody* sees your letters and *enclosures* to me, write nothing you dont want anyone to see, until I tell you when you can send to me privately and personally. If there are no letters to send me you can say, in your next, "there is nothing else of interest to write." With best regards to Mrs Schneider,

Yours, in haste,
B.H.

Provenience: UVa (ALS).

1. A clerk in the New York Customs House had disputed low values on invoices certified by the Crefeld consulate.

2. Samuel H. M. Byers (1838–1933), U.S. consul at Zürich, later consul general to Italy and Switzerland.

3. While in Switzerland, BH read page proofs of "The Twins of Table Mountain" (Byers, *Twenty Years in Europe* [Chicago: Rand, McNally, 1900], 176), which first appeared in the New York *Sun* (17 Aug. 1879, p. 1, col. 7–p. 2, col. 6; 24 Aug. 1879, p. 1, col. 7–p. 2, col. 6), prior to its publication in book form by Chatto & Windus the next month. Byers thought "the situations all seemed artificial and strained" and that BH "wasted little enthusiasm on the tale" (Overland, n.s., 42 [Nov. 1903]:429).

4. BH consulted a Dr. Cloetta, according to Byers "a distinguished professor and physician. The good doctor, who speaks but little English, put him on a lounge, examined him carefully, and said, 'Mr. Harte, I think

you got *extension* of the stomach.' Coming back to the boat, Harte laughed a good deal about this; cursed a little too" (Byers, *Twenty Years in Europe*, 177).

120. TO RUDOLF SCHNEIDER, 19 AUGUST 1879

Zurich, Switzerland
Aug 19th/79

My dear Schneider,

I enclose a reply to Mr Gross' proposition, which you will please put into your own elegant idiomatic German and transmit to him. I wish I knew what were the prices usually paid for translations; if so I might name a sum sufficient to make it worth while for Mrs Schneider to translate it—if she cared to—and send them the story in *German*.[1]

I have to thank you for the prompt remittance of 400 marks, and letters, and *The World* newspaper with that wonderful account of how I lost $10,000 through my diffidence![2] If I know Chicago well, and I think I do,—even if I had been *too diffident*—the Chicagoans would not have been so diffident as to keep the knowledge of an expected *dinner* from me. They would have published it a week before the party came off—and charged admission—25¢ for the spectacle, and so got their money back,—in advance.

I expect to return in a few days—without I fear having benefitted my health at all by my stay in Switzerland. The *Righi* gave me no stimulation whatever,—although I was there a day and night,—quite long enough to feel any exhilaration that might come from such an altitude. The only effect was a headache, and utter sleeplessness! The journey however was an amusing experience. It so happened that the day before I had decided to go with Mr. Byers, Mrs John Sherman—the wife of the Secretary of the Treasury[3]—and a party traveling with her, came to Zurich, and thence to "Bocken" at the invitation of Mr Byers, whom she knew slightly. Hearing of our intention to go to the Righi the next day, the whole party intimated that they would like to go with us, and as Byers did not like to decline the request of the wife of a Cabinet officer! they went with us. We hired a diligence to ourselves and made a very jolly party to Zug—

thence by steamer to Arth, and thence up the Righi to the Kulm. There were three young ladies to keep Callie company—two of them Washington girls—and a young officer of the Navy (detached from his ship at Antwerp, by orders of the Secretary of the Navy to keep Mrs Sherman company!!) It was a wonder that our friend Sandy[4] had not been telegraphed for also.

I enjoyed the ride over the hills to Zug greatly, and was really struck with the railway ride to the summit of the Righi. But I'll tell you all about it another time.

I hope to get back in time to be able to spend a week at the sea side in Holland or Belgium as a last hope of getting some *sanitary good* out of my vacation. The sea air always brings me up.

You need not send any more letters after this reaches you—unless you hear from me or unless you have important news—in which case a dispatch or letter to Consul Byers will always reach me. With best regards to Mrs Schneider, in which Callie joins

Yours always
B.H.

Provenience: UVa (ALS).

1. While BH's writings were often translated into German and published in such journals as the Vienna *Neue Freie Presse* and *Westermanns Illustrierte Deutsche Monatshefte*, sometimes even before they were published in English, Clara Schneider, the vice-consul's wife, did not subsequently translate any of them.

2. A sketch of BH in the London *World* for 13 August 1879 (cited in the *Chicago Tribune*, 29 Aug. 1879, p. 12, col. 3) gave new life to the rumor that, while in Chicago in February 1871, BH had lost $10,000 when he failed to attend a dinner party in his honor. For a vehement denial of the rumor, see the *New York Times*, 4 Sept. 1879, p. 2, col. 6. See also note 3 to letter 21.

3. Margaret Sherman, wife of John Sherman, the secretary of the treasury, later Republican senator from Ohio and U.S. secretary of state.

4. The unctuous clerk in the New York Custom House. See note 1 to letter 119.

1. Above, Bret Harte in 1870. Photograph by Bradley & Hulofson, San Francisco. Courtesy, Mark Twain Project, the Bancroft Library.

2. Below, Telegraph Hill, San Francisco, 1865. Photograph by T. E. Hecht. Courtesy of the Bancroft Library.

3. Above, Pine and Montgomery Streets, San Francisco, 1865. Photograph by T. E. Hecht. Courtesy of the Bancroft Library.

4. Below, A. S. Boyd's sketch of Bret Harte and Anton Roman accompanying Harte's "My First Book," *Idler* 4 (Jan. 1894):554.

5. Above, The Howells family circa 1875 (William in rear; Elinor, Mildred, Winifred, left to right in center; John in front). By permission of the Houghton Library, Harvard University.

6. Below, The Clemens family circa 1877 (left to right, Clara, Samuel, Jean, Olivia, Susy) at their Hartford home. Courtesy, Mark Twain Project, the Bancroft Library.

7. A promotional still of Bret Harte on the lecture platform, 1874. Photograph by Sarony, New York. Published in Charles Murdock's *A Backward Glance at Eighty* (San Francisco: Elder, 1921), opposite p. 80.

8. Anna Griswold Harte. Courtesy of John Bret-Harte.

9. Lawrence Barrett, circa 1870. Photograph by Bradley & Hulofson, San Francisco. Courtesy of V. B. Price.

10. J. R. Osgood. Engraving in *Harper's Weekly*, 28 May 1892, 508.

11. Bret Harte, circa 1876. Courtesy of John Bret-Harte.

12. John Hay in 1874. Published in William Roscoe Thayer, *The Life and Letters of John Hay* (Boston: Houghton Mifflin, 1915), I, opposite p. 388.

13. C. T. Parsloe as Ah Sin. Courtesy of the Hampden-Booth Theatre Library.

14. Stuart Robson as Colonel Starbottle. Courtesy of the Hampden-Booth Theatre Library.

15. Bret Harte in 1880. Photograph by Overbeck, Düsseldorf. Inscribed to Mme Van de Velde and reproduced as the frontispiece to Pemberton's *Life of Bret Harte*.

16. J. A. Froude. Published in *Bookman* 13 (Apr. 1901): 158.

17. Bret Harte's portrait by John Pettie, 1886. First published in *McClure's* 4 (Dec. 1894):39.

18. Bret Harte in 1887. Photo by Thomas Fall, London. Bret Harte Collection (#5310), Clifton Waller Barrett Library, Special Collections Department, University of Virginia Library.

19. Bret Harte in 1887. Photo by Hawker, Bournemouth. Bret Harte Collection (#5310), Clifton Waller Barrett Library, Special Collections Department, University of Virginia Library.

20. Above, Bret Harte in 1891. Photograph by Thomas Fall, London. Frontispiece to vol. 7 of *The Writings of Bret Harte* (Boston: Houghton Mifflin, 1896).

21. Below, Jessamy and Ethel Harte, 1891. Published in *McClure's* 4 (Dec. 1894):43.

22. Above, Bret Harte in 1894. Photo by Elliott & Fry, London. Published in *McClure's* 4 (Dec. 1894):43.

23. Below, Bret Harte at Arford House, Headley, Hants, May 1896. Courtesy of John Bret-Harte.

24. Above, Annie Russell in the title role of *Sue*, 1896. Photo by Pach Bros., New York. The Billy Rose Theatre Collection, New York Public Library for the Performing Arts, Astor, Lenox and Tilden Foundations.

25. Below, Family group circa 1900 (clockwise from upper left: Bret Harte, Anna Harte, Mme Van de Velde [?], Aline Harte). Courtesy of John Bret-Harte.

26. Kate Carew's sketches of Bret Harte. Published in the New York *World*, 22 Dec. 1901,

27. The last photograph of Bret Harte, 1902. Courtesy of John Bret-Harte.

28. The Red House, Camberley, where Bret Harte died. In Pemberton's *Life of Bret Harte*, opposite p. 260.

ROOMS OF
The Overland Monthly
San Francisco: Sept 1st 1870

My dear Sir:

I cannot, just now, forecast my work for the next year, but I think it possible that I may find the time, as I already have the inclination, to write for you. The main difficulty, I apprehend, will be in getting something to

29. The first page of letter 15 (Library of Congress).

74, LANCASTER GATE,
W.

June 29: 1900

Dear Mr. Gilder,

Mr Watt tells me that you would like me to submit the plot "H. H." of a proposed story for your magazine. Unfortunately I do not usually begin with a plot, but,— having a few characters and a situation in my mind,— I let them work out the plot in their own lines and generally find they do it better than I can! These characters and situations must, alas! be pretty well known to you and your readers during the thirty odd years that I have been story-telling, and consequently I am a little puzzled at your request. It occurs to me, however, looking back upon some past suggestions.

30. The first page of letter 251 (Morristown National Historical park).

121. TO S. H. M. BYERS, 27 AUGUST 1879

Crefeld, Aug. 27, 1879.

MY DEAR MR. BYERS:—We arrived here safely last night. *Of course*, the railways did not connect as you said they would, and *of course*, we did not go where you promised we should, but we got to Düsseldorf within twelve hours of the schedule time set and are thankful. Only let me beg you to post yourself a little on Swiss railroads before you travel *yourself*. Your knowledge does well enough for a guide to old experienced travelers *like us*!!! but it won't do for a simple, guileless, believing nature like your own. And don't let the landlord of the Chateau "Laufen" cook up a route for you.[1]

Our ride through the Black Forest was a delicious revelation. I should say it was an overture to Switzerland, had I entered Switzerland from its borders, but coming *from* Switzerland, I could not but think it was really *finer* than the Alps in everything that makes the picturesque, and that Switzerland would have been a disappointment afterwards. It was very like the California "foothills" in the mountain ranges, and the long dashes of red soil and red road—so unlike the glare and dazzle of the white Swiss turnpikes—were very effective. I wanted much to stop at Freiberg, still more at a certain ruined castle and "pension" called Hornberg,[2] which was as picturesque as Castle Laufen, minus the noise of "factory wheels and fulling mills" from those awful rapids.[3] Heidelberg was a sensation, with its castle that quite dwarfs the Rhine River[4] (as all these things do by comparison when one travels) and we could have stayed there two or three days and enjoyed ourselves.

The weather has changed back to the old wet season that we thought we had left behind us when we turned our faces Southward. It is dull and rainy. Nevertheless as soon as I get some work off my hands that has accumulated here I shall try the seaside for my hoped-for rehabilitation.

My cousin sends her regards. I suppose she will write or has written to Mrs. Byers. I hope you will not give up your Rhine trip (with a suitable guide) and that we may see you in Düsseldorf soon.[5]

With my best regards to Mrs. Byers,

Very truly yours, BRET HARTE.

Provenience: Samuel Byers, *Twenty Years in Europe* (Chicago: Rand, McNally. 1900), 183–84.

1. BH spent the night of 25 August 1879, his forty-third birthday, in company with Byers and his cousin Callie Cooper at the Laufen Castle on the Rhine north of Zurich (Byers, *Twenty Years in Europe*, 182).

2. Probably Schloss Hornberg northeast of Freiberg.

3. Byers, *Twenty Years in Europe*, 182: "That he might be right over the Rhine Falls by moonlight, the host of the Laufen Castle gave him the room with the balconies above the water. It was beautiful, but the noise of the falls kept Harte awake all night."

4. Actually, the Neckar.

5. Byers failed to make the trip. As he reminisced years later (*Overland*, n.s., 42 [Nov. 1903]:432), "When next I saw Bret Harte I was in London at the Langham Hotel. . . . Some way, somehow, he seemed another man."

122. TO ANNA HARTE, 29 AUGUST 1879

Crefeld,
Aug 29th/79

My dear Nan,—

I wrote you a few hurried lines yesterday as soon as I got back from Switzerland. I thought to write you a long letter describing some of the things I had seen, but I find the little enthusiasm I had has gone out—and I recall only a few things in which I was not disappointed.

Do you remember a certain ride we once took over the Sta Cruz range with Mr. Roman[1] & family. There was nothing in Switzerland more wonderful than that except that the roads are finer and better kept. There is nothing in Switzerland *grander* than the Sierras—there is much however more singularly *beautiful.* I was not struck with the isolated grandeur of the Rigi until I saw the clouds slowly forming on some peaks opposite, and really seemed to be *in the manufactory where they were made.* Not the usual misty sheets and vails and ribbons one sees on small mountains but these just piled up ice cream masses that lie high up in the sky before a thunder storm. I felt *no* exhilaration at this height 5000 feet, because perhaps I had often been 10000 feet up in the Sierras. The isolation of this great Sugar

Loaf rising out of Lake Zug was its point of interest to me, and at night, when the wind rose, I felt the joy as [if] I were again at sea. More remarkable to me were one or two days at Wesen on the *Wallen Sea* where I had the peak of *Glarnisch* before me and *Der Speer* behind me, all rising from a perfectly level billiard-table-like valley triangular in shape, having for its apex the *Glarnisch*. To watch the play of light and shade and color, the coming and going of clouds, the dream-like unreality of these great, lovable giants as they seemed occasionally to thrust a foot or an arm, or even to lift their *heads* up out of this wonderful shifting gauzing drapery was wonderful and rare to my eyes—accustomed only to the hard stern outlines of the atmosphereless Sierras I actually grew weak and faint with exhausted nervous sensation; "dazzled and drunk with beauty"[2] I suppose, but such beauty as makes all other beauty seem as naught—all other sensation as grossness. The alpine glow was also *not* a disappointment. I dont mean the rosy fire on the snow peaks known by that name—but the cold ghastly blueish white that succeeds it—which is *Death* made visible, and awfully beautiful. The *Jungfrau* one night looked to me as I suppose the Angel of Death looked in the days of Solomon when it was visible.

Between my awed and hushed reverence for the great, reposeful gentleman- and lady-like mountains, I had to struggle with a violent and active resentment against the natives—the "hardy," "liberty-loving" Swiss—who are the biggest frauds I ever met. A race of mean "yankees"—more intolerant and bigoted than the poorest down-trodden peasant I ever met—are these "hardy mountaineers," with their sham sentiments, their sham liberty, their sham chamois—(an ugly cross between a goat and a jackass) their sham *jodel*—that awful falsetto as musical as a cats serenade, and nothing real about them but their hideous *goitres*. How the mountains must despise 'em. I dont wonder that the *Matterhorn* occasionally yawns a *crevasse* to swallow 'em or that all the mountains every now and then take a shy at 'em with an avalanche. I saw the descendants of the survivors of three buried villages below the Rigi—I looked at them and looked up at the mountain, and thought it was merciful!

I spoke of Roman! Read the enclosed slip and imagine how furious I was to read it in Switzerland, where I couldn't get at anybody to set them right—or tell them that they *lied*! Do you remember the day you lay sick at *San Jose* and I read you the story of the "Luck," and took heart and comfort from your tears over it, and courage to go on and *demand* that it should be put into the magazine. And think—think of fat Mrs Roman claiming to be its sponsor!!![3]

Good night.

Limick

Provenience: UVa (ALS).

1. Anton Roman founded the *Overland* in 1868 and sold the magazine to J. H. Carmany in early 1869. See Roman's "The Genesis of the Overland Monthly," *Overland*, n.s., 40 (Sept. 1902):220–22. See also note 1 to letter 1.

2. *Childe Harold's Pilgrimage*, canto V, line 443.

3. BH refers in this paragraph to an interview with Roman entitled "'The Luck of Roaring Camp'/How Nearly Bret Harte's Story Was Once Refused by a Publisher" originally published in the New York *Sun* (20 July 1879, p. 2, col. 7) and widely copied (e.g., in the *Hartford Courant*, 29 July 1879, p. 1, col. 9; and *Chicago Tribune*, 14 Aug. 1879, p. 9, col. 7). In the interview, Roman offers an apocryphal account of the publication of "The Luck." He claims that BH assented to its suppression, agreeing that "his philosophic treatment" of the subject was "too real," and that BH planned to replace the story with "other matter." However, when Roman gave it to his wife to read in proof sheets, it reduced her to tears, and "That was enough. I rushed to the office, and, without explanation, ordered the article inserted." Later, "I told my wife that she was truly the sponsor of Bret Harte."

123. TO ELIZA KNAUFFT, 3 SEPTEMBER 1879

Crefeld,
Septem. 3d/79

My dear Sister Eliza,

You ought to remember how dreadfully negligent I was with poor Maggie[1] in letter writing and not expect better treatment yourself. I dont know but that I ought not to write to you until I have answered some of her letters. *I hate to write letters* especially *family* letters. I perhaps think more frequently of my family than most men who write letters—I sometimes think it is because I *do* think so much of them and have them so continually before me that writing becomes a superfluity and most inadequate way of expressing myself. My letters—the few I do write—never seem to contain anything that I am really concerned about, and perhaps I write so much of myself in my *professional writing*, that I always seem to be in artificial attitudes when I do so with letters. It was with the greatest difficulty that I could write to Frankie and Wodie even a rambling account of my Switzerland trip and experiences—it seemed like *business*, and business I ought to be doing better. There is really very little to say about myself—except always in the way of apology. And here is a fourth of this sheet gone already.

I was very much shocked to hear you were *seriously* ill. I was *surprised* too for I have never connected any *serious illness* with you, and I resented it. I am sometimes horrified to think how calmly I assume that the few people I love are immortal. That you ever could be *dangerously* sick I have never conceived, or that by any possibility you could not long survive me—or that at any future time, coming home I shouldn't find you always well and hearty, I never think of. I have always thought I would write to you at once if any thing *new* transpired or happened to me; but nothing new seems to happen; I am not well,—that is an old story; I am not sick yet—that is also nothing new, and I do not yet see a way to become sick—that is also one of my old experiences. Even in this strange land everything I have met seems to have been known to me before—or shorn of its marvellousness and novelty. I already seem to have been an exile for many years. Pecuniarily—and this is the only sign of our family's progress or decay—I am better off than I was during the two or three years previous to my leaving—but not as well as when I first returned to New York from California. I am saving *no* money—but I am not running into debt. Perhaps that is something.

I am disappointed with my post in Germany. Not solely because the climate does not agree with me—although that is much to a nervous irritable person like myself—but because I find that I can make nothing out of it in a literary way. It offers me *no* material. I think few American writers are helped by a contemplation of European life. Its incidents and episodes are all old, and if you treat them with American freshness, you only become a Mark Twain. I could write descriptions like the "Innocents Abroad"[2]—for much is here that is a sham—but I wont. Perhaps my inspiration will come.

The little work I have done here—excepting an attempt to describe German life in *Der Spion*[3]—is in my old field, of which I—and the public—are becoming heartily tired.

I am, as usual, undecided and *waiting*. Waiting to get an exchange if possible to some other post for I doubt if I can stay here and not become a confirmed invalid. I dare not ask for promotion from the Department, although this office has doubled its business since I took hold of it—and I have some right to ask;—the present Administration will do nothing for me. It would be madness to transport my family here until I know if I will be exchanged, and *where*? So I am—*waiting*.

You must remember me to all the children. And you must never think, dear Lize, that I ever forget *you*, or your trials, and the terrible weariness of your life. I know it *all*. I think of it *all*—as often and perhaps sometimes more surpassingly than you do. And however infrequent *my* letters may be, *you* must always write to me openly, frankly and lovingly. God bless you and remember I am always your loving brother. Frank

Provenience: Bancroft (MSS 88/181 C).

1. BH's sister Margaret Wyman (1838–1928), with whom he had sailed to San Francisco in 1854.

2. BH had helped Clemens edit the text of *The Innocents Abroad* and had reviewed the book favorably in the *Overland* 4 (Jan 1870):100–01.

3. See note 3 to letter 114.

124. TO CHARLES A. DANA, 1 OCTOBER 1879

Crefeld,
Oct. 1st/79

My dear Mr. Dana,

I enclose herewith revise of "Peter Schroeder" which will appear in *Belgravia* on the 28 October. You may publish a day or two before.[1]

I have not heard from you nor the *Sun*, since the publication of the "Twins,"[2] and a few days ago I wrote to the "Editor," asking "if a cheque had been sent to Mrs Harte?" I have since been advised by her that she has received $250 from the *Sun*—but I imagine not from *you* nor with your knowledge; you having not returned at that time from Europe.

Do you candidly think that $250 was enough for the sole first use and control of a rather good story of about 20000 words which occupied *two* pages of the *Sun*, from the pen of "B.H."—who isn't writing much, and only for you, in America? It is at all in proportion to what I have received from *you* before—or from *others*? I think not! But if you can lay your hand upon your heart, and say it is right, without your conscience punishing you, why, perhaps it is right, or journalism has ossified that organ.[3]

I was so sorry I could not meet you at Cologne. But I had been sent off to Switzerland by the Doctor who cheerfully tells me that the climate is killing me here in Crefeld. Can you do anything with the Washington people to get me exchanged or promoted?—although perhaps this last is too much? At any rate think of me occasionally these dark autumn days and write to your exiled friend,

Bret Harte

C. A. Dana Esq.

Provenience: Allyn Kellogg Ford Collection of Historical Manuscripts, Minnesota Historical Society (ALS).

1. Published in *Belgravia* 40 (Nov 1879):42–55; and the New York *Sun*, 26 Oct. 1879, p. 2, cols. 1–4.

2. "The Twins of Table Mountain," New York *Sun*, 17 Aug. 1879, p. 1, col. 7–p. 2, col. 6; 24 Aug. 1879, p. 1, col. 7–p. 2, col. 6.

3. Dana agreed, and he sent AH an additional $250. As BH wrote her in late October (UVa), "I am rejoiced . . . for it was *worth* $500—that Story!"

125. TO ANNA HARTE, 11 OCTOBER 1879

Crefeld,
11th October/79

My dear Nan,—

The English and continental newspapers have been circulating paragraphs about the effect of the Crefeld climate on my health, and that I am thinking of resigning. Many of the reports are very much exaggerated, and I fear may be copied in American newspapers and worry you.[1]

The facts are that I am far from well (although the neuralgia is better), but the famous German Doctor here—Dr Von Köhlwetter says I cannot get better in this climate, and I have written to the State Department, *first*, for a leave of absence of two months, *Second*, for an *exchange* of locality if I do not get better in that time.[2] I wrote a private note to Mr. Seward regarding it and have asked for an answer by telegraph. I suppose the newspapers got hold of it from some passage in a private letter to friends in England, and the newspapers here are as active in personal paragraphing as the American press—with the saving grace that they are more respectful and kind.

I have yours of the 17th & 26th. It cannot be helped if you have drawn from Schroeder. Your drafts there will always be honored as long as I remain here and dont get very sick. You understand that I expected you would get about $350 from the *Sun* $150 from Osgood—that was why I wrote.

Osgood is acting in that queer un-Osgood-like way in which he sometimes falls. I am asking no favor from him! He has taken the volume to publish, and he has always advanced the price of 1500 copies—$150—on the receipt of the MS. It is queer.[3] I am only afraid that some creditor may come down upon him. I have written him again.

I sent Dana another story for which he ought to send you $100.[4]

I will write again soon. I may probably go to Paris in a day or two.[5] But you shall hear from me as soon as I hear from the Department.

God bless you all.

Limick

Provenience: UVa (ALS).

1. BH's concern was well founded. For example, the *New York Times* for 29 Aug. 1879 (p. 4, col. 6) had reported that BH "is said to have experienced such ill-effects from the climate [in Crefeld]—generally reputed to be very salubrious—that he is doubtful if he can remain at his post." The San Francisco *Argonaut* (8 Nov. 1879, 6) cited the Vienna *Neue Freie Presse* to the effect that BH "is not greatly delighted with his Crefeld

consulate. In fact he likes Crefeld so little that he has moved his residence to Düsseldorf, and goes to and from his business office by rail."

2. BH wrote the State Department on 7 October 1879 (NA) that "the effect of the local climate upon my health is so unfavorable that I am compelled, under advice of my physician, to ask for a leave of absence" for "at least two months," to be spent, "if granted, in the restoration of my health elsewhere, or in travel." He also asked the department to consider "some exchange of position for me, whereby my services may be retained under more favorable climactic conditions."

3. The firm of Houghton, Osgood would publish BH's *The Twins of Table Mountain and Other Stories* in late October 1879.

4. "Peter Schroeder." See note 1 to letter 124.

5. In an undated letter to AH in late October (UVa), BH noted he had spent "a few days" in Paris "in the faint hope of getting some recognition from the newspapers and reviews of my rights to my literary property."

126. TO CLARA SCHNEIDER, 3 JANUARY 1880

London,
Jany. 3d 1880

My dear Mrs Schneider,

You must do without that "long letter[")] this time and put up with a few lines in answer to your kind remembrances. I have just returned from Bestwood but I could not write a line there. I was seldom alone and when I did go to my room in the day time I always found myself staring out of the window at the storm—for it was always storming—tossing the trees about in Sherwood Forest.

I spent Xmas very quietly at Mr Trübners; it scarcely seemed to be different from any other day. Trübner always has some company at dinner. I dined once or twice out, and once got quite lost in a London fog.

I saw the old year out at Bestwood where they had their regular annual Tenants Ball. It was a very pretty old English custom, but quite characteristic of the Duke and his wife in their way of treating it. They gave up the great drawing room to their guests to dance in—many of whom were their own household servants—and the Duke and Duchess danced very composedly and cheerfully in the same set with their valet and lady's maid. *I* divided my attention between my fair hostess and her French maid. Of course there were some friends of the Duchess also, like myself, come up from London at her invitation, but the Ball was for the tenants and servants solely. And very nicely gotten up too.

I understand the servants had looked forward to this for a twelve month and some of their dresses were remarkably fine. The most stylish man in the room, and decidedly the best dancer was the Duke's valet, who had but a few hours before, brought me my hot water! The dancing was kept up 'till 6 o'clock New Years morning.

I drove over to Annesly the next day with a party from Bestwood, and on the 2d left for London. But I could only get away by promising to return to Bestwood about the 10th. Besides I met the Webbs of Newstead Abbey at the ball and I must go there *first*, so I shall probably divide a week between the two places. I was obliged to return to London to keep some dinner engagements I had made. Very foolishly too, for this dining out does not agree with *me* any more than it does with your husband. But that is the only way people have of entertaining you here, and of showing their regard for you. If I could get out of it I would, and I am seriously thinking if I had better not "cut it" and go back to Crefeld first.

I have been quite free from neuralgia in spite of the depressing weather, and it is not improbable that I may not have to go to Italy at all but may keep my leave of absence to use later in the season.

I shall write a line to Mr Schneider to-morrow, meanwhile tell him I have no later letter from him than the one that enclosed the cheque which I received on the 30th. I hope all are well.

With a thousand good wishes for the New Year,

Always your friend,
B.H.

Provenience: UVa (ALS).

127. TO ANNA HARTE, 7 JANUARY 1880

London, January 7, 1880

My dear Anna,

I sent you yesterday a few New Year's and Christmas cards for

Tottie and Ethel—some of them sent by my kind hostess, Mrs. Trübner, and her little daughter. It is the European idea of a New Year's call, and is a very pretty custom, I think. In Germany it is sentimentality mixed up with Saint Valentine, but I sent the children the German cards and wrote all about it, I think, last year. Do you remember?[1]

I spent a delightful hour with George Eliot (Mrs. Lewes) on Sunday last at her house.[2] I was very pleasantly disappointed in her appearance, having heard so much of the plainness of her features. And I found them only strong, intellectual, and *noble*—indeed, I have seldom seen a grander face! I have read somewhere that she looked like a horse—a great mistake, as, although her face is long and narrow, it is only as Dante's was. It expresses elevation of thought, kindness, power, and *humor*. It is at times not unlike Starr King's—excepting King's beautiful eyes.[3] Mrs. Lewes's eyes are gray and sympathetic, but neither large nor beautiful. Her face lights up when she smiles and shows her large white teeth, and all thought of heaviness vanishes. She reminds you continually of a man—a bright, gentle, lovable, philosophical man—without being a bit *masculine*. Do you understand me?

Of course, her talk was charming. It was wise and sweet and humorous. It was like her books—or her written speech when she moralizes—but I thought it kinder and less hard than some of her satire. She said many fine things to me about my work, and asked me to come again to see her, which was a better compliment, as she has since Lewes's death received no one.

I saw Hardy—the novelist—at the club the other night.[4] A singularly unpretending-looking man, and indeed resembling anything but an author in manner or speech. I had a pleasant chat with the artist Du Maurier,[5] who draws the lovely children in "Punch," and met Henry James, Jr., the American novelist, who is creating quite a reputation here.[6] He looks, acts, and thinks like an Englishman, and writes like an Englishman, I am sorry to say, excellent as his style is. I wish he had more of an American flavor—but this is the effect of extreme Boston culture and European travel. The club is a new one—just being formed—the Rabelais Club it is called[7]—and I had been proud to become a member. At the dinner last night Sir Frederick Pollock presided as President,[8] and to my astonishment at the end of the dinner nominated *me* to preside as president next time, to everybody's apparent applause and satisfaction but my own.

The weather is gloomy and horribly foggy—worse than Crefeld was. I fear I will be obliged to cut short my stay, for my neuralgia is troubling me again. I will write you when I leave. Love to the kids.

Limick

Provenience: *Letters*, 162–64.

1. *Letters*, 117.

2. George Eliot, pen name of Marian Evans (1819–80), was the author of *The Mill on the Floss*, *Silas Marner*, *Middlemarch*, and other novels. Her companion, the editor George Henry Lewes (b. 1817) had died in November 1878. According to Joaquin Miller (*New York Times Saturday Review of Books*, 31 May 1902, 360), she told BH "that one of his poems was the finest things in our language."

3. Thomas Starr King (1824–64), minister of the First Unitarian Church of San Francisco from 1860 until his death.

4. Thomas Hardy (1840–1928), author of *Far from the Madding Crowd* and *The Return of the Native*. In 1883, Hardy invited BH to speak to the Dorchester Lecture Society (*The Collected Letters of Thomas Hardy*, ed. Richard L. Purdy and Michael Millgate [Oxford: Clarendon Press, 1978], I, 121–22). BH declined the invitation, prompting an "Absurdly offended letter from Mr. Hardy" which has not survived (BH diary, 26 Oct. 1883, Berg).

5. George L. P. B. du Maurier (1834–96), artist and, later, author of the popular romance *Trilby* (1894).

6. BH met Henry James (1843–1916) at the Howells home in Cambridge on 27 February 1871 (*If Not Literature*, 141). BH expressed similar reservations about James's stories, particularly *Daisy Miller* and "An International Episode," in a letter to the Duchess of St. Albans on 6 November 1879 (*Letters*, 158–59).

7. The membership of the club included Hardy, du Maurier, James, Lowell, Lord Houghton, and the English actors Henry Irving (1838–1905) and John L. Toole (1830–1906). The Huntington Library holds BH's copy of *Recreations of the Rabelais Club 1885–1888*.

8. The jurist Sir Frederick Pollock (1845–1937).

128. TO JOHN HAY, 20 JANUARY 1880

London,
Jany 20th/80

My dear Hay,—

Your charming Xmas-Eve note came to me like a ray of transatlantic sunshine in this foggy, stuffy London, where I have been spending my Xmas holidays on a leave of absence granted me by your predecessor. I should have long ago congratulated you upon your appointment but I did not know certainly if it was a subject for congratulation.[1]

Glad as I was to hear from you I confess to a grain of disappointment, as your letter evidently shows that you do not know of my application to the Department for an exchange from Crefeld. You make no allusion to it. Yet I sent the application formally to the Secretary, with a few informal lines to Mr. Seward, saying that the place was enfeebling me—mind and body. He replied that he would take pleasure in laying the matter before the Secretary. This was three months ago—before your appointment—and the matter evidently still "lies before the Secretary." About a month ago I had a pleasant Xmas note from Sam Barlow[2] who, referring to your appointment, suggested, quite of his own accord, that he and Clarence King[3] should speak with you about transferring me to some more congenial post—he having heard, but not through me, of my pitiable dislocation here. I told him to go on—try all his eloquences upon you, but I should not write you except officially and that my application was already before you. I believed, my dear fellow, that you did not require a formal appeal from me to do your best for our friendship. But your letter makes me fear that the whole application was pigeon-holed before you "came to the fore."

I told Mr. Seward that I did not believe there would be much difficulty in exchanging me, as my place, during my incumbency, has doubled its importance and its fees, and need not "go a begging." But I urged that I could not afford to take a place of less emolument.

This, my dear Hay, is my practical reply and return to your kindness. Do what you can for me—I should not have ventured to ask you informally, but for your note. The facts are that my physician says I will not get better of my neuralgia in Crefeld; my common sense and literary instinct tell me I can absorb nothing of value there.

There are changes being made continually in the Dept. At such times remember that I have been a pretty fair officer for nearly two years, have not embezzled any public moneys, but have sent considerable to the Treasury above my fees, and do what you can, for your friend,

Bret Harte

Hon. John Hay
P.S. I return to Crefeld to-morrow.

Provenience: Brown University Library (ALS).

1. Hay was appointed assistant secretary of state in November 1879 and served in the office for seventeen months.

2. Samuel L. M. Barlow (1829–89) was a prominent New York lawyer whom BH had met while residing on Long Island during the winter of 1877–78.

3. While in California, BH had met Clarence King (1842–1901), author of *Mountaineering in the Sierra Nevada* (1871) and the first director of the U.S. Geological Survey. See also James D. Hague's memoir of BH and King in the *Overland*, n.s., 40 (Sept. 1902):335–36; and Thomas Donaldson, *Idaho of Yesterday* (Caldwell, Ida.: Caxton, 1941), 356–58.

129. TO JOHN HAY, 11 FEBRUARY 1880

Crefeld,
Feby. 11th/80

My dear Hay,

I have just received yours of the 30th ult. Let me first say a word about your suggestion that the season is too far advanced for a change to a "southerly station." My dear Hay, I dont particularly care for a *southerly* station. I am not asking for a change of latitude nor of temperature, but only a change from the excessive *dampness* of this place. It is this which keeps up my neuralgia and from which my Doctor bids me fly. It is not the salt dampness of the British islands (which I *can* stand) but the dampness of a great river—the Rhine—

which loses its health and beauty as it enters my district *almost on a level with its banks*!

Any *dryer* climate or locality would meet the considerations of my *health*, and these were the only considerations urged in my official request. But as you invite me to write to you frankly and fully, and as your ideas of what I *want* may be quickened by knowing what I already *have*, let me tell you as briefly as I can how I am situated here. For I do not think I am overstating the case when I say that as a residence for a nervous impressionable literary man, practically, socially and intellectually, no place could be more outrageously absurd than Crefeld. And I have the mortification of knowing that this is glaringly apparent to everybody in Germany—not even excepting the people I am among and to whom I am preposterously accredited!

Have you—has anybody in Washington—the remotest idea what Crefeld is? Can you imagine a town about the size of Paterson, New Jersey, without its contiquity to a great city, without a horse railroad or a single improvement. Imagine the smart American inhabitants taken out and in their place substitute dull, materially minded, purse-proud, intensely conceited Teutons—the laughing stock and reproach of all the adjacent towns—speaking a *Platte* dialect, living within themselves, jealous of strangers to the extent that they will not have a decent hotel but oblige the commercial travelers to return to Cologne at night for lodgings? Can you imagine a town, so jealous of its security, that the only foreign representative there is obliged to live in Düsseldorf, because no one will disturb themselves to give him decent lodgings? Yet that is my experience. And during my eighteen months residence here I have not received the *first* official civility or even recognition from Mayor or Burgomaster. My cards have been unacknowledged. The consular Agent whom I superseded was a German,—a native of the town and the clerk of one of the Manufacturers—which seems to have settled the official and social *status* of the office.

All this, my dear Hay, is annoying but could be borne, if it were not for the ridiculous contrast and anomaly it presents to what is my real standing socially and intellectually in Germany. You cannot have—*I did not have before*—the least idea of my tremendous popularity as a writer here. My books are everywhere, my name is as well known as their own writers.[1] Bayard Taylor, philo-Teutonic as he was and translator of their Geöthe[,] occupies no such place in their reviews or their criticism. I do not say this from any exaltation; it is rather a subject for mortification to me. My pride would be less humbled if I were not known here, and the contrast between what Germany thinks of me and the value that my own Country officially sets upon me were not so shockingly fixed.

For, as I said before, everybody in Germany knows the exact value of my official position—and its absurdities. The effect of such an ambiguous position is by no means pleasant. When I visit the towns outside of my district I am treated with courtesy and distinction—but with a certain official restraint. People dont understand why I have been sent to Crefeld if I am a man whom the Government wishes to honor. You will not wonder that my amusement was mixed with some chagrin when a friend told me the other day that it had been intimated to him that I was in a sort of *degrading exile for holding political opinions adverse to the Government! You* will laugh at this! I would if I were, like you, three thousand miles away from it. But here, my dear fellow, with no company but your pen—and no material around you from which you may use it profitably,—here in this gloomy town, among a dull people, educated to believe that position is everything and Government rewards everything, taking this in with your sour view every day, one is apt to get morose and sulky!

My English friends get over the anomaly of my official position here—after the English way—by not believing it. Consequently I am ludicrously annoyed by receiving letters addressed to the "Honble Consul General for Westphalia" &c &c, and the Earl of Derby,[2] who ought to have known better, laid me flat on my back the other day by a large official invitation addressed to "His Excellency the American Envoy to Rhenish Prussia &c &c"

You ask me to tell you what I would like "best" and "better" and "pretty well." If I thought that the President or Mr. Evarts *wished to* reward me and *could* reward me in proportion to my literary standing as an American abroad—and that they were fully convinced *what* that standing was—I should very frankly say that I wanted Spain and Spain wanted me more than Genl. Fairchild. I might be very *humble* and let Fairchild go, and take his place at Paris.[3] I might tell you that the English would like very well to have me in London.

But *I know your limitations*, and the best I can do is to point out to you why I do not like Crefeld, as I have done.

Yet it is only fair to say that the Crefeld post might be made more profitable to a mercantile man. I dare say there are many in the Service who could make more out of it than I do—without an embarrassing literary reputation, and a still more enbarrassing literary appetite for material to digest. There are many triangular pegs ready for this rigid right-angled hole, which I rattle around in. The climate is not bad only for nervous diseases. I get out of the place $2500 yearly, which I send to my family (supporting *myself* by my literary work[)]. I pay the remaining $1250 allowed me out of my fees for rent and clerk, for the actual service. A smart *business* man might do better. I have, as the records show, doubled the business of the office and its fees—but there is considerable clerical work entailed in this increase.

I will look over the Register, which has not yet arrived, and send you some suggestions. All I can say *now* is that I do not want a place like Crefeld, and that I would not care to repeat the same experience elsewhere, that I can live in any climate (not absolutely unhealthy or damp), hot or cold, and that I could not afford to take a less pecuniary emolument than my present office yields.

You might telegraph me (at my expense) the name of any place eligible—if one should chance to occur. I have every faith in your good intent and kindness—I wish for myself, as well as Frank Mason, that your furies kept step to its music.

God bless you, old fellow,

Yours always,
Bret Harte

P.S. But why—O why, are *you*—rich, handsome witty, sweetly-wived, wealthily-fortuned, delicatedly-minded,—*where* you are?

B.H.

Provenience: Brown University Library (ALS).

1. For verification, see Eugene Timpe, "Bret Harte's German Public" (*Jahrbuch für Amerikastudien* 10 [1965]:215–20).

2. Edward Henry Stanley (1826–93), fifteenth earl of Derby, had resigned the office of foreign secretary under Disraeli in 1878.

3. Lucius Fairchild (1831–96) was a Civil War general, former governor

of Wisconsin, former consul to Liverpool, and consul general in Paris from 1878 to 1880. He subsequently served as U.S. minister to Spain from 1880 to 1882.

130. TO JAMES R. OSGOOD, 3 MARCH 1880

Crefeld,
March 3d 1880

My dear Osgood;

Chatto & Windus are about to bring out a "complete" edition of my writings in several volumes, and for that purpose have bought from Fred.[k] Warne the copyright of "Gabriel Conroy."

I am thinking of the advisability of your getting the American copyright from the American Publishing Co of Hartford, and bringing out a new edition of it. The book has never had a fair show in America—through its unfelicitous birth in Hartford. It is infinitely better known in England than it is in America, and to my enormous surprise it is the *one book* quoted by critics & read by the best people as the book upon which my literary reputation rests in Germany. All over Europe, readers who have never heard of the Luck of Roaring Camp and the "Heathen Chinee" know me by Gabriel Conroy.[1]

The American Publishing Co have *never rendered me any statement of sale, &c.*—alleging that the expenses and advances have or *had*—for it is nearly three years ago since I wrote to them—not yet been covered by sales and royalties. It is very likely so. The book never was a success—was unwieldly, expensive and unprepossessing for the retail trade, and as a subscription book took no hold on the usual buyers of subscription books. It was a wretched mistake, of publication.[2]

All of which would make the Am. Pub Co part with their interest in it on easy terms I imagine. Shall I or *you* sound them?

"Jeff Briggs" is an enormous success here—i.e. what is called in Europe an "enormous success."[3]

Yours ever,
Bret Harte

J. R. Osgood, Esq.

Provenience: Bancroft (MSS C-H 57).

1. According to Lewis Rosenthal (*Critic*, 21 Feb. 1885, 85), fourteen different German editions of *Gabriel Conroy* were issued.

2. In August 1896, BH's account with the American Publishing Co. was still over $4,000 in arrears—more than he received in advances while writing the novel—and Houghton Mifflin purchased rights to the novel early the next year for a mere $350 (F. E. Bliss, "The Sale of 'Gabriel Conroy' to Houghton, Mifflin & Co.," 1897 typescript, UCLA).

3. *Jeff Briggs's Love Story and Other Sketches* had been issued in England a few days earlier by Chatto & Windus. *Jeff Briggs's Love Story and Other Tales* had been issued on the continent a few days earlier by Tauchnitz.

131. TO ANNA HARTE, 1 APRIL 1880

Crefeld,
1st April 1880

My dear Anna,

I've been quite sick with a sore throat—(which clings obstinately to me—) since I wrote you last, and was ten days shut up in the house. During this time I saw a despatch in the London *Times* saying I had been nominated Consul to Glasgow.[1] Since then I have received all sorts of congratulations from England—the *Daily Telegraph* devoted an editorial of fervent welcome to me[2]—*but I have yet not a word from the Department at Washington*. Perhaps it may *not be true*. Perhaps it is the Department's brusque way of doing a favor, but I cannot help thinking it strange that *Hay* did not write me a line or send me a telegram. Possibly I may not be confirmed by the Senate.

If it is *true*, although the change is not all that I would seek in the way of a climate—it is better and more healthful than Crefeld. There are fogs—but they are *sea* fogs—and the winters are sincere and cold. In every other respect it is a grateful change and an improvement. *First* it is *promotion*. Glasgow is a *full Consulate* and is the second *largest* city of Great Britain. The salary is $3000 per year, and one of my colleagues writes me that there are other emoluments which make it at least $4000. Then it is near Edinburgh—and not very far from *London*, and, as my English friends write me "you belong now to *us*."

But I'm writing all this quite in the dark as to the future and quite ready to hear that there is some mistake. I must go to England on the 19th to lecture; before that time I ought to hear from the Dept, and while in England I will run up to Glasgow and examine the ground. It is scarcely possible, I am told, for all the formalities of the transfer to be concluded before two months.

I will write soon again. Tell Frankie I have his earnest, honest letter and will answer it as quickly as I can. Love to all. God bless you all.

Limick

Please pardon my scrawling hand to-day, but I've been writing much, and my eyes are giving out.

Provenience: UVa (ALS).

1. "The United States," London *Times*, 22 Mar. 1880, p. 6, col. 2.

2. The editorial in the London *Telegraph* was reprinted in the *New York Times*, 14 Apr. 1880, p. 2, col. 5: BH "may count with certainty" upon a "cordial welcome from the British people" like all those paid to American diplomats "when they come to us with literary genius to recommend them."

132. TO JOHN HAY, 2 APRIL 1880

Crefeld,
April 2nd 1880

My dear Hay,

Yours of the 19th reached me to-day. I had the news of my nomination, and even of my *confirmation*, delivered to me through the newspapers, but I would not believe them until I had your own word for it.

And now, my dear fellow, let me hasten to thank you. I believe you have had to work as hard and as conscientiously for this Glasgow Consulship, as if it had been a Mission to the Hague or Lisbon.[1] I *know* you have done your best. And I thank you very, *very* much.

It is indeed, as you say[,] "in every way better than Crefeld." And you have "builded better than you knew," as I shall somewhat later tell you—my only idea, just now, being to get this very grateful acknowledgement to you as quickly as possible from

Your friend,
Bret Harte

Hon John Hay. & & c
Washington.

Provenience: Brown University Library (ALS).

1. According to Joaquin Miller, Hay wrote him at the time: "We have got Glasgow for Bret Harte. It cost me friends, too, to do it, but I do not regret it" (*San Francisco Examiner*, 7 July 1895, p. 25, col. 2).

133. TO ANNA HARTE, 15 APRIL 1880

United States Consulate,
Crefeld
April 15 1880

My dear Nan,

I have just received yours of the 3d inst, and am greatly alarmed to hear you have had a return of the ear ache. I had hoped it was only a temporary trouble and that you would have forgotten it by this time. I wish you would at once *leave town*—unless the weather is very backward—and take the children with you to recruit in some little watering place. Above all, and over all things dont let yourself get "run down" now.

I am fearful that it may be *two months* yet before I can be formally exchanged—particularly as I have yet received *no official* notice of my promotion. I know it is all right—but it is very tantalizing this delay.

As I wrote you before I am all in the dark about my future movements in Scotland until I have seen my new post. I shall however see it within the next two weeks when I go to England to lecture, and I will write you *fully* all about it. I hear it is a rather *expensive* place. But Germany was always quoted as "cheap"—and is quite the reverse in my experience.

I have a dreadful amount of work and nervous anxiety crowded into the next two weeks. I must lecture three times—at Oxford, Cambridge & Norwich.[1] And here, at the last moment, I have a note from Sir Frederick Leighton that he expects me to answer to the toast of "Literature" at the R.A. Dinner.[2] I had hoped the rumor was *not true*. It will require me to prepare a speech—which I dont like—and speak it—which I *dread*. And besides there is all the work incident to the transfer of Consulate. And I am far from well. I ran down—five hours distant—to Holland on Sunday last and stayed three days. It broke up my cold I think. I'll write you all about it another time—as I will write you about England—but you must be content with a few lines only *until I have seen Glasgow*, and know what we can do.

Love to all. God bless you. Limick

The $50 was all right. The *Chronicle* offered me that sum for "Jeff Briggs" and I told them to send it to you.[3] I am too poor to lose $50 which I can honestly earn even of an enemy. They *might* have *stolen* Jeff Briggs and I couldn't have helped myself.

Provenience: UCLA (ALS).

1. BH lectured in Oxford on April 21, Cambridge on April 22, and Norwich a day or two later. Lewis Carroll, who heard BH's Oxford lecture, noted its "quiet humour" (*The Diaries of Lewis Carroll*, ed. Roger L. Green [New York: Oxford University Press, 1954], II, 387).

2. BH delivered the "Reply to 'Toast to Literature'" at the Royal Academy dinner in London on 1 May 1880. The most complete transcript of his remarks appears in the London *Times*, 3 May 1880, p. 10, col. 1. See also London *Daily News*, 3 May 1880, p. 2, cols. 6–8; *New York Times*, 18 May 1880, p. 2, col. 2; and *Harper's Weekly*, 12 June 1880, 371.

3. "Jeff Briggs's Love Story" was reprinted in the *San Francisco Chronicle* on 14 Mar. 1880 (p. 1, col. 9–p. 2, col. 4), 21 Mar. 1880 (p. 6, cols. 1–3), 28 Mar. 1880 (p. 6, cols. 1–3), and 4 Apr. 1880 (p. 6, cols. 1–4).

134. TO ANNA HARTE, 17 APRIL 1880

Crefeld,
Apl 17th 1880

My dear Nan,

No news yet from the Department. I go in a day or two to England to lecture. I may not have time to write you again until I return.

A line in Frankies letter, received over a week ago, alludes "to some trouble I had had in Germany." As I *have had* some trouble here—but only recently, and before you could have an opportunity of hearing it it surprised me.

I should not allude to it *now* and worry you with it if it were not all over—and settled. While I was confined to my room with sore throat, I received a paragraph cut from a German newspaper by an English friend in Dusseldorf. The paragraph said that I "was sick of Germany and was going to *resign*." It then added that it was "well known" that this "genial poet" was beset with an ungovernable passion for "fire water" (*feuerwasser*—brandy) brought on by his early habits in California; that his Government had sent him to Germany hoping to cure him of it. (Imagine a man addicted to drinking sent to this land of swilling sots for a cure!) but that, alas, it was all in vain, and now the "genial poet" was about to *return to San Francisco* where he could "indulge himself freely."

I need not tell you how furious I felt. I at once wrote to a lawyer in Berlin to demand a retraction or and [*sic*] began a prosecution against the paper.[1] Meantime the very few friends I have here, but who knew me thoroughly were indignant too. My little doctor Von Köhlwetter who is one of the most famous of physicians in this district was furious. He wrote an indignant letter to the *Kölnische Zeitung* saying that he had attended me *daily*, that it was all an infamous lie &c. &c and hinted pretty plainly that if all Germans were as abstemious as I was it would be better for them.[2] Mr Jentges, my old Crefeld friend, and a member of parliament, declared that I had been an inmate of his family, and he knew me perfectly, and that it was a gratuitous and infamous slander.[3] You see, any body who really *knew* me—or saw me in *company* or at dinners knew that I drank sparingly—(I think I told you that I *could not* take any stimulants here)—so that to them the story was absurd. Dr Von K. went further and said he knew from my nature and habits and above all my *symptoms*, that I not only *was not* but never could *have been* a drunkard, &c &c. Meantime the Berlin paper, frightened, apologized and took it all back. Another paper came out and said it was all an infamous lie. The other papers copied the retraction—and so the matter ended. I triumphed. But, Nan, *I knew*—what I didnt dare tell my friends—*that paragraph—that slander came from America!*[4]

God bless you all. Tell Frankie I will write to him as soon as I have seen Glasgow.

Limick

Provenience: UVa (ALS).

1. See, for instance, *Literary World*, 22 May 1880, 172: "Mr. Bret Harte has begun a libel suit against a German newspaper, for insinuating that he has an over-fondness for the cheering cup."

2. BH referred in a note to Rudolf Schneider on 27 March 1880 (UVa) to "this abominable and filthy slander"; and he advised Schneider on 3 April 1880 (UVa) that Von Köhlwetter had given the editors of the *Kölnische Zeitung* "the choice of correcting" their report "or of publishing *his* letter with his signature."

3. Wilhelm Jentges (d. 1884).

4. Duckett (188) speculates that BH believed Clemens the source of these rumors.

135. TO SAMUEL L. M. BARLOW, 5 MAY 1880

5. Onslow Gardens, S.W.
May 5 1880

My dear Barlow,

You will find enclosed my official Bond. Pray forgive my troubling you with an odd request.

Both of my sureties on my previous Bond were *not* rich men,[1] and the present Bond is a little larger than the one they signed. I hesitate about asking them again. Would you [one line illegible] by finding two men who would sign it? Perhaps Hay would be willing to be one of the sureties.

Would you then enclose it, and transmit it to Washington?

I dare say you know some of my friends—Dana for instance—who would take part of the trouble off your hands. But I can think of none at present. And I have not time to address them personally. So I must fain ask *you*.[2]

I am here in London on my way to Glasgow to take a [one line illegible] part.

They toasted me very kindly here at the R.A. Dinner, and afterwards. **H. R. H.** and the lesser swells all "wanted to know me."[3] I've had no end of invitations and a general kind of awful patronage from every body, but I shall be very glad to get back to Crefeld again, wind up my consular affairs there, and come back to Glasgow. And

I dont dare to confess, even to myself, with what longing I am looking over the great Atlantic to the land I left behind me. I am *very lonely* here.

Always, dear Barlow,
Bret Harte

P.S. My address will be Trübner & Co., 59 Ludgate Hill, London, E.C., or the Consul General at London, until I am fairly in the saddle at Glasgow. I am stopping at present with J. A. Froude—the Historian.

Yours
B.H.

Provenience: Huntington (BW Box 135).

1. David M. Cooper of the Bureau of Engraving, husband of BH's cousin Georgianna, was one of his Crefeld bondsmen.

2. As BH wrote AH on 2 July 1880 (UVa), "I had quite a fright in regard to my official bond last week. I had sent it to Barlow and as the amount was higher than the old bond, had asked him to find two bondsmen for me. Instead of receiving my commission . . . I got a letter from Barlow saying he could *get no one* to act as my bondsman, and that Dana and Musgrave *had refused*! I felt hurt and indignant, as you may imagine, but still more frightened, as, if the bond is not signed in a certain time, the commission *lapses*!" Finally, "I was relieved by a dispatch from Hay saying the bond was filed and the commission sent—but who signed it or how it was done I have not yet heard."

Thomas B. Musgrave (d. 1903) was a Wall Street broker to whom BH dedicated *Gabriel Conroy*. On Musgrave, see also Gary Scharnhorst, "The Bret Harte-Mark Twain Feud," *Mark Twain Journal* 31 (Spring 1993):31–32.

3. Among the celebrities who attended the Royal Academy dinner on May 1 were Froude, Robert Browning, T. H. Huxley, Lawrence Alma-Tadema, Arthur Sullivan, W. E. Gladstone, the archbishop of Canterbury, and the prince of Wales. See London *Daily News*, 3 May 1880, p. 2, cols. 6–8. BH wrote AH on 11 May 1880 (*Letters*, 178) that "I made a neat little speech—not bad and not very good—the Prince of Wales asked to be introduced to me (He's more like an American than an Englishman), a lot of swells were [']glad to make my acquaintance' &c. &c."

136. TO RUDOLF SCHNEIDER, 22 JUNE 1880

Trübner & Co. . . . *57, & 59, Ludgate Hill,*
London June 22d *1880*

My dear Schneider,

Thanks for your telegram and letter. I am more sorry for Mr Potter's enforced delay than I am for the change in our plans about closing my term of office with the fiscal year.

I *still think* you can act as Vice Consul in Mr. Potters absence without waiting for your final confirmation as Vice Consul.[1] You *did act so* as Vice Commercial Agent with the full knowledge of the Department and without criticism—when I first assumed the office. But Mr Potter is of course the best and only judge in this case. Does he propose to wait in Crefeld the action of the Department? Let me know.

And send me a statement of my a/c to the 15th with the Government. If the *Deutsche Revue* has not yet remitted the 600 marks due me, which Mr Rodenberg said would be sent 10 days ago,[2] *telegraph* him that I have instructed you to ask for it. D—m these lying Jew publishers!

Let me know what I owed the office on the 15th June and I will send you a draft. Send me some Department paper also, please, that I may write my "good bye" from the Crefeld office.

Thank Heaven the lecture is over! It was called a "brilliant success."[3] It was simply a room crowded by fashionable folk in *full dress*—in fact, more like a "small reception" than an honest lecture and what between rustling silks and laces *inside* and rattling carriages and bawling footmen outside—it was a most extraordinary and amusing affair. I dont think any one came really to *hear* me; many of them were my "society" friends and they nodded their heads at me and shook their faces and smiled graciously and chatted with each other and came to enjoy apparently "a very good time." I managed finally to frown them into silence, and then they all pretended to be vastly interested, and applauded in the wrong places, and said, in loud stage whispers, to each other "O isnt it perfectly charming! Really, how delicious! You know! The idea! you know!" At last they got me to laughing too—and so the lecture ended. It wanted only the handing around of ices and tea—to have made it perfect. Indeed one of the ladies said to me afterwards with the most charming frankness, "O dear Mr. Bret Harte, you know, you ought to have had—you know—one of those "recesses"—a kind of intermission of 10 minutes, when you could have come down and *talked with us* or had *us come up and talk with you!* It would have [been] *so* delightful!"

I shall leave for Glasgow about the 27th or 29th but I hope to hear from the Department before. I did not quite finish with the Dentist in Paris! He has turned me over to another Fraud in London.

Tell Mr Potter I sincerely condole with him. Give my best respects to Mrs Schneider, & believe me always

Your friend
Bret Harte

P.S. Pardon this scrawl—its all due to Trübner's bad pens and worse ink!

Provenience: UVa (ALS).

1. Joseph S. Potter (d. 1904), BH's successor in Crefeld, was U.S. consul in Stuttgart and had not yet transferred his office.

2. Dr. Julius Rodenberg (1831–1914) was founding editor of the *Deutsche Rundschau* (not the *Deutsche Revue*). BH had submitted the text of his lecture, "The Argonauts of '49," to the *Rundschau*, where it appeared in German translation under the title "Aus Kaliforniens fruhen Tagen" 25 (Nov. 1880):268–86.

3. BH delivered "The Argonauts of '49" in London on June 21 (London *Times*, 22 June 1880, p. 12, col. 1).

137. TO ANNA HARTE, 9 JULY 1880

London,
July 9 1880

My dear Nan,

I am still waiting for my commission. I cannot take charge in Glasgow until that comes, and so I wait in London where—as I am staying with the Trübners,—it is less expensive. I expect, of course, that the Government will allow me to reckon my salary from the time I left Crefeld, but I cannot draw anything until I actually take charge.

Since I wrote you from Scotland I have received yours of the 15th June. I am rejoiced to hear that you are out of town; even if Morristown is the same old bigoted, self righteous hypocritical place it is better than being in a N.Y. boarding house in summer. But could you not find some pleasanter place? As soon as I "take charge," I will see that you have the $200 regularly every month and will probably send it through some bank, but until then you may draw upon Schroeder as before.

The question of your coming over with the children this summer, Nan, is one that must be at once seriously considered. In the first place, we must both bear in mind that my position in the Government service is sure only up to the 4th of next March, and the duration of this Administration. I *believe* that Garfield will be elected; Captain Mason, who knows him intimately, says if he is *elected*, I may expect not only to be retained but promoted. Even if the Democrats succeed it is possible that they will not interfere with *me*—a literary man and not a political appointee. *But none of these things are sure.* I do not—I *must not* take them into my calculations. So that the real question is can we afford to undergo the cost of bringing the whole family over when the additional expense of *returning* may be added in 6 months? If I were to leave the Government service I could not make enough money by mere literary work in England to support my family. I should be obliged to return to America at once.

I can easily reckon what the expenses of the trip here and back would be, and when I get to Glasgow ascertain what the expenses of living there for six months would be and add these sums together for the total.

The question therefore is whether it is better to take this risk *now*, or wait until *after* the 4th of March, when the risk is past. If it is better to wait, I shall try to get a leave of absence this winter to visit America get promoted if I can and then bring you back with me—I hope *not* to Glasgow. For I do not think I could stand it long and I go there only with the hope that I may be "changed" with the change of administration.

I hope I may be disappointed in the Scotch people. All I hear of them is dreadful; all I have yet seen of them is not hopeful. The climate certainly is a very slight improvement on Crefeld. It rains every day, but I suffer most here from the utter absence of all the warmth and graciousness of summer. It is not to be found in Northern Europe. There are occasional *tepid* damp days, but never any dry sunny summer weather when the shade is really grateful. I always find an overcoat comfortable in England, but what is more perplexing I find that I seldom have an opportunity of *perspiring*. You remember how easily I always perspired; since I have been in Europe I do not know what it is. I think much of my neuralgia and throat-trouble is owing to this inactivity of my skin and its pores. Other Americans tell me the same thing.

Returning from Oban, by rail, I passed through the Highlands of Scotland. I never saw scenery that, to me, seemed to typify the character of the people so strongly. Rather, I ought to say, has impressed itself so strongly on the character of the people. I do no longer wonder that a Scotchman cannot take a joke. Nature never smiles upon him. I can understand why they are bigoted; their highest mountains never rise above the clouds and fog and mist of their own creating. There is not a mountain summit in Scotland above the clouds. Accustomed to see Nature stern and forbidding, and scant in her kindliness to him—he makes his own religion out [of] it. I wish you could see what they call a "fine day" in Scotland—you would understand their ideas of the Sabbath.

Apropos, I must tell you a good story of them—new to me. A gentleman going to church one Sunday, found himself too early for the service and would pass away the time by walking in an adjacent park. But the park keeper opposed him, and informed him he must not desecrate the "Sawbath" by walking in the park. In vain the gentleman pleaded that he was only *waiting to go to church.* The park keeper was unflinching. Then the gentleman, a little indignant, informed the park keeper that Our Lord not only walked in the fields with his disciples on the Sabbath day, but plucked some ears of corn and ate them. "Eye," said the park keeper. "And I'm *na thinkin' the better o' him* for that!!" This is the most perfect exposition of Scotch theology I ever heard.

I have been very kindly treated, and made much of during my stay in London. But I am more pleased at meeting my old friends of two years ago and finding them still loyal and true, than in making any new acquaintances. I have found the Webbs of Newstead, the

Duchess, the Froudes, and the Trübners, quite as I left them. The poor Duchess lost her mother lately in Ireland, and has gone over to stay there.

Kiss the kids for their Papa. Give my love to Lize. I'll write you *next* from Glasgow. God bless you all.

Limick

P.S. I add a line to tell you a bit of good news which I intended to keep until it was *better*. It has been suggested to me to publish a magazine here called "Bret Harte's Monthly" and, what is more to the purpose, certain printers and publishers have offered to bear the expense of it themselves. It would be *my own property*, the proceeds my own deducting the expenses of publication. It will enable me to control my own publications and really profit by my own stories. It would enable me [to] turn my editorial faculty to account. I am at present working it up. If it can be done, and made a success, I need not worry about the 4th of March, and I should arrange to stay here.[1]

Limick

Provenience: Boston Public Library (ALS). By courtesy of the Trustees of the Boston Public Library.

1. BH wrote AH on 12 November 1880 (*Letters*, 192) that "The magazine enterprise I fear will have to be abandoned on account of the introduction of an English edition of Harpers."

138. TO RUDOLF SCHNEIDER, 21 JULY 1880

London,
July 21st 1880

My dear Schneider,

Thanks for yours of the 14th. Cooper hung on,[1] under various pretences, until yesterday, when I took charge, although my exequatur is not yet issued. He had sent home *all* the surplus funds, and pocketed his own salary up to date, so I shall have nothing until the first of August. I send you a draft for £20⁰⁰, which you will please post to my credit, and I will send you the rest on the 1st. It is a very provoking piece of business—the more so as I found my sympathy with Cooper was entirely thrown away; he only wanted the office for what it was worth each day to him, and although he is, compared with myself, a rich man, he was quite willing to keep me out of it as long as he could. He is very mean and economical, saves nearly all his salary, and told me, with an injured air, that it cost him *as high* as £2 *a week to live*! That is the way the Government has been represented in Glasgow—and this is the man I was feeling so sorry for. I reckon he has "done me" out of $300 already—to say nothing of bringing me in at the end of a quarter into an empty treasury.

I have arranged with my Vice Consul only temporarily until I see how we suit.[2] He's a good fellow I think—*but we all can't be Schneider*, and I've been spoilt for any *other*. I am here for a day or two on business, but I am going to Paris to hear my niece sing at the *Concours* at the Conservatoire on the 29th[3] and return to Glasgow on the 1st. Tell Mrs Schneider I do not write because not only I have *no time* to write, but I absolutely have *no place* to write in. For nearly six weeks I have been "living in my trunks" as we say in America. Give her my best thanks for her bright, cheering letter and tell her as soon as I have a desk and a room, and a place where I can write to her *comfortably* I'll pay up my arrears.

With best love to the children from their "Uncle Bret Harte"

Always, dear Schneider,
Yours
B.H.

Provenience: UVa (ALS).

1. Samuel F. Cooper, BH's predecessor in Glasgow. BH had complained to Schneider on 8 July 1880 (UVa) that "Cooper is an awful old fogy. He is asking now for me to delay taking my office until the 15th."

2. The lawyer William Gibson, who had also served as Cooper's vice-consul.

3. BH wrote AH from Paris on 28 July 1880 (*Letters*, 186) that "Gerty has got the *first* prize and is immensely praised by the critics, and is thought to be 'the coming American Prima Donna.'"

139. TO SAMUEL L. M. BARLOW, 22 JULY 1880

London,
July 22d 1880

My dear Mr Barlow,

Thank you for yours of the 2d and the successful issue of my bond out of its difficulties. When I telegraphed you I was fearful that my commission might lapse through the delay. It is here now, but I am waiting for my exequatur from the Foreign Office.

I congratulate you on your happy deliverance from the burning Seawauhaka. After reading the first meagre despatch, I scarcely dared look at the list of the lost lest I should come upon the names of some of that cheerful group who used to meet in your little state room. How remarkable was their escape; your own seems to have been simply *marvellous*![1]

Dreadful as the whole thing must have been, the spectacle of you comfortable people being obliged to take to the water in ten minutes after you were leisurely seated on your pleasant homeward trip, has something ghastly ludicrous about it. How far did Dana have to swim?[2] Did you have any ladies in your party? How did Harper get ashore?[3] I see the whole thing very vividly.

Captain Smith showed great pluck.[4] I remember being with him and Dana in that great squall off Sands Point when the Seawauhaka took a heavy sea over her bows, dashing in the sliding doors forward and flooding the forward salon. He was very cool and averted a panic.

But all this you have forgotten by this time. It is very fresh in my mind now as I look over the details of your catastrophe.

The English people are very kind to me; indeed all Americans are "to the fore" just now. I try very hard to be all that they think I am. But I miss my countrymen and my country more and more every day. I have had some experience of what we, in America, fondly believe is especially admirable and superior in Europe. I know of nothing, except antiquity, that we have not at home in a better, purer, higher degree. I have become intolerant of even the most tolerant English criticism of our Life; there is so much more to be criticised in theirs!

Write me a line now and then wont you? With best regards to your wife & daughter

Yours, always,
Bret Harte

Provenience: Huntington (BW Box 135).

1. The steamer *Seawauhaka*, plying a route between New York and towns along the north shore of Long Island, caught fire in the water on the afternoon of 28 June 1880 with about three hundred passengers on board. About forty of them died. Among the survivors were both Barlow and Charles Dana. As this letter indicates, when he lived in Sea Cliff BH often commuted to the city on this boat. See the *New York Times*, 29 June 1880, p. 1, cols. 1–5.

2. In an interview the next day, Dana reported that he swam "about 175 feet" to shore (*New York Times*, 30 June 1880, p. 1, col. 3).

3. Probably J. Henry Harper (b. 1850) of Harper & Bros., who reminisced about BH in his autobiography *I Remember* (1934).

4. Though the captain, Charles P. Smith, was badly burned in the accident, he succeeded in running the boat aground near Randall's Island.

140. TO JOHN HAY, 5 AUGUST 1880

Glasgow
August 5th 1880

My dear Hay,

Dont think me unmindful or ungrateful for leaving your letter so long unanswered. I am sparing my eyes—which are greatly troubling me in this gray, Glasgow smoke—as much as possible. I try to think the trouble *is* the fog and the generally depressing effect of the Climate—or anything but the probable and unpleasant fact that I'm growing old!

My predecessor here—a singular kind of Western puritan—more Scotch in some things than the most rigid economical Scotsman,—clung tenaciously to his office until I got *all* my papers from Washington, two weeks ago, and, indeed, kindly offered to keep the position until the day he sailed for America.[1] I dare say he represented the Government in all that severe Republican simplicity which the Average Congressman demands of the American representative abroad. The Consulate in this second largest city of Great Britain resembled Mr. Micawber's office at the time of his unsuccessful coal brokerage.[2] I bought his furniture for £13 and at once rashly ordered a desk and bookcase at my own risk. If this momentous speculation of mine comes before you for endorsement, for Heaven's sake, Hay, dont go back on me! Had you been here and present at the solemn delivery to me of three chairs that had seen better days when the Century was young, a map of the U.S. on a conservative plan with the newer and younger states left out, a faded lithograph of Webster and a gorgeous one of somebody's "Reaper" and twenty six volumes of Congressional Reports you would have forgiven me. "That sofy," said the Colonel, pointing to a misshapen object in the last stages of mangy decline—"that sofy is my own. I shant say *what* I paid for it! Enough," added this noble man with a slight struggle, "that we wont count it as *extra. I* know what's due from one gentleman to another. Its yours—take it."

If you ever meet this remarkable man gain his confidence and try to find out what he had done with his salary and the emoluments of his office during these years. He has a wife and *no* children; he doesn't spend his substance on her clothes nor his own. He tells me that he has lived here on (2) guineas a week, but that Glasgow is a *dear* place. "Dont—" he said to me, seriously, when I had unfolded a plan of living out of town on the Clyde, "dont go to a watering place. It will cost you, Sir, *at least* 8 shillings a day!" Cultivate the Col. if you meet him. If he developes into a first class *millionaire* when he returns, let me know.

I know very little of the natives as yet. In the climate and in the scenery I see much to condone their faults. How can a Scotchman take a joke when Nature never smiles on him? Can you wonder at his meanness and economy when Nature sits him the example and is skimped and poverty-stricken; when the very hills are bare-legged and show their breechless bottoms in the wind. The kilt is a suggestion directly from Nature. And as for their *theology*! Think of a country where the mountains never rise above the fogs and mists of their own creating! There isn't a peak in all Scotland that ever pierces the Serenity of the Upper Sky!

But the Scotch are no *fools*. There is something tremendous in their common sense. In the pathetic bewilderment of English politics just now I should not wonder if the canny Scot should be the saving grace. And as I cannot help liking the English—for all their conceit and economies—I hope they may see their way out of their present perplexities.

I say this partly from a natural human gratitude—for these

English have been very kind to me—but partly because any honest American finds it quite impossible to overlook a great wholesome *manliness* in them, which they often misapply, but which is none the less *manliness*. They have a wonderful sense of *duty* and *discipline*, which often leads them to pathetically absurd extremes—but I wish *we* had more of it in America. I like them, also, because they allow me to air *my* American beliefs and convictions and I am vain enough to think they like me none the less for it! And, just now, there is quite an American "boom" in England. American artists, writers, actors, and even American ladies and gentlemen they have discerned to be as good as themselves, with an added originality, which although unprecedented is not altogether dangerous or subversive! And, better yet, they have discerned that the Boston or New York Snob who stands with his hat in his hand humbly apologizing for the faults of his countrymen, or worse yet, trying to pose as an Englishman—is not a genuine or representative American. Hay! I would give anything—even my prospects of being President of the Young Men's Christian Association—to have you here with me a few weeks that we might enjoy these people together, and that I might introduce a *real* Western American to some of them. There is one I know you would like, and you would forget she was not an American.[3] She ought to be living in North Perry Street Cleveland instead of a Castle in Nottinghamshire, and be a simple Ohio woman instead of a Duchess. She talks of coming over to America in the fall. I'll give you a letter to her, and if you dont go to see her and show yourself and your wife to her and make some things howl around her, I'll abuse you as a low politician!

I have had two or three delicious letters from Captain Mason—who, to use his own noble language, "drips down at one end of the historic Rhine as I *leak out* of the other."[4] I hope he'll have a leave of absence and come over here. I'm dying for a breath of Western slang—for the Americans one meets [are] the better class tourists, who dare not open their mouths at a *table d'hote* lest they should betray their nationality. It is delicious to see them "tumble" violently into English "form," and outdo the Englishmen.

Could you not come on after the 4th of March (if *I* am still here) and prowl around with me?

A number of English Capitalists offer to start me in a magazine of my own in London called "Bret Harte's Monthly." Will you write for me—if I do. I am serious—*they* are serious—be serious yourself and say "yes."[5]

Dont forget me, Hay. Remember me to Clarence King. And when you and he are sitting at the festive board and exchanging the gentle slang of the Wild West, think of *me* nobly striving to "keep up my end," on this gloomy sunless coast, and among these gloomy puritans. God bless you, old fellow,

Always Your
B.H.

Provenience: Brown University Library (ALS).

1. See note 1 to letter 138.

2. In Dickens's *David Copperfield*, Wilkins Micawber considers becoming a coal dealer (chapter XVII) before opening a corn brokerage (chapters XXVII–XXVIII).

3. The Duchess of St. Albans.

4. With the help of his friend Hay, Mason had been appointed U.S. consul at Basel, Switzerland.

5. See note to letter 137.

141. TO CLARA SCHNEIDER, 11 AUGUST 1880

Glasgow,
August 11th 1880

My dear Mrs Schneider,

I am afraid that if I wait until I am "settled" to answer your kind letters, you will lose even your gentle patience with me, so I sit down resolutely here, at the Queens Hotel, with my stupid trunks gaping their open mouths at me. I take from one a pen and a pair of boots, an inkstand and a hat from another, and at last find my envelopes wrapped up in a night shirt in a third, and then compose myself to tell you what I have *been* doing and *am* doing. It is easily told. *Nothing!* At least I find I have achieved so little since I left Crefeld in June last, and above all so little that would interest you that I really doubt, after all my promises about *that long* letter, if I've anything to say. I only know, very positively, that since then I've longed for my quiet bachelor "dew" in Düsseldorf, and for the hearty, honest welcome that always met me at my *other home* in the little house on Neue Liner Strasse.[1] I have a very good Vice Consul; he's a Scotch lawyer and an upright man; I've got a well meaning but stupid clerk[2] but these are only my *business associates*. So you readily see that I miss our old gossiping chats and the sympathy that was always ready for me when I used to come over growling and dyspeptic from Düsseldorf in the morning. I've been spoiled. I have become sentimental and *German*!! Think of it—what an awful retribution!

Not that I have anything to complain of here. These Scotch folk have been awfully kind and hospitable. The Lord Provost has put his yacht at my disposal; my foreign colleagues, Dutch and French Consuls, have been full of kindness. I have successfully avoided a public *dinner*; I've been up to Oban in the West Highlands; I've been down to a castle with an unpronouncable name—the seat of one of the Campbells; I've been to Loch Lomond and Ben Lomond, and have more invitations to "shootings" visits &c. than I can well attend to. But over all, and above all, is the dreadful, dull gloomy sky, *this damp depressing Scotch weather*—which is almost poisonous to me. Shall I ever live in the sunshine again or must I go back to America for it? I spent three blessed days in sunshiny Paris, when I warmed up my torpid blood on the Boulevards, and absorbed enough sun to last me two weeks in England. As to scenery &c, I think we saw more during our little trip into Holland last spring that I have seen during these last two months in England and Scotland.

The people are very quiet, very intelligent, common-sensical, and in some things very liberal. They are hard workers and intensely *practical*. They are not well-favored; men and women of upper and lower classes are quite plain. But I have found less of that Puritanism about them than I had been led to expect. The Sunday in many private homes is a *passable* day; but I miss the perfect freedom, and the pleasant outdoor Sunday life of the Continent.

At Oban I saw a little fellow of about 5 years—bare legged, fringy-haired and dirty who was selling papers. I suggested to my two friends that we might try the effect of 1/2 a sovereign on the boy and observe how he stood the present of such a vast fortune to him. I was overruled and a half-crown from each of us—(we were three—) making

7/6, was substituted. He received it with calm and practical satisfaction. "And now" said we, "what are you going to do with it?" The little rascal opened his keen grey eyes on us. "*Keep it!*" said he with perfect sincerity. We subsequently heard that he had 8 shillings already in the bank!

I am not yet certain about my residence here. I have not found city lodgings to suit me, but I shall probably go down to Innellan—a very pretty coast watering place with a fine hotel—to spend a week or two, coming up to town by train and boat every day. Its very little longer than the ride from Düsseldorf to Crefeld—lovelier, of course,—and about *1/2 the expense*! Indeed, one of the pleasantest experiences in Scotland is the cheapness of travelling. And all the fine scenery is quickly accessible. You can find yourself on an island—in the open Atlantic—in two hours and a half from Glasgow. Mr Schneider shocks me by telling me that Lulu is getting no stronger.[3] Why dont *you* come over here with her for a few weeks. Come down to Innellen, or Oban. I believe it would do you a world of good! Tell Mr Schneider he can get leave of absence for a few days—some of those *fest* days—to bring you over.

I fear that I must remain in daily intercourse with Glasgow for some time. The Webbs have invited me to come and spend a vacation with them at Newstead, but I must decline for the present. I have an ugly shipping case on hand; a brutal captain who is trying to get a crew together by "bull-dozing" them and I am staying here to stand between "poor Jack" and his tyrant.[4] I am rather glad of an opportunity to put my *foot down* on what I have long believed an act of injustice. Tell Mr Schneider it *is* rather livelier here at such times than it was in calm virtuous Crefeld. I wish he were here with me.

I am half-conscious I have not written all I intended. You know, of course, that my niece Gertie Griswold got the 1st prize—the first prize ever carried off by an American—or even an English-speaking girl. I'll send you a newspaper containing an account of it.

Remember me kindly to your mother and Mr Jentges and the other few friends I have in Crefeld. Write soon again.

Always your friend,
Bret Harte

Provenience: UVa (ALS).

1. The Schneider house in Crefeld.

2. See letter 167 and accompanying note 2.

3. Rudolf and Clara Schneider's daughter (d. 1890).

4. The case was more nuanced than BH here implies. Several crew members of the barque *Bessie Wittich*, upon docking in Scotland, had complained of the condition of the vessel and the "insufficiency of their food" and promptly deserted. Two (others?) were arrested for theft and jailed. The ship's captain refused to pay wages due them on grounds they had deserted. BH interceded on behalf of the jailed sailors, arguing that they were detainees, not deserters. "The record of the ships voyage was one of unseaworthiness, brutality, and inefficiency," he reported. "It is by no means improbable that some of the men were driven to desertion. The Captain was intoxicated, violent, and overbearing in the Consulate" (to the State Department, 14 Oct. 1880, NA).

142. TO M. S. VAN DE VELDE, 10 SEPTEMBER 1880

Glasgow, September 10, 1880.

My dear Madame Van de Velde,[1]—Why do you permit yourself to live at a place with such a name as "South Sheen?" What is the "sheen" anyway? Is it the glitter from the sea, or the genial effulgency of your presence that gives a name to your local habitation? And why "South?"

The photographs taken by——[2] are too atrocious to give to anybody, much less a critical and mischievous woman. So I have written to Germany for some of the old ones,[3] taken in *real* sunlight, and I will keep my word with you when they come. There was a portrait of me in a magazine. You should see that remarkable picture. It is so faint, so spiritual, so ghostly and apparition-like that I am afraid to stay in the room with it in the dark.[4]

The weather has been preternaturally (I didn't know that word was really so *very* long, please excuse me!) fine all over Scotland, but most gracious, I think, at Innellan—a charming little watering-place on the west coast, where I go every night from Glasgow. I am sorry you do not like the seaside; but you must remember *this* is not the staring, overdressed, negro-minstrel haunted, children-shovelling beach of Brighton, nor the fashionable, full-toiletted sands of Trouville or Etretat. It is a craggy shelf of tangled seaweed and rocks, blown over by foam and breeze; the gentlemen bathe from small boats in the offing, quite *au naturel*, and honest but awfully plain Scotch lassies apparently are baptized in long grey and black gowns and then stride home without stockings. But I have picked up some little health here and some little experience, both of which I need.

The Scotch people are very queer, but in the main very kind and hospitable. I have no reason to complain. On my birthday, which became quite accidentally known to a few friends in the hotel, my table was covered with bouquets of flowers and little remembrances from cigar cases to lockets.

As I am trying to get up a good reputation here I stay at my post pretty regularly, occasionally making a cheap excursion. This is a country for them. The other day I went to Staffa. It was really the only "sight" in Europe that quite filled all my expectations. But alas! that magnificent, cathedral-like cave was presently filled with a howling party of sandwich-eating tourists, splashing in the water and climbing up the rocks. One should only go there alone, or with some sympathetic spirit. Permit me to suggest that we go there together!

Write me again. I like your letters. I'll keep my promise about the photograph and anything else you may ask of yours always,

Bret Harte.

Provenience: Pemberton, 214–15.

1. M. S. Van de Velde (1853–1913) was an author and translator fluent in three languages; the daughter of Count de Launay, Italian ambassador in Berlin; the wife of Arthur Van de Velde, chancellor of the Belgian legation in London; and the mother of nine children. BH probably met the Van de Veldes, who lived at 15 Upper Hamilton Terrace, while visiting the Trübners in St. John's Wood. See also Mme Van de Velde's essays "Francis Bret Harte," *Belgravia* 45 (Aug. 1881):232–36, reprinted in *Potter's American Magazine* 17 (Oct. 1881):306–309; and "Bret Harte: First and Last Tales of the Argonauts," *Gentleman's Magazine* 295 (Dec. 1903):535–44.

2. The omission appears in the only extant text of the letter, printed in Pemberton.

3. As BH wrote Rudolf Schneider the same day (UVa), "I have some Scotch friends [*sic*] who have been very kind to me and I want *them* to

have the best pictures—which are the Düsseldorf ones." After BH's death, Pemberton published the photo BH gave Mme Van de Velde as the frontispiece to his *The Life of Bret Harte*. See photograph 15, Harte in 1880.

4. BH apparently refers to the cover of *Every Saturday* for 14 January 1871. See letter 20.

143. TO JOHN HAY, 11 DECEMBER 1880

Glasgow,
Decem 11th 1880

My dear Hay,

I thought myself, as an old newspaper man, quite an expert in tracing the genesis of most newspaper lies, but I confess the one that heads your letter completely gets me. I have never *written*, spoken nor intimated to any one that I intended to resign from Glasgow; I have never even *thought* it. I am, it is true, suffering from the detestable climate and its chemical smoke and fogs, but beyond the hope that I might be *exchanged* in due course of time I have had no other idea.

Who is the paragraph fiend who continually pursues me so? Could I buy him up; could you give him an office? Three months ago I met with an accident while shooting at Cumbernauld House. After the surgeon had sewn me up I swore all the other guns and the surgeon to secrecy, knowing that the paragraph devil might wound and torture some gentle hearts that love me in America, and went down to a quiet place to recruit—for a week. The result was that I had three cable messages to answer in a week. It appeared that I was thrown from my horse in the hunting field and had dislocated my shoulder; that I had been shot by a brother sportsman and seriously wounded, and last but not least that I and William Black (the novelist)[1] had been knocked overboard from a yacht and nearly drowned. The Newstead Abbey paragraph was nearly true. I had lost so much blood and was still suffering from what the surgeons call "shock" that I was quite an invalid, and very weak.[2] I went down to Newstead Abbey, whose kind-hearted hostess calls herself my English Cousin, and bids me treat it as my English home, and laid myself up to recruit. An unlucky note from me, declining an invitation to an Edinburgh public dinner was the basis of that paragraph.[3]

But its awfully kind in you, dear old fellow, to think of me, either amidst your official bother, or in the sanctity of the circle of wife and babies. I am very grateful, dear Hay. A line from you or Mason sets me up wonderfully above the loneliness that so often encompasses me. The people here are very hospitable; but they do not seem to understand that I am a "shy" man, that I like to dodge dinners and speeches, and that I fear I am not in that sense at all a representative American. I have made some dear friends in the United Kingdom, but not in that way. I wish I could "fill the bill" and fly the banner after the republican style. But if I could I have a faint suspicion that I couldn't write the stories you are good enough to like.

I hope, however, that I have convinced some people here that I am a different sort of animal from my immediate predecessor.[4] Hay,—if that hound, Cooper, ever crosses your threshold, dont wait to kick him, but grab the inkstand and go for him. The day he left Glasgow he told my Vice Consul that he, Cooper, had recommended me to retain him. "And thats worth something" added the ex-representative of the U.S. significantly. The V.C., a little astonished, but thinking it the custom timidly asked how much it was worth. "£20" responded Cooper. And he got it. I half suspected something and, at last, a few weeks ago drew this story, very reluctantly, from the lips of the V.C. Thus my dear Hay, does the pensive Iowa politician compass the "siller" of the canny Scotch barrister.

You have been kind enough to hint that I might have a leave of absence for three months with permission to visit home. After that hint I shall address myself to you, *formally*, in a few days.[5] If the climate still goes for me I may have to come home and arrange if I can for an exchange should Garfield[6] feel inclined to retain the services of your friend

Bret Harte

P.S. Love to King.

Provenience: Brown University Library (ALS).

1. William Black (1841–98) was the author of *White Wings* (1880) and *Judith Shakespeare* (1884).

2. A few weeks later, Hay remarked in an interview: "Harte met with

an accident last summer, about which nothing was said, but it disabled him for a while. He was shot in the hand while out gunning. He makes a good consul, and is doing considerable literary work for Germany and France" (*Springfield Republican*, 3 Feb. 1881, p. 3, col. 1).

3. The Edinburgh Philosophical Institution honored Lowell with a dinner on 6 November 1880 which BH failed to attend, as he explained in a telegram read from the podium, because he was "indisposed" at Newstead Abbey (London *Times*, 8 Nov. 1880, p. 10, col. 3). By the time the item was picked up by the New York *World* ten days later (18 Nov. 1880, p. 1, col. 2) BH was "seriously ill," perhaps even incapacitated.

4. See letter 140.

5. BH formally wrote Hay on 17 January 1881 to request "a leave of absence of three months" as well as "permission to visit the United States" (NA).

6. James A. Garfield (1831–81) had been elected president of the United States a month earlier.

144. TO ANNA HARTE, 10 MARCH 1881

Consulate of the United States of America.
Glasgow, March 10th *1881*

My dear Anna,

I was in London when your telegram came to Glasgow but it was at once repeated to me there. I immediately sent you the money, though I had to borrow it from a friend. The delay was unavoidable.

I have been unable, through illness, to do any literary work, so I am obliged to draw *all* my means from the Consulate. Before, when I was in Crefeld, I supported myself from my literary gains. *Now* we are *both* dipping out of the same dish, and as I am obliged every month to make a return to the Government of my fees I've no capital to borrow from as in the case last year. I shall send you to-morrow or next day another $100. I think it strange, knowing the regularity with which I have sent you money during the past two years that you should not have *credit* enough to enable you to bridge over a single month.

I have had no news from my leave of absence. My Cleveland friends Capt.[n.] and Mrs Mason came to London—Mrs Mason *en route* to Washington to see Garfield, her very near friend[1]—and I ran down to spend a week with them. It was, I think, a week well spent, as the little woman went home filled with a desire to have me promoted or at least retained in the service.

I am still suffering from this dreadful nervous depression and want of food and sleep. But I think I am a little better. Pray keep the boys from doing anything or committing themselves to any permanent profession until I come, or I *know what I am to do.* The next two months of the new administration will settle that.

Meantime God bless you all. Kiss my little girls for their papa

Limick

Provenience: UVa (ALS).

1. Jennie V. Mason (1844–1916) was, like Garfield and her husband Frank Mason, a native Ohioan.

145. TO ANNA HARTE, 11 NOVEMBER 1881

London,
Novem 11th 1881

My dear Nan,

I suppose you have been more or less alarmed at my silence, but I have been very ill, very uncertain *how* I should take my leave of absence, and I feared it would alarm you still more if I asked any one else to write for me. I have suffered terribly from rheumatism and dyspepsia and have been quite unable to walk or write. I stayed with some kind foreign friends of mine—Count Van de Velde and his family—for over a month at Bournemouth—a little watering place in the south of England, returned to Glasgow in company with one of my hosts, who thought me unfit to travel alone, and have again returned to London for treatment a week longer.[1]

I do not know whether I told you in a previous letter that my Washington friends thought it better for me not to come to America after all had been gossiped about my absences from Scotland.[2] If I did not tell you this I can add now that poor Garfields assassination made it most imperative that I should remain in Great Britain until the new officers were appointed and that even my hoped for trip to the Continent was lost.[3]

It seems a long time since I heard from you last. My hand is very stiff and cramped, and I must stop. I send you a telegram and some money, both I hope will relieve your anxiety, and I shall send again as soon as I can get my return of fees. God bless you, and love to the children.

Your Limick

Address Glasgow as before.

Provenience: UVa (ALS).

1. BH alludes for the first time to the Van de Veldes in a letter to AH.

2. While BH's request for a leave was granted, as he wrote AH on 22 April 1881 (Claremont), the Masons discouraged him from visiting the United States: "[T]here are thousands of people clamoring for Glasgow" and "my alleged absences from my post are brought to the fore," so "as a matter of selfish wisdom it might be well to hang round" Glasgow "until the pressure subsides." His friend William Black privately compared BH with a "globule of mercury" or a "wandering comet. The only place he is sure not to be found in is at the Glasgow Consulate" (T. Wemyss Reid, *William Black: Novelist* [New York: Harper, 1902], 216, 218). George Stewart reported in 1931 that there were 562 "letters and telegrams from Harte to Gibson" in the consular archives in Glasgow (since lost)—a number that "makes certain" BH "must have been away from Glasgow an extraordinarily large proportion of his time" (Stewart, 271).

3. Garfield had been shot by Charles Guiteau on 2 July and died on 19 September 1881. As BH wrote Clara Schneider on 1 November 1881 (UVa), "Guiteau's bullet not only stopped my visit to Washington but kept me in England. Diplomatic friends of mine thought it wiser for me to keep within the British Islands, and nearer my post."

146. TO THE DEPARTMENT OF STATE, 9 JANUARY 1882

. . . *United States Consulate,*
Glasgow, 9th January *1882*

Hon[l.] J. C. Bancroft Davis,[1]
Assistant Secretary of State . . .

Sir

I have the honor to report that on a recent visit to the island of Iona, within this consular district, I found in the consecrated ground of the ruined Cathedral the graves of nineteen American seamen who perished in the wreck of the "Guy Mannering" on the evening of the thirty first December, eighteen hundred and sixty five on the north west coast of the island. The place where they are interred is marked by two rows of low granite pediments at the head and feet of the dead supporting and connected by an iron chain which encloses the whole space. This was done by the order and at the expense of the lord of the manor—the present Duke of Argyll.

A record of the names ages and burial of these men is kept by the Registrar of the District, but there is no memorial upon the stone enclosure. The fact of their burial there and the story of the generosity of the distinguished nobleman is learned only from the lips of hired guides. The locality is picturesque and historical; the graves of the American seamen lie side by side with the tombs and sculptured effigies of Ancient Scottish Kings. It is a favorite resort of all tourists, but particularly of Americans, who are, however, for the most part, made first aware of the courtesy of the Scotch nobleman who has honored the remains of their unfortunate countrymen, or their own neglect which has left the names of these poor sailors and their foreign benefactor equally unrecorded on the spot where they are hallowed.

In view of this I venture to make these facts known to the Department satisfied that such recognition of the thoughtful courtesy of the Duke of Argyll as would seem most fit and appropriate to the Department will be made, and that possibly a record of the names of the seamen will be placed upon some endurable memorial erected upon the spot. I have the honor to annex herewith copy of a letter from a resident of the island, by which it will appear that the names of the deceased are easily obtainable. In conclusion I beg to state that should the Department deem any expenditure by the Government for this purpose inexpedient I am willing with the permission of the Department to endeavor to procure by private subscription a sufficient sum for the outlay.[2]

I have the honor to remain most respectfully your obedient servant

Bret Harte
U. S. Consul

Provenience: NA (LS).

1. John C. Bancroft Davis (1822–1907) was thrice assistant secretary of state (1869–71, 1873–74, and 1882).

2. In reply, Davis thanked BH for bringing this matter "to the attention of the department" and authorized him "to have erected at or near the graves a simple stone bearing the names of the deceased" (*New York Times*, 9 June 1882, p. 3, col. 5). BH commissioned an engraved granite obelisk. Davis also asked BH to express to the Duke the "thanks of the President of the United States and the State Department" for his "thoughtful courtesy in giving the bodies" of the shipwrecked Americans "careful and decent" burial (to the Duke of Argyll, 23 Feb. 1882, NA).

147. TO ANNA HARTE, 10 FEBRUARY 1882

Queen's Hotel, Harrogate,
Yorkshire
Feby 10th 82

My dear Anna,

I telegraphed you a few days ago £55. I should have sent it before but I did not have it to send. I was obliged to make up my accounts to the end of the year and send off a heavy balance to Washington. My silence so long was equally unpremeditated but I hope less unfortunate for I have been hard at work. I have just written and forwarded a story for the *Sun* and I have asked Dana to send you the money; it should bring from $200 to $300, but you must take what he gives. I hoped to have finished it on Xmas, that you should have had a cheque from the *Sun* before 15th Jany.[1]

After finishing my story I began to *write a new play*. I have stuck at it in spite of illness and interruptions, and last night at 11 oclock I wrote the last words of the last act. I know not what it may produce; I have scarcely spoken to any one of it; I have made this time no contract with managers. I have written it in *collaboration* with a friend, whose name I have solemnly promised *not yet to give*, but who is, without being professional, thoroughly competent at play-writing.[2] And what do you think is the subject? Think of it while you are in Morristown—think of it when you pass the Head Quarters. It is based on my little idyl "Thankful Blossom." It is wonderful how well and quickly it adapts itself to stage effect, and its dialogue keeps it *understandable* by all audiences, while all the old cant about my *coarseness* and *slang* certainly cannot be used against. The idea first came to me from seeing "Jeff Briggs Love story" made into a pretty little parlor piece for private theatricals where *every word of the dialogue was* taken from my own writing and even the descriptions of the book. It was so good that I began to think I would try once more to *adapt* my own stories for the stage.

What it may be in return; whether I shall ever get a manager to take it, and when and where it will be performed—are all things yet profoundly vague. I only know I have finished the work, and written it all since the 1st of Jany. I have not worked at it regularly, except within the last fortnight when I left Glasgow to come *here*, where I have done nothing else. Harrogate is a famous summer resort in Yorkshire,—the highest table land in England—which is not saying much—and has renowned sulphur baths. I took no baths, though I am suffering from rheumatism, I saw no sights—tho' Bolton Abbey and Fountain and Jervaulx Abbey are all near. I only *worked.* I have at least one satisfaction. During the last two years I have done scarcely anything in the way of literary work. I began to fear that I had lost the power. It is with heartfelt gratitude that I find I can at least *seem* to do it. As I said before, I know not what *the play may be.* You must judge for yourself of the little story "Found at Blazing Star" which you will find in the *Sun* about the 1st March.

All this must atone for my not answering your letters, and you must tell Frankie and Wodie why I have seemed to neglect them. Say to Eliza I will try to write her a few lines.

The trunk, I am told, arrived in New York and passed the customs safely.[3] But there may have been some mistake in the directions. I am making enquiries now.

I am hoping to hear you are better of your rheumatism as the winter passes. Kiss the girls for papa, cheer up the boys, always your

Limick.

Provenience: UVa (ALS).

1. "Found at Blazing Star" appeared in the New York *Sun* for 5 Mar. 1882 (p. 2, cols. 1–5) and 12 Mar. 1882 (p. 2, cols. 1–4).

2. Mme Van de Velde.

3. BH wrote AH on 28 December 1881 (UVa) that he had shipped "one trunk of clothing, consisting of suits worn by me—some only slightly—but which, since my illness, no longer fit me. . . . As I have an opportunity of sending them to New York at little expense I thought you might make use of them for the boys."

148. TO DONALD MACLEOD, 13 FEBRUARY 1882

Glasgow,
Feby 13th/82

My dear Doctor Macleod,[1]

Your frank letter of Jany 31th deserves a reply equally frank, but as the matter is between ourselves, you will take it as also answering the letter of your publisher, which exhibits a caution equally Scotch,—but not perhaps as genially worded—as your own.

I perfectly understand and appreciate your position. I trust you will do the same with mine. The patrons of "Good Words"—you must admit—although possessing the highest moral and intellectual qualities, are, alas, a very small portion of the worlds peoples who read English, while on the contrary I think I may say, without complacency, that I address a far larger and necessarily more catholic class. It would be unjust to the position I have won with them to restrict my work to the habits and tastes of a restricted and narrower class. Putting the question therefore on purely commercial grounds, it will not pay. E.g., I have just finished a story for *Belgravia*, which is not written for that magazine alone nor for any peculiar taste of its readers. It is however purchased for translation in Germany and France, and serves for my compatriots in America;[2] the pecuniary result of which is greatly in excess of any sum "Good Words" could afford to pay me for keeping out a single human character or human experience—not necessarily indelicate unusual or improper—but which might shock the over-fastidiousness of your subscribers. I agree with you that it might be easy to soften or even eliminate certain expressions which are original and give a local flavor to a character if they offend your readers, but it will not pay me to give up the character itself.[3]

I have tried to keep this discussion on the basis of a business transaction, but I am tempted to tell you that "The Luck of Roaring

Camp" was seriously objected to by the proprietor of the magazine of which I was editor and contributor, upon grounds I fear almost *identical* with those so frankly expressed in your letter.[4]

You see I have not "cussed."[5] At the worst, I have only expressed my opinion, when in any other case I should have simply declined contributing. Let me trust that we leave the subject here as kindly, and with as good understanding of and respect for each others beliefs, as when we approached it.[6]

I have referred Mr Isbister to you.[7]

Very truly, dear Doctor,
Yours
Bret Harte

Donald Macleod D D

Provenience: National Library of Scotland (ALS).

1. The Very Reverend Donald Macleod (d. 1916) was chaplain in ordinary to the king in Scotland and editor of *Good Words* from 1872 to 1905. See also Macleod's "Reminiscences of the late Mr. Bret Harte," *Good Words* 43 (July 1902):532–33.

2. In addition to its publication in the New York *Sun* (note 1 to letter 147), "Found at Blazing Star" appeared in *Belgravia* 47 (Mar.–Apr. 1882):46–60, 172–84; in German translation under title "Der Ring" in the Vienna *Neue Freie Presse*, morning edition, 1–4 Mar. 1882; in French translation by M. S. Van de Velde under title "La Trouvaille de Blazing-Star" in Paris *Figaro*, 13–18 Mar. 1882.

3. Macleod objected to the thinly veiled erotics of BH's "Flip: A California Romance." With her "shapely limb" and "lithe, nymph-like figure," the title character of "Flip" epitomizes BH's treatment of sexual themes. See Jeffrey F. Thomas, "Bret Harte and the Power of Sex," *Western American Literature* 8 (Fall 1973):95–96; and Gary Scharnhorst, *Bret Harte* (New York: Twayne, 1992), 78–79. Not surprisingly, BH and Macleod ended negotiations over the manuscript. The story appeared in the New York *Sun* for 2, 9, 16 July 1882 and locally in the *Glasgow Herald*. BH was not always so punctilious, however; see letter 251 and accompanying note 3.

4. See note 5 to letter 12.

5. As in "The Luck of Roaring Camp," BH invoked in "Flip" the deracinated epithet "d——d."

6. BH subsequently published his valedictory essay "Longfellow" in *Good Words* 23 (June 1882):385–87.

7. Probably the educational writer Alexander K. Isbister (1822–83).

149. TO ANNA HARTE, 25 FEBRUARY 1882

London,
Feby 25th 1882

My dear Anna,

I wrote you from Harrogate about ten days ago. Since then I have been here revising my play and waiting overtures from managers. As *one*, only, has read it yet I am still uncertain of its merits, its availabililty or its prospects of success. I am keeping it quite a secret yet as, if I should find that the London managers are in doubt about it I should quietly send it to America. I am unfortunate in the fact that McCullough, Booth, Barrett and Boucicault are not in Europe *now* and I have no one to consult with. The *one* manager I speak of is a Mr Gunn,[1] partner of my former agent D'Oyly Carte,—in the Savoy Theatre here. Carte, you remember, brought out the "Pinafore," "Pirates of Penzance," and "Patience." Gunn thinks that the play will be more assured of success in America than here.

I am prepared for any disappointment and should be willing even now to forego my work rather than have a public failure as far as *that* play is concerned. But I want you to try and think that I should not by any means be dependent on that particular result. The fact is, I have overcome all my difficulties regarding "construction"; Mr. Gunn says, what I see plainly myself, that the action and movement and technical arrangement are practically good—and that any failure must come from a want of interest in the *subject* here. Any ill luck I might have with *this* play will be quite recompensed by my knowledge that I have greatly improved in "dramatic construction.["] I know now how to begin and how to end a play. *That* will satisfy me if my present venture fails. I shall try again. And select a better subject.

So much for discounting already a possible loss. For the rest I am, thank Heaven! still keeping up my old desire for work wh. I once feared I had lost. I can even forget my rheumatism and dyspepsia—which still "go" for me at times—in work. I am hoping that I may make at least enough out of the play to justify me in beginning and giving myself up entirely to my American-English novel, which I am feverish to be at.

I have at times a certain flutter of anxiety over the new nominations for Consulships. Of course I have no right to think myself secure in even my present berth, let alone any hope of promotion—and I may be at any moment removed to make a place for some body. I do not think that Mr. Arthur[2] would do it willingly, but I have no one to intercede for me nor have I even asked any one to use any influence to have me retained. While Hay was Assistant Secy, of course I had a personal friend. On the other hand the Department have treated me with what I am sometimes vain enough to think, *peculiar consideration*. I have never asked for anything nor made a suggestion regarding my official business or the service generally that has not been attended to. I have been repeatedly thanked by the Department, and only a day or two ago, for the performance of a thoughtful little diplomatic courtesy outside of my usual routine, I was not only thanked by the Department for my thoughtfulness, and all my suggestions accepted, but I was selected by the Secretary to carry the thanks of the President and the Department to the Duke of Argyll.[3] Some particular attention to meteorological reports brought from the chief signal officer of the War Dept a handsome letter.[4] My office is capitally manned. My Vice Consul is a hard headed Scotch lawyer and devoted to my service. In fact I'm *rather* a good Consul. All I believe they can say about me is that I dont go much into society, and that I escape the fogs of Glasgow whenever I can. But even when I am away, all my letters and documents pass under my eye, and I telegraph often twice a day.[5]

I am writing all this as I suppose you want to know what I am doing and what are my prospects. Of the latter you must judge. I keep nothing from you.

I wish, by the way, you would promptly inform me when and how much Mr. Dana sends you, and if you have received anything from Houghton Mifflin & Co. It is necessary I should know this so as to be able to arrange the next draft I send you. Write me fully and frequently, and, above all, select *some permanent address*. Love to Eliza. Kiss the girls and give papa's love to the boys.

Always Limick

P.S. I enclose two photographs; price 1/6 to the public generally; to *myself* nothing. They're not worth *that*, but you might as well have what can be bought for even that sum here.

Provenience: UVa (ALS).

1. Michael Gunn, Carte's partner, was "a young man of decided business acumen," according to Herbert Sullivan and Newman Flower, *Sir Arthur Sullivan: His Life, Letters, and Diaries* (New York: Doran, 1927), 127.

2. Chester A. Arthur (1830–86) became president at Garfield's death in September 1881.

3. See note 2 to letter 146.

4. BH sent detailed meteorological reports for the Glasgow region to Gen. William B. Hazen (1830–87), chief signal officer of the U.S. Army, on 20 January 1882 (NA).

5. See note 2 to letter 145.

150. TO ANNA HARTE, 9 JUNE 1882

London,
June 9th/82

My dear Nan,

I have run down here for a few days to try for the last time to arrange my play for the season. But I find it will require so many alterations[1] that I have quite concluded I had better spend that time and labor *in writing a new one* rather than risk more on the old. If the new one should be a success it will help the other; if it should fail the public will only know of my one defeat. In either case I shall not worry much and I hope you will not. I am only too thankful to be able to still keep the ear of the public in my old way. For in spite of all the envious sneers and wicked prophecies that follow me I find I still hold my old audience and that the publishers are quite ready for me when I have anything ready for them. It is quite wonderful also what a large and growing audience I have all over the continent; anything I write is instantly translated. I should be indeed content if it were not that play writing is so vastly more profitable and that with all my popularity as a *Romancer* I fear I could not more than make a scanty living.

I wonder if you will care for "Flip."[2] It will remind you of "Mliss."[3]

It is odd that after it was finished I was visiting Tarbet, on Loch Lomond, with a friend who was looking for a country house and a shooting box. One of the estates was shown to us by a young Scotch girl—the "daughter of the house"—who might have sat for a portrait of "Flip." Except her dialect she was a mixture of Lily Hitchcock,[4] "Di Vernon,"[5] Bishop Odenheimer's daughter,[6] and "Mliss." My friend who had just read the proofs (and was in fact making the French translation for me) was as astonished as myself.[7] It was a marvellous resemblance for I had never seen the girl before.

I have not heard anything from Gerty Griswold lately, which is very singular. She was always a regular correspondent, writing often two letters to my one. I have no answer to three of my last letters. As I have not been to Paris since her *debut*, last year, I have not seen her since.

Charles Watrous' son (Harry I think) who has been painting in Paris wrote to me the other day asking to meet me in London on his way home. I replied by inviting him to Scotland as I could not leave at that time, but he wrote me since that he could not come, but that his father would be over this summer.

There have been so many changes in the Consular service that I do not know what will be done with me yet. I am trying hard to appear and to really be independent of the office, for this uncertainty is most trying. I fancy that I must have *some friends at court*, or I should have been changed about or removed with as good men as myself. I know that there are hundreds hungry for my place. But I hear nothing: the Department is kind and civil to me, and I remain. Dana offered to say a word for me in the right place.

I am here in the beginning of the London season, the city crowded over its vast proportions, and the weather abominable. The English come to town when we in America leave it for the Country. I go out little, accept few invitations. I refused one for Ascot yesterday. Would you believe it, I have never been to the Derby or Epsom. Of course you would—for you know I dont like it.

The Americans are coming over this summer by thousands. It makes my heart sick to see so much money thrown away by these people—many of whom are merely vulgarians—upon things not so good as can be got at home, and upon a people as effete as these Europeans. Every American who comes to England helps to swell the inordinate conceit of the English, even the journals openly say that Americans can not abide their own country and live only in the hope of coming abroad to really know what gentlemen & ladies are. You cannot conceive, until you have lived in England, the supreme contempt they have for all *foreigners*. They will flatter us occasionally to our faces, but let the slightest thing occur and they show their old hatred for us.

Where are you? I send this to Morristown, believing you have not yet left for the Adirondacks. My love to the kids big and little. Always your

Limick

P.S. I will try to write to Frankie & Wodie next week if I remain in London.

Provenience: UVa (ALS).

1. Boucicault had written BH with a detailed critique of the "Thankful Blossom" script (Pemberton, 261–63).

2. See note 3 to letter 148.

3. See letter 44 and accompanying note 5.

4. Eliza (Lillie) W. Hitchcock (1843–1929) was a popular San Francisco socialite and former Paris correspondent of the San Francisco *Daily Evening Bulletin*.

5. Eliza D. Keith ("Di Vernon") was a prominent San Francisco journalist.

6. William Henry Odenheimer (1817–79), Episcopal bishop of New Jersey from 1859 to 1874.

7. Mme Van de Velde. See note 2 to letter 148.

151. TO ANNA HARTE, 17 JULY 1882

London,
July 17th/82

My dear Anna,

I telegraphed in answer to your question, that Frankie must wait for my letter. There are two or three reasons why a visit as unprepared for and as unexpected as the one proposed would not be as pleasant to him or myself as it might be if made a matter of forethought and calculations. In the first place I have no "home" in this country beyond a hotel in Glasgow, or the home of a friend in London. If I have a vacation it is generally spent at some country house where I have been invited. My London friends, the Van de Veldes, who have been very kind to me, have a large family of nine children, but always keep a room for me. They have proposed to me to spend August with them at the sea side, and when I told Madame V. de V that Frankie might possibly come she of course offered him a room, which I of course declined, as it would be scarcely right to abuse their continuous hospitality. I have not the slightest doubt that he or *you* or *any of my family* that were with me would be promptly invited any where and everywhere I go, and most spontaneously, but it would take some time before people knew it, and most invitations, especially to country houses, are given months in advance. I know he would be a welcome guest at Newstead Abbey, but the Webbs are in Italy where two or three of the family are invalided. If he came to Glasgow at once—the only way I could amuse him would be to take him to the Western Highlands—for I have no acquaintances and there is nothing to do in Glasgow, but that would take me from the literary work I have cut out for this summer—the writing of two plays. This latter is really the strongest objection I see to Frankie's coming to me this summer. I shall be distracted and preoccupied in time and thought and could not do my duty to him here. I am determined to succeed with a play this season and at Boucicault's suggestion I have begun to dramatize the Luck of Roaring Camp. I have read him the first act and he gives me the greatest encouragement. Arthur Sullivan has proposed to me to write the theme and libretto of an opera on some Californian subject, and I have just sent him a sketch of one.[1] You see how my hands will be full this summer and how I require perfect isolation. I have just declined an invitation from the Duchess because I could not work in the fashionable whirl of Bestwood. If I had my own house Frankie and I might manage to get along; indeed if I had my own house and a decent one in England or Scotland we might all—but what's the use of dreaming? First let me get *the Play* written!

I've gone into these details, that you may fully understand how I am situated and how your sudden and rather abrupt suggestion has put me into the ungracious position of declining a visit from

Frankie. I dont think I am wanting in love for my children and do not believe you will think it inconsistent with that affection if I hesitate about the expediency of their suddenly taking a trip of three thousand miles to find their father unprepared for them. I should be glad to have Frankie with me. I wrote to him to-day in reference to his desire to go on the stage, and what you call "his disappointment" over McCulloughs broken promise.[2]

You have not yet acknowledged the receipt of my draft on Dana for $250 sent about June 23. I enclose you another for the same amt. payable August 1st making in all $500, which will be due to me from him by the 1st August. I hope you are better. Try to go somewhere this summer where you can have complete change and rest, and do not mind a little extra expense.

I wrote to Frankie that I hope to arrange for his visit later on. Love to all.

Limick

Provenience: UVa (ALS).

1. Sir Arthur Sullivan (1842–1900), English composer and collaborator with W. S. Gilbert in popular light operas. Sullivan declined the scenario in a letter to BH dated 2 February 1884 (Pemberton, 278–79).

2. In his autobiographical dictation Mark Twain offers a skewed version of FH's "disappointment" ostensibly told him by McCullough. In this account, FH at seventeen applied for a job with McCullough's company, presented a letter of introduction from BH, and was hired on the spot. In fact, according to Clemens, McCullough *ignored* BH's letter, written to warn him that FH was "stage-struck, but he isn't of any account, and will never amount to anything." Instead, "McCullough stood by the boy and pushed his fortunes on the stage and was the best father the lad ever had" (*MT in Eruption*, 288–89). However, this account is demonstrably untrue, if only because FH never acted in McCullough's company. In fact, as BH wrote FH on 15 December 1882 (*Letters*, 220), he had asked McCullough to "be frank with you; not to discourage you solely . . . but to show you what you can do in the way of a beginning." McCullough had told FH his father had asked him to "be rude to you if necessary to keep you off the stage," an allegation BH specifically denied: "It is scarcely worth while repeating that I never *could* or *did* say anything of the kind or write anything like it to McCullough. I told him only that if it were true that you were

physically not up to the active requirements of the stage, he ought to dissuade you from it."

152. TO JOHN HAY, 3 SEPTEMBER 1882

Sterling House, Bournemouth,
Hauts.
Sept 3rd/82

My dear Hay,

Before I received yours of yesterday I had accepted Osgood's invitation to meet you in London on Thursday. I am sure of you there, but why cant you run down here for a day with your wife, leaving your little Shrimps, on their native beach, at St. Leonards? At the dinner on Thursday I shall have to share you with the rest of those tramps Osgood had invited,[1] and I want one meal of you alone. When I say *you* I mean King too—so bring your Castor with you. You can manage it that we all can travel up to London together to the dinner. If you cannot stay over night come for a day. *I* should come up to *you* but I am doing some work which I want to bring up to London with me; its a play which I want to show Boucicault.[2]

Let me add to Madame V. de V's note that we all live here very simply and as members of a large family—in which "German, French, English and American are spoken," and that you and your wife will be most welcome. Present her my regards and respectful compliments and give to the Shrimps the love of your grey-headed, corpulently inclined friend.

B.H.

P.S. I dont ask after your health; I want to see it.

Provenience: Brown University Library (ALS).

1. Osgood hosted a dinner at the Hotel Continental in London on 7 September 1882. In addition to Hay and King, as BH reported to AH on 9 September 1882 (*Letters*, 212), the diners included Howells, Charles Dudley Warner, Thomas Bailey Aldrich, Henry James, the actor Edwin Booth (1833–93), the painter Lawrence Alma-Tadema (1836–1912), and the minister Moncure Conway (1832–1912): "It was a most wonderful coincidence to find all these men together in London—it would have been most

remarkable for New York or Boston." See also Howells's letter to Edmund Gosse dated 9 September 1882 in *Transatlantic Dialogue: Selected American Correspondence of Edmund Gosse*, ed. Paul F. Mattheisen and Michael Millgate (Austin: University of Texas Press, 1965), 98.

2. Howells wrote Clemens that, while they were in London, "Hay and King went to hear Bret Harte read a comedy he has been colaborating with a Belgian lady. He has turned the 'Luck' of Roaring Camp into a girl, and brought her to Paris, with all his Californians where she has adventures" (*MT-H Letters*, I, 416). BH tried to interest Augustin Daly in the script: "The first act—or prologue as it really is—is an almost literal dramatization of my original story, except that the child is a girl instead of a boy. The two remaining acts . . . take place in Paris, where the girl, grown a young lady, has been placed at school by her rough but devoted fathers of Roaring Camp. . . . It is a comedy, naturally—the humorous situations dominate, but the rough element is never low comedy—nor is it ever obtrusive or protracted. All my old characters appear:—Oakhurst, Stumpy, Kentuck and Skaggs" (Daly, 362–63). See also *Letters*, 218. The unpublished playscript, donated by Charles Watrous's heirs, is preserved in the Library of Congress.

153. TO ANNA HARTE, 11 OCTOBER 1882

Consulate of the United States of America,
Glasgow, Oct 11th *1882*

My dear Anna,

I enclose a draft for $250 which I send a few days earlier that you may certainly get it before the 1st Novem. I have heretofore been helped by that little balance in Dana's hands, due from my writings, but that is now exhausted and until I have something more to send him I must draw from my salary here. I only tell you this, Nan, that in case I may not be able to send quite as much next month you will understand it and not think it ungenerous or forgetfulness. You know I am only too happy when I can keep you and the children comfortably. I am trying to write a little Christmas Story (a pot boiler) "between the acts" of my play. I wrote you how disappointed I had been with the "Luck,"—in its construction.[1] I by no means despair however.

My health is better I think. I am stronger for my little change of air, for it is apparent not only to myself but to all who know me that this climate (the climate of *Glasgow*) is most depressing to me. I think I have said the same, however, about any climate to which I have taken my blessed nerves, but even the Glasgow people tell me they can see the difference in me. I cannot get acclimated. I cannot help feeling that I am living by gas light in a damp cellar with an occasional whiff from a drain, from a coal heap, from a mouldy potatoe bin and from dirty wash tubs. That is Glasgow to *me*, and worse that is all it has ever been since I have been here.

You ask me how I live. I thought I told you. The nearest approach I have to a home, is naturally, not where it ought to be—at Glasgow. I suppose I am most at ease with my friends the Van de Veldes in London. A friendship of four years has resulted in my making their comfortable London home my home when I am in London; their country home at Bournemouth my home whenever I can get a leave of absence for a few weeks in summer. I have a room there always known as mine, and always containing something of mine summer or winter. I have surely told you all about this family in previous letters. There are nine children in all and nearly as many servants. It is the most refined, courteous, simple, elegant and unaffected household that can be imagined. The father and mother are each foreigners of rank and title; Madame is the daughter of Count de Launay the Italian Ambassador at Berlin. Sir Arthur Van de Velde is the Chancellor of the Belgian Legation. They have adopted me into their family,—Heaven knows how or why—as simply as if I had known them for years. Perhaps there is a kind of sympathy in the fact that they are intensely *unEnglish*, and Madame as a girl thirty years ago visited America with her father and loved it.

When I first came to Glasgow I had "lodgings"—an institution even drearier than the American boarding house. I had two rooms to myself, where my solitary breakfasts were eaten in a loneliness so intense that I now shudder to think of it. No wonder that at the beginning of my illness I gave up eating breakfasts at all. My dinners were taken at a lonelier club—where I sometimes was the only diner. I could not stand the dull vulgar ostentation of the few people I met who were mostly retired merchants; I only knew one family, and in this country of classes and divisions, they wanted me to take sides and participate in their prejudices so I presently fell back into my first seclusion. I used to go to the theatre nights; or visit one or two men friends; dear old Lieut Tobin,[2] was a godsend to me—and the only American I met. At times some of my London friends were visiting in the vicinity and I had a call from them, or some actor or actress from America came here; Genevieve Ward[3] was here a week or two, Modjeska[4] another week, and Edwin Booth is here now. Black sometimes came here. Such *was* my life here—such it *is* now, with slight changes; I live at a hotel and have forsaken my dreary lodgings. It is some ones "folly"—a building too fine for the locality and is in bankruptcy—kept open by the creditors with a man in charge. Through this extravagance I am enabled to have two rooms handsomely furnished at a moderate sum, and the transient guests are company enough for me. I often wonder how many of the guests are creditors and whether the waiters are not bailiffs in disguise. As the hotel is run by a company of these creditors there is not of course the unpleasant perennial spectacle of a ruined landlord before our eyes. One can be quite heartless over the wreck of a joint stock company. The little entertaining I give in exchange for any hospitality thus becomes quite inexpensive, I can even offer some English or German friend a room for a night out of the dreary waste of unoccupied suites of apartments.

I have an odd idea I've told you all this before. But as you say I have not I repeat myself. My friends of the past few years I keep still; the Webbs of Newstead Abbey, the Duchess of St Albans, Froude, I visit them when I am very lonely. Only one friend I have been obliged to give up—Mr Trübner. His wife got to quarrelling with my other friends, because she and her husband could not "run me" and keep me as their peculiar property in Society. I'm sorry—because I liked the husband.[5] But this is the only social disagreement I have had and even that matters little as I do not go much into society.

I have written so much about myself to please you that I have no time now to scold you about your own carelessness regarding your health. I am always hearing from you that you are better and have been ill. Tell me all your troubles.

Kiss the children for Papa.—

Limick.

Thank Ethel for her dear little letter. I shall write to both the girls next time.
P.P.S. I find I've been tempted and led away by you into a long egotistical account of myself and "the way I live" but it is all your fault. I had many other things to say—but it is too late now.

Provenience: UVa (ALS).

1. BH had written AH on 26 September 1882 (*Letters*, 213) that "I've just finished two months work on the 'Luck,' and am somewhat disappointed to find from Boucicault, on submitting it to him, that the two last acts are radically wrong in structure—in other words, I must *begin it all over again*. . . . It seems I can write dialogue like an angel, draw character like a heaven born genius, but I cant make *situations* and *plots*."

2. As BH wrote AH on 12 December 1881 (*Letters*, 197), John A. Tobin (1850–1926) was "an officer of the U.S. Navy sent here on special duty by the Navy Dept. some six months ago. . . . We became fast friends and good Americans and he lightened up my exile considerably."

3. The actress Genevieve Ward (1838–1922).

4. The Polish-born stage star Helena Modjeska (1840–1909).

5. BH noted in his diary for 4 November 1881 (Berg): "Discover mischief to originate with Mrs Trübner write to demand explanation. her answer unsatisfactory inform her that our acquaintance is at an end." A subsequent entry for 1 January 1882 clarifies the source of the quarrel: "The V de Vs break off definitely with the Miles, who support the Trübners view of our friendship." Nor did the parties reconcile. BH wrote Clara Schneider on 1 January 1889 (UVa) that he had "not been 'on terms'" with the Trübners "for some time."

154. TO JOHN HAY, 3 DECEMBER 1882

London
15 Upper Hamilton Terrace, N.W.
Decem 3rd/82

My dear Hay—

I had returned to Scotland before your letter arrived;[1] it followed me there, but I waited until I could run down to London before I answered it. I wanted to send you my copy of our Club's

"Recreation"—which I finally hunted up and despatched to you yesterday.[2]

Walter Besant,[3] our Secretary, writes to me to "tell Col Hay that membership means no responsibility or liability whatever—except a distinct duty to dine with us whenever he can. He may also give us a ballad or anything else learned or otherwise." Later, in suggesting to me to select a day for our next dinner, he says "Let us have our next dinner when both Col. Hay and Clarence King (I read his book years ago) will be able to be present."[4]

Let me add to this official utterance the fact that we know nothing whatever about Rabelais, and that except drinking our one toast to the "Memory of the Master," it is considered bad form to speak of him. Nor do we, with the exception of Silenus Houghton, tell naughty stories.[5] In the matter of that I do not know that we do anything; we certainly dont discuss music, art or literature. I dont believe we like each other overmuch, and as we only meet to dine, and only then when we've no better engagement, I really think the only charm of the Club is the utter irresponsibility of its members. But, no matter the weather or the day there is sure to be enough together at the regular dinner to attract a lonely man. We have no dues; we pay for nothing but our dinner and that at a fixed price. We have no committees; only a chairman who presides at the dinner and two Secretaries. How we are evoked, who writes the invitations, does the printing or writes the verses, nobody knows and no one cares. With the solitary exception of the Knickerbocker Club in New York where I always believed that you used to hand the key to the policeman after we had breakfasted, I dont know of any club as fascinatingly unlike a club as the Rabelais.

The sole object of these five pages is to get you and King to run over here for a day and dine with me there as my guests—whether you have or have not yet received your notice of election. I will fix the day subject to your suggestion. Let it be within the next two weeks and I will come down from Scotland especially for it.[6]

Do you go out at all in Paris? Would you and Mrs. Hay care to see Mrs. Harte's niece, Miss Griswold, (who made her *debut* in the Grand Opera last year, if you remember). Although she belongs to my wife's family she is charming, and I can in some way make you acquainted with herself and her mother if you have the time.

Love to Clarence King and best assurances of profound homage to Madame Hay.

Yours always, B.H.

Provenience: Brown University Library (ALS).

1. Hay had written BH from Paris on 22 November 1882 (JBH), "I have been hungering for a membership of the Rabelais Club for years though I have never had the audacity to ask any one to propose me. But if it is an honor I must lay down—like a Lord Mayoralty—after a short term, I could hardly endure it. . . . Is it necessary to have written an epic poem to be a candidate? If so, let me know, and I will at once buy the stationery required."

2. See note 7 to letter 127.

3. The historian and critic Walter Besant (1836–1901).

4. Both Hay and King were subsequently elected to membership in the Rabelais Club.

5. Lord Houghton's collection of erotic books was "unrivalled upon earth," according to Swinburne (James Pope-Hennessy, *Monckton Milnes: The Flight of Youth 1851–1885* [New York: Farrar, Straus, & Cudahy, 1955], 114).

6. Hay replied from the Hotel d'Albe on 5 December 1882 (JBH), "I have just read over your letter for the third time, trying to get up steam enough to say I will come over to dinner. Mrs Hay stands over me, helping all she can—saying Go! But Harte, my dear Harte, I am not fit."

155. TO ANNA HARTE, 4 AUGUST 1883

Consulate of the United States of America,
Glasgow, Aug 4th *1883*

My dear Anna,

I have just written to Frankie (in your care) regarding the Play. He will show you the letter.[1] I have simply disposed of Mr Frohman's offer—the only offer I have.[2] If he accepts my terms—(which I doubt)—well and good; if he doesn't I must wait for another offer as good or better elsewhere. My terms are based upon the advice of good business men here—managers both in England and

America—as well as my own judgement.[3] The Madison Square Theatre, and its reputation and advantages are perfectly well known to me. You may tell Frankie that I forgot to write to him that Bronson Howard, one of the Madison Square Theatre dramatists, who lives in London and is an acquaintance of mine,[4] advises me that Frohman's offer is too low.

As to Boucicault's offer—if it can be called one—so unfortunate is his business reputation here that theatrical men do not scruple to say that his offer is *purposely* vague.[5] I do not agree with them as to his want of good faith in this matter, for I know how facile is this fashion to abuse certain men—but I *do* believe that he is really too doubtful of the success of the piece to make an offer. I think also he is more sensitive of my reputation and his own in such a play, than an ordinary manager would be—who would be quite sure to put enough money in his own pocket out of two weeks performances, to cover any expense. And it is really a question to consider if it would be well for me to risk a literary *failure* solely for the sake of a slight pecuniary success. In any event, as I wrote to Frankie I do not think that he (Frankie) should in any way depend upon the Play—or be equally handicapped by its good or ill fortune.[6]

But for something more important at present—as the Play can wait. My leave of absence for three months *has been granted*, with permission to visit the United States.[7] But—and there is a "but["]! You know that, although I have been keeping from any new debts while I have been abroad, there are old ones unpaid in America—and in some cases *judgements* have been procured. My creditors have not slept nor abated a single jot of their claims; nothing but a certain immunity I hold by being *here* keeps me from being harrassed perpetually by them. The Lelands have been bothering me with an old Sturtevant House note—which *here* cannot be collected as it is *outlawed*.[8] Teats & Throckmorton have a judgement against me for that very tailors bill[9] that Mrs Griswold declares Ned paid for me,[10] and Park & Tilford[11] have been pressing me through Walker my former lawyer. I hope to live to pay these bills—for *they ought to be paid*, (barring some extravagant interest) but it would only plunge me in debt again to attempt to pay them now. What I anticipate is that when it is known that I have returned for a leave of absence, they will all make a dead set at me—*at once*.[12] Even if I am protected by my consular shield which is doubted by some lawyers whom I have consulted—they might try to make a fuss by commencing suit, and I already have had proof of the delight with which the newspapers would comment upon my extravagance. My Vice Consul, who is a clear headed Scotch lawyer advises me to keep *this* country as a vantage ground from which I can settle matters and dictate terms. I should write to Walker—but he is also counsel for Park & Tilford—and it would scarcely be wise to put his slight friendship to such a business test. Even if he effected a compromise he would require *something down*, or a regular sum per month, which would hamper me. All this could be avoided if I could come over quietly and without newspaper heralding, but that I fear would be impossible. It is the penalty of my name that I must pay for as roundly as if it were a disgrace instead of an honor. It has even been suggested to me that, although the Department has granted me a leave my enemies, (and I have I fear, little else among the newspaper men) would make it a text for saying that I was not at my post. I am about as satisfied as if I read it already in print that I should see a paragraph to the effect that I had either *resigned* or been *removed*, and that the Department would be thronged with applicants for my position.

Can you believe that I never once thought of all this until about a week before my leave of absence arrived! But the more I think of it the more reasonable it appears. The legal question only sprang up in my mind in devising a plan to secure from attachment any money that might arise from the Play in America—by making it payable to my *collaborateur* here who is not an American.[13] I have always protected myself with publishers in America by getting the money *in advance*.

Will you think it over very calmly and seriously and tell me what you think. Do not let your judgement be influenced by the idea that it would be the only chance that you and the children would have of seeing me this summer or autumn, for if I did not come for [*sic*] I might still be able *to bring you here* on a visit a little later and go with you on a leave of absence on the Continent. The expense would not be much greater. You might see Walker, or some other lawyer, who was a friend, and find out if I would lose the vantage I have here, by coming to America just now. You might talk to Dana—if you could see him quite naturally, and get at his opinion of the policy of my making the visit. Perhaps I may be unduly sensitive, or perhaps there may be a little less unkindness among my brethren of the Press. Talk with Eliza about it. If you think it may be best for me to come I shall be delighted apart from all other considerations, for it is not pleasant to think, Nan, that one is almost virtually expatriated.

Write me as soon as you can. As far as the "leave of absence" is concerned *I can take it at any time*, within reasonable limits, so that except for the convenience and season of recreation there is no hurry.

I make Eliza's birthday an occasion to send her something—the best I can do. Kiss the little ones for me. I do not hear anything from Wodie—how is he?

Yours
Limick

P.S. Do not let the additional expense of a little tour to the Adirondacks keep you from going there, if your own or the childrens health requires it.

Provenience: Bancroft (MSS 77/166 C).

1. Published in *American Literature* 16 (May 1944):136–37.

2. Charles Frohman (1860–1915), the most prominent American theatrical manager of his generation, offered BH ten dollars per performance after a two-week tryout. Frohman added that the script of "The Luck," cowritten by BH and Mme Van de Velde, "would require a great deal of overhauling and and changing. *The chief novelty, however, would be the retaining of the original title*" and the sanction of the author (to FH, 4 Aug. 1883, UCLA). BH rightly suspected Frohman's offer was merely a ruse to acquire dramatic rights to his story and perhaps to resell them (to AH, 15 Aug, 1883, UVa).

3. BH demanded twenty-five dollars per night and a forfeiture fee of five hundred dollars if the play was "not acted in a twelvemonth" (diary, 4 Aug. 1883, Berg). He settled with Frohman for fifteen dollars per night, ceasing at ten thousand dollars (to AH, 15 Oct. 1883, UVa). Unfortunately, Frohman never staged the play, and BH was eventually paid a "small forfeiture" (*Letters*, 269).

4. The playwright Bronson Howard (1842–1908), author of such popular farces as *The Banker's Daughter* and the Civil War melodrama *Shenandoah*. On BH's friendship with Howard, see also Lorin A. Lathrop, "The Recollections of a Consul," *Saturday Evening Post*, 11 Apr. 1925, 185.

5. Dion Boucicault eventually tendered roughly the same deal as did Frohman, though BH declined it (to AH, 15 Oct. 1883, UVa).

6. Boucicault, in whose company FH was employed, had suggested that BH "make over the play" to his son "for some undefined consideration," whereupon BH wrote his son he "should not like your success as an *actor* to hang upon my success as a *dramatist*" (to FH, 4 Aug. 1883, UCLA).

7. BH wrote the State Department on 20 June 1883 (NA) to request a leave "to visit the United States or the baths of the Continent of Europe." The request was approved on 22 June 1883.

8. BH wrote letters (41 and 42) to Fields and Clemens from the Sturtevant House in December 1872, the only time he is known to have registered there.

9. According to a certificate of satisfaction (LC), the haberdashers Ralph Teats and John Throckmorton sued BH in a New York court for "damages and costs" amounting to $230.35 on 6 July 1874. The judgment was satisfied on 14 September 1886.

10. BH's nephew. BH had written AH on 14 June 1883 (Bancroft, MSS C-H 57) that he had received "a very insane and insulting letter" from Dora Griswold threatening to "*speak out*" unless he reimbursed her for those "*tailors Bills*" her son "*had paid for me*."

11. Joseph Park and John M. Tilford owned a chain of grocery stories in New York.

12. BH reiterated this fear in a letter to AH on 15 April 1884 (Bancroft, MSS 77/166 C): "You may be certain that the smallest most doubtful and forgotten bill in account against me will be actively revived when I return."

13. Mme Van de Velde.

156. TO ANNA HARTE, 17 SEPTEMBER 1883

Consulate of the United States of America,
Glasgow, Septem 17 1883

My dear Anna,

Since sending you a draft on the 15th I have received your two letters of Aug 26 Septem 5th and Dana's letter. I am glad to have the *legal* aspect of that question settled,[1] although judging from the paragraph from the *Tribune* which you send me, without comment,

I do not think the social aspect much changed. If a paragraph that seems to be apparently written in *good will* can contain a wanton fling at you, and an intimation that I do not live at Glasgow and have always been irregular there, what may not be said when the pen is sharpened by envy or malice.[2]

I dont remember if I told you that the Department once wrote to me very kindly that they heard reports regarding my absences from Glasgow and asked me to write a denial, which I did when they expressed their satisfaction.[3] I was told privately, that the reports were spread by people who wanted my place. The paragraph in question plays into their hands.

But I shall not let this stand in my way of my contemplated visit, though the season is now so far gone that I may take my leave a month or two later. Senator Cameron and one or two other Americans are in Scotland[4] and I should not like to be out of the country while they are here; and, more important I may be able to finish a play I have in hand. I should not of course expect to do any writing in America.

In yours of the 26th, you speak, and so does Eliza, of some picture you were to send me of yourself and Frankie. Up to this date nothing has come. I suppose you know that I have no photograph of you or either of the boys. I have written to Frankie, and shall send a few lines to-day to Wodie. I will write more fully of my plans in a few days. Unless Eliza were so situated that you could be with her and have room for us all when I come, without crowding, etc. etc. I think we had better go to a hotel. I would not say anything of it yet to Eliza—but wait for further advices from me. Do you not, yourself, think we would be better at a hotel? Only the thought that by coming to her I might help her in her affairs makes me hesitate. Perhaps you might enquire what it would cost for our family at a good hotel like the New York (as it was when I was there) or some other. The question would have been settled if I had been able to come in the height of summer, for we might have all gone to a watering place where I could have spent the whole of my stay. It will be autumn before I come now.

Nevertheless, I wish you would still consider if it would be pleasant, *looking at all things*, if you all came *here* to me—instead of my going to you for the *visit*. Perhaps you will smile at what I am about to say; it may be the weakest superstition, but I have a strange feeling about returning to America, that runs through all my longings and all my desires to return. I cannot call it a dread; the word is too large to express my meaning; it is not a *presentiment* exactly. Perhaps it is because I have been *singularly lucky while I have been here in Europe*. My affairs have prospered; I have a market for my wares; I am not dependant upon publishers whims or caprices. I have had no extraordinary expenses; I have been kept in my official position without any effort on my part and against outside influence. I have for the first time in my life known what it is to be independent. I dread some step—some unconscious act, that may change the luck.

I dare say it is foolish, so I merely reiterate to you that if you proposed to come to Europe for the visit—there would be more substantial reasons for that preference than my silly fancies. We could spend a month or so in the South of France or Italy if you liked in the autumn when England is unendurable. But if you think the other course advisable—and the visit to America better in all ways—I am quite willing to laugh at my fancies. I suppose *that paragraph* has not made me very hopeful. It is *hard*, is it not, that when I found that the American papers "were going for me" because I was being "lionized" in England and "becoming snobbish" and "unAmerican," and I gave up going into society because I feared that my name being in the papers with other visitors might give a color to these reports, that the only satisfaction I got from it, is the suggestion that I stopped it because I could work and do it, or rather that my friends had to drag me from it!

I shall write a few lines to Wodie—although I have written to him since he wrote me.

Much love to all.

Yrs Limick

Provenience: UVa (ALS).

1. BH was reassured he was unlikely to be sued for unpaid debts if he visited the United States while on leave.

2. In his diary under date of 15 September 1883 (Berg) BH had noted: "Mrs. Harte sends paragraph about the V de V's and self." He no doubt referred to a paragraph in "Broadway Note-book," *New York Tribune*, 26 Aug. 1883, p. 4, col. 6: "Bret Harte resides at St. John's Wood, London,

with the Chancellor of the Belgian Legation, Mr. Vanderveldt, a cultivated man whose wife seriously set herself to work to regulate Mr. Harte, of whose genius she had a high idea. He held the American consulate at Glasgow, but was there irregularly and yet he did not produce any literary work. She discovered that he required surroundings and conditions to stimulate his powers, of which, meantime, a great variety of result-killing society people were getting amusement at dinner parties. Mrs. Harte lives in this country upon her husband's consular salary, not being able to provide the conditions, as aforesaid, to decoy his fancy forth. But though he has slidden out of society since Mrs. Vanderveldt took him in hand, he has been productive again. She has ten children, is herself of a literary inclination and is fine at repartee."

3. On 2 December 1882, BH had written the State Department to deny the persistent rumors that he was delinquent in his duties. He was absent from his post, he insisted, only on holidays, Sundays, and "the very few days I was incapacitated" by illness. If the rumors "carry with them the imputation of any inattention, negligence or delay in my duties or those of my subordinates," BH added, "I thank the Department for giving me this opportunity of utterly denying them. If an invoice has been delayed, a signature withheld, an interview denied or any duty unfulfilled through my absence I have yet to hear of it, and it will be as new to the merchants of Glasgow whose good will I have had the satisfaction of obtaining, as I hope it will prove to be to the Department that has honored me with its trust" (NA).

4. J. Donald Cameron (1833–1918) was a Republican political boss and U.S. senator from Pennsylvania between 1877 and 1897.

157. TO ANNA HARTE, 8 NOVEMBER 1883

Consulate of the United States
of America,
Glasgow, Novem 8 *1883*

My dear Anna,

I have been waiting and hoping to arrange my affairs so that I might make it not only possible, but *best* to visit home this autumn as I proposed to do, but it is still so doubtful that it would be cruel to keep you longer in suspense, and it is better for us both to look upon it now as *postponed* until the spring. I say *postponed* because the same leave of absence will do and need not be applied for again.[1]

My most urgent reason of course was the financial one. Besides the Christmas story I am writing *now*,[2] I have an offer for another this winter to make up another volume for the spring.[3] Although I might, and it is possible *could* raise enough money now for my visit, I know my own unfortunate self too well to believe that I would be as able to work and complete this volume by spring, if I came to you as late as this. The offer is a *good one* and if I took it, I should be able to come home in the spring that much *richer*, and of course much easier in my mind and more able to fully enjoy my visit.

My next reason is that Frohman of the Madison Square Theatre is to bring out my play in the spring, and as it is to be altered and revised I should like to be there at the time and possibly oversee one or two rehearsals.

Another reason is that the State Department have in consideration a proposal to elevate my Consulate at Glasgow another step in rank, with an advance of $1000 on the salary. This has not been suggested by me, and may be only to prepare a more profitable berth for some one to succeed me, but as it has to go before Congress this winter, in either event it would not look well for me to be present.

I do not think you can be more disappointed than myself and I have tried to look at the whole matter calmly—but I still want you to write freely to me about [it] and point out any fallacy you may see in my reasoning. Your suggestion in your last letter to sacrifice yourself by letting the money I gave Eliza go as an advance on what I send you is kind and good, Nan,—but you know as well as I that it would not solve the problem. I should eventually and perhaps the more certainly if I were in America, have to assist Eliza in her present trouble.[4] It would be doubly difficult to refuse then, or even to refuse *more* if she asked it—as she probably would do—poor child. That is why I wished you not be mixed up in it. It goes to my heart to disappoint you all—to disappoint the poor children. I almost wish I had not asked for the "leave of absence" or told you of my intention. God bless you all. I'm too full of this to write much on any other subject, and must write you again.

Limick!

Provenience: UVa (ALS).

1. Two days later, BH wrote AH (Bancroft, MSS 77/166 C) that he "was almost tempted to tear up my last letter and write another, saying I would come in spite of everything. . . . I suppose I am 'a strange man'— but you must try to think Nan that I am trying to be a more practical one than I have ever been." At any rate, he waited until 26 November 1883 (NA) to request permission from the State Department to defer his leave until spring 1884 "owing to the lateness of the season and the postponement of my private business in the United States." His request was approved by the consul general.

2. "Left Out on Lone Star Mountain," in the New York *Sun* (23 Dec. 1883, p. 2, cols. 1–7) and in *Longman's* 3 (Jan. 1884):259–82.

3. See note 5 to letter 158.

4. BH had sent Eliza Knaufft two hundred dollars in late September 1883 "on account of her usual troubles and chiefly to enable her to get a house in New York" (*Letters*, 238).

158. TO ANNA HARTE, 5 FEBRUARY 1884

Glasgow,
Feby 5/84

My dear Anna,

I have yours (not dated) enclosing the newspaper slips about "Gabriel Conroy." But I had already (on the 21st Jany) a note of warning from Joaquin Miller, who wrote that McKee Rankin was using my *name* as well as my material,[1] and I at once telegraphed to Watrous that Gabriel Conroy was *dramatic* copyright of mine, and to notify Rankin of the fact. Today I have a note from Watrous, to the effect that a Mr Andrews, the adapter, says that the American Publishing Co of Hartford *sold* him the dramatic copyright, alleging that they had advanced me $1,000 on account of it![2]

I send you a copy of the letter I have written Watrous.[3] I do not honestly *believe* that I ever parted with my dramatic copyright to the Pub. Co. in any way—or particularly in the way indicated. But unfortunately my memory of that particular advance is somewhat confused. Although I do not doubt that it is as I have related it, I cannot *swear* to it, and I beg you to recall, if you can, all the circumstances of the transaction. It must have been while we were at Lenox—after Cohassett, and you will probably remember the worry and anxiety I had at that time for money and my journeys from Lenox to N.Y. and Hartford to get the advance. I cannot just now remember the name of the President of the Co—the man with whom I always dealt but I remember that Mark Twain used his influence as director in my favor,[4] but I am quite oblivious of there being any other security than the sales of the book itself. If I had been tempted to give my dramatic copyright as security I certainly should have *told you at the time*. And as the actors always wanted *me* to dramatize the novel—and no other person—I dont see what value the copyright would be to the Company—if I didn't covenant to dramatize the novel for them at the same time.

I think that Mr Walker, my legal friend, has the contract with the Am Pub Co in his safe. I know I once consulted him upon the advisability of forcing the Company to give me a Statement of a/c. If you remember anything of the transaction you might communicate to Mr Watrous.

But in any event neither Mr. Andrews nor McKee Rankin have any right to use my name as countenancing this dramatization of the novel.

I had Frankies letter and the notice from the Georgia paper. I was, I need hardly say, delighted with his making himself equal to an emergency—which I hold the greatest element of success in everything. I was rather proud of my boy, and read the paragraph to my friends here. I liked the letter which accompanied it—which was *modest* and *strong*, and as promising as the paragraph. But more of this and his future another time.

I have begun my new story for Longman, which will complete a volume to be published in July.[5] I have not been very strong in health this winter and if I had not been afraid of anticipating my leave of absence in the spring, I should have gone to the South of France or Italy for a few weeks. But I must wait now for the tonic and stimulation of my visit home. (Apropos of stimulation, I am quite a blue ribbon man. I have not touched any alcohol of any kind for a year. I am none the worse for it—nor much better!)

I spent part of the Xmas holidays at Bestwood Lodge with the St Albans. The Duchess Sister goes to America *en route* to the

Bahamas where her husband has been made Governor General.[6] I have half promised to run over with some of you when I come to America. It is only a few hours from Savannah.

I'll write again on the 15th. I sent you on the 15th of last month a draft on Dana for $250. With love to all and a kiss for the little ones

Limick

Provenience: UVa (ALS).

1. The actor Arthur McKee Rankin (1841–1914) had staged a "dramatization of Bret Harte's story of 'Gabriel Conroy'" consisting "of a number of scenes transferred almost bodily from Mr. Harte's story" in New York two weeks earlier (*New York Times*, 22 Jan. 1884, p. 4, col. 6). Rankin was best known for his role in Joaquin Miller's melodrama *The Danites*; however, Miller had sued Rankin in 1881 to enjoin the production of *Forty-Nine*, claiming the play was stolen from him. The case finally went to trial in February 1884. Miller's "note of warning" appears in Pemberton, 267–68.

2. The adapter was Lillian Leland under the nom de plume "W. S. Andrews." The original contract between BH and the American Publishing Co. of Hartford (UCLA) does not address the question of dramatic rights; that is, the publisher was not entitled to sell such rights. Nor does the firm credit the author with any proceeds of the sale of dramatic rights in its detailed accounting with BH dated 21 December 1896 (UCLA).

3. In his 5 February 1884 letter to Watrous (*Letters*, 248–50) BH insisted that "to the best of my recollections at no time" did the firm "ever contract for or pay anything on account of my dramatic copyright. . . . If, however, my memory is at fault, and there was at one time a *bona fide* transfer of the dramatic copyright to the American Publishing Company they must have some document . . . to show for it."

4. See letters 71 and 72 and accompanying notes.

5. According to his diary (Berg), BH started "A Blue Grass Penelope" on 12 February 1884. It was subsequently published in the New York *Sun* (29 June 1884) and *Longman's* 4 (July-Sept. 1884) and collected in *On the Frontier* (Boston: Houghton Mifflin; London: Longman's Green; Leipzig: Tauchnitz), which was released in late June 1884.

6. Grace St. Albans's older sister, the former Edith Bernal Osborne, was married to Sir Henry A. Blake (1840–1918), governor of the Bahamas from 1884 to 1887.

159. TO ANNA HARTE, 15 FEBRUARY 1884

Consulate of the United States of America.
. . . Glasgow, Feby 15th *1884*

My dear Nan,

I wrote you on the 6th, but it was about the business of the wretched plays, which so far at least, have only been a worry and annoyance to me. I often wish I had not touched them. I sometimes think it was only the belief *you* always expressed that I could write a good playing & *paying* play that has kept me at it. I have been calculating that in all I have spent over six months steady writing—(if taken together—) over my part of the *Luck Thankful Blossom* & *Germaine*,[1] including two scenarios or arguments of comic operas—all of which as yet is unpaid time and perhaps unpayable. Meanwhile people like the dramatizers of "Mliss,"[2] "Gabriel Conroy,"[3] "My Pardner"[4] and "49"[5] draw what little money there is in my dramatic work, by the most unscrupulous and unskillful means. I would not feel so indignant if their dramatizations were better than mine. It is possible that the failures of "Sandy Bar" and "Ah Sin" prejudice the American managerial mind against *my* work; here in London there is a deep-rooted suspicion of all American plays—and, sadly to say, with just reason. I do not expect to produce any of my present plays here.

But I am harping on the old string.

You do not tell me how the girls are getting on with their educations—(if such a word can be used to express the scant tuition I suppose they get on our small means). I know *you* will look after their *music*—but how and where are they taught the rest? I am worried about the outlook for Wodie; Watrous gave me a faint hope that he (Wodie) and Harry might together do something in the way of buying and selling pictures on commission—but it was rather a sanguine possibility than a business prospect. Is there any particular line of business that Wodie shows a liking for? I have examined and rejected a dozen plans by which I might have him with me here—but they all result *in the unalterable conviction that this country is no place for a young man to make his way*. The "go" and "dash" of a young American is looked upon with suspicion and what they call "business" here is so encumbered with useless superfluities and prejudices and lumber that even a bright young Englishman has to leave his own country to make his future—or rather to keep him from upsetting the drones and hangers on and leeches who confuse the conservatism of English business—in attempting to make it there. Fathers here pay premiums of from one to ten thousand dollars to get their sons in business places where they are paid the first year $200 salary or less. But all this we will discuss when I come over. Wodie can wait, unless there is something urgent.

But I do not know if Frankie's business will wait.[6] I shall feel less secure about him after he leaves Boucicault—who, even [if] he has not been able to greatly advance Franks future in a pecuniary way, I feel has been of inestimatable service to him. He could not have had a better master to serve his apprenticeship under than Boucicault, and it is a service that he can always look back upon proudly. No boy ever graduated under a more perfect professor! I do not know whether you at your distance appreciate as fully as I do at this, the singular good fortune that has befallen Frankie in his close relations at the outset of his career with this greatest Master of his Art. I know that *I* do—and thank Boucicault from the bottom of my heart.

How do you and Eliza get on in your new quarters? You say nothing about your accommodations. Let me also know, who, of our old friends, you see now. Where are the Schuylers,[7] the Godwins the Barlows—Mrs Sherwood? You never speak of them. I think I told you once that *I just missed* Mrs Robt Sherwood, of San Francisco, in Paris.[8]

Dont forget Wodies and Ethels and Jessamys pictures. And—by the way—where is the Christmas box promised to Papa? With kisses and love

Limick

Provenience: UVa (ALS).

1. BH had drafted a dramatic version of Edmond About's novel *Germaine* in collaboration with Mme Van de Velde. Genevieve Ward would have staged it in Great Britain, BH claimed, "but for the sudden squeamishness of the 'Censor of Plays,' who had been lately hauled over the coals for permitting 'Odette' and who suggested alterations and

difficulties" (*Letters*, 234). He then submitted the script to the impresario Lester Wallack (1819–88), who agreed to pay BH $125 per week and a $1000 forfeiture fee if he failed to stage it before March 1885 (diary, 7 Jan. 1884, Berg). In fact, Wallack did not stage it, and the *Brooklyn Eagle* reported (1 Mar. 1885, p. 2, col. 3) that he had paid BH the forfeiture fee. As BH noted laconically to AH (*Letters*, 273), "It wont hurt to let people *think* so—but I wish I had the money!"

2. In addition to pirated reprintings (see especially note 5 to letter 44) "M'liss" was the basis of several unauthorized dramatic adaptations. See "Drama," San Francisco *Argonaut*, 19 Oct. 1878, 12: "*M'liss* is advertised all over the country" because BH "[forgot] to copyright the story." Leander P. Richardson published a five-act version in New York in 1878, though it probably was never performed. The same year, Kate Mayhew [Widmer] (1853–1944) published a four-act version entitled *The Waif of Smith's Pocket* (San Francisco: Francis and Valentine). Mayhew debuted in the title role in New York in 1878 (*New York Times*, 24 Sept. 1878, p. 5, cols. 5–6; and 7 Jan. 1879, p. 5, col. 5). A third version of "M'liss," written by Clay Greene (1850–1933) and starring Annie Pixley (1858–98), soon opened at the Grand Opera House in New York (*New York Tribune*, 28 Mar. 1880, p. 7, col. 1). The Greene/Pixley version was by far the most popular, and BH eventually sued to enjoin its production in England (see letter 198). For photos of Mayhew and Pixley in the role, see George C. D. Odell's *Annals of the New York Stage* (New York: Columbia University Press, 1938–39), X, opposite 584, and XI, opposite 44.

3. See letter 158 and accompanying notes 1–3.

4. *My Partner*, scripted by Bartley Campbell (1843–88), was commissioned by and starred C. T. Parsloe in the role of Wing Lee, a Chinese type virtually indistinguishable from Hop Sing and Ah Sin. Parsloe made a fortune on the play, which kept the stage for years. See also the *New York Times*, 17 Sept. 1879, p. 5, col. 3; and Jeffrey D. Mason, *Melodrama and the Myth of America* (Bloomington: Indiana University Press, 1993), 138–43.

5. See note 1 to letter 158. See also *New York Times*, 2 Oct. 1881, p. 7, col. 4: "Carrots, the leading female character, is a weak reproduction of Mliss. The comical gentleman with a prevailing taste for whiskey is a cross between the boozy low comedian in 'Kit' and the drunken heroes of Bret Harte."

6. FH had written his father that he was in love with another member of Boucicault's company, an affair Boucicault tried to discourage, according to FH, by giving him only minor parts (to FH, 20 Apr. 1884, Berg).

7. Probably the New York journalist Montgomery Schuyler (1843–1914).

8. *Letters*, 186.

160. TO ROBERT BROWNING, 10 MAY 1884

Consulate of the United States of America.
. . . Glasgow, May 10th *1884*

My dear Mr. Browning,[1]

I have been waiting to thank you for your charming note of last month,[2] until I received from Boston a copy of a characteristic American edition of my latest story. It has just come. Will you kindly accept the little volume without troubling yourself to acknowledge it.[3]

Yours always,
Bret Harte

Provenience: UVa (ALS).

1. BH and Browning had met no later than 1 May 1880 at the Royal Academy dinner. Their paths crossed again on 23 February 1884, when both attended a dinner at the Reform Club (Philip Kelley, *The Browning Collections: A Reconstruction* [Waco, Tex.: Armstrong Browning Library, 1984], 519). The actress Sarah Cowell also remembered seeing them together at the home of the Duchess of St. Albans (Barnett, 120). As early as 1874, BH was accused to imitating Browning (*Springfield Republican*, 23 June 1874, p. 3; col. 3). According to S. H. M. Byers (Overland, n.s., 42 [Oct. 1903], 295), BH thought Browning's "How They Brought the Good News from Ghent to Aix" the "finest poem in the English language"; and according to S. R. Elliott (*Reader* 10 [July 1907]:127), BH "marveled" at Browning and was profoundly "affected by the man-flavor" of his verse.

2. Browning had written BH on 3 April 1884 (JBH) in reply to his request for an inscribed copy of a book of poems, probably *Jocoseria* (1883).

3. Kelley's *The Browning Collections* lists among the books in the poet's library a copy of BH's *In the Carquinez Woods* (Boston: Houghton Mifflin, 1884) inscribed on the flyleaf "To Robert Browning from Bret Harte May 1884."

161. TO ANNA HARTE, 15 MAY 1884

Consulate of the United States of America,
Glasgow. May 15, *1884*

My dear Nan,

You will have made up your mind for another delay in my coming before this reaches you; I began to fear as much myself after I had last written you when I found my work was getting on so slowly on account of my ill health through the spring, and particularly when I found that my *Christmas* story for Longman must be ready by the 15th of June![1] Then I *knew* I could not come in the middle of May—partly because I could not find time to do my work during my furlough, and most particularly because I wanted the money I should get from my work for my expenses. During my absence, you know, my Vice Consul is entitled to *all* my salary and actually gets the greater part of it.

I have been expecting a letter from you as Watrous has assured me from one written at the same time I wrote you last, and as he says you had called upon him and got my letters the day he wrote. His letter is not very encouraging regarding the money claims against me, as it seems they are not "outlawed" as I believed they would be, and I have no reason to suppose that any creditor I might have will not press his claims to the utmost when I come over. I wish I were in a position to compound with them. I believe I could settle for a very small sum comparatively. I suppose you think Nan, I am unnecessarily nervous and anxious, considering that my money affairs are no different from what they were the two or three years before I left, and I managed to bear up under them, but I think the five years relief I have had from the pressing and persistent clamor of debts, and the knowledge that I have not made any new ones, has made it all the harder for me to bear a return to it.

Perhaps I may be able still to devise some way to settle these claims and not make my visit a continual source of anxiety. I hardly think it will be possible for me now to leave before the latter part of June, which will make my coming back coincident with the time of the year when I first left America, as you remember—in July. It enables me to clear up my official accounts for the quarter ending June 30th. I know you are patient, but that these repeated delays are quite disheartening. Nevertheless I really think we are gaining more than we are losing by them, and that perhaps it is all for the best. I shall write again in a few days when I hope to have heard from you. I send you the usual draft for $250. God bless you all. Kiss the little ones for their papa! always

Limick

Provenience: UVa (ALS).

1. "Sarah Walker," *Longman's* 5 (Christmas number):28–41; also in New York *Sun*, 16 Nov. 1884, p. 1, col. 7–p. 2, col. 3.

162. TO ANNA HARTE, 15 JUNE 1884

Consulate of the United States of America, . . .

Glasgow, June 15 *1884*

My dear Nan,

I enclose the draft for $250.

I have not heard from you since the 19th ult, but I suppose you are waiting to hear from me about my coming home—perhaps even waiting my arrival. But my coming to America this summer seems to be now even a more difficult question than before. I can only make amends for your disappointment and my own by telling you that after you read this letter and consider it carefully if you think it better, I will come, or if you believe it better to come over yourself this summer, with the children and *pay me a visit*, I will arrange it.

The difficulty is no longer the one I spoke to Watrous about: *that* he thinks will be trifling.[1] The question now is only the advisability of my going over *before the election*. I have seen much of Col John Hay while he has been here this summer, he is quite *au fait* on the question, has great influence in Washington, and you will remember is the man to whom I entirely owe my promotion from Crefeld to Glasgow. I think he is a true, disinterested friend of mine; he advises me strongly *to wait until after the election* soley in references to the possibility of my bettering my condition, or *retaining it* through another administration. In the meantime he will do all he can to help me with the "power that is to be." His advice seems the more reasonable as *in any event* I should come to America after the election—either on a leave of absence if I still retained my place after the 4th March,[2]—or as a matter of necessity, if I lost my position. If I came in the present uncertainty as to whether I should not be *obliged* to come over again in the spring, I would also lose the credit I got from the Dept during the last campaign by being (with Capt Mason) the only consul who didn't ask for leave to come over and "help the election." This Hay used to quote in my favor; while even if I came over quietly, and did not even go to Washington—the fact would still go against me. The possibility that the Democrats may succeed also makes it advisable *that I should wait*, and not appear there as *affiché* to any candidate, as Dana (who has always promised me his assistance, and Barlow who is my friend)—could both help me better. I have considered the matter with great care and anxiety and after serious consultation with Hay and Clarence King, who is also here. It would be foolish of me to undervalue the importance of my keeping my consular position—I might almost say the *necessity* of it. $3000 a year could not be gained by me by the extra time I would give to my literary work in losing my official position.

Again I have before me a summer of hard literary work. I have concluded my story & Christmas story for Longmans,[3] but no sooner is it done than Mr Frohman, the manager of the Madison Square Theatre, comes over here with the MS of my Play, and the unpleasant information that it must be almost entirely rearranged and rewritten before it can appear. This was the play that I expected would be paying me a royalty this autumn! The work must be done at once—it will take the better part of two months to complete. I have also just concluded the rough draft of another play which I may substitute for the "Luck," but this will take almost as much time to complete.[4] You may wonder why I work so hard at a thing thus far so unprofitable. I do so only because, if I write a good popular play—it would take the place of my consulate, in eking out my income. A good play ought to give me certainly $3000 a year for a year or two.

I have no time to write on any other subject except to say that you may tell Frankie that Barrett,—Lawrence Barrett—has offered to take him into his company—immediately on his return to America, next month, and that I have not yet consulted Irving[5] (except to learn that his company is full). I will try to see him, but I should advise Frankie not to undervalue Barretts offer which will give him all the experience he asks for, and I think the best salary he can expect.

Write me at once, and write freely, dear Nan. And with my love to all of you,

Always
Limick

Provenience: UCLA (ALS).

1. See letter 155 and accompanying note 12 and letter 161 regarding BH's fear that he would increase his legal exposure to creditors should he visit the United States.

2. The date of the next presidential inauguration.

3. "Sarah Walker." See note to letter 161.

4. The script of "A Frontier Penelope," based upon BH's story "A Blue Grass Penelope," also written in collaboration with Mme Van de Velde.

5. Henry Irving would begin his second theatrical tour of the United States in September 1884.

163. TO THE DUCHESS OF ST. ALBANS, 15 AUGUST 1884

Consulate of the United States of America.
Glasgow, August 15, *1884*

The Duchess of St. Albans.
My dear Duchess,

Yours of the 9th came while I was out of town. I hasten to say I am as eager as ever to make the promised visit, and to come as early in September as possible, but I must crave your indulgence a few days longer, before arranging the date, as I am waiting letters from America regarding a projected visit from my two boys this autumn. The friends I spoke of also, to arrive on the 13th August, are already here, so that I shall be quite free as regards my duty to *them*. I only wait now to learn when the boys will come, if they are coming at all, to give you a positive date, when I shall be at your service.

Pray don't scent in this an impending repetition of former feeble failures. I am coming despite my promises.

Is Ireland as mellow as England in this weather? During the intense heat of the last week I was in an old country house that had, in fact, almost passed its maturity, and was exhaling itself in a *pot-pourri* odour of desiccation. The unwonted heat had taken away that treacherous damp which is to me an unpleasant reserve of the English climate, and always suggests the *deliquesence* of decay, but here was a fine mummified spice of Old England that quite interested me. I sat in an old church (tempus Edward III) redolent with the fragrant dust of somebody's ancestors, and sneezed, not unkindly, at one of their early parliaments. The past was in the sluggish, heated air, everywhere; it escaped under the effaced brasses of old tombs in the church, shook out of the tapestry and the walls of the old Manor House, and rose from the dust of oaken floors. Heaven knows how much of Conservatism I have inhaled during the past week.

I am waiting to get an American copy of "On the Frontier" to send you.[1] The English copies are in paper covers.

Always yours
Bret Harte

Provenience: *Letters*, 256–57.

1. The English edition of *On the Frontier* (London: Longman, Green, and Co.) appeared in early August 1884. The American edition (Boston: Houghton Mifflin) appeared in mid-August 1884.

164. TO ANNA HARTE, 15 OCTOBER 1884

Consulate of the United States of America,
Glasgow. Oct 15 1884

My dear Nan,

I enclose a draft for $250 as usual, but as my expenses are somewhat increased by Franks visit,[1] and as I presume yours are equally *lessened* by his absence, I hope you will try to economize a little, so that you can manage to make $200 meet your expenses on the 15th of next mo.

Frank, whom it is difficult to call "Frankie" any more in the face of his looks which are those of a young man of twenty-five, is here with me in Glasgow after having squeezed London dry of sight-seeing and amusement. He is a little stronger and in better health than when he arrived, but his voice has not improved in proportion, and I am taking him to-morrow to an excellent Homeopathic physician—an American—in Glasgow, with a view of getting another opinion in his case.[2] I shall go with him to Edinboro' Melrose Abbey, Abbotsford, Ayr (Burns birthplace,) and one or two other principal places, but I fear we have no time to make an extended tour in Scotland and go to Paris too. His great desire to go to Paris is quite professional, as he wishes to see the acting at the *Theatre Francois*. Indeed he seems to be more imbued with the idea of seeing plays and actors than anything else; he has already been to the principal theaters in London, and he signalizes his entry into Glasgow by going to the theater tonight to see Toole—the great English comedian. I have already written to Toole, whom I know—that I wished to introduce Frank to him, and I shall invite him to luncheon to-morrow. I hope however that Frank will not build up any hopes of an English engagement,—at least for this year—on these chances, but I fear he does. His voice would very badly prejudice him in the minds of English actors and managers.

He has enjoyed himself I think thus far. He has certainly had every opportunity. What he intends to do, or thinks of doing I cannot say. He is very impatient of control, very confident in himself as his first reserve wears off, and he lets every one see it. He does not invite much confidence from me, and I am held back from any suggestions by his general intolerance of any other opinion than his own.[3] Of course I have not yet offered any *decided objection, or adherence* to anything he says, and I cannot say whether he would treat the paternal *authority* any more gently than he treats the paternal *advice*. I gather one fact from his general manner as well as from his admissions to me. He has had a very easy time of it with Boucicault and the comparative success of his first entry into life, without any of its hard knocks and disappointments,—have set him up a little unfairly. He has been a trifle *spoiled* I think! Is it not so? I think too that one need not worry about him as his perfect self-confidence will always give him a certain kind of success. At least he will not suffer as others might—as others have—in early struggles.

I am looking for a letter from you daily. God bless you all.

Limick

Provenience: UVa (ALS).

1. FH visited his father in England and Scotland from 26 September to 13 November 1884.

2. To treat symptoms of dyspepsia and sore throat, FH's American physician had prescribed stimulants, including spirits of ammonia and camphor; BH's London physician urged him to stop using them; and BH's physician in Glasgow prescribed cod-liver oil and belladonna (to AH, 30 Oct. 1884, UVa).

3. BH wrote AH (*Letters*, 263–64) that their son "allowed Madame Van de Velde, whom he evidently admired, to control him with good humored advice more than he did me."

165. TO CLARA SCHNEIDER, 25 MARCH 1885

Consulate of the United States of America,
Glasgow, Mar 25th *1885*

My dear Mrs Schneider,

Just a few lines to prove to you I have not forgotten you and to ask your forgiveness for having so long delayed an answer to your welcome letter of Feby 6th. But I have been quite overwhelmed with literary work for the last six months and what with writing two stories for Longmans Magazine, one for the English Illustrated Magazine—a long one—and having just made an agreement to furnish another long one for the Summer number of the Illustrated London News my hands are full.[1] This and the regular Consular work, for I have taken no "leave of absence[,]" has left me very little time for any recreation. When my son Frank (who has been on the stage with Boucicault) was over here I could not even go on the Continent with him.

Warned by what you say I shall make no plans for Germany, but trust to my *wishes* coming true. I longed when I got your letter to go to the Melkarten Ball, again.[2] That is one of my pleasantest recollections of Düsseldorf.

Of course I am yet in the dark as to my remaining in office in Glasgow. The new administration may remove or promote me. The American office holders paradise is like the Mohammedeans "under the shadow of swords."

Will you accept a little book of photographs of this part of Scotland which will tell you better than I can something of the place I live. Always deduct 50 per cent from the prettiness—still, some of the places are not bad to look at. The atmosphere, thank Heaven! cant be put into the picture, so you can look at Glasgow in the book without crying, coughing or sneezing.

I also send you a copy of a New York Review with a German criticism on myself.[3]

Dont let my silence prevent your writing. With love to your children and no end of kind greetings to my dear friend Schneider, always

Your friend
Bret Harte

P.S. You ask me about Miss Griswold. She is in England, doing very well in her profession. My son Frank has been on the stage with every prospect of being a fine actor—you know he is not yet of age.

B.H.

Provenience: UVa (ALS).

1. On "Sarah Walker," see note to letter 161. On "A Ship of '49" and "An Apostle of the Tules," see note 2 to letter 170. In his diary for 15 March 1885 (Berg), BH wrote "Begin story for Summer number of the Ill. London News (Maruja) to be finished middle of May." It was published in the summer 1885 issue of the *News* and in *Harper's Weekly* between 13 June and 11 July 1885.

2. Writing Clara Schneider on 29 November 1890 (UVa), BH reminisced about "how you and your husband and Callie and I 'did' the Carnival Ball" in Düsseldorf during *Fasching* in 1879.

3. Lewis Rosenthal, "Bret Harte in Germany," *Critic*, 21 Feb 1885, 85–86.

166. TO ANNA HARTE, 15 APRIL 1885

London
April 15 1885

My dear Nan,

Just a hurried line to thank you for yours of the 1st and to enclose a draft on Dana for $250.

I am very glad you saw Dana and Barlow; indeed it is the first I have really known of what they were doing, and the prospects of success.[1]

Thanks for your defence of my absences from Glasgow. But isn't it hard! There are no *complaints*!—there cannot be; there may have been "reports" and jokes—but there is no "inattention"—and nothing to complain of at the Consulate. I am always there when wanted. No Americans come to Glasgow to *complain*. In fact it is this utter desolation and loneliness which often makes me run down to London to see the face of a fellow countryman. There is but one American resident in Glasgow, besides myself, and I am told *he* wants my place! I have never seen him! The merchants here naturally prefer to do their purely clerical business with my Vice Consul—their own countryman—who is one of the best and most efficient lawyers in Glasgow. *They* dont complain. *The Department* dont complain of inattention. Who does?

I have just now run down to London to read proofs and see the artist who is illustrating my new Story for the Summer number of the *Ill. London News*.[2] The drawings are perfectly charming. I have never had anything like them before.

I am still hard at work, grinding out my 600 words a day Sundays and holidays, sick or well.

Apropos of my *absences* again! Regularly every year I have always received an invitation from Berlin to the Court Ball given by the Italian Ambassador, (Madame Van de Veldes father) to the Emperor Wilhelm. I never dared to go on account of the possible criticism there might be of my absence from Great Britain, on the occasion—as it is an affair of public ceremony. Only a few days ago I declined to accompany the Van de Veldes, who have gone on there for the Ball of this year—for the same reason. And now I hear that there are "complaints" made of my absences at London! It is a little too hard! Young Bismarck gave me an invitation to come to his fathers house and stay;[3] it would have been an affair of only two days but—you can imagine what would have been said in America! And yet I have taken no "leave of absence" since I came here.

I wrote you how pleased I was with the Xmas box. Tell Frank I'll answer his last letter soon. God bless you all.

Limick

Provenience: UVa (ALS).

1. *Brooklyn Eagle*, 1 Mar. 1885, p. 2, col. 3: BH "expects to lose the office soon after the change in our Presidential administration."

2. R. Caton Woodville (1856–1926).

3. Herbert Bismarck (1849–1904), member of the Reichstag and undersecretary of state in the Department of Foreign Affairs. BH had met the son of the German chancellor at a dinner in August 1884. He wrote Rudolf Schneider (23 Aug. 1884, UVa) that young Bismarck "reminded me very much of a young American—or even Californian in his manner."

167. TO THE DEPARTMENT OF STATE, 28 APRIL 1885

United States Consulate,
Glasgow, April 28th *1885*

Hon[l]. James D. Porter,[1]

Assistant Secretary of State . . .

Sir

I have the honor to acknowledge the receipt of despatch No 67 under date of April 15th 1885.

I exceedingly regret that the Department is obliged to call my attention to an apparent disregard of its instructions in Circular of July 31st 1882, as, since the receipt of these instructions I have regularly signed the lists and given them to the Chief Clerk, Mr Peter Firgie, with explicit directions that no invoices were to be sent without a descriptive list. This clerk, who was an old employé of my predecessor and retained by me on taking office, I was lately, however, obliged to dismiss on the discovery of evidence of his irregularities, disobedience and negligence.[2] I now find on examination of the books that there has been no omission of descriptive lists in the Invoices to New York, Boston, Philadelphia and other more important posts, but that the omissions must have been the result of positive disobedience in the cases of simple invoices to unimportant posts, or these of two or three only.

I have to repeat my mortification that this apparent disregard of positive instructions has occurred in this Consulate, but I venture to submit to the Department that it was beyond my power or that of my Vice and Deputy Consul to foresee the disobedience and negligence of a long trusted, tried and hitherto unsuspected employe, or to discern it without the assistance of the Department records.[3]

I have the honor to remain
Your obedient Servant
Bret Harte
U. S. Consul

Provenience: NA (ALS).

1. James D. Porter (1828–1912), former governor of Tennessee and assistant secretary of state from 1885 to 1889.

2. BH wrote AH on 14 June 1885 (SFPL) that the "chief clerk whom I retained in my Consulate, after my predecessor had left, and who was a legacy of two previous consuls, behaved so dishonestly lately that I was obliged to dismiss him—(I had evidence enough to have remanded him to jail." Firgie retaliated "by charging me with paying him only a part of the salary allowed by law" and putting the balance "in my own pocket," and the State Department was obliged to investigate the allegation. By all accounts, it was baseless. BH had instructed William Gibson on 11 April 1885 (JBH) to "settle with him for his services up to the day he was actually suspended, deducting the amounts due the Government and the office and to allow him his share of the $250 which we have claimed from the Government for extra service for Reports."

3. This letter was apparently used to build the case for BH's dismissal. It is glossed "Copy to aud[ito]r May 25th 85."

168. TO A. P. WATT, 21 MAY 1885

Consulate of the United States of America.
Glasgow, May 21, *1885*

My dear Mr. Watt,[1]

In sending you back the last proofs of *Maruja* to transmit to the publishers, I want to thank you for the trouble you have taken in connection with this part of your service to me as my agent—not the least of your valuable help to the literary man in his relations with his publishers. It is hardly necessary for me to repeat what I have already told you of my satisfaction with the financial result of your business arrangements with the publishers, both here and in America. Your disposal of *Maruja* to the two largest illustrated weeklies in Great Britain and America was managed with great tact, delicacy, and patience, and I can believe that you have pleased the publishers as much as the author.[2]

No recommendation from me to my brother authors can be as potent as a recapitulation of these facts, and I doubt if you require anything more. Until authors know a little more about business, and are less likely to feel that it interferes with that perfect freedom essential to literary composition, it seems better that they should employ a *business man* to represent them with those other *business men*, the publishers. And I hope I won't shock your modesty by adding that I don't think they can find a better man for that purpose than *yourself.* For *myself* I am quite convinced that *the commission I pay you has been fully returned by the appreciation of the market value of my work through your efforts,* to say nothing of the saving of time and trouble to me during the progress of that work.

I am, dear Mr. Watt,

Very truly yours,
Bret Harte.

Provenience: *Letters Addressed to A. P. Watt* (London: A. P. Watt, 1894), 33–34.

1. Alexander P. Watt (d. 1914) was a pioneering literary agent who represented, among others, Hardy and Rudyard Kipling. Nearly seven years later (*Letters*, 365) BH found "nothing that I would alter of the full praise" he expressed in this letter.

2. See note 1 to letter 165.

169. TO CLARA SCHNEIDER, 25 MAY 1885

Consulate of the United States of America,
Glasgow, May 25th *1885*

My dear Mrs Schneider,

I know you will forgive my two months delay in answering your kind letter, but every moment of that time was taken up in work—which when published I'll send you not as *compensation*, but as corroborative evidence! Since the 30th March, I have written 42,000 words of composition—which is much for *me*, who am slow and not over-prolific.[1]

In the midst of it, I had to give up a chance I had of going to Germany, which would have brought me eventually—and at about this time! to see you in Crefeld! The wife of my host—an old diplomatic friend—in London is the daughter of the Count de Launay, the Italian Ambassador at Berlin, and the Countess had sent me a special invitation to come to their Ball, which the Emperor and the Crown Prince always attend, and stay at the Embassy for a week or ten days. I hoped to see Herbert Bismarck too,[2] and then—to work my way back *via* Düsseldorf and Crefeld where I hoped to stay a week longer! Alas! the work could not be left behind, and I knew that I could not and *should* not work *en route* and I had to give it up. It was awfully mean—wasn't it? And I expected to take you by surprise!

I am still at Glasgow. I know nothing of the intentions of the present Administration regarding me. My friends in America are doing all they can to keep me here, and all write to me that the Government does not look upon my appointment as a *political* one—like the others. But I shall be surprised at nothing. I neither allow myself to expect or hope or fear. Perhaps they may "eat me last."

I have no picture of my boy Frank, and can give you little idea of him except that he *doesn't* look like me. The people here thought him very refined and graceful and intelligent looking—at least that [is] what they told his flattered papa—who was however only stupified at the grown up size of the little boy he had left behind. Its of no use to say that you dont *feel* old—these children *will* grow up and then—where are you?

I am so glad to hear such good accounts of your own family and that dear little Lulu is so much better. She was always pretty and more than that, spiritual looking, in spite of her figure. I am glad she has got rid of her stomach—I wish I could get rid of mine! Tell your husband that I am afraid I am getting stout, and I am envying his "slim and genteel" figure. Give him my affectionate regards, write me in reply, and believe me

Always your friend
Bret Harte

P.S. Do you think you ever will make a visit to England?

Provenience: UVa (ALS).

1. "Maruja." See note 1 to letter 165.

2. See note 3 to letter 166.

170. TO JOHN HAY, 25 JUNE 1885

Consulate of the United States of America,
Glasgow, June 25 *1885*

My dear Hay,

Your last letter, two months ago, dropped in upon me when I was half-through a story, and in the usual interval of disgust and doubt of my work, and your cheering words about the Frontier volume quite pulled me together for a fresh start.[1] I had just finished the "Ship of '49" and the "Apostle of the Tules"—two stories I thought you would like,[2] and the latter particularly you would understand for its picture of a certain Western religious life which you must have seen. At that time I was writing "Maruja" for the Summer Number of the Ill. London News,[3] and indeed had been in harness since December last. I had one of the best illustrators in London to follow me in "Maruja," but although I had to stand over him with a club some of his ideas of Californian life and character are startling.[4]

Thank you, dear Hay, for all you have done and intended to do for me in Washington. Your word was of inestimable service to me in the Department, as you knew and could speak with confidence of my consular record. I am still in office—that is all I know! Whether at this moment my successor is walking around the streets of Washington with his commission in his pocket I can't say, but like Bryant's friend I try to "live" meanwhile so that when my "summons comes to join the innumerable caravan that moves," my official "drapery" will be decently disposed.[5]

Let me hear from you soon again. If you knew what a comfort your letters are to me out here in this stony labyrinth of smoke and mist and orthodoxy you would write oftener. With best regards to Mrs. Hay,

Always yours,
Bret Harte

Provenience: Brown University Library (ALS).

1. BH had sent Hay an advance copy of *On the Frontier.*

2. "A Ship of '49" appeared in the New York *Sun*, 22 Feb. 1885, 1 Mar. 1885, and 8 Mar. 1885; and in *English Illustrated Magazine* 2 (Mar.-May 1885). "An Apostle of the Tules" was first published in *Longman's* 6 (May 1885):67–88.

3. See note 1 to letter 165.

4. See note 2 to letter 166.

5. BH cites the concluding stanza of Bryant's "Thanatopsis."

171. TO ANNA HARTE, 13 JULY 1885

Consulate of the United States of America,
. . . Glasgow, July 13th *1885*

My dear Nan,

I enclose with this a dft for $450—being $200 more than your usual monthly draft, which I wish you would apply to the expenses of some summer recreation for yourself and the children—either in the Adirondacks or the seaside, whichever may be most pleasant or beneficial to you all. I beg you not to use it for any purpose other than this *change*—which I think will do you all good. I only wish I could go with you—but there seems to be no chance of my coming over until something is definitely settled about my continuing in Glasgow. I may go over to Ireland about the 1st of August to visit the Duchess of St Albans for a week or ten days, but I shall not be able to take any extended recreation or rest at present.

Do you see Harpers with the reprint of "Maruja"?[1] I will send you a copy of the English one. I will ask you in return to send me any notices you may find of it or of "Shore and Sedge" in the reviews or newspapers.[2] I never see *any* American notices. I wonder if they are any kinder to me—those critics—than they were.

Apropos, whenever I read the New York papers or hear from my countrymen socially, I am heartsick and consumed with shame to observe how despicably and shamelessly "English," we [are] becoming in American society. When I think of how much we have that is real and true and refined and *original*, the thought that *we* should ape the customs and manners and follies that the best Englishmen are ashamed and sick of, I am lost in mortification and sorrow. Englishmen have the excuse of a climate, of a certain education and a certain conservative habit which makes them what they are; we have no excuse for slavishly imitating them in everything, as I hear we do. With all the talk of international good feeling etc. etc.—of which so much is due to Mr Lowells Bostonian—New *England*—predilections, if people like Curtis[3] and others could see as I do, the amused and self-satisfied contempt the average Englishman feels for these feeble Americans who are trying to ingratiate themselves by their ludicrous imitation of small things, they would change their belief and stiffen themselves into something like manhood. I really believe that the American reverence for the aristocracy and their habits is greater than it is among those to the manner born, and it is most humiliating to think that at a time when the best of England is seriously skeptical of the old and conservative, or honestly striving towards the new and democratic, American flunkeyism, in borrowed plumes, and ill-fitting cast off clothes, swaggers into the sand before it. Most Americans think it their first duty to impress Englishmen with the fact that they are still as English as they are, and ignore the fact that an hundred and fifty years of isolation and independence has made us a new and distinct people. With much that I honestly like in the English character, I cannot help seeing how great is the difference between us, and apart from any patriotic feeling, how far we have left them behind in all things that tend to make humanity better and broader. I think this would be my belief if I were a foreigner to both nations. I think it *is* the belief of many Germans, Frenchmen, Russians, Spaniards, &c. And yet we are always striving for the good will of only one nation—the English!

Heaven knows how I have come to write all this to you—instead of writing more about myself or you and the children. I suppose the fact that my official position, stays my pen at all times and with all others makes me pour out all this stuff on poor, unoffending, helpless Nan! Put it aside to read some day when *you* are a little discontented with your life *at home*, and when you think *I* am quite contented with my life here.

I hope to get some more work done this autumn, to be able to put a little money "by." I have been trying to negotiate through

Watrous to pay off more of my debts—a "judgment.["] I am fairly well, except that some of my complaints have become chronic with my age (I scarcely dare to think *how old* I am, although my white hair continually obtrudes the fact upon me), and I regularly look for a return of my rheumatism every spring and autumn.[4] The other trouble that once startled me and shocked me, as being so *unlike* me—I mean the *piles*—has, to my great horror, made its appearance two or three times since I wrote you. Yet I believe I am still able to do good work; God grant I may continue so, a little longer, for the sake of you and the children.

Write me as soon as you get this. And give me all the family news. Make Frank and Wodie go with you on your "outing." Tell Eliza I'll write to her before her birthday. God bless you all.

Always
Limick

Provenience: UVa (ALS).

1. See note 1 to letter 165.

2. *By Shore and Sedge* (Boston: Houghton Mifflin; London: Longman, Green; and Leipzig: Tauchnitz, 1885).

3. George William Curtis (1824–92), travel writer and editor of *Harper's Weekly* from 1863 until his death, had been offered a diplomatic appointment to England by Rutherford Hayes.

4. BH was not yet forty-nine years old when he wrote this letter.

172. TO ANNA HARTE, 3 AUGUST 1885

Glasgow,
Aug 3d/85

My dear Nan,

Since I read in the London Times telegraphic news on the 18th of July that a new Consul was appointed to Glasgow[1] I have been daily and hourly expecting a telegram or letter from you. Now that I have official notice from the Department that my successor *is really appointed* it matters little, but it would have been some satisfaction for the last two weeks to have had a line from you of explanation or sympathy. Everybody here was asking me, "but what do *you* hear from America and what do your friends say." I was ashamed to tell them that my friends did not seem to concern themselves much about it in any way, and I said nothing. I was so certain that some cable despatch would come from you or Dana or Watrous, that I was inclined to doubt if the news had been made public in America. Since then I have seen in the *Sun* the full details of my removal (and not couched in the most complimentary or kindly sense)[2] but I have no letter from any one.

It is fortunate that I have been always, to a certain extent, prepared for this change, and never, as I have written you, really believed the easy assurances of my friends that I was sure to retain my position. I was quite unprepared however for the excuse that I was removed for "inattention to duty," and this gratuitous insult galls me. I never should have blamed this present administration for removing me but I do not think it necessary for them to anticipate criticism by reviving a wretched newspaper squib as an excuse for getting my place.

I have made no plans yet—except that I shall remain here long enough, at least, to finish some more literary work. While I am expecting my successor I shall go to visit the Duke of St Albans in Ireland for a week or ten days in fulfilment of an old promise. When I leave Glasgow finally, I shall probably accept the Van de Veldes invitation to their country house "to do my work" there, and make the most I can of the English demand for my work just now. I hope to make enough to cover the loss to my income of the half years salary. This will bring me to the middle of October. After that—we shall see. Frank made a suggestion (that was somewhat of a presentiment) in his last letter, that I should, if I returned, "lecture" again. It is something to consider. In great haste, but with love to all, and anxiously expecting a letter.

Limick

Provenience: Berg (ALS).

1. BH's diary entry for 18 July 1885 (Berg): "See in the *Times* the nomination to Consulate Glasgow. First intimation." See "The United States," London *Times*, 18 July 1885, p. 7, col. 3: "The President has appointed Mr. Francis Underwood, of Massachusetts, American Consul at Glasgow."

2. "Bret Harte Must Go," New York *Sun*, 12 July 1885, p. 2, col. 6: "Bret Harte, as everybody knows, is to lose his Consulate for inattention to duty. He has made a great struggle to keep the place, but he must go." An assistant secretary of state visited the Glasgow consulate looking for BH, only to be told by Gibson that "Mr. Harte is never here. He lives in London and devotes himself to literature."

173. TO ANNA HARTE, 17 AUGUST 1885

Glasgow.
August 17th/85

My dear Nan,

I got your good sympathizing letter in Ireland during my visit to the Duke of St Albans. It relieved me greatly to hear from you for I was much depressed in spirits with a severe cold that continued throughout my stay, and although my friends and entertainers were as good and sweet as they always are, I had somehow lost my capacity for enjoyment. I was glad to find you still hopeful and confident; it gave me courage to go on and try to make up the palpable loss to my income of $3000 a year—by extra work—perhaps by some position in which I could use my *editorial faculty*, which is a capital I have not drawn upon for years and has always seemed to me a pity to allow to remain idle. This is something to be considered. There is also the chance of *lecturing* here; I have not lectured since I first arrived, and I have had many invitations which I have declined hitherto.

As far as I can judge hastily, my chances, for the present at least, are better *here*. I have never stood so well in regard to the *market value* of my works in any other countries as here; with all my patriotism I am forced to confess that I do not stand as high in my own country; indeed not a few Americans are kind enough to intimate to my friends here that I am no longer a popular writer in America, and have done nothing since the days of the "Luck of Roaring Camp! and The Heathen Chinee," etc. etc. etc. and I was told that Mr Sargent of California, while Minister to Germany,[1] intimated to the Countess de Launay in Berlin that he was surprised at my German reputation as I was completely "played out" in America. The attitude of the press in my own country shows me very plainly that there is no personal sympathy whatever for me there, and I think—indeed I *fear*—that if I returned, as if to earn my bread among them once more, the value of my work would be lessened because the publishers would think I was *dependent* upon them. With the solitary exception of the "lecture field," which might be open to me as an American fresh from abroad (as Frank has wisely suggested,) I see nothing for me to do there. But *that will always be open when I return* and can be used as a *dernier resort*, while the demand for my work here must be met while it is good and profitable. Summarizing my reflections thus hastily, it would seem wiser if I did not return at once. If I found it better after experience to stay here permanently, we could next consider the question *of our all living here*. For the next two months at least, I shall quietly continue my literary work. I am afraid however you are wrong as to the time when my successor takes possession. By the statute he can take office *temporarily* until Congress meets, and from the action of the Department and their instructions to me I judge that that is the case. So he may arrive at any moment.

Console yourself, my dear Nan, that with the sole, (and I admit the *important*) question of income, my removal from Glasgow in no way else affects me here. None of my best and most influential friends here *care* if I am Consul or not; many of them did not at first know that I was— Some do not yet know it! I can fairly say, without the least vanity, that my personal position in Europe is not only independent of my Consular position—but immeasurably above it. In fact it has somewhat humorously perplexed some of my official friends in matters of etiquette and procedure, at dinners and social gatherings, where I *personally* "ranked" those officially above me, even of my own countrymen, and yet was a plain U.S. Consul. I know that my removal from a subordinate official position was by no means *desired* by any U.S. Minister, including even Mr Lowell, who was himself a great *personal* favorite, but who unfortunately valued *his* official position more than I did *mine*. Thus free I cannot complain, and if I can only make you believe that I am quite as respectable as plain "BH" as U.S. Consul anywhere I shant be ashamed of having written to you with such apparent egotism.

I am sorry I could not send Eliza anything for her birthday this year. But you will comprehend that just now I must be careful of my smallest expenditure. I send you however the usual monthly draft for $250. Make it go as far as you can, Nan, in case it may not be followed next month by a sum quite as large. Believe however that I am doing my best for you and *ours*. God bless you and the children.

Always
Limick

P.S. In some other letter I will tell you all about Ireland. Enough that one never can understand the Irish people without first seeing them at home, and under their own conditions of life. A more hopeless outlook to a political question I never saw before; nor a more utterly helpless, *unhelpable* and weakly incorrigable *nation*! They are a race of badly brought up *children*—whom we can only hope *will never grow up*! God help them; no one else can; least of all *themselves*!

Yours
Limick

Provenience: UVa (ALS).

1. The former congressman Aaron Sargent (1827–87) was appointed the U.S. minister to Germany in March 1882.

174. TO ANNA HARTE, 3 APRIL 1886

15, Upper Hamilton Terrace, N.W.
April 3d/86

My dear Nan,

I got your letter of the 19th March, and at once set about trying to get the money you asked for Eliza. I succeeded finally in getting an advance of $150 on some work I am doing—the only work I have secured as yet for this year![1]—and sent it to her. I wrote to her at the same time telling her frankly my situation—which I think not only *she*, but you *all* ought to forever consider—that I am getting $3000 a year less than before;—in other words, I am losing the fixed income which I have been sending you for the last three years, and I am living myself and trying to send you the same sum *in the amount I get from my literary work alone*—an amount always precarious and uncertain, and, in America, discounted to one half. I can understand your feeling sorry for Eliza and your wishing me to send her money, but I cannot understand *where* you expect me to get the money—and how! You have never intimated you could get along for less than what I send you—you have never been able to *save* anything from the $3,000 a year you receive; you *know* I have $3000 less a year than I had when I sent you that sum, and that my literary gains are less, and yet you ask me to send Eliza some money as quietly as if I had a capital to draw from, and need only to be assured of the necessity of the case to do it, at once.

I dont want to seem cruel or selfish—I do not think I am either—but when you tell me that Eliza has nothing left to her—nothing between her and starvation but the prospect of going to live with her son, in his house, I must ask you if *I* have even *that* prospect! If I were to be ill or helpless tomorrow, have I a son that could offer me a home—have I even a family that could support me? I think not. I believe they would *try* to do it—but they could not. Yet I am supposed to be the fit person to apply to obviate the painful contingency of another being obliged to accept a security *I* have not, myself.

I have not heard from Wodie nor the five pound note I enclosed in his letter as a little gift to cheer him in his business disappointments.[2] It was not much, but as I wrote him, five pound notes that are not fully bespoken, do not often fall in my way. I dare say, however, he may not have had time to write.

I hope Frank will not lose by the change from Barrett to Boucicault.[3] He writes to me that he hopes I will invite him to come over here this summer. I am afraid from the present prospects of my literary income this year I will have very little left to bring anybody to me or to go to anybody myself. God bless you all.

Yours always
Limick

P.S. This is not a very cheerful letter, but I am not cheerful.

Provenience: UVa (ALS).

1. BH was writing "Struck at Devil's Ford" for the Central News Agency. The story was also serialized in the Sunday editions of the New York *Sun* between 30 May and 13 June 1886.

2. Griswold Harte had been employed as the business manager of *Town Topics*, a New York society magazine, the previous autumn (*Critic*, 5 Sept. 1885, 119). However, as BH noted in his diary on 1 Feb 1886 (Berg), "Wodie lost his situation."

3. FH acted in Barrett's company during the 1885–86 season. Though BH thought his son "*morally* better off with Barrett than Boucicault," he believed Boucicault "far cleverer than Barrett" (*Letters*, 301). When Boucicault offered to "pay him as well if not better than Barrett" (to AH, 15 July 1886, UVa), FH agreed to rejoin his company.

175. TO ANNA HARTE, 26 APRIL 1886

15 Upper Hamilton Terrace N.W.
April 26th '86

My dear Nan,

Wont you thank Jessamy and Ethel for their pretty Easter gifts, and tell them I will write as soon as I have a moments leisure in the country—where I am going in a few days for rest and recovery.[1] I need not say I was touched and grateful for your own little present—accepting it as a kind of propitiatory offering for an inexplicable passage in your last letter that intimated I had done or said something that caused you pain. Let me say now that I am utterly at a loss to understand what it meant, or what I had written in any previous letter to produce such an impression or put you into that attitude towards me. I was so surprised that I at first attributed it to my remarks on Eliza's application to me for money, when I reflected that you could not possibly have received my letter yet. If I remember well, the letter to which you allude, was the one in which I discussed the possibilities and probabilities of our being all together, somewhere, this summer. I certainly did not dream of saying anything that could by any interpretation to cause you pain. I wish you would say *what* it was—for I know you must have misunderstood some word or expression.[2]

I received by the same post that brought yours the first numbers of the *Greene Co Advertiser.*[3] Here again, I was astonished. I knew that Wodie was at Cairo on some one of his business enterprises with a paper about to be started, but until I read his name as "editor," and more remarkable—as part "*proprietor*" I did not know or dream of the *extent* of his venture. The papers are accompanied with no note or explanation from him. I knew nothing whatever of his responsibility or prospects in this enterprise; all I know is that he seems to be *the editor and proprietor* of the first number of a very respectable county newspaper. To reconcile this with what I have heard from you of his subordinate prepossessions, and my recollection that, not very long ago, he was getting—or rather *not* getting—six or seven dollars a week salary in a smaller capacity, and that he had got himself into almost compromising trouble by a certain want of business experience,[4] I confess is very difficult. I would be delighted if I knew more—or less! At present I am simply amazed—and a little uneasy—until I know more. Why does he not write? Who is Mr Lemmon? Who furnishes the capital? What equivalent for capital does Wodie give? Is his salary and proprietorship contingent upon the success of the paper? Has Cairo any other or older established newspaper? Is it a large town? Dont think I am ungracious or skeptical;—I am pleased—and more than pleased at the appearance of the affair *on the surface*; the paper strikes me as being very well conducted; I like the modesty and self-contained reticence of Wodies first editorial introduction. There is nothing that worries me, or detracts from my gratification except the absence of any other information about it than that offered by the paper itself—which is nothing.

I will write to you again from the country, but meantime I hope to hear something more of this venture from Wodie or you. I am driven out of town for a change from my work, and my failing health. I have just finished a story at a certain length for a contract price. But I found I could not finish it to suit me except making it a longer story by three or four thousand words than I had contracted for. I am sorry to say the contracting party did not pay me any more for my conscientiousness![5]

With love to the children always dear Nan, your

Limick

Provenience: UVa (ALS).

1. Jessamy (born in May 1872) was not yet sixteen; Ethel (born early in 1875) was eleven.

2. AH apparently had replied to letter 174.

3. Griswold Harte briefly edited the Greene County *Advertiser*, published in Cairo, New York.

4. See note 2 to letter 174.

5. See note 1 to letter 174.

176. TO ANNA HARTE, 15 MAY 1886

Bournemouth,
May 15 1886

My dear Nan,

I had been so run down by worry and work this winter that I was obliged to come down here in the hope of driving away my persistent headaches and being strengthened by the salt air. I have been here two weeks and am already sleeping and eating better! though my return to work—even writing a long letter—brings back the old symptoms. I expect to be here a week longer, although I would require at a least a month of this channel air to blow out of my wretched carcass the accretion and deposits of last winter's work and confinement. This is unfortunately, an expensive watering place—and, as you wisely suggest, I have an expensive predilection—so I cannot afford to stay here long. The cheaper places are farther from London, and my ideal of a French fishing village, or a quiet Dutch seaport are impossible with my working connection with London.

I have a very sad but very grateful letter from Eliza thanking me for the money I sent her. I am myself very thankful that I was able, by any means, to help her—though I still dont quite understand from her letter *how* I have helped her. She seems to be with Fred and yet in Plainfield, and she says nothing of the home—or of you and the children who occupied it with her. Your letter of the 15th April does not tell me whether you are leaving her, or if so when.

I shall only speak of that letter, Nan, as something you have written hurriedly, under a strong misconstruction of the meaning of my few words of caution to you for your own sake and that of the children. I have never asked for an account of your stewardship; I have only tried to make you understand, ever since I have been away from you, that my income, though better than in America, was not permanent, and thus consequently it could not indicate what we could afford to spend. I think you will remember that I only spoke of it seriously after I had lost the *fixed* income I had from the Consulate. You quite frighten me, however, when you tell me that during the first three years of my absence the income of $150 a month "did not cover the expenses of your living." If I had not been *promoted to a larger salary*, I tremble to think what would be your condition now. I would rather have you generous and uncalculating, than selfish and exact, as you well know, and I do not question your bounty or necessary charities, but I only spoke to warn you of the possibility when there was not enough to divide. And now let this talk pass, Nan; there is no one but yourself to whom I should, could, or *would* trust these matters, and whether you like it or not, you must continue to act for yourself and the children and me equally as steward of what I gain in this world. And you must not be angry nor hurt when I venture to hint that the income is *uncertain*; it is the least I can do, as the one who creates it.

I have nothing from Wodie personally and know nothing more of his ventures. I hope Frank has received the plays I sent him.[1] I have lately made another venture *in collaboration*; this time with a well-known English dramatist, but I dont know yet what success will attend our efforts.[2] It is still a secret and I hope you will not repeat even this much to any one. God bless you all.

Frank

P.S. I enclose dft for $250.00, which I have just procured from London.

Limick

Provenience: SFPL (ALS).

1. FH was apparently trying to interest Barrett in "Thankful Blossom," "Germaine," and/or "A Frontier Penelope," the plays (excepting "The Luck," which was still with Watrous) BH had written in collaboration with Mme Van de Velde. All of these scripts are now lost.

2. BH was collaborating with J. L. Toole, the actor and theatrical manager, on a comedy, "Furnished by Bunter," which was never produced and is also lost.

177. TO ANNA HARTE, 19 SEPTEMBER 1886

Johnson Hall,
Eccleshall, Staffordshire.
Septem 19th/86

My dear Nan,

The draft for $250 has been delayed until I could finish "copy." I have been writing about 1000 words a day since I wrote you last, and have had to give up all idea of having a holiday rest. The whole of the "copy" for my Xmas Story must be done before the 1st Oct.[1]

I have nothing from Toole to whom I sent the play that for the last two months has cost me so much worry and labor.[2] It will be too late for the Season now, if it appears at all, and I suppose I must put it among my failures!

Thank Ethel for her kind little note for my birth day. I had no letter from you, but a birth day note—dated Cairo the 25th August from a Messrs Lynn & Lemmon of the Columbian Hotel, threatening "Griswold Harte" with law suits and even "arrest" if a board-bill of $68.00 was not paid by me. They say *you* promised to pay it, but didnt. I suppose you can explain it—as of course there is no reason why you shouldnt have paid the bill, if it was all right.[3] Of course *I* shall take no notice of it until I hear from you.

As soon as this pressure is over I will write again. I am greatly hurried, and greatly worried just now. With love to all, Nan, always

Limick.

Provenience: UVa (ALS).

1. "A Millionaire of Rough-and-Ready," originally serialized in *Harper's Bazar* between 4 Dec. 1886 and 1 Jan. 1887.

2. "Furnished by Bunter."

3. BH commended AH the next month (18 Oct. 1886, UVa) for demanding an "explanation of Lemmons bill" and awaiting "a reduction of it, but after that has been made I beg you to settle it at once."

178. TO ANNA HARTE, 16 OCTOBER 1886

15 Upper Hamilton Terrace, N.W.
Oct. 16/86

My dear Nan,

I have nothing from you later than the 6th of Septem, and now Jessamys letter which I received only yesterday, was dated the 17th Septem.

I returned to London on the 13th after having been ten weeks in the country. As I wrote to you, all but the few last days of that vacation were spent in work; but I must have been kept up and invigorated by the fresh air and simple life of the country, during that time, since I find London on my return so depressing and so unbearable. I may be obliged to go away again for a few days to the sea side while I am arranging proofs for my new volume.[1]

I have heard nothing more from Toole about my play:[2] it is very evident however that it must go over for this season. It is a great disappointment and I beg you not to be discouraged if you will be called upon to share that disappointment with me—for it will *delay my leaving for America*! I cannot go now until I have done some more work and made some more money. It may not be until Christmas—it may not be until early spring. But it cannot be later—of that I am at least certain.

It is simply a question of *money*, and I scarcely dare to confess to you, how, as I grow older, and my best days are behind me, *that* assumes a paramount importance. I could not and *would not under any circumstances*, again go through what I did in New York the last two years and particularly the last winter I passed there. And from all that I *have* experienced there, from all that I hear now from there, there is not the least chance of my doing any better now. I am paid in America less than half what I get here, and while I am there I should lose *all* that I am able to get here. If I could even have the $3,000 a year which I send you now, *assured* to me, I should not hesitate.

Our old friend Dana of the *Sun* was here in England a few weeks ago, and on the invitation of my host, came down to the country and spent two days with me. But even he offered me no encouragement to return.

My visit therefore to you must be first *earned* here, and I must have a little money, *over and above my actual expenses* while there, in my pocket when I come. I presume that is only a question of time now but I must make the most of my opportunities, while I can. Just now in England there is no one who can fill a certain want as I can—or as the English publishers *think* I can. I dread by my absence at the exact moment they might want me, to have them find out that they *could* do without me. I would like to *fill* the market for a few months, by work ahead, and then take that opportunity to make my visit—and return before they knew I was gone. If I lose the hold I have upon them here, Heaven knows what would support us. America alone would *not*!

I want you to think over these things when you are getting disappointed and discouraged, 'though I know you cannot see them as clearly as I do. I have put early spring as my limit; if I dare not leave then you must come over here, and I must make a home for you as best I can in England or Germany. You must look at *that* contingency with the rest.

I enclose the dft. God bless you all; I will try to write a few lines to Tottie.

Always
Limick

Provenience: UVa (ALS).

1. *The Queen of the Pirate Isle* (Boston: Houghton Mifflin; London: Chatto & Windus) appeared in early December 1886.

2. "Furnished by Bunter."

179. TO ANNA HARTE, 16 NOVEMBER 1886

15. Upper Hamilton Terrace. N.W.
Novem. 16th/86

My dear Nan,

I am afraid I can send only a few lines with the draft today. I have received an order for *another* novel from the *Ill London News*—of nearly double the length of the Christmas story—and I am already hard at work on it. It must be ready by the 1st of January—that is my extreme limit. Of course, I am hoping to finish it much before that time, and naturally *before* Christmas.[1]

I write this knowing that you will not be able to look at this *possibility* of delay beyond Christmas in anything but the light of another disappointment, but I wish, my dear Nan, you could see it as *I* do. Before accepting the offer I looked at it in every light and I came to the conclusion that I ought not, on your account and the childrens, lose the opportunity of securing three or four more months income, merely to gratify myself by making my coming at Christmas a *certainty*. I may still finish the story in time to do it.

I had a foolish idea, which I quickly abandoned, of beginning the story here and taking it with me to finish in America. But I know my own weakness too well, and remembered my old attempts to finish a story when I was on my lecturing tour—and the failure and anxieties I suffered. I had either to give up the story, or do it at once.[2]

I did not expect this offer—following so quickly on the heels of the other—and from the same people. But I have a very good agent here, who looks after my interest, and to whom I pay a percentage, and who relieves me from all the horrible torments of being obliged to offer my MSS personally to publishers, as I used to do in America. It takes away half the pains of authorship.[3] I generally know before I trust pen to paper that my work will be disposed of and the amount it will bring. You can imagine how I dread to lose this great relief—and the terror with which I look upon the prospect of wearily going the rounds of New York publishers with my MS in hand. When I have finished this work I shall have earned two months holiday when I need not think of publishers and work.

Forgive my taking so much space with my business, solely. I am afraid I am thinking of nothing else—but I have some excuse as this affects *you*. Cheer up, Nan, and if you are disappointed again—think it is because I am working hard for you and yours. Tell Wodie I will answer his letter soon. I shall try to write to you next Sunday. God bless you all dear Nan. Always Limick

Provenience: Bancroft (MSS 77/166 C).

1. "The Crusade of the Excelsior," originally serialized in the *Illustrated London News* between 1 January and 7 May 1887 and reprinted in *Harper's Weekly* between 8 January and 14 May 1887.

2. See letter 58.

3. See letter 168.

180. TO ANNA HARTE, 17 APRIL 1887

Newlyn's,
Royal Exeter Hotel, Bournemouth.
April 17th/87

My dear Nan,

I send you the draft to-day from Bournemouth, although I shall not have any news for you until I return to London next week. I am getting a little better, and have been lingering here in the hope of more decided improvement than I have yet experienced. I was very much below par when I came; more than I imagined and as I grow older I fear I recuperate less and less quickly.

Apart from your letters and those of the children, the tidings I get from America are seldom promising hopeful, or calculated to make me anticipate much pleasure from anything there—out of my own family. I am either written to about old obligations or asked to grant favors to strangers, or informed that my literary work is of less value intrinsically and commercially there, every-day. My publishers Houghton Mifflin & Co of Boston have just written to me that they cant afford to pay me even as much as their *already reduced* prices—and have actually offered me less for my new book—"The Crusade of the Excelsior" than for my previous *smaller* volumes, and less than I can get for the *translation* of it in Germany.[1] I am inclined to believe that they are swindling me; I cannot think that my prices have gone off so tremendously in America, and that I am no longer read. Unfortunately, I am in their hands, as I signed a contract with their predecessors, J. R. Osgood & Co—as you remember—to give them all my books, when I left America.[2] I trusted Osgood—but he failed and turned over all his contracts to these men. I can readily believe that I am not as popular as formerly—but I cannot think the change is so great.

I will write as soon as I get back to London and have time to make my calculations for the next month. Until then, dear Nan, with love to all. Always

Frank

Provenience: UVa (ALS).

1. *The Crusade of the Excelsior* (Boston: Houghton Mifflin; London: F. V. White, 1887). The novel was translated into German by W. H. Meyer under the title "Der Kruzzug des 'Excelsior,'" *Romanwelt*, 1 (1894), *passim*.

2. BH's account is not entirely accurate. On 4 June 1878, before leaving for Europe, he transferred to the new firm of Houghton, Osgood his copyright to fourteen books and gave the publishers the right of first refusal to all future books. They in turn paid him fifteen hundred dollars and removed all "pecuniary indebtedness appearing against him on their books" (Ballou, 252). A year later, BH asked Osgood about the contract (diary, 4 May 1888, Berg) and was told he "cannot break it."

181. TO CLARA SCHNEIDER, 8 MAY 1887

15. Upper Hamilton Terrace. N.W.
May 8th/87

My dear Mrs Schneider,

You will see that I am better than my promise, and send you *two* photographs instead of one. The full length was taken in London in early spring and the other in Bournemouth (by the sea) a few weeks ago[1]—while I was recruiting after a hard winter of hard work. The delay was partly owing to my health and partly to the weather; when the sun was shining, I was *not* and *vice versa.*

I thought of sending you a large "photogravure" of the big portrait of me by Pettie, R.A. painted for the Royal Academy a year ago, but I was afraid that you might not be any more able to give house-room to the copy than I have been to the original picture. For to my astonishment the other day Mr. Pettie after exhibiting it in the Royal Academy and at Berlin presented it to me as a gift![2] Imagine *me* with a portrait of myself as large as the "Fritz" Mr Jentges lent to my cousin Callie to copy! I suppose I shall have to send it to America—perhaps present it to some association as I cant afford to keep a picture worth at least six or seven hundred pounds sterling. Im not sure that *I* would fetch half that amount myself.

Shall I send it to Düsseldorf to one of the galleries?

Seriously, if you *would* like this photogravure copy I will send you one.

I have not been to America this year, although I expected to go at Xmas. In fact my literary work in England is more pressing—and more *profitable*—than it would be in America, and I can't afford yet to leave so good a market behind me. Besides, I am enabled through an English residence and publisher to keep my French and German copyrights. I know you will be glad to hear that my German readers are still loyal to me, and they do not appear to be yet tired of translations of all I do.

Is that not enough about *myself*? Now, you will be good, and let me have something about *you*—your family your house,—your plans and whatever has lately interested you. I suppose your husband is too preoccupied to write. Does he never come to England now? Where are you going for the summer? For myself—(again!) I make no *plans*. I live from one piece of work to another. I have always a vague belief that we shall all meet again—but *how* or *where* I dont know.

I suppose Crefeld has changed—at least the picture I have of it in my memory, no longer exists. I wonder if I could find my way from the Bahnhof to Neue Liner Strasse without the inevitable droschky![3] Give my love to your husband and let me know if you get this—

Always yours
Bret Harte

Provenience: UVa (ALS).

1. Photographs 18 and 19, Harte in 1887.

2. Photograph 17, Harte in 1886. BH had sat for the portrait painter John Pettie (1839–93) in early 1886. "I was very thankful to sit to him," BH remembered in March 1893. "But I was greatly astonished, and I think very honestly touched, when the picture, handsomely framed, came to me on the following Christmas, as a free gift" (Pemberton, 311–12). The portrait was hung prominently in the dining room of the Van de Velde home (*Letters*, 362–63).

3. *Droschke*, or taxi.

182. TO ANNA HARTE, 15 SEPTEMBER 1887

Buckenham Hall,
Mundford, Norfolk.
Septem. 15th/87

My dear Nan,

I got your pretty birth day gift soon after I arrived here. The views of the hotel and lake were very charming, and very comforting to me as they gave me some idea of the place where you and the children were enjoying yourselves, but I think I would have preferred those promised photographs of *yourselves*. You know I have **no** picture of you now, since the singular disappearance of the photo you sent me in Scotland, during my absence. I also want to see Jessamy as "grown up"—so as not to be *too much surprised*, when I see her in the flesh again.[1]

It will be rather monotonous for you to hear that *my* vacation was spent in the same uneventful way that it was last year, in

Staffordshire. I came here a month ago to *work*. Since then I have written 29,000 words, or nearly 1000 words a day—to have my Christmas Story for the *Ill London News* finished in season.[2] It will weary you to hear me repeat, as I did last year, that I will never do it again! But I *did* do it—going out a little in the morning before I began my work, and in the afternoon, after it was finished—but making no excursion and giving myself no holiday. My working room overlooked a beautiful park through a open window and over a stone balcony—and this was my only extended view of the country. The house itself, one of the old Norfolk country seats, was nearly as large as your hotel. The Van de Veldes who, with their servants, number eighteen, were quite lost in this great English country house which, you can tell Frank, is much larger than Oakham Park. The length of the library and drawing room conservatory—is 124 feet; it is quite a walk from the central hall, through one of the wings to the stables, whose courtyard would completely enclose Elizas old country house at Morristown. This estate and the *adjoining* one *five miles* away belong to one man—a member of Parliament—whose *income* is over $500,000 a year. Near at hand is Lynnford Park,[3] belonging to an old lady who has £80,000 or $400,000 a year to spend on it. And all these vast properties are simply kept as *sporting* estates—Norfolk is a great sporting country—where partridges and pheasants, fed and preserved like barn yard fowl—are kept for a *two weeks battue* or shooting party of the proprietor and his friends in one month of the whole year. In plain English about 20 square miles in the middle of this densely populated country is turned into one vast green park, where nothing is cultivated but game, where the birds are so nosy and so tame that they have to be driven away from under your carriage wheels in the road, where not a shot is allowed to be fired until a few weeks in the year when the proprietor and his friends engage in, not sport, but wholesale *butchery*. One of the keepers told me that it took a van with four horses to carry the game away after one of these battues. All this wild extravagance and waste for the delectation of a *few*—is a story repeated in most of the English counties.

I am an earnest Republican—and I think a *just* one—but I can understand how a man feels when he is a Communist and a Socialist—and what makes him one![4] I like these people very well—but Heaven help them, when the day of reckoning comes.

I have, in my Christmas story, treaded lightly upon English country life—putting the last chapters here in England, and describing an old English country house. I dont know how it will be liked. Did you read the "Crusader of the Excelsior"? I am rather disappointed in it, myself. I had really only one strong character on which to base a long story—the character of the wild mercurial fillibuster.[5] The wife of Hurlstone was a study from some of my recollections of Ada Isaacs Menken, in the old California days.[6] But I fear they were each not sufficiently treated to make the story interesting.

Since writing you last month, I have seen and known nothing but my work. I know nothing yet of my prospects for the autumn. I enclose the usual draft. God bless you all and dont forget

Your
Limick.

Provenience: UVa (ALS).

1. Jessamy Harte was fifteen when this letter was written; BH would not see his daughter again.

2. BH's "A Phyllis of the Sierras," in the Christmas 1887 issue of the *News*.

3. Lyndford Park is east of the village of Mundford.

4. BH wrote AH on 15 February 1886 (*Letters*, 302), during a period of civil disturbance, that he had "seen the English upper classes shaken in their firm belief in their own superiority and eternal power. I have seen them brought face to face, through their own plate glass windows, with the howling, staring mob they and their fathers have trodden upon and despised for all these years, and they have grown pale, as the plate glass shattered around them."

5. BH modeled the character of Leonidas Bolivar Perkins in "The Crusade" on William Walker (1824–60), an American adventurer and erstwhile president of Sonora and Nicaragua.

6. The actress and poet Adah Isaacs Menken (1835–68) was famous for playing the title role of *Mazeppa* in flesh-colored tights. She performed in San Francisco in 1863.

183. TO JOHN HAY, 27 NOVEMBER 1887

15, Upper Hamilton Terrace, N.W.
Novem 27th/87

My dear Hay,

You certainly understand the perfection of all compliments—opportuneness! Or I can say of you what a Western friend once said to me of another: "Its the d——d *contemporaneousness* of that man's judgement that gets me every time." Your pleasant note reached me at one of those "contemporaneous" moments—when I was grinding away at "copy" and fighting at the same time a very uncomfortable sensation that all the extra pains I was taking was only another proof of a consciousness of failing spontaniety. You see therefore, my dear Hay, how happy was your interruption. I had seen very few criticisms of the "Crusade" and as they all were based upon a foregone conclusion that I couldn't write a story beyond a certain length they weren't very flattering. Your unlooked for praise was a great help to me[1]—none the less of course that the critics might have been right too.

I suppose I ought not to complain of *them*, when the public (through the publishers) seem to want me to go on. I find myself generally "bespoke" for a story or two ahead of the one I am writing,—and the actual £.S.d. value of the work remains unchanged.[2] Perhaps its this which makes me a little sensitive. They have been so *trustful* of me—this good-humoured public—that to deceive them and myself would be as mean as deceiving a woman—and as easy.

I dont suppose that in your bigger work you suffer from this conceit of the poor romancer. I envy your calm reposeful rest on Abraham, Lincoln's, bosom, and your consciousness that you are equal to the result, whatever it may be, as you have shown yourself equal to the work. I am proud that you have done it. What I have read of it has given me the clearest idea—I mean the only *clear* idea—I have been able to get of the genesis of the Anti-Slavery struggle and the political advent of Lincoln in our history.[3] Fortified by you and Nicolay, my dear Hay, I have been able to add gleams of intelligence and occasional data to my usual violent political discussions with Englishmen.

That reminds me that there is nothing going on here in London, except the usual one-idead stupidity of the governing classes, and the feeble revolutions of Trafalgar Square, which like the English thunder-storms, thicken, without clearing the air.[4] The upper classes go on with their pleasures just the same—conscious only of the vices of the lower class. Everybody is shrieking for a stronger government, and calmly adding to its weakness.

Sullivan (J. L.)[5] has not yet taken Lowells or Buffalo Bills place in Society; Phelps is still embracing the Royal Family whenever he can get a chance,[6] and will have touching and tender memories to take back to Vermont, that will make the Green Mountains white with envy. Give my love to Mrs Hay and the children. Madame Van de Velde and her children are off in Switzerland visiting the de Launays. V. de V. and I are quite alone in the Season.

Write me soon again.

Always Yours,
Bret Harte

P.S. I enclose a characteristic notice from the London Times. You observe that they dont even "read my title clear."[7] They call it "The *Cruise*."[8]

Provenience: Brown University Library (ALS).

1. The same day BH replied to Hay's letter, the *Louisville Courier-Journal* (27 Nov. 1887, p. 19, col. 5) carried an article in which Hay listed BH among his favorite writers and *The Crusade of the Excelsior* among his favorite novels.

2. Pound, shilling, pence value. Axel Nissen of Oslo University has estimated BH's income from writing in 1887 at $9,350.

3. *Abraham Lincoln: A History*, by Hay and John G. Nicolay (1832–1901), Lincoln's private secretaries, appeared serially in *Century* beginning in November 1886. In its final form, written between 1875 and 1890, the work ran to ten volumes.

4. BH refers to the Trafalgar Square riot on "Bloody Sunday," 13 November 1887, when a mass meeting of the unemployed was dispersed by soldiers.

5. The pugilist John L. Sullivan (1858–1918).

6. Edward J. Phelps (1822–1900) was Lowell's successor as U.S. minister to the Court of St. James.

7. Isaac Watts, *Hymns and Spiritual Songs*, book 2, hymn 65.

8. London *Times* reviewed *The Crusade of the Excelsior* on 9 November 1887 (p. 4, col. 5): "Its characters are crisp, its situations . . . interesting, and yet—alas! that there should be a yet—the book is unsatisfactory as a whole."

184. TO ANNA HARTE, 20 DECEMBER 1887

15. Upper Hamilton Terrace. N.W.
Decem. 20th 87

My dear Nan,—

I read the account of Franks accident in a Glasgow paper nearly *three* weeks before your letter came with an allusion to it. I had treated it as a gross fabrication,—based upon the fact that I had heard personally nothing about it, and told everyone so. I am still at a loss to understand why you kept silent about it, after it had appeared in the New York papers, as, unless it was telegraphed directly to the Glasgow papers—which is most improbable—it must have been known to you three weeks before I saw it. You may be certain that it appeared here in its most exaggerated form—of Franks *fainting from fright*—of your own carelessness which even kept *you* from discovering your own mistake,—and of the *twelve* hours incessant labor to save Frank from death. I confess therefore I was more alarmed and indignant when I found that *something had* happened unknown to me, than when I believed it an utter falsehood. I had poo-poohed the whole thing, and told my Doctor that it was ridiculous from the fact alone that you were not only excessively careful and chary of drugs, but that you were a homoeopath and never had laudanum in your house. I had thought so little of it that I did not mention it to you in my last letter. Of course I am deeply thankful it was no worse; the only unpleasant suggestion left behind is that Frank is obliged to take such sedatives as "hips," &c&. I am worried about his state of health and his impatience of illness and discomfort which obliges him too often to seek relief in anodynes.[1]

I generally pay little heed to rumours from America concerning myself or family, and I have learned by sad experience not to look for anything kindly or truthful. But I was a little surprised the other day to hear that some Americans had gossiped at the Hotel, and at the U.S. Legation here, to the effect that you were left in such poverty by me that you were obliged to borrow money to keep yourself and children from want.[2] Luckily one of the Englishmen present happened to be connected with the Bank here which draws on the Bank of British N. America through which my monthly drafts to you pass, and he expressed his surprise pretty freely, and thought it strange that £600 a year—which he knew was *more than the income* of even families of officers, and even of younger sons of the nobility here—was not enough to keep mine "from want." I wish you would try to trace the origin of that story in N.Y. It seems hard to exile myself here at hard work in order that my family may live *comfortably*, and be met by such gratuitous falsehoods.

Watrous and his wife have been here two weeks on their way to the Continent. Charley and I have been discussing my affairs, and I think he understands exactly the value and importance of my *practical* position here. We have been discussing also the probability and the *practicality* of my arranging my business so that I can return *with him and his wife* to New York in the early spring—if only a visit. I'll write you again, about it, when my present work is off my hands. I have had a year of very hard labor. I cannot yet say what the next may bring forth.

I enclose the usual draft. I dont want you to live meanly or stingily—but *I wish* you could put by a little something—against the next year. You do not seem to care particularly for society or the city—could you not find some little country place, where you could begin in a small house to make the nucleus of a home for us. There are cheaper places than Plainfield:—are there not? and more independent homes than a boarding house offers. Try and look about you, Nan,—and write to me what you think— God bless you all.

Limick

P.S. I sent you $50 on the 11th which I hope came safely to hand for Christmas.

Provenience: UVa (ALS).

1. In a letter published in the *New York Times* (19 Nov. 1887, p. 5, col. 2) FH corrected the "sensational" press reports of his recent poisoning: "Mr. Harte was given by mistake a teaspoonful—not tablespoonful—of laudanum instead of the medicine prescribed for him, and upon the discovery of the error a physician was promptly summoned, an emetic administered, and 15 minutes after the occurrence Mr. Harte was completely restored to health. The physician remained with him half an hour instead of 12 hours, as was reported, and he emphatically denies having fainted or having evinced the slightest fear, as he was perfectly aware the dose was powerless to cause any serious injury."

2. In fact, AH had written S. L. M. Barlow on 6 July 1887 (Huntington, BW Box 183) to borrow one hundred dollars: "By the death of two brothers and a sister, I have been called upon to share some family expenses, which has fallen heavily upon my income this Spring. . . . I beg you to keep the matter *strictly confidential*."

185. TO ANNA HARTE, 18 JULY 1888

15. Upper Hamilton Terrace. N.W.
July 18th/88

My dear Nan,

Since I wrote you last I have been having great annoyance and greater disappointment with the dramatization of "Gabriel Conroy" which seems to be going the way of all my dramatic ventures. The man who undertook to make all the preliminary arrangements for me—as my other literary work prevented my doing it myself—has bungled so frightfully, that I fear the scheme is not only ruined for the present, but that he has got himself in the hands of some of the literary thieves that hang about the theatres and so spoiled the prospect for the future. He was a young man accustomed to do certain work for actors and managers, had that access to the coterie who surround the stage in London which I have not the time nor disposition to cultivate, and seemed to me trustworthy and competent. In the present state of literary property in novels, I had only the choice of selecting a man who would steal from me and pay me part of the profits, among others who would steal from me and pay me nothing. It would be unfair yet to say that *he* has helped to deceive me—but there is little doubt in my mind that he has been deceived.[1] The annoyance and worry that the affair has cost me is worse than any actual loss I have yet sustained. I have just finished the last proofs of "Cressy" my lastest story,[2] and am trying now—in the few days of leisure left me before I begin again my mere bread-and-butter work—to learn how the matter stands and what hope, if any, remains.

I'll write you again the result. I am anxiously waiting now to hear when you are beginning your summering. God bless you all.

Your Limick

P.S. I enclose the draft for $250.

Provenience: UVa (ALS).

1. According to BH's diary (Berg), one H. Bray wrote him about dramatizing *Gabriel Conroy* on 29 March 1888. Bray contacted, among others, Arthur Wing Pinero about adapting the novel, albeit to no avail.

2. *Cressy* was originally serialized in *Macmillan's* between August and December 1888.

186. TO ANNA HARTE, 20 NOVEMBER 1888

15. Upper Hamilton Terrace. N.W.
20 Novem./88

My dear Nan,

I am a few days late in sending the enclosed draft as the extra amount I sent you at the beginning of the month considerably cramped me. I have been also very much disappointed over the results of my last business arrangements with American publishers. One of them has backed out of a contract, leaving a story (which I had given up my holiday to write) on my hands, while another has not yet paid me for work already done, and published by him.[1] Heaven help me, if I had to depend upon my country alone for my support! The pittance I get from the publishers of my *books* in Boston—to whom I am bound by the old contract with Osgood—is so small that I am ashamed to speak of it to my business agent here. Yet they can afford to pay English writers *there* treble what they pay me *here*, and as England and the continent pay me more than most English writers get *here*, I must be content.

But if it is hard to be *financially* depreciated in ones own country, it is still harder to hear abuse and misrepresentations from ones own countrymen! And I was startled out of my usual patience a few weeks ago to find an article in an American paper, (twice copied) alleging that I was a ruined spendthrift living in England "on money I borrowed from my English friends," and that I would probably stay abroad as long as I could borrow money from them. To make it appear the more plausible the article was written with an air of affected regret and commiseration over the decadence of a once brilliant "over-praised," but now "played out" and "broken down" hack.

I was so angry that I was foolish enough to write to Dana begging him to advise me whether to sue the newspaper proprietors or if he could point out the outrageous falsehoods in his own paper, the *Sun*,—which he could do of his own knowledge—as he has seen me here, living in my almost *too*-methodical business like fashion, and was fully aware of my position in every respect. He has since written to me, and I find a denial of the slanders in his paper of the 8th Novem.[2] Perhaps you have already seen it; perhaps you have seen the poison too, as well as the antidote.

Since I wrote you last I have yours of the 26th Oct, and this morning yours of the 9th. What I meant, in speaking of the effect of the Newport air upon your health previously, was your own statement that I remembered, that it made you *sleepless* and *intensely nervous*—in which the doctor agreed with you I think.[3] I think this was quite a distinct symptom—from your *other troubles*, which I did not mean to refer to and am glad to know were purely *local*. I was very much worried over your illness, and in the belief that you might require to stay at Pittsfield longer than you thought you could afford to, and in order that you should want for nothing I sent all I could get \$150—by cable—(as you requested.) The \$50 I sent the boys, was a previous present for themselves—before I knew of your illness—to mitigate Franks disappointment over the clothes I couldn't send him, and to help Wodie in his summer "outing." *He* has not however, written to me, and except from your letter I should not know that he had received it. I read the newspaper extract of his "correspondence" which you enclosed. He writes well enough for the *papers* (if he doesn't often give his *father* a taste of his quality) and I liked the extract you sent me—because it was simple, and without any "attitude"—or affectation.

I am greatly pleased with Jessamys photograph. Tell her so, and say I will thank her later. Everybody here who has seen Frank says she looks like him. I *do wish* you would send me *yours*. Make a *duty* of going and having it done—if you do not find it a pleasure!

My work is waiting me, and I must halt at the end of this page. I'll manage to write again before the end of the month. God bless you all.

Limick

Provenience: UVa (ALS).

1. BH agreed on 14 August 1888 to write an 8,000-word story for *America* for £120; he finished the manuscript of "Captain Jim's Friend" on

4 October 1888 (diary, Berg), though the story did not appear until January 1889. BH had also sold *Cressy* to the McClure Syndicate in the United States; it appeared in the Sunday editions of such papers as the *San Francisco Chronicle* and the *Louisville Courier-Journal* throughout November and December 1888. McClure sent BH £80 "on account" in late October 1888, the balance to be paid later.

2. Dana replied to the allegations, which had appeared in the St. Louis *Globe-Democrat* and the *Boston Herald*, in an unsigned editorial (New York *Sun*, 8 Nov. 1888, p. 4, col. 3): "Mr. HARTE'S habits both of life and of work in England we happen to know of our own knowledge, and nothing can be more regular, industrious, careful, or successful. . . . His mode of life is perfectly moderate, his labors most methodical, and his income almost as steady as if it were derived from cash investments."

3. See note 2 to letter 31.

187. TO JOHN HAY, 22 NOVEMBER 1888

15, Upper Hamilton Terrace. N.W.
22nd Novem./88

My dear Hay,

I think I was, at first, too unselfishly delighted over the triumph of our party to speculate upon any individual benefit that might come to me from a change in the Administration.[1] But, alas! the mere effort of throwing up my hat reminds me—by certain rheumatic twinges—that I am no longer young, and that, tho' I ought to be grateful at having been able to support my family confortably by my literary work alone, during these past years; I have not got *laid up* enough for the coming time when this pen will be supplanted by younger and better ones, and perhaps "cease from troubling"[2] altogether, I ought not and *do* not complain; like the tradesman I am thankful to the public "for past favors," but unlike the tradesman, the literary man does not "build up a business" that is pecuniary capital, after he is gone, for his family.

Wherefore, my dear Hay, I want to ask your opinion of the chances of my getting a post again over here. I believe my record in the State Department is a good one, although a travelling Assistant Secretary of State, I am told, did not find me at home one day,[3] and I have reason to think that the affairs of my Consulates in Crefeld and in Glasgow were so well administered that the fact of my being absent, could have been only known by actual personal enquiry. At least the Department never complained to me of the *conduct* of the office or the inefficiency in its working, or its results.

Drop me a line, at your leisure to say what *you* would do (if you were not a rich man and independent equally of literature and politics)—and what can be done, and advise me, always dear Hay, in advance,[4]

Yours very gratefully
Bret Harte

Provenience: Brown University Library (ALS).

1. The Republican candidate Benjamin Harrison (1833–1901) had been elected in presidential balloting earlier in the month.

2. Job 3:17: "There the wicked cease from troubling; and there the weary be at rest."

3. See note 2 to letter 172.

4. Hay later wrote Joaquin Miller that BH had been "a first-rate Consul, square, accurate and efficient in all his work" and that he had expected BH "to be reinstated" in a diplomatic post (*San Francisco Examiner*, 7 July 1895, p. 25, col. 2). Hay made some discreet inquiries and was told by James G. Blaine (1830–93), the new secretary of state, that BH "has injured himself in these prosaic days by making himself (so says the Consular Bureau) the worst consul thus far recorded" (Blaine to Hay, 31 Dec. 1889, Brown University Library).

188. TO ANNA HARTE, 15 FEBRUARY 1889

15. Upper Hamilton Terrace. N.W.
Feby. 15 '89

My dear Anna,

If it is painful for you to have to ask me for another extra $100 this month, it is still more painful for me to be forced to confess to you that *I have not got it*, and *cannot get it* to send. I have never before been obliged to say this; I have hitherto always managed to scrape together enough to send you these yearly increasing "extras."

But at last what I have always warned you *might* happen at any moment *has* happened. I simply have not received enough from my work to meet this unlooked-for demand, and I have no means of getting any money except what I earn, day by day, and month by month. If it is possible for me to raise $100 before the next $250 is due—without taking it from *that*—I will send it to you.

I need not say more than this; you know, at least your experience has taught you that if I had the money I would send it without comment if I thought it an *extravagance*. But I cannot help adding that in this case, it seems to *me* an *improvidence*. It is not an emergency of sickness or accident! It is a *school bill* which might—I must say *ought*—to have been paid out of your $3,000 a year. If you find you cannot support yourself and four children—two of whom are young men whom I suppose earn at least their pocket-money and clothes—on $3,000 a year, we may well despair of the future![1] And I am afraid we cannot ask for *sympathy*—much less *assistance* from our friends! There are families of 5 and 6—living here in *expensive* London—who live respectably on £500 year—($2500). I know that some of my literary friends, in New York with families as large as my own, do not receive more. *I* could not expect to get much more were I *there*—yet you write to me and I dare say *think* me wanting in natural affection, because I do not return to perhaps run in debt on $4,000 a year, which would even be an extravagant permanent increase to expect from what I know of my prospects in America!

I should of course be delighted to hear that poor dear Wodie is at last making his way for I grieve for and pity him. But I am *prepared* to hear that his sanguine expectations have come to naught, and I dont *expect* that letter you speak of. For Frank, I am equally hopeless. After four years of stage experience, under exceptional advantages and patronage—advantages that many a striving young actor, of more than Franks ability, would have deemed himself blessed to have—with even the possible advantages of his fathers name and his fathers friends to make his apprenticeship light,—he now finds that he does not "like the stage" for which a few years ago he thought he had a "special talent."[2] If I grow sometimes impatient to find that he is led to believe that this experience of his is supposed to be in some vague way of *value* to him hereafter, I hope you dont think me unreasonable. Knowing that the purely artificial life he has been leading—without the distinction of a fixed purpose or special aptitude for the profession is not calculated to encourage any faith in honest endeavor, prudence, stability, economy, principle, or even the simple self-sustained modesty of a gentleman, I am thankful that he has not been more affected by it. But it has given him very foolish ideas of what makes or constitutes success. He probably knows more of the world than I do at this moment; that it will ever enable him to grapple with it or use it any better,— I doubt.

For myself I am getting too old to look forward to much now, and what I do see, or think I see, is not particularly cheering. Its bad enough to be forced to look for the appreciation of my work from strangers—and not my own countrymen—for my support, and to be obliged to look to another household than my own for the conditions under which I can do that work—but it is still worse to find it [unrelenting?]. If I write seriously to you now, it is for your own sake. I have been working pretty steadily for the last few years—with the exception of *five* days in Yorkshire (where I took my work with me) at the beginning of this month. I have had no change or relaxation. The machine works a little slowly at times. To guard against your utter helplessness when it shall break down for a time or all time, is the only reason why I write you this. God bless you all and keep it grinding on for your sakes is the purpose of

Your Limick.

Provenience: Berg (ALS).

1. At the time this letter was written BH's sons were in their mid-twenties; his daughters were teenagers.

2. FH acted in Edwin Booth's company during the 1887–88 season. As BH wrote AH on 15 July 1887 (*Letters*, 318–19), "there are lots of young fellows here who would have been glad to have graduated as he has, under such men as Boucicault, Barrett, and Booth—and have had them for personal friends! Everybody here thinks him intensely lucky."

189. TO ANNA HARTE, 19 MARCH 1889

15. Upper Hamilton Terrace. N.W.
19th Mar./89

My dear Nan,

I enclose the usual draft for $250.

I have just got your letter of March 8th. At another time I will answer it at length. I can only say now that I am grieved that you should misunderstand the object of my last letter,[1] or believe that I do not perfectly understand that you are no more happy than I am in the position we are placed. That is the reason why I beg you to give me some reason at least to *hope* from something you are doing and the children are doing, or better still the practice of some trifling economy in our expenses, that this position may be changed, and that I can support myself and you and the children as well living together in America, as I am doing, in the lonely and not very happy life *I* am living here. If any of my friends speak to you of my life here that is what they mean—at least, that is what they say to *me*. And I do not know one of them who would raise a hand to help me in America—or who is willing, even now, in the mere matter of assisting me to secure some position under the Government that would increase my income and enable me to return there—to take the least trouble in my behalf. They believe that I am doing better here than there, and would be the first to exclaim against our improvidence. And they know—as well as I do, if not *better*,—that we could not afford to remove and live in London all together as a family, keeping our own house and servants in the most simple manner. It would cost us double; to say nothing of the hopeless outlook for the boys, and the still more hopeless chances for the girls.

I do not complain about my work as long as I am able to do it, but when you say you are sorry that I have no recreation or rest, you should remember that, if through an extra expense, I am unable to take even a few weeks recreation out of London how hopeless becomes the prospect of my making a visit for two or three months to America, to say nothing of the risks I run of losing an order, while I am away.

I have not heard from Wodie, as I suppose the poor boy has again been disappointed. God help him, and help us all.

Your Limick

Provenience: UVa (ALS).

1. Letter 188.

190. TO ANNA HARTE, 17 AUGUST 1889

17th August/89

My dear Nan,

At last I have got away from London for a while, and am here with the V. de V.s at a "hunting box" in Gloucestershire—a very quaint, pretty place that they have taken for the summer. The house is most picturesque looking, with the never-failing charm of ivy wall and green lawns, which look well at *all* times. I will send you some photographs of the place, when I can get them.

I wish that it meant *rest* for me, for I am tired of work, and what is worse—empty of material and vapid as the public will soon find out. I have only just finished one piece of work when I am obliged to set down to another, and I see six weeks of *daily* work before me already. And alas, it means no more than my yearly income—with nothing ahead, and nothing decreased in expenses. Like the old Californian miner who works "for grub," I have always the hope of "striking something"—in a play perhaps—that may lift me out of this drudgery—and always the disappointment.[1] But I fancy I've said all this before—and you must be tired of it. It comes home to me when I get your letters, half-hoping that I may be able to come over to you, and I only see this dreary sentence of a six weeks treadmill before me to be worked out.

I enclose the draft. My difficulty in getting returns from the American Syndicate has resolved itself into their paying me in small monthly instalments—which keeps me always limited in means.

I hope you are enjoying yourself with the children at Little Neck, and getting up some strength for the winter. I only wish the house was your own and I could think of you and the girls at some fixed spot where I could come to. By the end of September I suppose Little Neck will be as deserted as Sea Cliff.

Do you ever see Dana on the boat? I think it is the same boat that touches at his place on the sound. I hope you understood from my last note that you need not put yourself out to see Lady Shrewsbury.[2] It was only a politeness I thought she would appreciate if you left a card for her, and she was always very civil to me here. I dare say she will not lack attention. People of title generally get it among my republican countrymen! And the American abroad—simply worships it!

I can think of nothing else to say, and dread returning to my old querulous indictment of myself, my fate my work, and my exile. I'll try to write a more cheerful letter soon—out of the regular draft-day, which always brings me anxiety—but just now even the sunshine and shadows on the lawn beyond my window, and the cheerful oasis on the terrace only reminds me of "Bonnie Doon"— and the birds that would sing although the poet was "nay more and fre' a' care."[3] God bless you all

Always affectionately
Limick

P.S. I see I have called it "Little Neck" instead of "Great Neck." I hope I havent made that mistake in addressing a previous letter. Shall I send there or to Plainfield?

Provenience: UVa (ALS).

1. BH had written AH on 20 July 1889 (UCLA) that he was working on a play "with a collaborateur who is in the profession" and it "looks more practical than my other ventures of the kind." He was cowriting a dramatic version of "M'liss" with the author and journalist Joseph Hatton (1841–1907).

2. Anna Theresa (Cockerell) Cherwynd-Talbot, nineteenth countess of Shrewsbury (1836–1912), left for New York on 7 August 1889. In a note dated 6 August 1889 (*Letters*, 340) BH had asked AH to call on her "with one of the girls" if "you happen to be in town."

3. BH alludes to Robert Burns's lyric "The Banks o' Doon."

191. TO ANNA HARTE, 17 SEPTEMBER 1889

Trewsbury, Cirencester.

Septem 17/89

My dear Nan,

I have been waiting for a few photographic views to send to you and the girls, but I fear I cannot get them now before Saturday. So I wait no longer to enclose the draft with the letter I wrote you a few days ago to go with the photographs.

"The play" still lingers on the stocks; the man who is collaborating with me is, I fear, too sanguine about its merits and its success, but as I am very anxious that it should not be a *fiasco* again I decline that it should even go before a manager before it satisfies me.[1] The result is that we [are] still working at it—although I hoped to be able to write to you something more definite by this time. It seems to be my only hope of getting some relief to this perpetual grinding out of literary copy which is exhausting me, and no doubt the public. If I could afford to be on my own a few months, I might recoup, and so might they. This summer I was in the two principal illustrated papers, and will appear in another at Christmas.[2] I would rather write a long story—but I must take what I can get.

I hope you are enjoying and have enjoyed Great Neck. I hardly think that Franks going to the Adirondacks was a *sanitary* necessity. I agree with you in being very anxious about him. I think he has not the least conception of what is good for him—or indeed good for anybody—yet he firmly believes that he has both. He lives in a world of the feeblest expediencies and makeshifts, and thinks they are wise. He has no idea of a long aim in anything. He mistakes his indulgences for experience. He profoundly believes that his errors will pull him through. You may ask me why I write this to *you* about him. Simply because it is of no use to write to *him*. And I should hardly say as much as this to you but I see that you are terribly troubled about him—and while, woman-like, you have helped to make him think lightly of these troubles. Frank is like all spoiled men and women—most impatient of those that have spoiled them. I hope and pray as he is still young he may change yet—perhaps from some influence or accident that wont seem to him so unimportant and mistaken as yours or mine. I hope so for *his* sake—even more than yours or mine. A spoiled child of thirty is a monstrosity even the gods must permit, much less womankind. With the graces and possibilities of youth that condones and blinds everything, *gone*—the awakening is more terrible to the victim. He has evidently been greatly influenced by women; I believe that even an unhappy marriage would save him, by turning his mind and attention to something else. I dont mean to say that I think him at all a roué; perhaps he might be less influenced if he were; but I mean that he *is* sentimentally influenced by them without believing that he is—which is much worse for his making a career of any kind. I may be wrong in imputing this dominant influence to him; but I cant find out that he really *has any other* bent. His love for the stage!—you see that it is not the hopeless passion you once imagined it. He has already deserted it for another light o' love—dramatic literature! I cant discover that he really has a bent for either.

I can understand, poor Wodie, struggling along, handicapped by circumstances and very little talent, and make allowances for him. He, at least, has clung to the newspaper work—that the poor boy stumbled into so far as I can see. I have more hope for him than Frank, at the moment. I don't think that Wodie ever will make a great newspaper writer; but he may make a successful *journalist* and be able to run a paper for his sympathy with his calling even if not very effective is at least sincere. I have written to Mr Dana about him[3]—and I wish you would tell him I shall write to him soon. I have not heard the result of his Yacht reporting though I have the newspaper slip you sent me.

I will send you a few lines when the photographs come. God bless you, dear Nan,

Always Limick

Please send me your photograph.

Provenience: Bancroft (MSS 76/192 C).

1. "M'liss." See note 1 to letter 190.

2. "The Heritage of Dedlow Marsh," *Graphic*, summer 1889; "A Secret of Telegraph Hill," *Illustrated London News*, summer 1889; "The Chatelaine of Burnt Ridge," *Pictorial World*, Christmas 1889.

3. Griswold Harte was subsequently employed by Charles Dana at the New York *Sun* (*New York Times*, 14 Dec. 1901, p. 9, col. 5).

192. TO JOSEPH HATTON, 24 SEPTEMBER 1889

Trewsbury. Cirencester.

Septem. 24th/89

My dear Hatton,

When you and Mr Willard[1] and the work are ready for me I shall be in hand.[2] I am glad we so nearly agree where the difficulty lies, and I hope when we overcome it the result will be what we expect. Does Mr Willard look at it merely as a consulting friend or a possible manager for it?

Yours always
B.H.

Provenience: Texas (ALS).

1. The popular actor Edward S. Willard (1853–1915).

2. Hatton reminisced in 1902 about his efforts to recruit Willard to play opposite his daughter Bessie in a production of the "M'liss" script he had cowritten with BH (Texas): Hatton had invited Willard to lunch "to meet Bret Harte (he was *very* anxious to meet him). . . . It was a good luncheon and the champagne was a fine Mumm. Perhaps Willard had too much, though I had never seen him in that condition. . . . Willard was very arrogant in his remarks after luncheon. . . . He never had good manners; they were damned bad on this occasion. He spoke as if he had never had any intention of considering the play—M'Liss—though I had talked the part [of the Schoolmaster] over with him and he had read it. . . . Harte was very indignant, never forgave him thought him a boor and impertinent."

193. TO HAVELOCK ELLIS, 21 DECEMBER 1889

15. Upper Hamilton Terrace. N.W.
21st Decem/89

My dear Sir,[1]

I beg to acknowledge the receipt of your favor of the 18*th* inst.

I am afraid I have not given that attention to my ancestry which distinguishes my republican fellow countrymen in Europe, but in reply to your enquiry I think I am safe in saying that, to the best of my knowledge, my *mother* and her immediate ancestors were descended from the Early Dutch (Holland) settlers in America, while my *father* and his immediate ancestors were as distinctly English in origin.[2]

I am very much interested in your theory. You possibly remember the remark of a California teamster who was remonstrated with for objurgating his refractory mule with unnecessary severity. "Yes," he said, "but you see what riles me is that the derned fool seems to forget everything but the *hoss* side of his ancestry!"

A wholesome belief in the efficiency of mixed races might have saved him from this dangerous conceit. I have possibly escaped it, by not clearly knowing in my own mind which was the *hoss* side of mine!

Believe me, dear Sir,

Yours very sincerely,
Bret Harte

Provenience: Texas (ALS).

1. Henry Havelock Ellis (1859–1939), best known today as a sex psychologist, was trained in medicine before turning to literary and scientific work. In *The New Spirit* (London: George Bell & Sons, 1890), 86, Ellis ranked BH with Hawthorne, Poe, and Mark Twain among the "imaginative writers . . . America has produced . . . of world-wide significance."

2. BH fails to mention that his paternal grandfather, Bernard Hart (1764–1855), was an orthodox Jew. See Helen I. Davis, "Bret Harte and His Jewish Ancestor, Bernard Hart," *Publications of the American Jewish Historical Society* 32 (1931):99–111.

194. TO FLORENCE HENNIKER, 13 FEBRUARY 1890

Royal Hotel, Ventnor, I.W.
13th Feby/90

My dear Mrs Henniker,[1]

I have let your note lie reproachfully on my desk for a day, as I wanted to ascertain definitely and positively *when* I could be in London. And now I find, unfortunately, that I cannot get away on account of this dreadful work—to say nothing of the dreadful weather—until after the 20th. The work is for the Illustrated[2]—the weather is for my sins, I suppose. A hideous East Wind shakes its fist at me through the window as I plod along at my work; when I go out and engage it it unvariably gets the better of me; there is nothing to see or hear but the "low wash of leaden coloured seas,"[3]—(which is Tennyson for the Channel), and I am altogether so miserable that I suppose it is doing me good.

Make my apologies to Lady Ashburton,[4] and say that I trust that "even this will pass" and I shall still meet her in another and a better Island than this—when I return. As to yourself!—I am hopelessly culpable! I cant find here at Ventnor a copy of "Dedlow Marsh,"[5] and I cant find the leisure and happiness to write the verse in the Book of Rondeaux.[6] I am afraid everything must stand over until I return. I would send you a valentine but, as far as I can see, the birds do not pass on this island until later in the season and I cannot yet find a swallow "flying flying *North*."[7]

I shall try to find a copy of Tennysons last here and read the poems you speak of.[8] I have been reading nothing but *proof*—the dreariest form of remorse and self-examination!

Did you ever read any of Emersons (R.W.) verse? You have read so much that is smooth and flowing I'd like you to see something rugged.[9] Thats the effect of Ventnor on

Yours always
Bret Harte

Provenience: UVa (ALS).

1. Florence Henniker (1855–1923), younger daughter of Richard Monckton Milnes, Lord Houghton, was a distinguished writer and hostess. In his *Reminiscences* (New York: Harper, 1899), II, 61, Justin McCarthy recalled that "Mrs. Henniker's is just the house where one who knows his way about London would naturally expect to meet Bret Harte; and I have been happy enough to get the chance every now and then of meeting him there." Henniker dedicated her novel *Bid Me Goodbye* (1892) to BH.

2. "A Ward of the Golden Gate," *Illustrated London News*, 96 (Summer 1890):1–38.

3. Tennyson's "Enoch Arden," l. 608: "the low moan of leaden-color'd seas."

4. Lady Louisa Ashburton (d. 1903).

5. BH's *The Heritage of Dedlow Marsh and Other Tales* (Boston: Houghton Mifflin; London: Macmillan, 1889).

6. Henniker had sent BH a keepsake volume with a request that he write in it a parody he had promised her.

7. A bit of wordplay on the first line of Tennyson's "O Swallow, Swallow": "O Swallow, Swallow, flying, flying south."

8. *Demeter and Other Poems* (London: Macmillan, 1889).

9. BH remarked in a letter to a Mrs. Jamieson on 3 August 1889 (Harkness Collection, Rare Books and Manuscripts Division, New York Public Library, Astor, Lenox and Tilden Foundations) enclosing a copy of Emerson's "Forbearance" that "I used to think it very noble when I was a younger man, and even believed I *understood* it; its rather unfair of me now to add *illegibility* to a poet whom some people think not sufficiently *intelligible*."

195. TO FLORENCE HENNIKER, 5 OR 12 (?) APRIL 1890[1]

15. Upper Hamilton Terrace. N.W.
Saturday P.M.

My dear Mrs Henniker,

I have just written to you at 23 Hill St to say I would come to Kent House after three to-morrow, but it has since occurred to me that you may go to Kent House first.

I am sending there also Longmans Magazine which contains an effusion of your friend Mr Kipling which I grieve to say *I* cannot make head nor tail of. Perhaps *you* may. To me it carries no consecutive thought, whatever, of incident, suggestion or object![2]

Since you wrote to me of him, I turned to the "Plain Tales from the Hills," which I had bought but had not yet read, and read the ones you said you liked.[3] I liked the freshness of *choice of subject*, and the apparent *truthfulness of character sketching* but I was repelled by a certain smart *attitude* which struck me always as being in excess of the *actual smartness of the work done*, or of any smartness *that the character of the work required.* Of course this is only partial and unfair criticism. I shall certainly read the others and a volume of "Indian Tales" which has been lent to me,[4] before I judge—and then I may be no judge at all!

However there is always room for anything new and good, whatever the critics may say. I am no critic but

Yours always
Bret Harte

Provenience: UVa (ALS).

1. Tentatively dated by reference to the story in *Longman's* cited in note 2 below and BH's 23 April 1890 letter to Florence Henniker (UVa).

2. The uncollected "For One Night Only" (*Longman's* 15 [Apr. 1890]:611–20) is a strained satire of salon society. Writing to Florence Henniker on 13 January 1891 (UVa), BH complained that "there is a little too much of 'Bill Sykes' and 'Nancy'" in Kipling's 'The Record of Badalia Herodsfoot.'" BH first met Rudyard Kipling (1865–1936) on 3 May 1894 at a dinner in London hosted by William Waldorf Astor (*Letters*, 386), though they did not hit it off. Still, Kipling as a child read BH's tales (*Something of Myself* [Garden City, N.Y.: Doubleday, Doran, 1937], 39); and

when he visited California in 1889 he was continually reminded of BH (*From Sea to Sea* [New York: Scribner, 1899], II, 82–90; *American Notes* [New York: Standard Book Co., 1930], 24–25, 67–69). On his part, though he publicly professed admiration for Kipling (New York *World*, 22 Dec. 1901, p. 5, col. 3), BH parodied him in "Stories Three, by R-dy—d K-pl—g," *Saturday Evening Post*, 30 June 1900, 1219; 7 July 1900, 2; and 14 July 1900, 14, collected in *Condensed Novels, Second Series* (Boston: Houghton Mifflin, 1902).

3. London: Thacker, 1888.

4. New York: U.S. Book Co. 1890.

196. TO FRANK HARTE, 16 MAY 1890

15, Upper Hamilton Terrace, N.W.
May 16, 1890

My dear Frank,

I have asked Mr. Boucicault seventy-five dollars per week instead of sixty dollars—his offer for the use of the name, characters, and incidents of "The Luck of Roaring Camp."[1] This is the *lowest* figure you suggest in your letter to me, and if the play is a *success* will be of little moment to him. However, if *you* think he *cannot* give any more, I will take his offer of sixty dollars, and I authorize you to tell him so if there should be any difficulty as to the terms.

More important to me is the consideration that he shall not use any of the characters of incidents in my story of "M'liss," nor of "A Blue Grass Penelope," nor of *any story* I have written within the last three years. This is only due to my collaboration with Mr. Joseph Hatton in my play of "M'liss," and Madame V. de V. in "Penelope."[2] I cannot imagine, however, that Mr. Boucicault will require any of these as the characters he proposes to take from my "other works."

I am glad to find that you anticipate my judgment in your feelings in regard to any connection of yours with the play. As a mere matter of *business*, it is better that the *contract* should be made with *me*, and the *payments* likewise, even though I transfer the latter to your mother instead of my monthly drafts; and in regard to the new use of *your name*—if that is what Mr. Boucicault suggests—I cannot see what reputation that will give you except *he* takes *you* as collaborateur in dramatizing *my* story. I fear it would be more confusing than advantageous to the play.

If, of course, any of the material that Madame Van de Velde and myself imparted into the play is used by Mr. Boucicault, I shall pay Madame V. de V. for the use of her collaboration out of the royalty Boucicault pays me, and I therefore hope you will let me know if such is the case.[3] She sends you kind messages and would have written, but says you owe her a letter. I have not been very well lately and have been obliged to go for two weeks to the country.

Your affectionate father
B.H.

Provenience: *Letters*, 355–56.

1. BH to Dion Boucicault, 16 May 1890 (American Antiquarian Society).

2. See note 4 to letter 162.

3. A dramatic version of "The Luck of Roaring Camp" produced in New York in May 1894 was ostensibly based on a script by Boucicault (*New York Times*, 15 May 1894, p. 5, col. 5). Whether or not Boucicault had a hand in it, it did not rely upon the Harte/Van de Velde treatment.

197. TO ANNA HARTE, 16 MAY 1890

15. Upper Hamilton Terrace. N.W.
16th May/90

My dear Nan,

I have just returned from two weeks absence in the country where I went to work and recruit, for I am not yet quite strong. I do not think the change did me any good, and I fear I shall have to try some other locality in a few days. During the last week of my stay I was scarcely able to do any work—a serious thing to me with all my engagements.

I have just written to Frank and Mr Boucicault in reference to a dramatization of The Luck of Roaring Camp which "B" has suggested.[1] I hope something may come of it. My own play of "Mliss" I fear now will go over to the autumn before it sees the footlights for the first time. I am greatly disappointed as I hoped to have it launched this spring. But the delay for a success is better than haste for a failure. And I, and my collaborateur, Mr Hatton—whose daughter is to play in it—are of course anxious that *all* the chances shall be favorable.

I hope so. I am getting very weary of this monotonous work 'though it is better paid here than in my own country, where I believe I should starve from all appearances if I depended solely upon my stories. Messrs Houghton, Mifflin & Co sent me last week *$30.00* as a munificent royalty on my two books "Cressy" and "The Argonauts of North Liberty" for six months![2]

With love for the children always dear Nan,

Affectionately,
Limick

Provenience: UCLA (ALS).

1. See letter 196.

2. *The Argonauts of North Liberty* (Boston: Houghton Mifflin; London: Spencer Blackett), published in the United States in May 1888; *Cressy* (Boston: Houghton Mifflin; London: Macmillan; Leipzig: Tauchnitz), published in the United States in February 1889.

198. TO JOSEPH HATTON, 12 NOVEMBER 1890

15. Upper Hamilton Terrace. N.W.
12th Novem./90

Dear Hatton,

I asked my solicitor, (the same who advised us about the right to enjoin Miss Pixley's "Mliss,") to draw up the accompanying letter, which is based, as you will see, on the suggestion of your last note to me.[1] It leaves you free to make what arrangements you can for the production of the play, with such complications as may arise from your daughter's acting in it, only providing that you shall pay me half-profits *on the play*, as you receive them, and relieving me from any liability for cast and expense of production.

It seems to me that a success in America would be enhanced if the play had been first produced in London, but if you see a chance of success in the first opening in America of course you will follow your own judgment.

On the second leaf of my enclosed letter, you will find a copy of the note that you are to sign and return to me to complete the agreement.

I also enclose a letter I lately received in regard to "Mliss" from a Miss Kate Mayhew. It may be of use to you, and you can return it to me later. It is possible that when unauthorized adapters fall out, *bona fide* authors may get their due! I shall prefer Miss Mayhew to *you*![2]

Drop me a line—with your agreement—as soon as you get this. Let me know if you hear anything of Boucicaults dramatization of my "Luck." I had a line from him a few days before his death saying that it was complete and in the hands of Abott & Teal managers. I have written to the legal representatives, of Boucicault, stating my claims under agreement with him, and forwarded it to New York to a friend to present for me.[3]

With kindest regards to your wife and daughter and best wishes for your Business success

Yours always
Bret Harte

Provenience: Texas (ALS).

1. Though the letter of agreement between BH and Hatton is lost, the instructions BH sent his solicitor Stephenson on 4 November 1890 (UVa) are extant: "You will say that in *consideration* of my dramatizing—in collaboration with him—'The Story of Mliss' under the title of 'Smiths Pocket' or any other name to be agreed upon, and of my permitting and authorizing such dramatization he is to pay me one half (or 50 per cent) of the *profits* (or the sum received by him as royalty on the play) whenever the play is represented. 2d. That his daughter, Miss Bessie Hatton, shall have the refusal of playing the part of the heroine, 'Mliss' for the space of one year from the date of the contract, but if she does not begin such representation of the heroine during that time, the part may then be offered to some other actress." On a separate page accompanying this letter, BH again insisted he "is not to be held responsible for any debts or expenses incurred in the bringing out of Mliss or connected with its representation."

2. See note 2 to letter 159.

3. BH wrote Boucicault's legal representatives on 5 November 1890 (LC) that he had authorized Boucicault "to dramatise my novel 'The Luck of Roaring Camp' and to produce the play under that title," that he held "a written promise . . . to pay me £15 weekly as long as the said play is

acted," and that he would honor the contract if paid "the same royalty on the same play." BH added that Boucicault had written before his death the play "was finished and on the eve of being produced by Messrs Abbot & Teal." See also note 3 to letter 196.

199. TO ROBERT B. CUNNINGHAME GRAHAM, 28 NOVEMBER 1890

15. Upper Hamilton Terrace. N.W.
28th Novem./90

Dear Mr Cunninghame Graham,[1]

I hope you will believe that I cordially enter into your feelings in regard to our Indian troubles, even though I cant see my way, just now, to other expression. It is the old story of our Anglo Saxon Civilized aggression, yet I have thought that during the last fifteen years of our Indian administration, it has not had to be told so often, and I have been hoping that it was of the Past. Of course the desire to "improve" people off the face of the earth with a gun, and then to punish them for learning how to use the weapon will continue to exist, yet I think that my Western friends have lately proposed to act up to their doctrine that "the only good Indian was a dead one."

And I think that the reports of the present crisis are exaggerated by the press. Significant as "poor Lo's" dancing has been, you will remember that there was always more of it than fighting.[2] Indian uprisings have usually *begun* with the maneuver. I hope—I believe—there is no great, vengeful outbreak. There may be some wave of religion passing over them,—boisterously and tumultously[3]—but it would seem to require a Booth rather than a Miles[4] to understand and take after it.

Yours very Sincerely
Bret Harte

R. B. Cunninghame Graham. Esq. M.P.

Provenience: National Library of Scotland (ALS).

1. Robert Bontine Cunninghame Graham (1852–1936) was a writer, a Scottish landowner, and a Liberal member of Parliament who had traveled

extensively in Mexico, in Argentina with the gauchos in the 1870s, and in Texas in the 1880s.

2. BH exploits a popular pun on Pope's "Essay on Man": "Lo, the poor Indian! whose untutored mind/Sees God in clouds, or hears him in the wind."

3. BH remarks on contemporary news reports about Indian resistance and the practice of the Ghost Dance religion among the Sioux in South Dakota. His tone of racial condescension notwithstanding, his comments are mercifully free of the hostility which led a month later to the Wounded Knee massacre.

4. Gen. Nathan A. Miles (1839–1925), commander of the Division of the Missouri. BH thus avers that the Ghost Dance is more theatrical performance than military threat.

200. TO ANNA HARTE, 18 AUGUST 1891

15. Upper Hamilton Terrace. N.W.
August 18th 91

My dear Nan,

I am sending you a draft for $300, $50 of which is to go towards your summer outing, and I shall send you an additional $50 at the time I send the next draft. I am still in London, very much unsettled and uncertain where to go, and rather ailing, nervous, weak and miserable generally. The Doctor says I ought to go for a "cure" to some of the French or German watering places, but I am not quite fit to travel *alone*, and I have no one to go with me. The fact is that I have always been so steadily working in one place—only because I *could work there*, that I dread journeys and moving. And there is the expense!

I have been looking anxiously for a letter from you. I hope you are already in the country and better than when Jessamy wrote me. As soon as I know anything of my movements, more than I do now I will write to you, at once. I owe the girls a letter, but I am scarcely fit to write, and I have just been called upon hurriedly to say something about poor Lowell in a magazine.[1] God bless you all, always

Your affec.
Limick

Provenience: UVa (ALS).

1. In his commissioned valedictory, "A Few Words about Mr. Lowell" in *New Review* 5 (Sept. 1891):193–201, BH mustered few higher words for the poet than these: "Mr. Lowell was more of an Englishman than an American." See also letter 24.

201. TO ANNA HARTE, 16 DECEMBER 1891

15. Upper Hamilton Terrace. N.W.
16th Decem. '91

My dear Nan,

Even if I had been quite able to come home for Christmas, I could hardly have started upon so short notice as your last letter,—for a two or three months trip! I had still some of my Christmas work for the periodicals and the proofs of my new book to finish.[1] But what was more important than that, I *was not well enough* to undertake so long a journey! I am afraid, Nan, you do not appreciate that I am no longer young, nor even that dubious thing—middle-aged—but that I am really *old*, and have the infirmities of age to contend against.[2] I am easily exhausted by exertion, and can no longer travel as I once did. I was obliged last week to give up a pleasant country visit to an old friend, because I could not bear the few hours journey. One of the first things I must try to do is to get a *slighter* and not *too* violent a change, and I do not think that I was quite up to a plunge into a New York winter—(much as I sometimes long for it)—in my present condition. This has been the worst season yet known for transatlantic journeys—and December is seldom a favorable month for changing climate. As soon as I got your letter I consulted my Doctor—a homeopath—and he advised me to wait a month or two at least, and to prepare myself by *stopping work*, and going to the South of France until I was stronger—which was of course, impossible!

So I can only send my Christmas wishes, and my little gift of $75.00, for you and the children, and my love which goes always with it. I am sending $50 to Eliza and $25 to Maggie,—who I fear have not much to make them happy. God bless you all, and give you a happy Christmas and New Year, always

Your affectionate,
Limick.

P.S. I enclose the draft for $325.

Provenience: UVa (ALS).

1. BH was remarkably prolific at the time, writing stories for the Christmas number of both *Black and White* ("In a Pioneer Restaurant") and the *Illustrated London News* ("Their Uncle from California") while reading proof of *A First Family of Tasajara*.

2. BH was fifty-five years of age at this writing; AH was fifty-nine.

202. TO ANNA HARTE, 23 JANUARY 1892

15, Upper Hamilton Terrace, N.W.
23 Jany '92

My dear Anna,

I have been so poorly, with a succession of colds, that my work is greatly in arrears and I have only just been able to get the enclosed draft. I ought not complain, for I have been in the midst of much more serious illness, resulting from this dreadful influenza and the poison that seems to be in the air everywhere.[1] Mr Van de Velde the head of this house—a middle aged man, whose strength and youthfulness I have always envied—has been lying *critically ill*, with nurses, doctors and consultations and the whole household—like many others—is ailing. I have given up for the present my intention of going away, for I should not like to fall seriously ill, as so many have—among entire strangers—with no relations here, and 3000 miles from my family. There is no place exempt from the scourge—although probably there may be spots where the weather is less depressing. Here it has been fittingly dark and gloomy; days when one exists only by artificial light and the streets at noon are like midnight. London has well earned the title of the "City of Dreadful Night"! The oldest Londoners remember nothing like it. Everywhere we hear of friends—whole households—stricken down.

My work is so far *behind* that I must keep all my strength for that. You must write to me more frequently; I was quite worried at receiving no Xmas letter until a few days ago. *Some* of you certainly can find time to send me a few lines once a fortnight. I will write again soon.

Always your affec
Limick

I hope you and the children are keeping well. Eliza says she has had the *grippe* three times! It must be in some mild form.

You do not say where Frank is. Is he still in Europe?

Provenience: UVa (ALS).

1. Influenza and pneumonia death rates in London increased from 9.83 per 10,000 persons in 1889 to 16.5 in 1890, 21.9 in 1891, and 19.8 in 1892. In all, some 5,800 people died during the epidemic (K. David Patterson, *Pandemic Influenza 1700–1900* [Totowa, N.J.: Rowman & Littlefield, 1986], 73).

203. TO FLORENCE HENNIKER, 8 FEBRUARY 1892[1]

15. Upper Hamilton Terrace. N.W.
Monday AM

My dear Mrs Henniker,

Thanks for your kind words about "Tasajara."[2]

My old friend, the head of this household, Mr Van de Velde died yesterday morning. The shock was unexpected—as these things always are—although he was very weak and had never really rallied from his first illness. Its the more dreadful for the family that *at the same time* they were receiving telegrams from Berlin of the critical state of Madame Van de Veldes stepfather Count de Launay, and they could not send anyone from the bedside of Mr Van de Velde to be with the Count in his last moments and comfort Madames daughter Marguerite, who was the only one of the family that was with him and was alone in her sorrow.

It makes a sad break in a household which the kindness of Monsieur & Madame has made my home in London, so many years.

Yours always
Bret Harte

Provenience: UVa (ALS).

1. Dated by its reference to Arthur Van de Velde's death.
2. See note 1 to letter 201.

204. TO ANNA HARTE, 19 MARCH 1892

15. Upper Hamilton Terrace. N.W.
19 March '92

My dear Nan,

I am still here, awaiting the return of Madame Van de Velde and the part of her family that were with her at Berlin.[1] I am expecting them to-night, and when I am relieved of my charge and the responsibility of looking after the orphans I shall go to the seaside to recruit. I will then write to you more fully of myself and my plans.[2] Meantime I enclose a note from Madame Van de Velde, which came yesterday. I suppose it is in acknowledgement of your sympathy which I had conveyed to her. She sent it to me to be addressed to you.

I have not heard from you since that letter, although I have received only a few days ago a nice long one from Jessamy—which I will answer as soon as I can get away from my work here. My health has been so poor that my writing is sadly in arrears and I must try this year *some change* to prevent me becoming a confirmed invalid. My doctor wants me to go to Bath for my gouty tendency, and take the regular "cure" of three weeks. But I am puzzled what to do, and shall, I think, consult others before entering upon an experiment of this kind. Everything is called "gout" here, and the British Doctor doesnt quite understand the American constitution, even when it has become partly acclimated like mine. The "cure" would have no reference to any other changes—as, for instance, my coming to America, or going on the Continent.

My love to the children; God bless and keep you all till our next meeting! Affectionately, dear Nan

Limick

I enclose the dft for $250.

Provenience: Bancroft (MSS 88/146 C).

1. On the same day Arthur Van de Velde died in London, Mme Van de Velde's stepfather, the Count de Launay, died in Berlin. "Madame has

gone to Berlin with her eldest daughter to settle the Counts affairs," BH wrote AH on 20 February 1892 (*Letters*, 364). "I have been left in charge of the London house."

2. See letter 205.

205. TO ANNA HARTE, 15 APRIL 1892

Cavendish Hotel, Eastbourne.
15th April '92

My dear Nan,

Your kind, loving letter came a day after I last wrote you. First and foremost I want to say that I *never for an instant* ever conceived of the girls coming here *without you*, and much as I want to see them, I would not have had them separated from you, even for the shortest visit. My idea has always been that we should be *all together* again, or if that were impossible that it was more important that *you and I* should meet and that if there were any sacrifice, at first, it must be of the girls. That is why I have thought more of coming to America than I have of bringing you here; and the obstacles to the latter, have only been the same *practical* ones that worry me now.

Cruel as it seems to weigh them against the love that prompted your letter and a love *I* feel, appreciate and have always felt and appreciated, I am only kept from saying to you "come at once! dear Nan!" by the thought that I could not, at this moment, see my way to make my invitation result in anything but a bitter disappointment. That I can *later*,—perhaps in a month or two, or surely *this summer*, manage it I am *quite confident and hopeful*! To come here to London to a hotel, or even to lodgings—living as you ought to live as my wife—even in the plainest way, would cost more than my income would permit, and much more than for me to come to New York—or rather to New Jersey or the country for an equal length of time. I have been able to live in London solely because I lived with the Van de Veldes, half as guest, under circumstances that enabled me to send you $3,000 a year. That $3,000 would not give you the same *comfort* here as in America. But it *may be possible* to find something, out of London, or in the vicinity where we could make at least a *temporary* home; for I should never consent to have my daughters educated or even reside permanently in England. Or, after a slight visit to London and the Van de Veldes, if they are in a new house in town or country, we could go to the Continent, where I would *first* find some place in Switzerland or Germany for a longer stay. Travel would be too expensive *at first*, until after we had tested what it cost us to remain comfortably in any one place.

This is what I am considering now and enquiring about, and of which I shall write you as soon as I return to London. I am a little better since my weeks sojourn here, but I am yet far from strong. I go back next week. I still remain with the Van de Veldes, until they move to a new house.[1] With love to the children, always your affect

Limick

I am hurrying this off to catch the Post on Saturday, as there is a Bank Holiday and Good Friday hiatus at the Post Office.

Provenience: Bancroft (MSS C-H 57).

1. See letter 210 and note 1 to letter 211.

206. TO CLARA SCHNEIDER, 23 APRIL 1892

15. Upper Hamilton Terrace. N.W.
April 23d '92

Dear Mrs Schneider,

Many, many thanks for your charming Easter gift! You could not have sent me anything that was a more pleasant reminder of yourself, or a more convincing token that in the past *twelve years* (is it *really* twelve years?) you are unchanged from what you were in the pleasant days of Crefeld. If anything you look *younger* I fancy, and the flesh you have gained is far from unbecoming! I am glad to see that in spite of illness and household worries you are looking so bright and cheerful, and that the dark days have left no shadow. What do your husband and friends say? Do they not think you are looking wonderfully well?

I am afraid that I on the contrary, are much *thinner* than when I first came here, although perhaps not much thinner than when I first came to Germany. I am sending you a copy of a new magazine called the "Idler" which contains some *real* and some *fanciful* portraits and descriptions of your old friend—some of which you may recognize. The large portrait at the beginning of the Magazine you will remember as the photograph I sent you last.[1] It was taken from that. One of the "interviews"—you will also know *which*—was the result of what I supposed was a merely *friendly visit* from a gentleman I had received a letter from. But they may amuse you.[2]

I am still here and may probably remain until my friends move to the country or some larger London house, but I may go to America for a short visit during the summer or have a part of my family visit me and perhaps spend a few weeks on the Continent. I should so like to see you all again, in any event, and wish if I cross the channel it could be arranged in some way, at some watering place or some pleasant spot on the Rhine!

Thank you for all the Crefeld news, which bring the old days back. Why doesn't your husband write a line to me. Give him my love and believe me

Always yours
Bret Harte

P.S. I have only just returned from a fortnights trip to the seaside.
Yours B.H.

Provenience: UVa (ALS).

1. Photograph 20, Harte in 1891.

2. Luke Sharp [Robert Barr], "Francis Bret Harte: Two Interviews with Him on Somewhat Dissimilar Lines," *Idler* 1 (Apr. 1892):301–11. The frontispiece to this issue is a sketch by A. S. Boyd from photograph 20.

207. TO BRAM STOKER, 8 MAY 1892

15. Upper Hamilton Terrace. N.W.
8th May '92

My dear Bram Stoker,[1]

I am sending you by Parcel's Post a copy of "Thankful Blossom," which I have just unearthed among my papers, in obedience to your rash desire to read it again![2] There are a great many alterations, emendations and suggestions; whether they were there when you read it I dont know; but I think you can easily follow the rivulet of original text that runs through them. Some of these suggestions were poor Boucicaults, although *he* wanted me to retain the long rhetorical scene with Paulding which I had concluded to leave out. You will also observe a suggestion of omitting much of the first part of Act IIII, and partly gagging that noble but oppressive Lady Washington.

I have not looked at it for five years. But it strikes me, in glancing over it now, that my collaborateurs (Madame Van de Veldes) management of the two Frenchmen—which is very much amplified, extended, and recreated from the novel—is *good* work!

Supposing there is any constructive basis for a play, or any connected dramatic work here *at all*, I still have certain doubts. *First*; if the historical subject is interesting to an English audience. *Second*; if any audience cares to see a girl change her love during the play, (however they do it in real life). In the play the first lover is her *cousin* also, but I doubt if it alters the sentimental consideration.

Let me know when you get the package.

Yours very Sincerely
Bret Harte

Provenience: The Brotherton Collection, Leeds University Library.

1. Bram Stoker (1847–1912) not only wrote *Dracula* and managed the career of Henry Irving but managed the Lyceum Theatre in London. BH had met him no later than January 1891, when he inscribed a copy of *The Heritage of Dedlow Marsh and Other Tales* to him (*National Union Catalogue*, vol. 232, p. 634).

2. BH refers, of course, to the playscript of "Thankful Blossom" he cowrote with Mme Van de Velde. See letter 147.

208. TO ANNA HARTE, 22 JUNE 1892

15. Upper Hamilton Terrace, N.W.
22d June '92

My dear Nan,

I've just got your letter of the 7th inst, but I am so hurried with the finishing of a long novel (which must be ready without fail on the 1st July)[1] and have been so troubled in getting together enough for the monthly draft, that I have no time to answer it at length. Only I beg you to believe that I am doing everything I can to expedite matters and for the best, for us all. Do not, however, pay much attention to the opinions of others in regard to expenses here. I have lived long enough in London—and I know enough of the "American gentlemen" who live here—to know that my estimate is more likely to be right than his. Three thousand dollars in N.Y. is only three thousand dollars in London, and goes no further *nor as far* and if you have not been able to save any thing out of it in N.Y. but neither have run in debt on it,—we would certainly run in debt on that sum here. I have had an unexceptionally fortunate position in living with the Van de Veldes, and *I* could not expect to repeat it—either with you and the girls or with myself again. The whole scheme of living here is different; every body here has some small capital or *assured* income, and they know how much they can spend from year to year—I have nothing but this wretched hand of mine—already growing weaker by age—to support us year by year and none of my children are likely to help me.

I cannot trust to the hope that we are going to be any luckier in our expenses here than elsewhere. In the matter of illness alone, we would be at a disadvantage. We have been accustomed to Doctors who have been friends and content with small fees, and long credit. Think of paying a guinea ($5.00) to a Doctor for every visit, and paying him on the spot!

You must leave it to me, Nan, to do the best I can to bring us together and decide where it shall be, and not trust to our wishes alone, or other peoples opinions who would hardly help us in an emergency. Poverty is dreadful anywhere. Here, among strangers, it is terrible.

I will write you again as soon as this book is off my hands. God bless you all.

Always affect
Limick

P.S. I enclose a letter which evidently was intended for Frank or Wodie.[2] It came to me here through the Legation. It is a sad commentary on what I have just written.

Provenience: UVa (ALS).

1. *Susy: The Story of a Waif*, first published serially in the New York *Sun* between 7 August and 25 September 1892. In this novella, as I have argued elsewhere (*Bret Harte* [New York: Twayne, 1992], 108–10), BH encoded his "conflicted relations at the time with AH and Mdm Van de Velde."

2. According to his obituary in the *New York Times* (14 Dec. 1901, p. 9, col. 5), Griswold Harte studied briefly at Oxford. BH nowhere mentions this detail in his extant letters, though it may be implicit here. Certainly the father and son were estranged in their final years (see letter 254); their estrangement and the silence about his elder son in BH's surviving letters date from this period.

209. TO ANNA HARTE, 21 JANUARY 1893

15. Upper Hamilton Terrace. N.W.
21st Jany '93

My dear Nan,

I have been suffering a good deal lately with persistent neuralgia in my head and face so that I have barely been able to sleep but a few hours—and what is even more important to us all—barely able to work! I suppose it was brought on by the severe weather, but I fear, by what is less changable—age! So I cannot ever look forward to improvement, and for the first time, in many years, I am beginning to lose heart, and faith in myself. And as I have long ago lost it in the ability of others to help me the outlook for a few years more of helpless drudgery is not a pleasant one. The New Year has not set in very joyfully to me.

I have yours of Jany 4th in regard to your Christmas presents. I dont want to complain, Nan, but for several years both you and the children have been sending me your little Christmas offerings *long after* everyone else has, who cares to remember me, until it seems to have become a *habit*. Surely, you have the whole year to prepare some trifles in time—and not make me feel every year that it was the *last* thing you thought of. I send you your money regularly, and I believe I have never missed, beyond a few days, your extra Xmas draft. I will not believe it is forgetfulness—but it affects me almost as painfully to think it is that dreadful hand-to-mouth, slip-shod want of foresight and preparation which has been the curse of our family. If you sent me a few things,—the merest trifles—one or two handkerchiefs marked with my initials—that would reach me in time I should be, as you know content and happy. I do not think it is a sufficient answer for you to say that each year you have been expecting me home—for you would not even then have anything ready for me.

Madame Van de Velde sent Jessamy a "Bret Harte Birth Day Book"[1]—a volume which she compiled and published herself here—but she tells me she has never heard from Jessamy if it was received, and you do not speak of it in your letters. I knew nothing of it—in fact I knew little of the publication of the book, for I was away from London part of the time, and Madame V. de V. was in Berlin when it was prepared. But it is a very *pretty looking* volume, and has been highly praised in England. I am sorry to add, however, that *in my own country, my publishers would not take it,* (so Madame's publishers tell *me*) and she is recouped for her expense by my European readers. I believe she has written to Jessamy about it, but I told her I would enquire myself.

I may go to Oxford for a few days to stay with Froude. Everybody tells me that I ought to go to the Riviera or the South of France for my health. This was where I hoped to take you and the children if you came this winter—but I have no money now to go to that expense. The Vandeveldes are still looking for a new house; when they make the change I shall, in all probability, leave them and go elsewhere to live, but where I do not yet know. With love to the children always, dear Nan,

Yours affectionately
Limick

Provenience: UVa (ALS).

1. London: Osgood, McIlvaine & Co. The volume was designed for autographs and inscriptions, with pages entirely blank save for printed days of the year and apothegms from BH's writings. As BH wrote Clara Schneider (20 Dec. 1892, UVa), "*I* have nothing to do of course with the *selections*, or the *publishing of the* volume. I think you will find it a pretty book to look at; but I am afraid my writings dont lend themselves to *complementary* or *pretty sayings*, and some of my friends find some funny things opposite to their birth dates! At least they pretend to be furious!"

210. TO ANNA HARTE, 21 JUNE 1893

15. Upper Hamilton Terrace. N.W.
June 21st '93

My dear Nan,

This is just a line to say I returned a few days ago from Wales—and to send the draft. I did not profit much in health by my visit, although I felt a little better at the end of ten days, when I had to return to London—and to a *heat* that was unexampled for England. It was more like our hot weather in America as I remember it—without the thunder storms. Here one is so unprepared for anything warmer than 60°—that the thermometer at 85—is startling. I think this just knocked out of me whatever good I got from the country. But thank Heaven! I was able to do *some work*, and have wiped out a few of my old delayed engagements.[1] Yet I have scarcely dared to read what I have written—lest I should destroy it in disgust. I do not know if you read all that I write—it is almost always republished in America (at *half price*! for America no longer recognizes me as an *American*!), and generally in the newspapers. Sometime ago I asked my American publishers to send you my books regularly. I do not know if they have done so; they are so mean and I dislike them so that I hate to ask favors of them—and as they never *push* my works and scarcely pay me anything for them—I would rather *buy* them elsewhere. It is always ridiculous to attempt to *send you anything from England.* The freight is so much and the duty so high—in spite of the copyright act.[2]

I do not know yet what I am going to do, nor where I am going. In a week or two I shall have to go *temporarily* with the V. de V, or find myself lodgings elsewhere,—or make a visit to some convenient friend. I can see nothing *ahead* of me or *around* me but work! work!—promised or unfinished work!—and I dare not lift my hand from it to look beyond. With love to the children,

Always your affect
Limick

Provenience: UVa (ALS).

1. BH's next published story was "The Heir of the McHulishes," *Century*, n.s., 24 (Sept.-Oct. 1893):763–71, 921–26.

2. Like most writers, BH was an ardent supporter of international copyright. Soon after leaving the Glasgow consulate, he signed a memorial sent to Congress in support of it: "I am in favor of any and all legislation that recognizes the equal rights of any and all authors to their own property in any and all countries" (*Publishers Weekly*, 7 Nov. 1885, 639). The Berne Convention first published an international copyright policy and established the International Copyright Union in 1887.

211. TO CLARA SCHNEIDER, 26 AUGUST 1893

109, Lancaster Gate, W.[1]
August 26th '93

My dear Mrs Schneider,

Your very welcome letter came punctually to me yesterday,[2] although it had been forwarded from my old address at Hamilton Terrace. In the bustle of moving, and during the little while that I was in the country, when my friends were changing their houses, I had quite forgotten my birthday, and I actually only was reminded of it by thinking, the other day, that it was almost time that I should hear from *you*! It is so good of you to remember your old friend.

No, I have not been out of England since I wrote you last. I really have not had time to go to the Columbian Fair[3] although I wished to go, for I was not well last winter and my work—which is always pressing—got very much behind. So I have been scarcely out of London, except for a week or two, and during the moving, and my friends (on account of changing to their new town house) did not take their usual summer home in the Country. So I have been quietly plodding along here, without incident or new experience, very much in my old fashion. Thanks to the public, who still read my stuff, I have always work enough to do, and work enough ordered to keep my hands full. I suppose I ought to feel grateful, but I would like a holiday—now and then—without the atmosphere of pen- and-ink and paper. I had a hope of going to Homburg this season—but like all my projects for recreation it came to nought. I used to have dreams of going to Germany and stopping at some little place on the Rhine where you and your husband could join me! I have that *hope* still!

But why dont you run over here, with your husband, when he goes to Manchester? Then we could talk about it. At all events he must not pass through London without calling upon me here. Although this house is still in confusion, I should like him to see it, as it contains all of the Countess de Launays furniture, tapestries, portrait etc. etc. which Madame Van de Velde succeeded to when her mother died—and for which she has taken this larger house. Her salon looks like a German drawing room!

I am very much concerned with what you tell me about your eyes! I know the German oculists are good, but you ought to be very careful and have the best treatment. My own eyes are very poor—but that is *age*! I cannot read without glasses and lately I have taken to wearing mild ones in the street—that I may recognize my friends more distinctly. But *you* ought not to be troubled, and I am worried about you! Do scrawl a few lines to let me know how you are.

With love to you husband and children, believe me always

Your old friend
Bret Harte

Let me know if you need any of my books—although I have nothing later than "Sally Dows."[4] Did I send you my last photo? I wish you would send me a good one of yourself!

Provenience: UVa (ALS).

1. On 23 August 1893 (Wesleyan), BH wrote AH from 109 Lancaster Gate in Hyde Park to explain that "As my things were moved here from Upper Hamilton Terrace, I came here also, and shall remain, at present, whatever I may do, *later on*."

2. BH's fifty-seventh birthday.

3. The Columbian Exposition in Chicago.

4. Both the American and British editions of *Sally Dows and Other Stories* (Boston: Houghton Mifflin; London: Chatto & Windus) had appeared in May 1893.

212. TO ANNA HARTE, 24 SEPTEMBER 1893

109, Lancaster Gate, W.
24th Septem. 93

My dear Anna,

As soon as I received your very appealing letter I telegraphed you that it was impossible for me to arrange for your leaving by the first of October. The despatch was returned to me from America with the remark that you were not to be found at Plainfield, and then I directed that it should be forwarded to your new address.

One would think that it was not necessary that I should be put to this trouble and expense, and that you might have known that as soon as I could send for you, or go myself to America, I should do so without your having to write me such a letter, and without your laying such stress upon the circumstance of your being *ashamed* of not coming after you had told your friends that you were. I do not know what business it is of theirs, and I do not know one of them, who, if they heard that we all were living in poverty or *in debt* in London, would not hold up their hands in horror at your foolishness in going there and my recklessness in bringing you with my knowledge of our old shiftless, hand-to-mouth, life in N.Y. I do not know any of your or my friends that would advance a single dollar toward bringing you here, or helping to keep us together here. You have no reason to be *ashamed* of the manner in which I have treated you since I left, the amount of money I have sent you, or my joy and willingness to receive, from time to time, such of my family as I could afford to entertain here in the only way that I have been able [to] live here. Every one who knows me here, or in N.Y., knows too that I could not make a third of the money in N.Y. that I make here—and it would be rank folly for me to return unless I could afford to live without it. Yet notwithstanding this ever since I first wrote to you of coming I have been trying hard to make arrangements, and planning how I could manage to keep you and the family with me in London on my present income—which you know is not an *assured* or a regular one—but dependent upon my health and the amount of work I can do. All I have assured to me here from year to year, is the *demand* and price they pay for my work. Every month, as you might have seen by the lateness of my drafts I have been more or less troubled to get the amount I regularly send you, on account of my health having interfered with the amount of work I can get off, and this is one reason why I have not yet been able to perfect my plans. Again, this year, on account of my health and the change of houses, I have been living in the country, *alone*,[1] at small hotels, and, in spite of economy, I have been frightened at the expense—so unusual to me—and have had great difficulty to meet it. Yet all the while, I have been racking my brain to find ways and means for bringing you here—while you are writing to me as if it were only a question of my assenting to your coming. Madame V. de. V has kindly offered to invite each of you, *in time*, to this house for a *visit*, or until we found a house, for she could not keep us all together with her own large family, but this would mean for *a visit*, and I know that if you were ever here *you* would not want to go back without me—even if we were living in the direst poverty and confusion—nor do I know that *I* would be strong enough to insist upon it. That is the reason why I have to look forward to *all contingencies*, and that is why you *must* wait *patiently* and *believingly* and *trustfully* until I can meet them. No one thinks more and worries more over it, than your affectionate husband

Frank

Provenience: Bancroft (MSS C-H 57).

1. BH underlines the word, apparently to allay suspicion.

213. TO ANNA HARTE, 19 NOVEMBER 1893

109, Lancaster Gate, W.
19th Novem. 93

My dear Anna,

After writing to you very fully about the difficulties and prospects of your coming here speedily,[1] the first letter I receive from you is on the 17th of Novem. asking me to try to make arrangements for your passage to Paris *in about ten days*, on the first steamer after the 1st December. This I could barely do in time, even if I had the money for your passages and was perfectly satisfied with your plan.

Now, first of all, I have *not* got the money for your passages, nor could I raise it in time; I have not even got the money for your monthly draft yet, and will not have it until some work—delayed by my wretched state of health—is finished and paid for. I hope to get it by the 22d to go by the steamer of that day. I have told you, until I was ashamed of the repetition, that of late I have had great difficulty in getting money for the draft before the 20th, and you yourself might have noticed how, without reducing the sum I have sent you, I have been gradually obliged to protract the time of sending it from the 10th to the 20th. Yet you do not seem to have considered this more than to simply suggest "if it can be arranged."

Secondly. When you do come to Europe you must come where *I* am, to your *husbands house*, or wherever he may be living and among his friends. I am willing to believe that you are speaking with temper and do not mean what you say when you write of your reception in England being "a nightmare to me" and that you want to "place yourself respectably in Paris without bothering me." Your coming to Europe with the two girls *is* a very *serious practical* question of our living and our finances—apart from any sentiment whatever—and we have both suffered enough from shiftlessness, carelessness, want of judgement, and extravagance to make you understand this. So I shall not discuss the "respectability" of your coming to Paris when I am living and working in London *before you come to me*, nor the sentiment of it—but I only say that it seems to be ill-advised, thoughtless and far more likely to give me the bother and expense you say you wish to avoid—and that I *strongly object to it*. After coming *here* and being received by me and my friends, if you still think it expedient to go to Paris with the girls, there will be ample time for us to discuss it much more intelligently and with the facts before us, and when *I* should have the opportunity of knowing something more of the tastes and capabilities of the two girls who are to be benefitted by it. My experience of Franks choice of a profession and its result I think would justify a little more care in the future.

For this reason and others I am far from being sanguine of your plan as you show it. If Jessamy can already turn her talent to profit in America,[2] why should she come to Paris, where she cannot earn a penny in the same kind and quality of work, and where it will cost her more than either you or I can afford to teach her to do something else in Art, for which the poor child may not have capacity, and where she will have a hundred rivals. Have you the slightest idea of the expense or methods of Art Student life in Paris? *I* have, I know the Art Colony of Americans there. They come with capital for a three or four years study under expensive masters, and expect simply to spend their time and money there. Few succeed in doing anything as well as young Watrous—who had a special talent for imitative figure work. Callie Cooper at Düsseldorf spent her money hopelessly with the Professors—and yet she had great talent, and had painted some large pictures—and good ones too—before she left Washington. The first thing her French Master will do will be to make her *unlearn* everything she already knows, and prevent her from doing the work that she has found profitable. I cannot of course judge of her capacity except from the work she has sent me—the magazine cover design of flowers and the sketch. You, perhaps, have better opportunities of judging—but you have a terrible responsibility on your shoulders, if you listen to the dictates of your affection or the praises of her friends—alone.

You know my feelings about my daughters being educated in, and living in, and leaving their own country. Much as I want to see them I would not care to have them *live* in Europe. American girls—thanks to their own snobbishness, want of patriotism, and utter vanity—are already *passee*, *suspect*, and ridiculed abroad.

To sum up: 1st. I could not *promise* to do anything in the way of sending you passage money before a month or the 1st of January at the earliest. 2d. You must come *here* with the girls *first*, before you go to Paris—if you go there at all. 3d. You must leave the plan of Jessamy's Art education in Paris for further discussion.

Nothing that I have said refers in any way to the Magus School.[3] I believe it would be a very good place to go to *en pension* or for general tuition, and I have always liked the Magus.

I will write again when I send the draft. With love to all, always your affectionate

Limick

P.S. I have been very much run down with a severe cold the first of the season—and I have been suffering tortures with my teeth. I have been oscillating between the Dentist and the Doctor—going to the former every other day. It appears that I have neglected my teeth until my whole jaw is in a dreadful state.

Provenience: Bancroft (MSS 76/192 C).

1. Letter 212.

2. Jessamy Harte had exhibited her art at the Women's Building at the Chicago World's Fair in 1892–93 (San Francisco *Argonaut*, 5 Feb. 1894, 5); and she published an essay, "A Camp in the Adirondacks," in the *Ladies Home Journal*, n.s., 9 (July 1892):3.

3. BH probably means the Magnus School, a type of vocational institute with a curriculum designed by the British educator Philip Magnus (1842–1933).

214. TO ALEXANDER S. BOYD, 27 NOVEMBER 1893[1]

109, Lancaster Gate, W.
Monday Night

Dear Mr Boyd,[2]

I've just seen the Pall Mall Magazine. The illustrations of "The Mystery of the Hacienda" came out splendidly![3] All the delicacy of your pencil is retained, none of your grace of style is lost—they are admirable as they were in your drawing, and seem to me to be quite worthy of you. I only wish I thought as well of my own work!

I think "Rosita" on the garden bench perhaps takes my fancy most, although the running is between her and Cecily in the bed room scene. "Don Vincente" is a charming ghost; there is a delightful half-devilish, half-spiritual gallantry about him which puts him on the level of his companion spook Rosita. But they're all good—and the tail piece,—which I had not seen before—is a success!

Thank you so much for the corrections.[4] I know that you and your wife both loathe my feebly vile caricatures of Scotch—or as you say "Scorch"—character, and it was good of you to lend yourselves to make it less vile. But you will say "he meant well!—this Poker Flat Californian—and perhaps he never saw a Scotch girl in the whole wurrrrrld!"

Hoping to call soon

Always yours
Bret Harte

Provenience: UCLA (ALS).

1. Dated by the canceled stamp on the envelope.

2. A. S. Boyd (1854–1930), a Scottish artist, illustrated BH's "The Mystery of the Hacienda" (note 3 below) as well as his essay "My First Book" (*Idler*, Jan. 1894) and his story "Johnnyboy" (*Idler*, July 1894). See also sketch 4, Harte and Roman as drawn by Boyd.

3. BH's "The Mystery of the Hacienda," *Pall Mall Magazine* 2 (Dec. 1893):315–39.

4. BH invited Alexander and Mary Boyd to correct his Scottish dialogue.

215. TO CLARA SCHNEIDER, 30 AUGUST 1894

Imperial Hotel, Malvern.
August 30 *1894* . . .

My dear Mrs Schneider,

I hope you will not blame me for being so late in answering your always welcome letter, but when I came here from London I was very much run down, and was trying to escape to some more bracing air—where my usual *holiday work* had to be done. Your letter was forwarded to me from London, and this is my first chance to reply. I have not yet found the great benefit of the place—indeed I think your "birth day" letter to me, the satisfaction of your remembrances, and my own recollection of my pleasant days in your house cheered and "braced" me more than the climate. It seems that you go once a day to the top of the highest hills here for the bracing air, but as it is a ride and toilsome climb of three or four hours, and that the hotel in which you eat and sleep simply stifles and stagnates on the hillside below I cant see the benefit to *me* who have to work at least *six* hours out of the *24* in my room. How I wish I were sometime in that delightful dreary old hotel at Rolandseck—where I once had a holiday with you and your husband[1]—or the better, your Dutch hotel at Cleve where we all went with my cousin![2] You must not be surprised if some day, I drop into Crefeld and seize you and your little girl and "Rudolf" and carry you off for a week to one of those strongholds, as the old robber knights used to do!

It is very odd, but someone sent *me* a copy of that same *Washington Post* with the ridiculous photographs and quite as ridiculous biography. You have seen some of my photographs of the "*present day*"—but I think I must send you another taken a week or two ago to show you that I do not *look* like President Cleveland!—however good he may be.[3]

The summer has been dull and rainy and *dark*—as the English winter. I went once or twice to stay with an old friend (Lord Compton) at Compton Wynyates in Warwickshire—a wonderful old medieval house, with drawbridge, and quadrangle and an old hall with minstrel gallery, and the old *hole in the roof* (now boarded over) to let the smoke of the fire escape.[4] My bedroom was over the old postcastle's—and was on *two floors*—that is, one end of the room was lifted higher than the other like an altar or dais with an oak railing across and I went up four steps to my drawing table and fire place and down four steps to my bed!

I was also a little while in Wales—and a little while at Weybridge with *my son* and his wife—who are staying there.[5] I do not know if I told you that he had married a *rich* young widow older than himself! Think of my being a grandfather!—but I wont believe it—its all wrong!

I thought I had written to you, my dear friend, *after* the loss of your mother—but you know how deeply I sympathize with you.

I will write you soon again. I must close now to go *to work*! With love to you all believe me

Always affect[ly]
Bret Harte

P.S. Pray pardon this greasy hotel paper—and greasier hotel ink. I am afraid it makes my usually illegible scrawl—undecipherable! You can write to 109 Lancaster Gate, London—my letters are forwarded here.

P.P.S. I am sending you some little photos of Malvern.[6]

Provenience: UVa (ALS).

1. Writing Clara Schneider on 5 September 1889 (UVa), BH had reminisced about "the little hotel opposite the Drachenfels where you and I and your husband stayed on one of our excursions. Do you remember how we all took our dinner *al fresco* on the terrace, and then went for a sail on the Rhine ferry boat?"

2. Writing Clara Schneider on 29 November 1890 (UVa), BH had recalled "the small frontier town in Holland" where "the queer streets went upstairs and the hallways of the houses were painted, and where we had dinner at a deserted watering place hotel."

3. BH refers to Edward Marshall's "The Novelist of '49," *Washington Post*, 15 July 1894, p. 17, cols. 1–3. The article is illustrated with a line drawing based on photograph 22, Harte in 1894.

4. The ancestral home of Lord Alwyne Frederick Compton (1855–1911). Built between 1480 and 1520, Compton Wynyates is one of the most famous Tudor mansions in England.

5. FH and Aline Harte (d. 1920) had been married early in 1894. However, they may have been together as early as late 1890, when BH wrote his sister Eliza (14 Sept. 1890, Bancroft, MSS 88/181 C) that his son "seems to be the victim of a woman who has sacrificed everything to him, *but* her income of $6000 a year—for which she holds him in debt for $10,000! This may be '*infatuation*' as Anna calls it—on her part. I dont see it!"

6. BH encloses several postcards.

216. TO CLARA SCHNEIDER, 20 NOVEMBER 1894

109, Lancaster Gate, W.

Novem 20th '94

My dear Mrs Schneider,

I had been suffering from a heavy cold when I got your charming letter, but I read every line of it, and then sent off the book that you might know I was thinking of you, intending to write you later, when I was a little less stuffy and stupid. Alas! my cold still hangs on, although I went out of town for a day or two thinking the change of air might break it up, and I am afraid you must take me as I am—sniffling, and heavy,—fluent only in the eyes and nose!

I have not been at all well since I wrote you from Malvern so I fell an easy prey to the first cold of the season—which has been very wet and damp and depressing. But I think I was a little overworked to finish a long story,[1] and that left me rather weak. But enough about *myself*!—I began it partly to answer your question about my health, and partly to excuse the delay in answering. I wish I had something to tell you that was interesting; your letters will always be more entertaining than mine for you tell me of people and things I knew in dear old Crefeld and Düsseldorf, and I cannot, I fear, interest you in my surroundings which you dont know. I wish I could see you; I have always been hoping that I might come to Germany again; now I am wondering if *you* will ever come *here*; doesn't your husbands business sometimes bring him to Manchester or Birmingham—and couldn't you accompany him? But I shall try very hard to get across the channel this winter; (I have not been out of England for eight years!), and once I am on the continent—it will be easy to come to you at Crefeld. Then we will go and dine at

Düsseldorf at the "Door Nail" Restaurant,[2]—and if it shall be Carnival time we will all go to the Melkarten Ball![3] But I am forgetting that you are in mourning[4]—I am afraid I am forgetting the flight of time and all the changes since the old days. However I believe it is best to forget these changes, and keep our youth, and if we do meet, it will be exactly as then—we will believe we are not a day older, (I *know* that I am not a bit *wiser*), and you and I and your husband will enjoy ourselves just as foolishly as we did in the brave days of the Consulate, and you and Rudolf will perceive and pretend that you dont see any wrinkles or crows feet on the brow of the "Herr Consul" of old days, who is always your affectionate friend

Bret Harte

Provenience: UVa (ALS).

1. The serial novel *Clarence*, syndicated in the New York *Sun*, *San Francisco Chronicle*, and other papers between 25 November 1894 and 20 January 1895.

2. Writing Clara Schneider on 29 November 1890 (UVa), BH had reminisced about "a dinner I once gave, at the Thurnagel Restaurant, to you and some Düsseldorf friends."

3. See note 2 to letter 165.

4. See letter 215.

217. TO T. EDGAR PEMBERTON, 15 JANUARY 1895

109, Lancaster Gate, W.
Jany 15, '95

My dear Pemberton,[1]

First, let me say that during several visits lately to the vicinity of Birmingham, I have always been regretting that, what I supposed was your *complete* removal to Broadway,—prevented me from reviving an old acquaintance.[2] I am delighted *now* to find that you are dating your letter from the pleasant suburb where *I* once enjoyed your charming hospitality.

Now, as to the possible play that is in the little romance of "Bolinas Plain:"[3] you know, there is always the doubt if what is dramatic in ordinary *prose narrative*, is equally dramatic in *theatrical representation*. The story is but a single *episode*, and I am afraid that much would have to be imported into it that might weaken its dramatic intensity!

But I am far from dissuading you to make the attempt, and perhaps we could *together* make something out of it, or I could at least make some suggestions regarding it. You might give me an idea of your conception. Perhaps we might talk it over. I think of coming up again to the vicinity of Birmingham, *next week*, and we might—(if you are still there,) meet at your home at Edgbaston. With regards to your wife

Yours always
Bret Harte

P.S. I removed some two years ago to 109 Lancaster Gate—and your letter was consequently delayed by redirection.

Provenience: Berg !ALS).

1. T. Edgar Pemberton (1849–1905), dramatic editor of the *Birmingham Post* from 1882 until 1900.

2. BH had first corresponded with Pemberton in February 1879 before his lecture in Birmingham the next month.

3. "The Judgment of Bolinas Plain" appeared in *Pall Mall Magazine* 5 (Jan. 1895):7–26. The BH/Pemberton theatrical adaptation would be entitled *Sue*.

218. TO ANNA HARTE, 30 MARCH 1895

109, Lancaster Gate W.

30 Mar '95

My dear Anna,

I have waited until the last moment to send you this draft in the miserable hope that that miserable Frank would pay me back the £20 that he borrowed from me out of the sum I have raised to send your monthly £50. I told him that I had no money—you know I have not as much to support myself, you and the children as he has for himself and wife and one child—and that if he did not repay me I would have to send you only £30. I need not add that he has *not* repaid, nor do I see the slightest chance of getting it from him.

I at first thought that, as you were so exceedingly sympathetic over him, you would be content to get along with the £30 until he could pay the remaining £20 to you, but as there seems no prospect of his doing anything of the kind, I had this morning myself to borrow enough to make up your monthly draft. He probably thought that I *might*, and is quite satisfied with himself, his conduct, and his extraordinary sagacity, as he has always been brought up to believe. When you tell me that he is my own son, I do not see why that should blind me to faults in him which *I* know I never had, whatever others I may *have*; I know I never lived on any *woman*—mother, wife or mistress—but was content to do any honest work that would support me, without believing myself elected to superior work or to be supported by others. I fail also to see where Frank "has suffered"; during his whole misplaced career on the stage, he had advantages that the greatest actors have never had, and availed him nothing. He risked a scandal by marrying a women with $5000 a year,[1] and since is content to live on you or me also. And all this without having any irresistible vices—like gambling and drinking—but being inordinarily conceited and satisfied with his own sagacity. Your motherly tenderness to him is quite natural but you will forgive me if I sometimes think you have unwittingly nursed his vanity and self approbation.

I do not know how or where it will all end. I only know that my hope in him—and the feeling that I had after his marriage, that *one*, at least, of our children has completely settled—although not exactly as I would wish—is gone!

Your affect
Limick

Provenience: SFPL (ALS).

1. See note 5 to letter 215.

219. TO GERTRUDE GRISWOLD, 28 MAY 1895

28th May '95

My dear Gerty,

I could scarcely believe it was your familiar handwriting again when I opened your letter, although I dont know *why* you should doubt if I would *answer* it, unless your conscience has been frightfully worrying you for *not* having written to me in all these years! But I forgive you my child, and am sorry to hear that you have been ill—even though it may be a just punishment for your neglect of your noble and beautiful uncle, and that Christian and perfect example he set you and your mother—often at considerable pains and anguish to himself—during your last stay in London.[1] I may even go further and say I will be glad to see you! That is the kind of forgiving pere I am!

I expect to be in London when you arrive, but I have been working so hard during the winter and spring, and have not been out of England since you left, that I have thought of taking a holiday *on the Continent—in August*. Perhaps you might go there too, and we could make a little party in which you might utilize your invincible charm of manner, your delicate effrontery, your sublime mendacity, your knowledge of foreign languages and cheap hotels and act as one Cook—I mean the great expediter and courier, and not the culinary servitor—and be the guide philosopher and friend! Perhaps we might go to Paris. Of course, my dear child, although this is an advanced and liberal age I know that you would not take me anywhere where you would not go yourself or even take your sainted mother![2]

Since I left St Johns Wood I know very little of it, and couldnt give you any advice about lodgings—nor tell you as much about it as Miss Carmichael. I am still with the Van de Veldes, but in a new house at Lancaster Gate, which Madame bought after her mother's death when she came into her property. But the *household* has never been the same since her husbands death, and since the children—(the children who were to come with me in the carriage when I called on you in Baker St!) have grown up, gone away or married! It is almost a foreign household to me now, with these changes and their new relatives, and there only lingers the memory of the old London house I came to—and where you met me years ago! I am away from it often; so are the family; so if you write to me *here* perhaps you had better make sure by *also* writing to me at my club—"The Royal Thames Yacht Club, 7 Albemarle St" in case there is no one at home. Meantime I will make some enquiries about lodgings, but I think you will find St Johns Wood changed and not as pleasant and quiet as it was. London, however, is never quite full at the end of July and you might have no difficulty in finding something to suit your fancy, at your own figures, a little nearer the Park.

I find I have written you a long letter. Loquacity is the fault of old age I know! (I forgot to say I was quite senile and doddering, and only remember things that happened forty years ago!) but I dont let loquacity affect my pen, which, Heaven knows! has enough to do for me as a bread-winner! I will write you again. With affectionate remembrance to your mother. Accept, Mademoiselle, the distinguished sentiments of my profoundest considerations!

Your affec. uncle
Bret Harte

Provenience: Huntington (HM 25924).

1. BH and the Griswolds had often visited in London in the mid-1880s, prior to the Griswolds' departure for America on 23 October 1886 (diary, Berg).

2. BH subsequently traveled to Warwickshire in company with his niece. See letter 221.

220. TO T. EDGAR PEMBERTON, 11 JUNE 1895

11th of June '95

My dear Pemberton

I am sending you Act 3d with the interpolated pages and changes—in all about 10 pp. of new matter. That isn't much, but it has taken me *nearly a week* to do it! and I have a horrible feeling that it may be only that much time—taken from my work—and thrown away! I should like to have *finished it*, but my own work has been looking up at me so reproachfully that I feel I really could not spare another line. So I have left it for you to wind up with the reconciliation of the parties in the good old stage way. I even dare to hope that I have made that winding up easier, by the half humorous half realistic disposal of the Vigilance Committee, and the release of the Sheriff. *His* release is a sort of climax, which I have also left to you to use as you choose—merely indicating it in my text. As there is now no "killing"—the end need not be so grim. I have, as I before indicated, softened Silas brutalities a little, and even subjected him to the punishment of a ridiculous attitude at the end, which I think the audience always enjoy quite as much as more active castigation. I have made the Judge more of a character—and really the symbol of the reckless, illogical but sincere Lyncher. I have kept his historic name—"Lynch." I like Silas immensely and you can add anything you like to him—in the new lines we have laid down. I have given the acrobat a *professional chance* to save his life as you see, which will account for his appearing in his costume (as the Constable nabbed him at a performance).[1]

I should be delighted to come to you about *the 24th* to that week end, and think I can manage to do so. We ought to then *finish* the play *completely*—if not really *before* then. Perhaps I may even be able to run up this week-end (to keep you over Saturday night only.) But it should not interfere with, nor take the place of, my B'way visit—from the 24th to 29th—if I do so.

Will you forgive me for not having acknowledged your newspaper and the cuttings in regard to your success with "Edmund Kean." You *knew* I was delighted with them—even if my congratulations were forgotten in my preoccupation with "Sue." And the article on "plagarisms"—was capital, and read better even than in your *MS.*[2]

I quite agree with all you say and suggest about the Kendals.[3] I met Tom the other day at luncheon at the Garrick Club and he was, as usual, wondering "why" I didn't write a play![4] But then all actors say that to me—it is merely talk—and, of course, I said nothing to him about our little experiment.

Drop me a line when you get this. With kindest remembrances to your wife

Yours always
B.H.

Provenience: Yale (ALS).

1. The character Jim Wynd escapes from Judge Lynch's courtroom at the close of *Sue* by leaping through a window. His "leap for life" is, as one reviewer suggested, "possibly the most sensational incident in that picturesque play" (*Boston Herald*, 20 Dec. 1896, p. 31, col. 4).

2. A copy of "Plagiarism Extraordinary" (Birmingham *Town Crier*, 8 June 1895) survives in the archives of the University Research Library,

UCLA. Pemberton suggests that G. B. Burgin's "The Dance at the Four Corners" is modeled on BH's "Tennessee's Partner."

3. In 1900, Pemberton would publish a biography of William Kendal (1843–1917) and Madge Kendal (1849–1935).

4. Probably the actor Thomas W. S. Robertson (1858–95), who was the Kendals' nephew.

221. TO MARY S. BOYD, 15 JULY 1895

Manor House Hotel, Royal
Leamington Spa. . . .
July 15th 95

My dear Mrs Boyd,[1]

You will smile at this familiar paper and wonder that in my wanderings I have got no further from London than this. But I am here with my niece, Miss Griswold, and her friend and fellow traveller Miss Neale, and I have just despatched them to Warwick Castle to see the sights together, for I really cannot "do" the old familiar "shows" again! The house at Lancaster Gate is topsy turvy, and the servants are going, and like the raven that went out in the Ark, I find no "rest for the sole of my feet," and I am here *en-route* to *I dont know where yet*! I have many plans—but no preferences nor any certainty of movement. Colonel Collins[2] wants me to go to *Aix la Chappelle* with him—where he has to undergo "the Cure"; my niece wants me to go with her and her friend to Paris; perhaps I may combine both and so, for a while, get out of this island—but all is yet unsettled. I shall, I *expect*, return to London, day after to-morrow, then I may go to my friend Pemberton at B'way for the week end. I may go to Crewe[3] or I may go later to Compton Wynyates—they are all "on the cards." But I do not see where I am to find the *rest* and the *quiet* I am supposed to want. As my niece has her friend with her—(who is an enthusiastic sight seer and a worshipper of Gerty) they take the trouble of sight-seeing off my hands—and leave me to myself and that aforesaid "rest." They are both enthusiasts of a new kind of religious "fad," which they tell me is sweeping America called "Christian Science"! They wonder I have never heard of it! Have you? They have books upon it; they expound it to *me*! Our conversation is not flippant, nor wildly entertaining. My niece is serious, and her friend teaches *Latin* and cognate things in a Seminary at Baltimore!

It was very nice of you to write to me, and overlook my long silence—which was only that I was greatly preoccupied with many things for the future, which have to be settled *now*. And I never can write letters "on the wing"—it always seems like having a protracted conversation on the street corner! I will write to you again, as soon as I know anything definite of my movements. Do send me that book of Mallocks[4]—if not too late. I should like to read it—though I may not agree with you about the hero (I will afterwards send it to Mrs Hindley, and pay you the difference between the reduced market values! Eh! Sirs! but I'm getting "corny" in my old age!) Give my love to your husband and as much of it to Stuart[5] as will do him good;—dont spoil him with sweets as is your fashion! Pity me in my roving loneliness!

Always yours
Bret Harte

P.S. You will have to send to the Club—The Royal Thames Yacht Club—which will always forward my letters to me, until I advise you of a more settled address.

B.H.

Provenience: UCLA (ALS).

1. Mary Boyd was the wife of Alexander S. Boyd. See also her memoir "Some Letters of Bret Harte," *Harper's* 105 (Oct. 1902):773–76.

2. Arthur Collins (1845–1911), Gentleman Usher to Queen Victoria and later to King Edward VII.

3. BH had befriended the Earl of Crewe. See letter 226.

4. Mary Boyd had offered to loan BH a novel by W. H. Mallock (1849–1923), perhaps *A Human Document* (1892), his most recent.

5. The Boyds' son.

222. TO CLARA SCHNEIDER, 20 AUGUST 1895[1]

Hotel Jung, Rudesheim . . .
den Tuesday afternoon

My dear Mrs Schneider,

Your telegram reached me just as I was leaving the hotel for the day, as we were engaged to come here to-day, or should certainly have come to Crefeld which I would have much preferred. I expect to return to Cologne or Bonn to-morrow—unless I should receive a telegram bidding me come at once to *Switzerland*![2]—and if I do come to Bonn I shall certainly see you at Crefeld in a day or two.[3] But I will write in ample time.

I would much rather see you than hear your voice through a telephone. I know I shall find *you* looking just as you always did, but you forget that years have changed *me*—who was so much your *elder* in the old days, and I tremble! Perhaps Mr Schneider may have returned by the time I can get to Crefeld.

It has been a very hot and crowded journey here—not nearly as nice as the journey you and your husband made with me and Callie in the old days. In great haste.

Always your old friend
Bret Harte

Provenience: UVa (ALS).

1. Dated by reference to BH's letters to Clara Schneider (22 Aug. 1895, UVa) and T. E. Pemberton (23 Aug. 1895, Yale).

2. There can be no doubt who would summon BH: As he wrote A. P. Watt on 18 August 1895 (*Letters*, 407) Mme Van de Velde had already left for Switzerland.

3. BH hastened to Switzerland, then returned to England via France. "I found I could not return by way of Germany when my holiday was ended in Switzerland; I had already overstayed my time," he explained to Clara Schneider (28 Dec. 1895, UVa). He never saw the Schneiders again.

223. TO ANNA HARTE, 25 AUGUST 1895

Hôtel Byron
Villeneuve (Lac de Genève)
Villeneuve, le August 25th *1895*

My dear Nan,

At last after being nearly twelve years in England without change of scene or climate, I have managed to get a holiday for a few weeks in Switzerland. I wish it could be, as the Doctor orders, a complete *rest* and change, but alas, I must still work only I hope to do so under better conditions, and perhaps freshened by the pure air of the lake—although I am not "up" in the "bracing" air of the higher altitudes. Some of my doctors think I am better out of an exciting air, and that I dont require much stimulation. However, this is only an experiment, for if I do not find myself much better I shall go somewhere higher up. This whole country you know is simply given up to hotels and *pensions* that invade the very crags of the mountains, and give an artificial ballet-scene to everything. The dear old Sierras are, after all, infinitely finer with their freshness, their beauty, their absolute and wholesome rudeness and sincerity, and I never knew before how I really loved them, and how they have taken such a hold on my life; here everything is grand and spectacular—but in the very heart of the wilderness there is a suspicion of *drains* and the smell of French cooking comes in at your window with the breath of the pines. I have never been to this more popular and frequented part of Switzerland before; when I was last on the continent I went to Zurich and along the Wallen See which were not as tourist haunted.

I am sending this to the London Bank with the request that they will enclose a draft to you in another envelope, beneath the one I shall address. You had better however write to me to the care of "The Royal Thames Yacht Club, Albemarle St, London," and I can have the letters forwarded to me to any change of address, as the house at Lancaster Gate will be closed while the family are visiting their relatives in Belgium and Berlin.[1] I was a few days in London and at Folkestone with Frank and his wife before I left; his affairs are still very hopeless and his creditors are resolved upon bankruptcy proceedings.

I wish of course I was with you in the Adirondacks rather than here, but I have been very much alarmed at the effect of the recent hot weather—which has been phenomenal on the continent—and is certainly as extreme as anything I ever experienced at home. I have for the first time *in eighteen years!* known what it was to drip with perspiration *all day and night!* and it has left me as limp as a rag. I will write you soon again; with love to the children, always your affectionate

Limick

Provenience: UCLA (ALS).

1. His implication here notwithstanding, BH has joined Mme Van de Velde in Switzerland. See note 2 to letter 222.

224. TO FLORENCE HENNIKER, 31 AUGUST 1895

Hôtel Byron
Villeneuve (Lac de Genève)
Villeneuve, le 31st August *1895*

My dear Mrs Henniker,

Your thoughtful note reached me here a few days ago, where I am "holidaying" on the Continent for the first time in twelve years. Indeed I hardly know how I got here nor why I came. I started from Cologne with Colonel Collins and a young friend of his to "do" the Rhine, by boat and rail, as I had so often done it in my old German days, but we dropped into stifling weather, and into *local* holiday crowds, and after four or five days of torrid American heat we parted—at Bonn in the garden of the dear old Grand Royal Hotel, and I escaped by night over Strassburg and Bâle into this lake—which I had never visited in the old days—but where I am better than ever! Of course the air is exquisitely light and balmy but I came abroad to be "braced[")—and here I am lotus eating in the shade of these lovely terraces—with a panorama before me which is more unreal and about as impossible as a stage effect! Indeed I dare not go up to the houses at Montreux and knock at a door lest I should find it canvass. I sit very carefully on the stone benches, lest they should collapse suddenly, and I shouldnt think of picking a flower *anywhere* without expecting to find it "wired" by the Great Hotel company who run Switzerland as Daudet suggests.[1] There is a fine fleet of mechanical toy steamboats which pass my windows with musically tinkling bells, but I fail to find Chillon gloomy, and I dont think anybody ever suffered there but the tourists. I believe the Dukes of Savoy ran it as a hotel in the old days and there is a frightful similarity in Bonivards column to the gorgeous pillar that is on my balcony. I went up Territet-Glion, in an exaggerated "lift" with the sensation of being pulled up by my coat collar and thence to Caux by an incredible railway and further up to Rochers d'Naye—about

6000 feet—and got back to the hotel for dinner—but I wasn't braced! There was the usual panorama of snow peaks to be sure—not as fine as the Righi—but I only got homesick. I wouldn't give a mile of the dear old Sierras for 10,000 kilometers of the Vaud!

I shall linger here longer—I really haven't the energy to change—and eventually go on to Chamonix, or perhaps back to Germany when it is cooler and visit some friends.[2] Write me again from Marienbad; I'm glad you like it. Even if I shouldnt be here, your letter will be forwarded to me.

I got Mr Watsons book and liked it very much.[3] Thank you both. I have not heard from the Comptons since they went to Southend.[4] I called there a few days before I left London, but didn't see them and was much disappointed. But I believe Lady C. is much better.

Yours always
Bret Harte

P.S. Pardon the chromatic and lithographic epistle but I havent any other paper.[5]

B.H.

Provenience: UVa (ALS).

1. Alphonse Daudet (1840–97). BH cites Daudet's *Tartarin on the Alps*, first published in English translation by Henry Frith in 1888.

2. See note 3 to letter 222.

3. Probably *At the First Corner and Other Stories* (London: John Lane; Boston: Roberts Bros., 1895) by Henry Brereton Marriott Watson (1863–1921).

4. See note 4 to letter 215.

5. BH refers to the hotel stationery on which he is writing.

225. TO ANNA HARTE, 30 NOVEMBER 1895

109, Lancaster Gate W.

Novem 30th '95

My dear Anna,

I wish I could send you this draft *earlier*, but I am still behindhand in my work. Since my return to England after that six weeks sojourn in Switzerland, I have contracted a severe cold, and have quite lost the vigor and freshness of mind and body which I brought back with me. I, who never had a *cough* among *my many ills* before, am getting one settled upon me as a winter burden. I had one last year, and unless I can get rid out of this foggy, damp island for a month or two again, I fear it will become chronic. So do not be surprised if I write you some day that I am trying to "winter" in Switzerland or the South of France! Frank is in London, and I am trying to make him believe that he would be much better in future on the continent. With love to the children always, dear Nan,

Your affec
Limick

Provenience: UVa (ALS).

226. TO ANNA HARTE, 18 DECEMBER 1895

Fryston Hall, Ferrybridge,
Yorkshire.
18th Decem 95

My dear Nan,

I tried very hard to get the enclosed draft for $300.00 early, but it has only just followed me here, and I am posting it in great haste that it may reach you about Xmas time, so that you can use the extra $50.00 for presents for yourself and the children.

I am here on a visit to the Earl of Crewe[1]—the son of the late Lord Houghton, whom you remember breakfasted with us once at Eliza's in Fifth Avenue[2]—and though I have often been invited before I have never yet succeeded in effecting my intention. Even now, I have only come on the promise of Lord Crewe that I should be allowed to work while here, and I have brought with me some unfinished MSS which I want to complete by Xmas, if I consent to stay during the Holidays. Everybody here is very much excited over the Presidents Message, which they all believe means War between the two countries![3] Heaven forbid!—for *all* reasons—and not the least, the selfish one, that it would be ruinous to my future, for I should of course no longer remain in England—the only place where I could earn my daily bread. For much as I love my own country—it does not love *me* sufficiently to enable me to support myself there by my pen!

Frank is getting along much better in his new economics and I hope soon will be out of debt. God bless you and the children, Nan, with love and Xmas greetings from your ever affectionate

Limick

Provenience: UVa (ALS).

1. Robert Offley Ashburton Crewe-Milnes, Earl of Crewe (1858–1945), was a prominent Tory politician, member of the House of Lords, and president of the Royal Literary Fund.

2. See note 6 to letter 66.

3. In a message to Congress on 17 December 1895, President Cleveland threatened war with Great Britain over a disputed boundary between British Guiana and Venezuela.

227. TO T. EDGAR PEMBERTON, 18 DECEMBER 1895[1]

Fryston Hall, Ferrybridge,
Yorkshire.
Wednesday

My dear Pemberton,

I enclose the *Scenario* of the 3d Act of "Rushbrook." It seems to me perfectly satisfactory, as a whole, and I think the details will fill the Act completely when they are elaborated.

Wyndham[2] seemed to me to be greatly interested and sincere, and a *little disappointed* that *more* had not been done on the play itself—and that he was only to have the *scenario.* He seemed to think it almost a *fait accompli,*[3] and spoke to one of the guests at the luncheon—Sir Gerald Fitzgerald[4]—*jocularly,* regarding a difference of opinion between us, that he was obliged to be very civil and polite to me for I was writing a play for him! Of course Fitzgerald was very eager to know all about it, but as he was an old acquaintance of mine, I begged him not to ask any more questions, and to let the knowledge go no further.

I am writing this in a great hurry to catch the post. I shall be here a few days longer but if I return I will telegraph to you where to send the *Scenario.*

Yours always
Bret Harte

Provenience: Yale (ALS).

1. Dated by Pemberton's gloss on the holograph.

2. Sir Charles Wyndham (1837–1919), a prominent actor-manager, subject of a biography by Pemberton (London: Hutchinson, 1904). BH had seen him about the play on December 15.

3. Nothing came of this overture. BH wrote Pemberton on 18 December 1896 (Yale) that he still had received no reply from Wyndham "regarding the *scenario* of Rushbrook. Shall I write him?—or shall I accept, what is possible the fact—that he is not particularly interested in it?" BH and Pemberton returned to the scenario several months later and developed it into a full script. See letter 237 and accompanying note 2.

4. Sir (William) Gerald S. V. Fitzgerald (1841–1910).

228. TO ANNA HARTE, 26 FEBRUARY 1896

74, Lancaster Gate, W.[1]
26th Feby '96

My dear Nan,

I have been through quite a siege of rheumatism, which is giving way now to one of my winter colds in the head and throat! For three or four weeks my right hand was so cramped and painful that I could hardly write and the little finger is still so swollen at the second joint—that it reminds me of my poor mothers hand in the later years of her life. The doctor says it is a kind of *gout*—and proposes that later I should go to some Baths—here or on the Continent. It is too bad as I have a big job of writing—a long novel on my hands—cramped as they are! It has been of course a little more expensive to me since I have left Madame Van de Veldes house—although I have now much more freedom and independence than when I was in a private family—but even that little expense is a good deal to me just now and a "cure" at a watering place is a *luxury*—in the sense of cost. I dont want to be a cripple quite yet however, and I must try to get rid of my *gout* some way.

I suppose you know Frank is at Brighton—but if Madame V. de V. takes a country place, (as she thinks of doing,) she might let it to Frank and I, when she is in her town house and doesnt require it. It would be a great change from London, which is always unsuitable to me in winter. I should have gone to Switzerland this last winter, but I dreaded being so far alone, and among strangers.

I am so sorry, Nan, to hear of your repeated illnesses. Surely, what you call the "grippe" must be very different from what we call the "influenza" here—people dont have it *so many times*! They *cant*—it is too *severe*!

I enclose the draft which I had hoped to send you earlier in the month, but I am afraid I will not be able to do so before the spring—May—when my novel will be finished. With love to all the children always dear Nan affectly Your Limick

Provenience: UVa (ALS).

1. BH has moved into a flat a few doors from the Van de Velde home.

229. TO ANNA HARTE, 30 MAY 1896

74, Lancaster Gate, W.
May 30 '96

My dear Nan,

I have had a very hard spell of work which I am just finishing, and I hope next month to send you the draft a little earlier. A good deal of this work has been done in the country for I was really too exhausted to do it in town. Frank and his wife were with me, visiting Madame Van de Velde in her new country home—a little cottage in a very rural but very delightful part of Hampshire.[1] I was consequently kept up by the pure air and healthful surroundings, and was enabled to do my work better. But *Holiday*!—I have had none!

I and my collaborateur a very pleasant literary man and dramatist of some ability, have completed a contract with an *American Manager* for the production of a play we have written together.[2] You may remember that I told you I was engaged upon it some time ago.[3] We did not think to produce it first in America—but we thought it advisable not to lose the offer. I will write you the particulars later, but *please dont say anything about it* yet. I *hope* something may come of it to relieve me of this continuous strain. With love to the children!—always, dear Nan, your

Limick

Provenience: UVa (ALS).

1. Arford House. See photograph 23.

2. For details about this agreement, see "How Frohman Got 'Sue,'" *Boston Herald*, 29 Nov. 1896, p. 29, cols. 1–2.

3. BH had first mentioned to AH his collaboration on the play on 26 January 1895 (*Letters*, 397–98).

230. TO FLORENCE HENNIKER, 4 SEPTEMBER 1896

Arford House, Headley, Hants,
Septem. 4th '96

My dear Mrs Henniker,

It seems a very long time since I received your "Scarlet and Grey"[1]—yet I have only, just now, found a moment to write—or rather *talk* with you about it. First of all, let me say, very honestly, that I think it is *a very marked advance* in style and conciseness on your previous work much as I was pleased with that. You seem to hold yourself more securely and confidently—to "ride straighter," but why, in the name of heaven!—which I believe is really a *happy* place!—do you ride through such gloomy bye-roads, and to such a dismal home-coming in the end! You must be awfully young yet and awfully happy to be able to think of such hopeless things! The stories are all well told, and strong, but the short ones are too continuous, some of them are too sad and hopeless to be even *pathetic*. Do you not know that human nature revolts at too much suffering and takes refuge at last in apathy or incredulity! And where the *fateful* and "hopeless" come in, human sympathy steps out. But luckily, in real life, there is always some relief, some hope, and it is with *that* we sympathize and cry over! Your stories are, to my mind, too "grey" and I dont see where the "Scarlet" comes in—except it is in the soldiers' coats, and that seems only to pick them out for your own sharp-shooters! Now, please be more cheerful, and take a few, healthy, strong soldiers to play with, the next time, who haven't got the seeds of consumption or fever germs in them, and dont succumb to disappointment but let them go *roaring* out of your pages, even if they take the wrong girl or somebody's wife with them! Perhaps this is only *my* taste, or I am getting too old to be made unhappy without growling, (for it is only the young who can fasten upon sorrow.)—and I read these stories in bed, and rose up in the morning embittered against the world! and found fault with my bath, and distrusted the servants!

Even your lighter story the "Successful Intrusion"—which is full of fine strokes of character-drawing, and delicate touches of observation—has a *denouement* too sad for its previous comedy. That wretched Dick Turpin had to break *two* womens hearts before you let him go—which wasn't at all *necessary* to his amusing imposture. In *real* life I dont think he *could* have done it! A woman can stand being made a fool of—alone by herself—but she *cant* stand it, and *wont* stand it to be made a fool of with *others*. If your Dick Turpin had run away with *one* of the women—it doesn't matter which—it would have been all right! But when he left them *both* and didn't run away with anything but *money*, depend upon it, they got together and just *loathed* him—but *didn't* break their hearts![2]

For all that, as I said before, I think the book is very strong, and I congratulate you upon your success—whether its too sad for *my* amusement or not. And you can remember always that with a majority of story readers as "Tony Lumpkin" says, "the more they liked it, the more it made 'em cry."[3] Let me know where you are and how you are! I am sending this at a venture to your London address to be forwarded.

Yours always
Bret Harte

Provenience: UVa (ALS).

1. *In Scarlet and Grey* (Boston: Roberts Bros.; London: John Lane, 1896) includes "The Spectre of the Real," written by Henniker and Thomas Hardy in collaboration.

2. BH compares Oswald, the villain of "A Successful Intrusion," to the English brigand Dick Turpin.

3. Oliver Goldsmith's *She Stoops to Conquer*, act II: "They said they liked the book the better the more it made them cry."

231. TO T. EDGAR PEMBERTON, 4 OCTOBER 1896[1]

Arford House,
Headley, Hants.

My dear Pemberton,

I am returning the notices with Frohmans letter—which is, I suppose, the most satisfying of all. I dare say the critics are right in pointing out the anticlimaxes of the latter portion of the play, which I think came from our endeavors to make a *conventional ending.* (I am always convinced this is more or less *a mistake*, and *always a blunder* in plays that are *on unconventional subjects*!) But I am amused at what they call the *unreality* of the *characters*—these critics who smothered *Trilby*![2] and know nothing of life outside of New York—although this incongruity of subject and ending was doubtless what they had in their minds.[3] I quite agree with you that Frohman's act—in taking the play on tour for the season—is a fair augery of success, and the evidence that Miss Russell had made a "hit" in the character is strongly corroborative.[4] But we shall see! If we can get the play "on" here—*we* could make the alterations *ourselves* and see to the rehearsals *ourselves*!

I hope your wife got the 5 o'clock tea table I sent her in good condition. I shall be here for a week or two. Are you really *better*—or are you humbugging again?

Yours always B. H.

P.S. I am very much inclined to like Frohman as he reveals himself in his letters—honest, straightforward, genuine, and energetic!

B. H.

Provenience: Yale (ALS).

1. Dated by Pemberton's gloss on the letter.

2. Paul M. Potter's dramatic version of *Trilby*, based on the immensely popular romance by BH's fellow clubman George du Maurier, opened at the Garden Theatre in New York on 15 April 1895 and held the stage for 208 performances. It was later performed 254 times at the Haymarket Theatre in London.

3. *Sue* premiered at Hoyt's Theatre in New York on 15 September 1896 and ran until 10 October 1896. The reviewer for the *New York Times* (16 Sept. 1896, p. 5, col. 2) complained of its "lack of rational motive," and the *New York Tribune* (16 Sept. 1896, p. 7, col. 1) asserted "there is no truth in it, nor any depth. Every character is extravagant and every incident improbable." Howells lambasted the play in *Harper's Weekly* (10 Oct. 1896, 998): it was "almost as bad in structure and false in motive as a play could very well be." On the other hand, BH's old nemesis, the New York *World* (16 Sept. 1896, p. 9, col. 5), declared it was "almost a great play," and James

Stetson in *Life* (1 Oct. 1896, 252) praised its "wholesome tone" and "literary quality."

4. The American actress Annie Russell (1864–1936) was famous for playing ingenues and rustic maidens.

232. TO ANNA HARTE, 11 OCTOBER 1896

Arford House
Headley, Hants, Octo 11th '96

My dear Nan,

I was obliged to *wire* you a draft on the 9th as I *only then* received a remittance from my Boston publisher, for which I had been waiting two months, and which had been promised *positively* by the 25th September! I am dreadfully sorry—and you must have been amazed at receiving no letter—but I think you got the money, almost as quickly as if I had sent it by post on the 1st inst, though not as quickly as you wished for this time.

Your letter about "Sue," which I received two days ago,[1] was very appreciative and rather *charming* although I am still very uncertain about the actual *success* of the piece. Of course I have received the critical notices, some good, some bad; and the letter from Mr Frohman, announcing the fact that *the actors* seemed to have made "a hit" in the leading roles, but all is yet too vague for any reliance on the future. You understand that I dont care for *criticism*, that I am quite content if the papers abuse the play as long as the audience like it, and the thing pays. For the rest, I know it is a *wholesome* play, and my conscience is clear. I am even quite willing that my *collaborateur* Mr Pemberton, should receive *all* the praise for its success—as he has worked very hard upon it, and it is *he* who succeeded in placing the play with Frohman, who, I dare say, would not have looked at it in *my* hands—nor would any other American manager have troubled himself about it. Mr. Frohman now writes to my *collaborateur* that it is "booked for a tour" and that is about all *I* know of it. He communicates with Mr. Pemberton directly, who in turn communicates with me. *I have not sold my rights in it*, but expect to receive a share of its profits as long as it keeps the stage. It is yet too soon to even imagine what *that* will be, or if it will be anything!

I thought all your criticisms *very good* and just. I believe they (in N.Y.) will try to work up a denouement that shall be less hopeless and more satisfying to the audience than it seems to be at present, and I believe that if either Pemberton or myself had seen the rehearsals, we could have arranged it.[2] You know we always expected to *produce it here first*! If it is only a fair success in America we will still do it, if we can get as good an actress as Miss Russell seems to be to take the part of "Sue." I should have a better hearing here than in my own country. The London audiences and critics are not afraid of being thought *vulgar* if they like to hear of "common" people or American subjects. But that is all in the future. Meantime I and Pemberton are hard at work on a dramatization of "Clarence," which we think will be much better than "Sue."

I have barely time in my hurry to tell you how grieved I am to hear of poor Doras death[3]—nor can I write to poor Lize my sympathy at such a moment. But I will later.

What terrible proportions that strange disease you call the "grippe" assumes in New York and particularly in our family! I cannot comprehend it! With love to the girls, always your

Limick

P.S. I am here for a week or two longer, but you can still write to the Club for I do not know how long I may remain out of London.

Provenience: UVa (ALS).

1. Though AH's original letter is lost, BH quotes it extensively in letters to Pemberton on October 9 (Yale) and FH on October 12 (*Letters*, 431–32). AH called it a "perfect play," with no line "that does not *tell* with the audience." The Vigilance Committee scene "brings down the house every time," and the trial scene in the third act "went off splendidly!" She also reported that Frohman "*is trying to get another theatre to continue the production of Sue in New York!*"

2. BH continued to tinker with the final act. See, for example, letter 245. Also, on 2 May 1900 (*Letters*, 470) he wrote FH that he was "writing a new first scene to Act 3 of 'Sue.' Perhaps you may remember that I told you I was going to change it, so as to show Sue and Wyand escaping after the murder and the discovery by Sue of Wyands selfishness and perfidy, and their separation! I had written to Frohman about it, and he was pleased and has said that he would in future have it played with that change."

3. BH's niece Dora, the daughter of his sister Eliza.

233. TO ANNA HARTE, 29 OCTOBER 1896

74, Lancaster Gate, W.
Oct 29th '96

My dear Anna

I lost yesterdays (Wednesdays) post, through not getting my draft from the Bank before 6 P.M. and I fear this will not leave here until Saturday; I hope you received the previous draft by cable, without any trouble.

I have not very satisfactory news from my play; indeed I dare say *you* hear more about it than I do. Mr Frohman writes to my collaborateur, and has all his dealings with *him* directly. We have had accounts of the first four weeks receipts and two *little cheques*, but no letter of advice or information since the one that told us that the play would be taken "on tour." I am afraid the election excitement will affect it, very badly,[1] but I still *hope*—Nan! It is something to have got the play *on* and *fairly* off before the public and I hope better luck for the next!

I am back again in London, in the fogs and smoke. I am afraid I cannot stand the whole winter here; year after year it seems the more terrible, and the days of semi-darkness harder to bear. Yet everything I get, in the way of criticism, advice or comment from America, tells me how utterly *alien* I and my writings have become in my own country—and how I must depend upon my appreciation and standing here. When "Max Nordau" the celebrated German philosopher and novelist, lately wrote that I was the "Columbus of American Fiction"[2] (whatever that may mean!) and that my own countrymen did not appreciate me sufficiently, I thought it might strike some echo in America—but alas! I have not seen even an allusion to it in my American publishers *advertisements*! while here it was copied largely and discussed! I dont believe, Nan, that even *you* ever heard a word of it!

I have a sad very sad letter from poor Maggie, and a request for money. God knows I should be too happy to support her—but what can I do beyond a few pounds a year!

Give my best love to the children, and let me soon hear from you. Always affectionately

Limick

Provenience: UVa (ALS).

1. In national balloting on 3 November 1896, William McKinley was elected president.

2. In an interview (*Literary Digest*, 12 Sept. 1896, 621) Nordau had described BH as "a Columbus" who "discovered a new world in fiction."

234. TO T. EDGAR PEMBERTON, 8 NOVEMBER 1896

74, Lancaster Gate, W.
November 8th 96

My dear Pemberton,

Thank you so much for the photographs of "Sue." I dare say they are very *effective* but still I'm afraid we cant call them exactly "*picturesque*"! But then, I don't know if we can call the story—or the play—picturesque either! Nevertheless, I wish they had made something prettier out of the love-making in the barn. Those cold stone steps and the posturing attitude of the acrobat are positively chilling! Why couldn't they have let the hay be scattered over the steps—as it really would be—and bursting out of the door? And a *stone* barn!—on a *frontier* ranch! where everything is of *wood*—will make them laugh "out West."

I wish we had a photograph of Annie Russell, herself, as she really looks! She looks very sweet in her *pose* in the scene where she is "mixing drinks" for the sheriff and deputy,[1] and Ira's doubting jealousy is good! In fact, it's the *best* and most *dramatic* scene of all!

I am anxiously awaiting news from "Sue," after the Brooklyn "lift." I wonder where she went afterwards.[2]

I'm glad to hear that your getting on with "Clarence," and look forward to seeing the complete M.S. soon.[3]

Did I ever thank you for the old Stamps? If not, let me do so now and forward Madame Van de Veldes grateful acknowledgements.

Yours always
Bret Harte

Provenience: Yale (ALS).

1. See photograph 24, Annie Russell as Sue.

2. *Sue* was produced at the Montauk Theatre in Brooklyn the week

of October 12, in Pittsburgh the week of October 19, in Toledo the weekend of November 12, in St. Louis the week of November 16, in Philadelphia the week of November 23, and at the Boston Museum between November 30 and December 26. It was subsequently performed in Providence, Washington, Brooklyn (again), Harlem, Bridgeport, Lowell, Newport, Brockton, Lynn, Hartford, and Buffalo before it closed on 13 February 1897.

3. Pemberton had begun to write a theatrical version of BH's novel *Clarence*, fragments of which survive at UCLA and Yale.

235. TO ANNA HARTE, 30 MARCH 1897

Arford House
Headley Hants
Mar. 30th 97

My dear Anna

I am very sorry I cannot increase the dft. this month by even ever so little! for although I have been doing my usual amount of work my agent has had some delay in disposing of it, and I presume he does not wish to push the market. Alas! it would not be strange if, after these years, people should not be quite as keen to buy or read B.H's stuff as ten or twenty years ago! Another reason for my financial "tightness" is that for nearly a month I have heard nothing from "Sue," and even the small cheques—that were always welcome however small they might be—have not come in. Except through my collaborateur—and *he* through Charles Frohman—I have no means of hearing anything about the play—whether it has been taken off or not. It was "flickering" out when I last heard from it, but was supposed to run until the 1st March in or about New York. Do you hear anything of it? Nor have I any word from *Danl* Frohman[1] who has our play of "Clarence" under consideration for nearly a month, now. We have been hoping that Annie Russell might come *over here* with "Sue" but we have no news of that either. "Sue" has never been played here and it ought to "run" moderately well in the provinces.

But I hope no news may not be bad news. Your last letter to me is dated Feby 19th. I did *not* get any Xmas letter, nor did anything come with the presents. I am so glad that you have not had your regular household "common or garden" grippe—though I say "*unberufen*"[2] to myself as I write and tap the desk! I have kept fairly well—though I have suffered dreadfully from neuralgia in my face and jaws.[3] The doctor says it is not from my teeth—(I have very few left!) but a general condition—that I think has been bettered by my coming into the country for a couple of weeks. Nevertheless I look forward to a siege with the dentist when I get back to London. With love to the children dear Nan and yourself

Yours affect
Limick

Provenience: UVa (ALS).

1. Daniel Frohman (1851–1940) was manager of the Lyceum Theatre in New York and brother of Charles Frohman.

2. "Touch wood."

3. By date of this letter, BH had been suffering with a persistent cough for over two months. The symptoms would gradually worsen until he was diagnosed with throat cancer.

236. TO T. EDGAR PEMBERTON, 4 APRIL 1897

Arford House,
Headley, Hants,
April 4th '97

My dear Pemberton,

It *is* very bad news, but I dont feel so sad about it as I ought—for, Cassandra like, I saw it all a month ago, and *discounted* it. I did not expect that Frohman's financial experience with "Sue" would make him look very kindly or hopefully upon any future play of ours,[1] but I agree with you that one can hardly call a play "a failure" which has made the amount of money that "Sue" has. Still we do not know what *expenses* the Frohmans had in *advertising* &c &c. which they certainly did not stint. I think he might have written us that "Sue" was "taken off" on such and such a date—as even his note which you enclose is not precise in its "sometime in February."[2] And "Sue" has never been *South*—to "New Orleans" for instance.

I think we ought to get something out of "Sue" in England. I believe it would make a good *provincial* play, and we might try it—

failing other arrangements—in Birmingham! Then we could see it rehearsed.

Oddly enough I received another letter this morning from Kirke La Shelle,[3] which I enclose. I received one from him scarcely a month ago—to exactly the same effect. Unfortunately we do not know anything about his financial responsibility. But wouldn't it be well for me to write to him, asking for references, and amount of royalty proposed, should he accept it? Perhaps I might get McClure's Syndicate, who publish all my stories in America to ascertain his *status* and perhaps take charge of the MS. At all events we are no longer bound to Frohman—and we must try for ourselves.

Kindly return La Shelles letters. I reenclose them for you. I am looking forward eagerly to seeing you on the 17th.

Yours always
Bret Harte

Provenience: Yale (ALS).

1. Frohman has refused "Clarence." For the reason, see letter 237. BH wrote Pemberton on 5 January 1897 (Yale) that the last week of the play's run in Boston had not "been very successful and I do not think Frohman would feel like continuing the tour on houses that dropped below $2000 per week. Their expenses must be nearly that!"

2. See note 2 to letter 234. BH complained to FH on 12 April 1897 (UCLA) that the play "is evidently off—although we have not had a line from Frohman since his last statement of a/c to Feby 20th. These managers are truly 'a law unto themselves.'"

3. Kirke La Shelle (1862–1905), a Chicago journalist, playwright, and theatrical manager.

237. TO ANNA HARTE, 14 JUNE 1897

Arford House,
Headley Hants,
June 14th 97

My dear Nan,

I have succeeded in getting the draft earlier this month and I hope you will receive it by the 1st July as I am hurrying this off to catch the post to-morrow. Frank and his wife have been visiting here with me, and lately I have had my dramatic *collaborateur* Mr. Pemberton and his wife here also through Madame V. de V's kindness—as I had some work to do with Pemberton. I am afraid "Clarence" has been anticipated here by Gillettes "Secret Service"[1] or at least put off, as *two* American plays on nearly the same lines wouldn't succeed. I think I told you that Frohman would not take "Clarence" for America—because he said the War plays were overdone. P. and I have some hope of bringing out "Sue" *here*—but it is only a hope—and we have no "Annie Russell" to insure its success. We are also at work on another play—a dramatization of my "Mæcenas of the Pacific," which will be offered to Frohman.[2]

I am keeping out of London and the confusion and snobbery of the Jubilee.[3] I am sorry to say that my countrymen—the Americans in London—are among the most vulgar and ostentatious in the display. I shall not go up for the Jubilee. I detest crowds, and a London crowd has not even the humour of an American crowd to make it bearable. As for seeing the Royalties together—the few I *have* seen are not striking enough to make a spectacle, and I am afraid I have no other feeling about them.

I am sorry that my being away from London has prevented my seeing Maggies married daughter "Maud Wyman Eberts,"[4] who is in England and who has written to me. But I may see her later—after the sawdust and orange peel of the big Jubilee show is swept out of London and people have recovered their senses.

I have been very *proud* and pleased by a letter I have received from a Mr Thomas of Council Bluffs who writes to me that in "making researches["] for the "Sons of the Revolution" he has discovered that his *great*, grandfather was *my great, great* grandfather (on my mothers side)—a Revolutionary soldier—whose daughter also married a Capt Truesdale a Revolutionary officer—so that I am a "Son of the Revolution."[5] I remember my mother had often talked of her Revolutionary ancestors but it was odd to receive this confirmation from a stranger. I dont know what the "Sons of the Revolution" are as *a Society*, but I am much more pleased, I am afraid, than if I had been told that I had a Peer among my ancestors—or had come into a little property through a distant nobleman.

I hope you will enjoy your outing at Norfolk—and though you may not believe it—I wish I could be there this summer! We had a few days of quite hot weather like an American summer—and then a drop of 20° *in one night* into the usual chilly, damp English summer. Yet we believe that it is only in America that we have these sudden changes. With best love to the girls

Your affect
Limick

Provenience: Bancroft (MSS 79/47 C).

1. The Civil War melodrama *Secret Service* by the actor and playwright William Gillette (1853–1937) opened at the Garrick Theatre in New York on 5 October 1896 and the Adelphi Theatre in London on 15 May 1897.

2. The script of "Rushbrook" was based on BH's "A Mæcenas of the Pacific Slope," which had been syndicated in such U.S. papers as the *New Orleans Times-Democrat* in January 1890. Charles Frohman rejected the play although, as BH wrote AH on 23 September 1897 (*Letters*, 450), he "*promised* to do his best to dispose of 'Clarence' and 'Rushbrook.'" A fragment of "Rushbrook" survives in the Beinecke Library, Yale.

3. The celebration marking the sixtieth year of Victoria's reign.

4. Maude Wyman Eberts (1861–1953), daughter of BH's sister Margaret.

5. Probably Jesse Truesdell, who enlisted in the Westchester County, New York, militia during the Revolution, was later promoted to captain of its 4th Regiment and to major of its 2d Regiment.

238. TO ANNA HARTE, 29 OCTOBER 1897

74, Lancaster Gate, W.

Oct. 29 '97

My dear Anna,

I am afraid this is a very late and somewhat hurried letter for I have only just returned from Worcestershire, and some work with my collaborateur, Pemberton, in a dramatic version of "Snowbound at Eagles," one of my old stories.[1] You see I am always *hoping* for some success with my plays. I am also hopeful of the production of "Sue" in London, by a very good actress—(Miss Annie Hughes[2] who saw Miss Russell act in America)—this winter, and the possibility of making a little more money out of it than I made in America. Frohman acted very queerly about "Sue" as well as some other plays that I and Pemberton wrote *at his* suggestion. All the English actors who saw "Sue" acted in America, and many Americans whom I have met here since agree in saying it was a *good success*—yet Frohman wrote to Pemberton that financially it was a failure![3]

I hope you and the girls will be preserved from "grippe" and early colds this autumn. I have a cold and cough I cannot shake off—although I stayed in the country as long as possible to try and get rid of it, before coming up to gloomy and foggy London. I wish I could go away this winter somewhere but I cannot afford it.

Frank is up in London for a few weeks. With love to the children, always your affectionate

Limick

Provenience: UCLA (ALS).

1. "Snow-Bound at Eagle's," first serialized in the New York *Sun* in November-December 1885. The four-act play *Held Up* was produced at the Worcester Theatre on 24 August 1903. A fragment of an early draft survives in the New York Public Library (Berg); a copy of the complete and final version survives in the Library of Congress.

2. The actress Annie Hughes (1870–1954) would drop the project when she was unable to book a theatre.

3. See letter 236.

239. TO FRANK HARTE, 3 JUNE 1898

74, Lancaster Gate, W.
June 3d '98

My dear Frank,

Certainly, I will ask Frohman for stalls for you and your wife next Friday.[1] He has asked me for a list of those of my friends whom I would like to have.

I have seen Annie Russell and have attended *one* rehearsal of the play.[2] She is very charming; I can quite understand her popularity in America, and certainly there is no *ingenue* on the *English* stage comparable to her. But at the rehearsal, I was pleased to see that other American actors were equally good in their *roles*, and while the play has certain inherent defects it is by no means as bad as the American critics made it. The Lynch trial was wonderfully good—and unless I am mistaken in what I know of English audiences—it will "go" with them.

I ought to be at Miss Froudes at Padworth Croft to-day,[3] but I have been rewriting one of the scenes this morning and have to go to a rehearsal to-morrow, so my visit to Aldermaster may go by the board.

In haste, with love to your wife,

Your tired popper
B.H.

Provenience: UVa (ALS).

1. *Sue* was first staged in England at the Garrick Theatre in London on 10 June 1898.

2. According to John D. Williams (*Century* 91 [Dec. 1915]:179–80), when Russell collapsed from exhaustion in rehearsal at the close of act II BH thought it part of the scene and was delighted.

3. May Froude, J. A. Froude's younger daughter, lived near Reading. See also letter 103 and accompanying note 3.

240. TO ANNA HARTE, 8 AUGUST 1898

Compton Wynyates, Kineton
August 8, 1898

My dear Nan,

It was very foolish and inconsiderate in me not to write to you for so long a time, but ever since I heard of the possibility of my play of "Sue" being brought out in London—ever since I saw it in rehearsal—ever since it made an *artistic* success here—and during its run for a month at one of the West End theatres,[1] I have been *waiting* and *hoping* to be able to tell you that it was also a *financial success for me! Alas!* I have been once more cruelly disappointed; in spite of the praises of press[2] and audiences; in spite of the attractions of a perfect actress, like Annie Russell, and a splendid company—in spite of everything that goes to make the success of a play—*it never paid!* I cannot understand it—the manager, Mr. Frohman, is equally bewildered and confounded, although he is much more *satisfied* with the money he has undoubtedly *lost*, and the artistic success the play has gained, than we are. I need not tell you how *for six weeks* I had hoped to delight and astonish you with news of a good fortune that would spare me all the trials and troubles I have had lately over my literary work—and how deeply disappointed I have been! I have had no heart to write to you, or to Jessamy regarding her affairs, and even now I can only congratulate her upon finding a husband who can take the place of her father and his precarious fortunes.[3] It is hard to face this fact, which for the last six months I have been trying to avoid.

I will try to send your next draft by the middle of this month. I am visiting one of my old English friends here, but I shall return to London next week. Write to me soon, no matter how remiss *I* am, or how hopelessly I write. I am always, dear Nan, your affectionate

Limick

Provenience: *Letters*, 455–56.

1. *Sue* ran at the Garrick Theatre in London between 29 June and 26 July 1898.

2. On balance, the reviews in London were favorable; e.g., the London *Speaker* (18 June 1898, 759) opined that the play "delights by its very artlessness," and the *Athenaeum* (18 June 1898, 800) thought the title character was "finely conceived by the dramatists." BH was particularly pleased by Clement Scott's notice in the London *Daily Telegraph*, which described him as "a born dramatist" (Pemberton, 273–74). See also note 3 to letter 231.

3. Earlier in 1898, Jessamy Harte had married Henry M. Steele, a Colorado mine owner and financier.

241. TO T. EDGAR PEMBERTON, 2 NOVEMBER 1898

74, Lancaster Gate, W.
Novem. 2d '98

My dear Pemberton,

I did not acknowledge your letter enclosing the replies of Frohman and Willard, as I was very busy just as I was leaving Fareham.

I was not surprised at either letter; "Clarence" is not a prominent enough part for Willard—nor indeed for *any* actor who wants a play for *himself*.[1] As to "Held Up," Frohman told me substantially what he wrote to you, but he did not say anything about the situation lacking novelty—and I do not agree with him *there*, however I may accept his other evaluation. I am pretty familiar with "situations" in literature and the drama and I certainly know of none like the principal one in "Held Up."[2] That the interest may be *divided* among *too many characters* to make a popular play, at present,—is quite understandable—and the money-making manager may fairly see it.

The greatest trouble we have, is that our experience of "Sue" has been so utterly confusing, conflicting and astounding that it *teaches* us nothing by way of example, monition, or encouragement! We may say that it had faults of situation, but that did not seem to abate the interest of the audience who appeared certainly to be delighted with a play that *did not draw* audiences to the house! I have sometimes thought that *my material* was not the kind from which a popular play could be made—that it was not sufficiently convincing or absorbing to our audience—but then the critics, at their worst, *didn't say that*, nor did our audiences seem to act so. So that we have absolutely nothing to go upon by way of guide to our other ventures! We are, if we consult the notices and critiques of "Sue," the authors of a highly successful and much talked of play—even a distinctly "novel" one—yet we couldn't draw a paying audience for that one, nor can we get an order for another from actor or manager—or know precisely what was the matter with the last. Verily a dramatists life is not a happy one!

I am so sorry to hear of Miss Pembertons ill health, but I think the air of Devonshire, which they say is very soothing, may sustain her.

Yours always
Bret Harte

Provenience: Yale (ALS).

1. See note 2 to letter 192.

2. BH outlined the final scenes of the scenario to FH (9 Mar 1898, UVa): "'Zeenie' has *met Lee and Falkner on the road* sent them in hiding until Harkness and the deputies shall pass—and brings to Kate a farewell

note from Falkner. Zeenie has taken in the situation at once—and tries to help Falkner with Kate, and has a good characteristic scene with the two women. The next entrance is Hale Rawlins and Clinch (as in the old form). Having left Hennicker a couple of hours before *Harkness* they naturally *precede* him. But on the road *they* have learnt of the civil action against Harkness, and are in possession of that fact, when he arrives. Zenobia is not on the stage when these scenes take place but when all is over and Hale knows *everything*, the women implore him to ask Ned Falkner to return. Hale declines with indignation, but Zenobia comes in from behind, and (unknown to the other women) with a few words half-playful and half threatening says she is Falkners messenger and induces Hale, from his anxiety to get rid of her, and his fears of her revealing the 'John Brown' episode, to write the invitation. With its delivery into her hand—the curtain falls. The audience know that Falkner will return[,] Lee go to the Wars, and all will be happy."

242. TO FRANK HARTE, 14 DECEMBER 1898

74, Lancaster Gate, W.
December 14th '98

My dear Frank,

I am greatly surprised by your letter, as your mother never intimated to me her intention of coming to England, nor have you ever told me that you were sending for her or intended to send for her. In her last letter to me, while acknowledging the receipt of the $250.00—which in my straightened circumstances that month I had to borrow[1]—she hoped that I would still be able to send her that *full* amount, monthly, for the rest of the year, as she could not reduce her expenses, at once. But she said nothing whatever of her coming, nor of your proposals to her.

Of course I can only hope and wish that the arrangements you have thus made may prove perfectly satisfactory to you all, and that in being able to share your house with your mother and sister you may have all the pleasure you have looked forward to.

Your affectionate father
B.H.

P.S. I sent this morning a line to Madame Van de Velde, as you wished, informing her of what you found yourself able to do, and had done.

Provenience: UVa (ALS).

1. BH first drew an advance on royalties from his agent, A. P. Watt, in April 1897 (UVa) and the practice soon became routine.

243. TO ANNA HARTE, 23 DECEMBER 1898[1]

74, Lancaster Gate, W.
Friday P.M.

My dear Anna,

I heard of your arrival[2] and was very sorry you have been in such poor health—although I think the air of Caversham—and a little quiet in the country—will do you a world of good. But that is one of the reasons why I am so utterly surprised to hear of Franks new intentions—which even now I can scarcely comprehend. Does he know of any other place where you could all live as cheaply together as in that house he had proposed for you? Is he in financial difficulties in Caversham, which forces him to leave? All these things cost money, as you know, and make all changes even when they seem cheaper, a great deal more expensive in the long run.

I am very hardly worked now—(even writing at night)—to do some *extra* and *unpaid* work on a story in order to dispose of it—a story which I supposed had been already accepted![3] I have very little time to myself, but I shall run up for a day—or at least *part of day* very soon. With love to Ethel and thanks for her nice letter, and hopes that this trouble of the house will be soon got over.

Always your affectionate,
Limick

Provenience: UCLA (ALS).

1. Dated by reference to letter 242; BH's 20 December 1898 letter to FH (Wesleyan); and his 27 December 1898 letter to AH (Wesleyan).

2. AH and Ethel Harte probably left New York on the White Star liner *Majestic* on December 13, arriving in Queenstown on December 19.

3. Probably "Mr. Jack Hamlin's Mediation," first published in *Frank Leslie's Popular Monthly* 47 (Jan.-Mar. 1899).

244. TO FRANK HARTE, CIRCA JANUARY 1899[1]

74, Lancaster Gate, W.
Sunday

My dear Frank,

I wrote to your mother yesterday that I was coming soon again to see you at Caversham.[2] I will come to luncheon, if you like; I am afraid I would not achieve a dinner as it would involve a late journey and I am obliged to work at night now. I have been very busy, but I am glad enough to be so, if it will bring me more quickly the money I am very much in need of.

I am afraid that I thought more of the inevitable *expenses* of your new house than the glories of its "Sheraton and Chippendale" furniture. Unless you are in receipt of a larger income than formerly, I am afraid you will find yourself in difficulty with this increased expenditure. I think that the amount you ask your mother to contribute is very reasonable and fair, and I can quite believe she could not be comfortable anywhere else in a low sense,—but as she tells me that on account of her debts and other expenses, she can barely get along on £30 a month, and as, at present, I can with great difficulty assure her of *that* amount, it doesn't seem that the new arrangement will relieve *me* much!

I wrote to your mother that I didn't think the special music lessons and drawing lessons for Ethel an advisable expense just now. *She* can keep Ethel in practice with her own knowledge of teaching, if necessary. The Piano I suppose is unavoidable—unless you can lend them yours—and the purchase system the best I dare say—if the instalments can be paid *regularly*. Otherwise it would be better to hire, and you would lose less if you got in arrears. I am afraid you dont understand the difficulties I have had for the past few years in sending your mother $3000 a year, in that both you and she had had a very exaggerated idea of my income.[3] Your wife's income is a fixed one—or at least assured whether you work or not—or are sick or well and yet you managed to get into debt in spite of it. Mine is not, and although I labour all the year round—taking no absolute holiday—in an exhausting profession—I never know what its profit may be. I can only look forward to a helpless old age. Until the past year I have regularly sent $3000 a year to support your mother, Ethel and Jessamy,—three people—and a decrease of that sum brings your mother here in debt! Yet I have sounded this note in my letter to her for years; perhaps I have cried "Wolf" so often that it has got to be a familiar warning. Yet it is at the door now, and you must not wonder if I do not get very hopeful or enthusiastic over the "Sheraton & Chippendale furniture," and the other expenses you talk of so lightly. Perhaps you can manage it; perhaps you considered it all before you persuaded your mother to take this extraordinary step upon your and her joint responsibility. I hope and trust you have!

I will send you a line,—or if hurried—a wire to say when I am coming. Tell your wife I will not forget the chocolates this time. I shall have a shilling or two left!

Your affect. father
B.H.

Provenience: UVa (ALS).

1. This letter is tentatively dated by its reference to FH's "new house." Soon after the arrival of his mother and sister, as letter 243 suggests, FH moved his family into a larger house in Caversham. BH had visited them in late December 1899 (to FH, 27 Dec. 1898, UCLA) en route to Birmingham; the present letter promises a second visit.

2. This letter is lost.

3. In 1891, BH's annual income was estimated to be in excess of $16,000 (*Critic*, 30 May 1891, 293). More recently, however, Axel Nissen of Oslo University has estimated his 1897 income at $9,610, his 1898 income at $6,760, and his 1899 income at $5,945.

245. TO T. EDGAR PEMBERTON, 9 MARCH 1899

The Red House
Camberley, Surrey, March 9, 99

My dear Pemberton,

I had barely time to acknowledge your last letter as I had posted down here—to Madame *V. de V.'s* new country home—to finish some work in a great hurry.[1]

I had no idea that "Sue" would be produced again in America and I wanted to alter that last Act before it was played again.[2] This

I must and *shall* do if there is any hope of its being brought over *here* once more.

Who played "Sue"?[3] What kind of a company was it? But I dare say you know no more about it yet—unless you have access to the American dramatic papers.

As I told you the Maurices came to see me.[4] They wanted me to do "Mliss" for them, and Miss Maurice was to send me *her* idea of what she wanted done.[5] But it may be very difficult for me to construct something without running over the lines on which Hatton and I worked, and I have not seen him yet. I tried to make her understand that the episodes of the *story* would not make episodes of a play—as for instance Mliss's declaration of heterodoxy at the end of a chapter! Besides the charm of Mliss is that she is a mere *child*—and it is very difficult for a grown actress to represent such a character—in love!

I hope to be able to come to Pye Corner at Easter. The weather will not prevent me for I know that this country at Easter is wilfulness and caprice itself. But I will let you know in due season.

With love to you all

B.H.

Provenience: Berg (ALS).

1. Probably "Liberty Jones' Discovery," first published in London *M.A.P.*, 17 June 1899, 590–95.

2. The Frawley Company took *Sue* on tour, producing it, for example, in San Francisco between 4 and 7 October 1897 and in Denver from 31 July through 6 August 1898. See also note 2 to letter 232.

3. Ethel Browning acted the part on tour in fall 1898.

4. Probably the actor-manager Edmund Maurice (1863–1928) and his sister (?) Annie Sturghes.

5. Within the month, Annie Sturghes sent BH "a sketchy *scenario* of 'M'liss,' from her point of view. It had some good things in it, but I wrote her that I much doubted the success of 'M'liss' as a play, and advised her to read" his story *Cressy* (*Letters*, 460).

246. TO ANNA HARTE, 30 MARCH 1899

74, Lancaster Gate, W.

March 30th '99

My dear Anna,

I'm sending you a cheque for £30.0.0 for this months remittance. I have dated it to-morrow, to give the Bank time to receive a draft from me, which I only got this morning, and unfortunately I have had no balance for some days to my credit.

And now, I am dreadfully sorry to say that I cannot come to Caversham to-morrow—but that I must stay *here* and work, morning and night, to finish a story for which I have got a partial advance.[1] I have had to wire to Pemberton at Broadway, where I expected to spend my Easter holiday, for I *cannot really spare the time to go and come*—which would mean nearly *two days* out of that brief vacation of four. I cannot even spend *the day* at Caversham—but must plod at my work here until it is finished. But I expect to be free by the fifteenth, April, and then I will come. I am sorry to disappoint you again—but it is really harder upon me than you.

In great haste, with love to Ethel and Frank, to whom I am writing.

Your affectionate
Limick

Provenience: UVa (ALS).

1. See note 1 to letter 245.

247. TO HAMLIN GARLAND, 3 MAY 1899

74, Lancaster Gate, W.
3d of May '99

Dear Mr Garland[1]

I would call at your hotel if my work did not confine me so closely to the house for the next few days. But if *you* could drop in *here* on Friday (5th) at about 1/2 past 4, to tea, *I* should be delighted![2]

It was a rare pleasure to get a line from Howells[3] and to find him, once more, the very charming flesh-and-blood creature I knew of old, and not only the distinguished author who of late years I merely know from his books.[4]

Yours very Sincerely,
Bret Harte

Provenience: University of Southern California Library (ALS).

1. The writer Hamlin Garland (1860–1940) had discussed BH's writings in a lecture, "Poets of the New Eldorado," in 1885–86 (Donald Pizer, *Hamlin Garland's Early Work and Career* [Berkeley: University of California Press, 1960], 13); and he had favorably reviewed BH's *A Millionaire of Rough-and-Ready and Devil's Ford* for the *Boston Transcript* (3 Feb. 1887, p. 6, cols. 4–5).

2. See *Hamlin Garland's Diaries*, ed. Donald Pizer (San Marino, Calif.: Huntington Library, 1968), 143: "I then went to call on Bret Harte, whom I found living in the West End. Lancaster Gate. Bachelor apartments. He was affable and polite but looked old and burnt out, his eyes clouded, his skin red and flabby. He has lived hard and fast, that is evident." Reminiscing about their visit more fully in *Roadside Meetings* (New York: Macmillan, 1931), 447–49, Garland added that BH reportedly "was living on the bounty of a patron" and "the gossip about him was not reassuring."

3. Howells had given Garland a letter of introduction to BH.

4. BH had urged the Duchess of St. Albans on 6 November 1879 to read Howells's *The Lady of the Aroostook* and "give me your opinion. I have my own" (*Letters*, 159). Writing to Mary S. Boyd in mid- to late-1894, BH was more forthcoming in his criticism of Howells's *A Traveler from Altruria*: The characters "seem to me rather colourless and even flavourless. . . . There isnt a sensation of any kind in the book, nor an out-and-out laugh in its pages" (*Letters*, 382–83).

248. TO FLORENCE HENNIKER, 30 SEPTEMBER 1899

The Red House,
Camberley, Surrey.
Septem 30th '99

My dear Mrs Henniker,

I was very glad to hear from you for I have been out of London—in Surrey and Oxfordshire—nearly the whole of this exceptionally hot summer. As I usually go into the country to work I unfortunately find the weather made me lazy, and now I am obliged, at the end of my vacation, to make up arrears—and linger here to do it. The flowers have gone, and the birds are going—but I and my work remain; I can only hope that I can get *my* leaves off before the trees do theirs. Really, however, I expect to be in town in a week or ten days. Then I hope to see you, and you will tell me all about your new collaboration.[1] Meantime, let me bespeak you all success!

I do not see why so clever and charming a fellow as your husband should not have a chance to kill somebody in South Africa if he wants to![2] Whats the use of having a kind heart, a loveable and loyal nature and a keen sense of humour—if it is to go unrewarded like this!

Personally, I think that married men ought *not* to go to the wars! Tennyson thought differently; but I never took any stock in that wife whose "voice was heard through rolling drums" and whose face coming "across" "his fancy" "gave the battle to his hands."[3] I always believed that a woman with a voice so preternaturally dominant and a face that the mere imagining of her are incentive to manslaughter must have been hideous!

Can you tell me how Lady Northampton is?[4] I have not heard from her or her husband for a long long time and fear she is not so well.

With love to Arthur, and wishes for the speedy realization of his most sanguinary hopes in the exercise of his vocation!

Always yours,
Bret Harte

P.S. I hoped to have had your husband and Major Norris[5] dine with me at my Club—but Norris was called away to South Africa by "rolling drums" some time ago!

Provenience: UVa (ALS).

1. Henniker had earlier collaborated with Hardy on the story "The Spectre of the Real." See note 1 to letter 230. BH apparently alludes to a proposed dramatic adaptation of one of her tales which was never produced or published. As Hardy had written her on 25 July 1899, "Which of your stories is the play to be based on?" (*One Rare Fair Woman: Thomas Hardy's Letters to Florence Henniker 1893–1922*, ed. Evelyn Hardy and F. B. Pionion [Coral Gables, Fla.: University of Miami Press, 1972], 80).

2. Arthur Henry Henniker-Major (1855–1912) commanded the second regiment of the Coldstream Guards during the Boer War, after which he was promoted to major-general. BH's pose here is ironic: he referred disparagingly to "this useless War" in a letter to Clara Schneider a few weeks later (22 Dec. 1899, UVa); and he described it still later to Pemberton (25 Jan. 1900, Yale) as "one of the most fatuous, inadvisible, unreasoning, incoherent and ghastly-miserable wars" in history.

3. *The Princess*, part iv, lines 577–80.

4. Lady Northampton (d. 1902), the former Mary Florence Baring.

5. Richard Joseph Norris (1854–1935) married the Van de Veldes' daughter Beatrice in 1894. Decorated in 1898, he was promoted to lieutenant colonel after his tour of duty in the Boer War.

249. TO T. EDGAR PEMBERTON, 12 FEBRUARY 1900

The Red House,
Camberley, Surrey.
12th Feb. 1900

My dear Pemberton,

I have been looking for that completed act of "Held Up," but it has not yet arrived from your daughter. I trust there are no domestic illnesses, of which you certainly have your full share already!

I saw a notice of your book on the Kendals.[1] Make your publisher send me a copy. How does the Bret Harte biography get on?[2]

I fear that De Beck is an illusion! I saw him, and he agreed to take the story of mine—but as I demanded payment on delivery of copy—he *put off receiving it, just yet!* but promised to take it this month. The new magazine—which by the way is to be called the "Universal" instead of the "Midland"—*vide* his note paper—was to come out on the 10th. I have heard nothing of it—except through him.[3]

I am here "snowed up"—or "Snowbound at Camberley." Bitterly cold, but the snow white and sparkling and the sun unimpeded by fog when it does shine. Exercise by walking almost impossible on the snow clogged roads; I get mine by shoveling out the paths, and am complimented by being told that I handle a spade well—the gardeners and odd man referring it vaguely to my early life as a gold digger! There is a great tonic in this air but a good deal of rheumatism and neuralgia in my bones and muscles. Yet it is better than dreary *dark* London! I can write without artificial light which was killing me—and can dress in the morning without it and without putting on trousers and coat of a different pattern! And then think of *you* at West Bromswich—and shudder—and am infinitely sad![4]

Yours always
Bret Harte

Provenience: Yale (ALS).

1. *The Kendals* (London: Pearson; New York: Dodd, Mead, 1900).

2. In an attempt to preempt the publication of an unauthorized BH biography, probably Henry W. Boynton's *Bret Harte* (1903), Pemberton offered to write one with BH's help and approval. BH was pleased by the result. As he wrote Pemberton on 27 August 1900 (*Letters*, 477), "You have done your self-imposed, self-denying task *wonderfully, generously, delicately* well!" Four days later, BH sent a formal letter of thanks which Pemberton published as a preface (*Letters*, 478). With Mme Van de Velde's cooperation, Pemberton revised and expanded his *Bret Harte: A Treatise and a Tribute* (1900) into his *The Life of Bret Harte* (1903), the standard biography before George Stewart's *Bret Harte: Argonaut and Exile* (1931).

3. BH published "A Romance of the Line" (July 1900), in the short-lived *Universal Magazine* (Feb. 1900–Jan. 1902).

4. Pemberton suffered from Bright's disease. As BH wrote AH (*Letters*, 493), he "has been a marvel to the Doctors, who tell him he should have been dead fifteen years ago!"

250. TO T. EDGAR PEMBERTON, 25 APRIL 1900

The Red House,
Camberley, Surrey.
April 25th/1900

My dear Pemberton,

I have just received the enclosed from Frohman's Secy, and when you have sent me that copy of the 3d Act, I will return it to you, with the changes, for a cleaner copy to send to Frohman. Of course subject to your suggestions!

Should "Held Up" fall through with Bourchier,[1] we ought to try Frohman again. You know it was *he* who suggested the changes we have made. *He* liked the play greatly, but thought the interest became *divided* by the Hennicker Act[2]—which we now have suppressed. What do you think? I dont think he has been very successful with his new ventures.

Yours always
Bret Harte

Provenience: Yale (ALS).

1. The actor and theatrical manager Arthur Bourchier (1863–1927) became joint manager with Sir Charles Wyndham of the Criterion Theatre in London in February 1900. Though Bourchier kept the manuscript several more months, he never staged the play.

2. As in the story "Snow-Bound at Eagle's," the play featured a shady hosteler named Hennicker.

251. TO RICHARD WATSON GILDER, 29 JUNE 1900

74, Lancaster Gate, W.
June 29 1900

Dear Mr. Gilder,[1]

Mr Watt tells me that you would like me to submit the "plot" &c. &c. of a proposed story for your magazine.[2] Unfortunately I do not usually *begin* with a *plot*, but,—having a few characters and a situation in my mind—,I let *them* work out the plot in *their* own lines and generally find they do it better than I can! These characters and situations must, alas! be pretty well known to you and your readers during the thirty odd years that I have been story-telling, and consequently I am a little puzzled at your request. It occurs to me, however,—looking back upon some past suggestions of yours—that there are *some* situations and characters you would prefer I *shouldn't* touch in a story of your bespeaking![3] Is this so? If it *is*, could you not indicate those points on which you, or your readers, are sensitive? Perhaps you could tell me better what you *dont* want (before I begin)—than what you *do.*

I should like to resurrect "Enriquez"—if I may use that word in reference to a character I never intended to kill, but only to make mysteriously disappear. I propose to put him in another episode, haunting his faithless wife, who believes him dead.[4]

I have a conception of a California millionaire who comes to Europe with his family, and their experiences in Society in England—on somewhat different lines to the usual story of the "American girl" abroad—as written by most American and some English writers on that subject. I have also an idea of an American-German Romance, somewhat on the lines of "The Indiscretion of Elsbeth."[5]

Perhaps you can see your way to indicating your preferences from these.

Yours very Sincerely
Bret Harte

Provenience: Lloyd W. Smith Collection, Morristown National Historical Park (LWS-109).

1. Richard Watson Gilder (1844–1909), the editor of *Century*.

2. BH subsequently published "Trent's Trust" in *Century*, n.s., 40 (Sept.–Oct. 1901):769–83, 892, 901; n.s., 41 (Nov. 1901):124–35.

3. Henry Adams once noted BH's insistence "on the power of sex . . . as far as the magazines would let him venture" (*The Education of Henry Adams* [Boston: Houghton Mifflin, 1961], 385). Robert Underwood Johnson (1853–1937), the associate editor of *Century*, had written Watt on 17 February 1893 (UNC) to solicit a story from BH, albeit with a condition: "the absolute necessity of considering very carefully the limitations under which a writer is who contributes to a family magazine. . . . We know that this rule is more rigid than prevails in Mr. Harte's environment, and he may easily have forgotten it without impropriety." Writing Watt on 3 July 1900 (UVa) to solicit a story from BH, Gilder sounded the same cautionary note: "I only want you to have in mind for avoidance the kind of thing that you are aware an American 'family magazine' has to be careful about.—A book is one thing—but a magazine that the subscriber bets $ on (in advance) will not too greatly 'shock the proprieties' is another." In a memoir (*Boston Transcript*, 10 May 1902, p. 18, col. 3) Gilder observed that he "always found Harte quite ready to revise any work and use the criticism of others as far as it was serviceable to him."

4. Enriquez Saltello was a recurring character in BH's late fiction, appearing in "Chu Chu" (1894), "The Devotion of Enriquez" (1895), "What Happened at the Fonda" (1899), and "The Passing of Enriquez," *Century* 34 (June 1898):230–47.

5. This story was not written. "The Indiscretion of Elsbeth" appeared in the *Ladies Home Journal*, n.s., 13 (Aug. 1896):7–8, 23.

252. TO CLARA SCHNEIDER, 28 AUGUST 1900

The Red House,
Camberley, Surrey.
August 28th/1900

My dear Mrs Schneider,

You must forgive my delay in answering your always-welcome birthday letter for I have been making a round of visits in the country and my letters follow me rather slowly. I had quite forgotten it was my birthday, until some friends reminded me of it in the same pleasant way that you have. *Then*, I need not say, I was daily looking for *your* letter, and would have been dreadfully disappointed, besides being alarmed—if I had not received it.

Its budget of Crefeld news always carries me back to the old days of my consulate, and for a day or two after I often, in fancy, walk the streets that are familiar—(I wonder if they are changed now)—from the little hotel of "Der Wildeman"—where I spent my first night in Crefeld[1]—to Mr Jentges house, your own, and the street of the shops, where you used to help out my bad German, when I was shopping! I remember the street where you are living now—though I have forgotten its name, and cannot make out (from your writing) what it is. It looks like "Oedwell." Please let me know the correct spelling of it, for I am sending this still to Neue Liner Strasse.

Oddly enough I can remember but few *faces* in Crefeld. Of course there was your own family, and your husbands brother, and the Jentges but the rest are quite indistinct, I own—I suppose it is one of the failings of age—always surprised to think of your children as grown up and married!—I cannot get beyond the period of "Uncle Bret Harte!"—and, if I come back to Crefeld, should expect to see your household just as it was—and resent any change! I always regretted that I did not see you that brief day I spent in Cologne a few years ago—it would have bridged over the interval.[2] All I can do now is to felicitate you upon the *marriage* of your *youngest* son!—and scarcely believe it!

I would send you my last book, but I can get it only in London and must wait until my return.[3] With kindest wishes to all and love to yourself and husband, believe me at all times—whether birthdays or not—

Your old friend
Bret Harte

Provenience: UVa (ALS).

1. BH had written FH from Crefeld on 25 July 1878 (Pemberton, 174) that he had "lived for some days at the 'Hotel Wildenmann,' *i.e.* 'Wildman.' a very old and very uncomfortable building. But a day or two ago one of the wealthiest men in this place asked me to come and stay for a few days at his house—a very beautiful place with a large garden." On 23 August 1884 (UVa) BH had thanked Rudolf Schneider for asking Wilhelm Jentges "to drag me out of the unutterable loneliness of 'Der Wildmann,' the first week I came to Crefeld."

2. See letter 222 and accompanying note 3.

3. *From Sand Hill to Pine* (London: Pearson; Boston: Houghton Mifflin, 1900).

253. TO T. EDGAR PEMBERTON, 5 DECEMBER 1900

74, Lancaster Gate, W.
Decem 5/1900

My dear Pemberton,

I had written to your wife yesterday for news of you, and I was delighted this morning to see your handwriting again, quite as much as I was with the good news it brought. "Good old Sue"! She has such a charming way of cropping up when we least expect it! And you are quite right about her "vitality." A play that can pay its authors $300 for a *weeks royalty* is "no slouch"! And as Annie Russell was, or *is* playing in another piece in New York, "Sue" can surely claim the merit for *herself*. I am glad you wrote to Frohman about it, and I am curious to know if he has used the altered act.[1]

Do you ever see the *Era*? *I* do not, but in the American theatrical news we might find something about that Pittsburg work.[2] Pittsburg, you know, is a kind of Manchester, but if a play can do well there for a week—(& *then* your old play at that!) surely it ought to be doing some business *elsewhere*. If Frohman's ways were not so inscrutable—we might find out. I return the accounts as I suppose you want 'em.

Anyhow, I was delighted with the news, and equally delighted that you are better. You must be careful of yourself.

I can sympathize with you—for, although I have got rid of my cold, I have not yet got rid of my *Dentist*! This is the *fourth week* of his almost *daily* visitation! In that 4 weeks I have had crammed the dental experiences of a whole *life-time* of ordinary humanity,—(to make up for my previous immunity I suppose—) and I really dont believe there can be anything new in the way of its tortures in store for me now, although I have still a week of it more to go through with. But then I think of *you*—and am silent![3]

Yours always
Bret Harte

Provenience: Yale (ALS).

1. See note 2 to letter 232.

2. *Sue* was staged at the Grand Opera House in Pittsburgh during the week of 5 November 1900 with Victory Bateman in the title role.

3. See note 4 to letter 249.

254. TO ANNA HARTE, 15 SEPTEMBER 1901

Camberley,
Septem 15th 1901

My dear Anna,

I returned from my brief holiday to find that wretched batch of lying, begging letters which you had forwarded to me in explanation of your again sending money to America, and diverting a part of the sum which I can only get with difficulty for *your own* needs, to other purposes. I need not say that the letters are utterly unconvincing. Fraud and Incompentancy are written all over them in letters large enough for the most self-blinded and doting mothers to read! I cannot believe that even *you* were deceived by them! If you believed in them, and that it was your mission to sacrifice yourself and others for Wodie, you would never have left America, where, with the money I sent you, you could have easily taken Wodie into your house and looked after him—instead of now expecting the father of *over sixty years*, in his old age to support a son of *nearly forty*! You would not have wished to add a dubious grandchild to my decreasing income and increasing years, when you could have made part of your household *them* with very little extra expense. Yet you now propose to help support them without personal supervision and without the least surety of its being a *necessity*.

Even the letters laugh in your face at the suggestion. A man who is able to earn $10.00 a week—or even £2-0-0,—a sum on which many gentlemen in this country are obliged to support themselves—is not the subject of charity. It was for *him* to say—not *you—how* his child should be looked after—and for *him* to do it! You have not even the power to take the child, and keep it—even if you had the money.[1]

If you were a rich woman and able to support yourself—or had a husband who was not obliged to work unceasingly, without help from any of his family, even in his old age, you might indulge in such folly. If you had saved anything out of the $60,000 I have sent you in the last twenty four years, you might do it. But you are still in debt after spending that money. And this mismanagement—or wilful blindness as to my income and its insecurity—you recognize in Wodie as a reason for your supporting him!

For the last 7 or 8 years I have been warning you of my decreasing income, and my ill health. A months illness would stop your income, three months incapacity for work would be more apt to make *me* a subject for charity and the hospital than it would Wodie![2]

When you came to England, without my knowledge or consent, I was told by Frank that you expected in that way to reduce your expenses by living with him, and *that*, I conceived to have been his reason for advising you to such a rash and expensive step, and becoming himself responsible for it. But that expectation has not been realized. You found it *necessary* for Ethel to study in Paris,[3] and although I finally consented to it, I must tell you frankly, now, that I couldnt afford it, and had to get money advanced on my work to do it—and am by no means certain that it ever was a *necessity*! And now, I gather from Franks letters that his plan of making a home for you in his home, and so dividing the expenses is, for some strange reason or other no longer possible. At least *he* proposes now to go to London, and put you in lodgings somewhere near him! On the income that I give you, with his own, you could all live comfortably in the country, as thousands of well bred people do. You could have that house which *I* cannot afford to have, who, but for the kindness of friends whose houses I visit could scarcely keep up my own lodgings in London for my work when I am there.

But I have told you all this before, and am heart-sick with repeating it. It is only when you now calmly propose "a friend" for the maintainance of a man like Wodie and his child that I do it. You told him that "I had reduced your income"! This is hardly the way to express *my* diminished income but even then it is not quite correct as *to the facts.* I had during many years sent you £50 per month—when the children were younger, and the family larger; it was only at about the time of Jessamys marriage that I reduced it—through necessity—to £30. I never "reduced your income" even after my own *regular* income—the only one I had here—as Consul, was taken away.

I look upon Franks idea of taking you to London for the winter as mad and preposterous! It would be quite impossible for you and Ethel—as I know you—to live with decency and comfort there on your income. I do not say anything of the normal and numbing effect of this hardening existence for a few weeks or months in lodging houses and boarding houses—but I must look at it—as the only breadwinner in the family—for its wastefulness, and *it is wasteful.*

I am writing to Frank about it,[4] but I hope in the meantime you will think better of it, or at least defer it until other plans are formed.

I expect to be in London in a few days to see my Dentist who has been away. With love to Ethel,

Your affect.
Limick

Provenience: UVa (ALS).

1. Griswold Harte died at his home in Brooklyn on 11 December 1901, less than three months after BH wrote this letter. According to obituaries in the *New York Herald* (p. 3, col. 4) and *Brooklyn Eagle* (p. 2, col. 1) for 14 December 1901, he had been married for thirteen years to the former Alice Chapin of Norfolk, Virginia. They had one child, a daughter named Helen. The official cause of his death was consumption.

2. BH's finances were as precarious as he claimed. His estate at his

death some eight months later totaled only about eighteen hundred dollars (*New York Tribune*, 3 Jan. 1903, p. 6, col. 6).

3. Ethel Harte had taken private voice lessons in Paris.

4. This letter is lost. However, BH wrote FH on 30 September 1901 (Wesleyan) to reiterate his "belief that your removal to London, even temporarily, is ill advised as regards *expenses* and *comfort* now and for the future."

255. TO FRANK HARTE, 1 DECEMBER 1901

74, Lancaster Gate, W.
Decem 1st 1901

My dear Frank

I came to town to see the Dentist, and since then I have been oscillating between the Doctor and the Dentist, and suffering painfully from neuralgia. I have had teeth pulled out and operated upon to no purpose, and have been taking quinine till I am dizzy. The Doctor sends me to the Dentist and *vice versa*, till I am quite worn out, and miserable.

So I can only thank you for your letter, and try to answer it another time, and swiftly send the usual draft for your mother. Tell her I have received Ethels letter with all the hopeless enclosures and *disclosures*, and I see nothing to alter my opinion—or my competency to do anything more.[1] I am myself becoming an invalid, and one scarcely able to work more than an hour or two a day.

I shall try to go for a day or two to the seaside to see if it will strengthen me. With love to all

Your affec. papa
B.H.

P.S. As I cant *register* this letter today I must trust it to the ordinary post and beg you to drop me a line back at once, to know that you have received it. B.H.

Provenience: UVa (ALS).

1. An oblique reference to Griswold Harte. See letter 254.

256. TO ANNA HARTE, 17 JANUARY 1902

74, Lancaster Gate, W.
17th January 1902

My dear Anna

Your little note was very kind and sympathetic, and I know you would do all you could for me in my illness if you had the opportunity. I thought you might have had that—if I had come to "Pangbourne,"[1] as it at one time seemed probable, but the Doctor thinks I had better go to the *seaside* for a more *decided* change and I am going to Southsea to-morrow for a few days. Had you been in the country this winter with Frank, I should have probably been with you, and you would have had an invalid on your hands! My principal trouble now is a very sluggish *sore-throat* (ulcerated,) which puzzles the Doctor with its slowness of improvement, although he says now it is mending.

If the air of Southsea does *not* improve me—or even if it *does*—I still hope to come down to Tunbridge Wells while you are there. With love to all—

Your affect,
Limick

Provenience: UCLA (ALS).

1. A village on the Thames where AH and Ethel Harte were wintering.

257. TO FRANK HARTE, 1 FEBRUARY 1902

No 2 Beach Mansions
Southsea,
Feb. 1st 1902

My dear Frank,

I have been here for a fortnight—pointlessly I fear—for my throat is no better, and I shall have to return to London and a Specialist and perhaps be obliged to have one of my tonsils excised. It has been a very protracted case, and I cannot help thinking a very much mismanaged case from the beginning. When Dr Dyer Browne sent me down here, he told me my throat was *improving*—there was nothing in my case to give me the slightest uneasiness and as soon as I presented myself to the Doctor here (whom he recommends) the man told me the case was serious enough to have the tonsil out!

But what concerns me more than all is, that besides these expenses, I have been unable to work since the 4th of December, and I have had to borrow the money to send you this month.

Tell your mother this and impress upon her the necessity of being careful of the little I am still able to give her. Tell her I will write to her again when I know what the specialist says, and what must be done. I should only bother her now with my fears and depressions. Give my love to your wife and Ethel, and believe me your affectionate but invalid father

B.H.

Provenience: UVa (ALS).

258. TO A. P. WATT, 22 FEBRUARY 1902

The Red House, Camberley,
Surrey.
Feby 22 1902

Dear Mr Watt,

In reply to yours of yesterdays date, I will accept Mr Tillotsons commission for three stories, not to exceed 5,000 words each, based upon the career and adventures of "Colonel Starbottle."[1] I will leave it to you to arrange and determine when the copy should be delivered, after consultations with me.

Yours very truly
Bret Harte

Provenience: UNC (ALS).

1. At his death, BH was writing "A Friend of Colonel Starbottle's" in fulfilment of this agreement (Pemberton, 340).

259. TO T. EDGAR PEMBERTON, 12 APRIL 1902

My dear Pemberton,—I had heard that published story of Clara Morris before.[1] I am glad it touched you, for *she* told me it herself! She was a strange, passionate, uncontrollable genius, yet in many ways as *simply* fine as any actress I have seen.

I am still very poorly; everything is against me—even this smileless, joyless, "sere and yellow"[2] spring! I get no stimulus from it. I can scarcely write a letter. The grasshopper is indeed a burden!

Nevertheless—Yours always,

Bret Harte.

Provenience: Pemberton, 96–97.

1. In her autobiography, the actress Clara Morris (1849–1925) recalled that, when she had to cry on stage, she would think "of poor old Tennessee's partner as he buried his worthless dead, with his honest old heart breaking" (*Life on the Stage: My Personal Experiences and Recollections* [New York: McClure, Phillips & Co., 1901], 316–17).

2. *Macbeth*, V. iii: "My way of life/Is fall'n into the sear, the yellow leaf/And that which should accompany old age,/As honor, love, obedience, troops of friends,/I must not look to have."

Bret Harte died on 5 May 1902 from throat cancer. Mme Van de Velde remarked at his funeral (London *Times*, 9 May 1902, p. 10, cols. 1–2) that in "the very brief moments which elapsed between his sudden attack of hemorrhage . . . he was surrounded only by intimate friends (one myself) and passed away without struggle or pain."

Harte's fears for his family, most immediately for his wife and daughter Ethel, were largely realized after his death. His modest estate, about £360, supported them only briefly. Ethel's health failed in a vain attempt to earn her living on the London stage, and in July 1905 a number of prominent British writers, including Sir Arthur Conan Doyle, Sir Gilbert Parker, and George Meredith, raised a "Bret Harte Assistance Fund" that provided her with a small annuity. She returned to the United States in 1924 and eventually settled in southern California. Anna Harte died of asphyxiation from choking on food in Hove, England, in 1920. Jessamy Harte and Henry Steele separated in 1906 and divorced in 1910, she alleging extreme cruelty and he claiming desertion. After a failed career as a cabaret singer, in destitute circumstances and with a history of mental illness, she was committed to the St. Lawrence State Hospital in Ogdensburg, New York, in 1915. She died there forty-seven years later. Frank Harte moved with his family to the continent after his father's death. He died in Monte Carlo in 1917, and his wife, Aline, in failing health for several years, died in London in 1920. Their son Richard, an aspiring painter and writer who had been twice married and divorced, committed suicide in Paris in 1925. His death was reported on the front page of the *New York Times*, a paper that had relegated to page 9 the news of his grandfather's passing in 1902.

Index

*(Illustration pages are in **bold** face.)*